Civil Society and the State

V

Civil Society and the State

New European Perspectives

Edited by
JOHN KEANE

VERSO

London · New York

First published by Verso 1988
© 1988 The Individual Contributors
All rights reserved

Verso
UK: 6 Meard Street, London W1V 3HR
USA: 29 West 35th Street, New York, NY 10001 2291

Verso is the imprint of New Left Books

British Library Cataloguing in Publication Data
Civil society and the state : new European
    perspectives.
    1. Europe. State. Theories
    I. Keane, John, 1949-
    320.1'01

Library of Congress Cataloging-in-Publication Data
Civil society and the state.

    Bibliography: p.
    Includes index.
    1. State, The.   I. Keane, John, 1949-
JC325.C55   1988   320.1   87-35827

ISBN 0-86091-203-5
ISBN 0-86091-921-8 (pbk.)

Typeset by Leaper & Gard Ltd, Bristol, England
Printed in Great Britain by Biddles Ltd, Guildford

Contents

Part Three: **Eastern States and the Possibility**
of Civil Society **261**

Introduction

After more than a century of neglect, the old topic of civil society and the state is again becoming a vital theme in European politics and social theory. This topic first appeared at the end of the eighteenth century. Thereafter it enjoyed a brief but remarkable career in Europe until the second half of the nineteenth century, when it fell (or was pushed) into obscurity and disappeared almost without trace. The renewed popularity of the distinction between civil society and the state during the past several decades thus comes as something of a puzzling surprise. It prompts a succession of questions: What precisely is meant by the distinction between the state (and its military, policing, legal, administrative, productive, and cultural organs) and the non-state (market-regulated, privately controlled or voluntarily organized) realm of civil society? Why is this distinction again topical? Does its renaissance constitute little more than a nostalgic rummaging through the past? For what intellectual and political purposes is this theme capable of being used? Whose interests might it serve?

The principal aim of this volume of essays is to provide some answers to these difficult questions. It seeks to shed light on the present 'rediscovery' of the theme of civil society and the state by examining its analytic relevance, normative significance and political potential. This task is more complicated than might initially be expected. The revival of interest in the theme of civil society and the state is propelled by a variety of overlapping and contradictory forces. This complexity is reflected in the structure and content of this volume. Its contributions – a small sample of the best European writings produced on the subject during the past two decades – are broad in scope and written from a variety of perspectives. They examine the late-eighteenth-century origins and early-nineteenth-century development of the distinction between civil society and the state, as well as its contemporary philosophical refinement and development. The usefulness of the distinction in analysing past events – such as the European civilizing process and the growth and decline of absolutist states – is illustrated. The contemporary sociological relevance of the distinction is discussed in relation to phenomena such as households, labour markets, trade unions, voluntary associations, political parties and state bureaucracies. And consideration is given to the political implications of the distinction – its capacity for making sense of such disparate phenomena as the resistance to totalitarianism, the rise of neo-conservatism, the growth of social movements and the future of the welfare state.

Central and Eastern Europe

Why is the old theme of civil society and the state enjoying a renaissance in Europe today? The reasons are perhaps easiest to discern in Central and Eastern Europe. Within the one-party systems of countries such as Poland, the GDR, Yugoslavia, Czechoslovakia and Hungary, and especially among their democratic oppositions, the growing intellectual and practical interest in the subject of civil society and the state has been encouraged by the evident failure of reform Communist attempts (as in Czechoslovakia in 1968) to modernize these systems from the top downwards. It is also propelled by the widespread sense that these one-party systems can function only by frustrating or extirpating this region's old traditions of civil society and, thus, by denying any difference between political and social power, public and private law, and state-sanctioned (dis)information and propaganda and freely circulated public opinion. The basic political, economic and cultural means of production of these systems – according to the contributors to part 3 of this volume – are monopolized by a bureaucratic apparatus supervised by the Party. These command states are mobilized against the formation of independent centres of power. All individuals, groups and organizations are supposed to be their property, and in this sense – as Jacques Rupnik explains – these Soviet-type systems are totalitarian. They seek to extinguish civil society by absorbing it fully into the crystalline structures of the state. In effect, they place all citizens under permanent surveillance and subject them to a form of permanent internment, while public opposition of any kind is always regarded by the state authorities as seditious.

This kind of ideal-typical description no doubt conceals important differences among the regimes of Central-Eastern Europe. Mihály Vajda emphasizes that the totalitarian political systems in this half of Europe have highly variable modes of operation, due in no small measure to the very different historical developments of the respective countries. Their unevenly developed traditions of 'instinctive' individualism and social organization ensure different types of conflicts with – and different types of response from – states claiming total power. In Poland, for example, the recurrent head-on confrontations between civil society and the state have not been resolved, and continue to shake the one-party system to its very foundations. In Czechoslovakia, political power has until now attempted to defeat civil society by annihilating it completely. Elsewhere (in Hungary and Yugoslavia) the state has successfully maintained a formal framework of total power, but in order to avoid protracted confrontations and open chaos it has been obliged to reduce its monopolistic power claims and to make small concessions to quasi-independent strivings for civil liberty.

The model of totalitarianism sketched here also conceals some important temporal changes. Since the death of Stalin, the Soviet-type regimes of Eastern and Central Europe have come to exhibit some decidedly novel characteristics. Their former brutality and monstrous delirium have given way to modes of control which are less brutal and more anonymous, selective and calculated. The utter disregard for productive and organizational efficiency characteristic of the Stalin period has also been abandoned. Moreover, while the ruling *apparat* still attempts to maintain its cohesion and smother public life through an institutionalized ideology of clichés ('The Party leads the struggle for socialism', and so on) which functions as 'the vital link holding everything together, with billions of tiny fasteners, several dozen to each individual',[1] almost no one, probably not even senior party officials, believes any longer in its pantomime of ritualized claims. Finally, no longer do these regimes strive to control fully the bodies and souls of their subjects, to bind everyone together into a single will, crystallized in the Caesarist leader. The contemporary totalitarian regimes of Central-Eastern Europe typically demand the opposite of their populations: moral torpor, mediocrity and an exclusive concern with minding one's own business and cultivating one's personal career, family life and other 'private' concerns. These regimes are content to regulate *apparent* behaviour: so long as their subjects only disagree silently (or engage in bellyaching) and avoid independent civil initiatives, they are normally safe in their servitude.

To highlight the *absence* of a division between civil society and the state within these state-dominated regimes – as Rupnik, Havel and Vajda do – is not to imply that they are free of structurally induced crises or independent forms of resistance. An example of the former is the way in which their systems of centralized state planning produce a kind of permanent bedlam. Despite the constant official boasting about planning, efficiency and other 'advantages of socialism', these systems are marked by chronic planning failures, technical stagnation, waste and scarcity, and a staggering overdevelopment of an unproductive apparatus of bureaucratic organization and control. These morbid symptoms stimulate attempts (evident in Kádárism and the Gorbachev campaign to 'widen and deepen socialist democracy') to increase the efficiency and effectiveness of the one-party system through reforms. These include the introduction of market mechanisms – whose scope, however, must be limited officially lest they develop into a countervailing principle which erodes the power and privilege of the Party-dominated state in favour of civil society.

Central and Eastern European regimes are also troubled by the growth of independent citizens' initiatives and (especially in Poland and Yugoslavia) social movements. These are catalysed, paradoxically, by the state's attempt to prevent a genuine pluralism in the distribution of power. Inspired by memories of besieged democratic traditions and driven by the sense that the socialist project is now exhausted, suppressed social interests of various kinds learn that they can protect themselves only by forming alliances based on the principles of openness, solidarity and 'living in the truth' (Havel). This dynamic explains why these regimes tend to produce regular social eruptions – campaigns for the free development of civil society against the state apparatus as a whole. Their capacity for rapid growth indicates that totalitarian state power is stable only if civil society is forced underground, shackled by fear and apathy, and thereby reduced to 'the safety of the mousehole' (György Konrád). Whenever civil society becomes more confident, however, the state rapidly loses its grip;

its structural weaknesses and *powerlessness* become evident. Civil society tends to swell rapidly from below. It feeds upon whatever gains it can wrench from the state, which normally lapses into confusion and paralysis. This pattern of development, as Pelczynski indicates, was strongly evident during the Polish events of 1976-81. Their historical novelty consisted in the struggle, led by workers, to establish a civil society [*społeczeństwo obywatelskie*] alongside a totalitarian state [*państwo*]. Solidarność sought neither to form a political party nor to 'capture' state power. It sought neither the restoration of capitalism nor the withering away of the state. Rather, it pursued a self-limiting 'evolutionist' strategy (radicalized during 1981 into the idea of a 'self-governing republic' and modified several times during the period of martial law). Its ultimate goal was – and remains – the cultivation of solidarity among a plurality of self-governing civil associations capable of pressuring the state from without and allowing various groups to attend peacefully to their non-political affairs in accordance with an old Central-Eastern European maxim, summarized by Vajda: 'Let me be, leave me alone, don't try to tell me how to live.'

The Withering Away of Civil Society

One fundamental issue raised by the renewed interest in the state–civil society relationship concerns a *qualitative* difference between the institutional arrangements of the western and eastern halves of Europe. Under the one-party systems, civil society is always on the verge of extinction. Attempts to establish it from below are inherently risky and dangerous and threatened from all sides by the Party official, psychiatrist, soldier, secret agent or vigilante. In the western half of Europe, by contrast, the elimination of the difference between social and political life is not yet a reality. The persistence of (ailing) representative democratic mechanisms, the concrete possibilities of legally establishing independent associations and movements, and the ongoing tensions between capitalist and state bureaucracies – among other factors – ensure that these systems do not 'converge' with their Soviet-type counterparts. Western European civil societies are threatened constantly by the activities of states and private corporations, yet they survive, and even display a remarkable capacity to deepen and extend their reach. Under Western European conditions, in short, social fermentation does not have to begin anew, as it does under totalitarian regimes.

This fundamental difference between the 'capitalist' and 'socialist' halves of Europe is sometimes ignored or explicitly denied. According to some observers, the distinction between civil society and the state may have obvious normative relevance for the opponents of Soviet-type systems, but it has become obsolete in Western European systems. It is claimed that the idea of a civil society independent of the state obtains only for the earlier, 'liberal' phase of modernity. Under present-day conditions, the 'classical' boundaries between public and private, state and civil society have been dissolved. It is observed, for instance, that welfare-state intervention is geared to solving basic economic and social problems, and thereby touches on and redefines the most intimate areas of private life; and that private corporations are regulated publicly (for example in the name of safety and consumer protection) and even compelled by law to perform services for public purposes (such as collecting taxes and providing statistics). It is argued that the whole system tends towards a modified corporatist regime, in which certain traits of the stateless medieval order reappear. This renders meaningless the old divisions between state and civil society, the public and the private. They are replaced by a 'magma' of overlapping, hybrid institutions no longer describable or recognizable as either 'political' or 'social' entities.[2]

This type of argument is at best a half-truth. It points correctly to the growth of attempts, since the nineteenth century,[3] consciously to mediate the state and civil society, and to integrate key social power groups into the structures of the state. Consequently, it helps to clarify the fact that the daily lives of most citizens of Western Europe have become highly dependent upon a mix of public and private regulations and provisions. This type of argument also implies, again correctly, that within any national context 'the state' is becoming less of a unitary agent than in the nineteenth century and that it is flanked from above by an interdependent system of transnational power groupings and from below by a multiplicity of sub-governments operating their own systems of decision-making.

These insights are valuable. They serve as a reminder of the vast distance separating the early modern and late modern European worlds. Nevertheless, the argument that the state–civil society schema is obsolete (at least in Western Europe) is unconvincing on two counts. It fails to distinguish between the analytic, tactical and normative dimensions of the schema – examined below – and overlooks a number of contemporary counter-trends. Three types of development in Western Europe – the restructuring of the capitalist economy, the embittered political controversies surrounding the Keynesian welfare state, and the growth of social movements – are examined in part 2. These trends, introduced and summarized below, suggest *prima facie* that the state–civil society distinction remains relevant in the western half of Europe. These trends also help explain why, in that region, old nineteenth-century controversies about the relationship between the state and civil society are currently being revived and extended.

(a) The current restructuring of Western European capitalist economies is among the key factors contributing to the renewed interest in the state–civil society relationship. This process of *economic restructuring* has been prompted by the exhausted growth potential of the 'long wave' of post-war investment and prosperity. It has brought sharply into focus the crucial dependence of many state policies upon the relatively independent processes of commodity production and exchange within civil society. It provides the reminder – sobering for those who still believe in the 'mixed economy' – that a permanent 'mismatch' between the economic and the political spheres is a defining characteristic of modern capitalist systems of production. During the decades after World War II this fundamental tension seemed temporarily to have been resolved in favour of the political sphere. The proportion of civil society structured by markets was dramatically reduced by state-organized processes of de-commodification. This trend had precedents, of course. Capitalist-dominated markets which utilize labour-power as if it were a commodity have always been contingent upon institutions (such as households and state bureaucracies) which are themselves not subject directly to the commodity form.[4] Even so, this decommodifying trend has accelerated considerably in recent decades. The welfare-state strategy of underwriting the commodity form has weakened its grip upon civil society by developing policies and building institutions (hospitals, schools, housing estates) exempt from this form.[5]

The present restructuring of Western European capitalist economies has begun to reverse this trend. The ability of states to anticipate and control their respective economies has decreased visibly in recent years. Even governments with previously buoyant economies (notably the Federal Republic of Germany) are experiencing growing unemployment, deindustrialization and jobless growth trends. The sources of this 'revenge' of the economic against the political are numerous. They range from centrifugal trends in the international monetary and trading systems and private firms' attempts to recoup the gains made by trade unions, to the emergence of a new international division of labour. A particularly important factor is the disintegration of the old technological paradigm based upon continuous-flow industries and the assembly-line system and the introduction of a great number and variety of process innovations (as distinct from product innovations) based on new microelectronics technologies.[6]

Such factors are having unsettling effects upon the whole global capitalist system. They have forced trade unions into defensive (and often self-regarding) strategies. They have thrown into question the official post-war commitment to greater equality of opportunity for the less powerful social groups. And they have severely undermined the capacity of the Keynesian welfare state to fulfil effectively its commitment to high levels of employment. Hinrichs, Offe and Wiesenthal concentrate on this latter development. They observe that the present economic crisis sharply exposes the deep functional dependence of the welfare state upon the labour market and the household, which they consider to be the core institutions of (what remains of) civil society in Western Europe. They argue that most proponents of the welfare state supposed – quite unrealistically, in retrospect – that nearly all adult males would be employed full-time within the labour market, while the household would be the principal agency of material and cultural reproduction. Thus civil society was supposed to be separated into two sharply divided but complementary spheres: workplace and household, employment and consumption, male and female domains.

Hinrichs, Offe and Wiesenthal argue that the present employment crisis throws this conventional view into disarray. It casts doubt upon the existing range of proposals (such as accelerated growth rates or trade-union campaigns for reducing worktime) for 'restoring' full male employment. It thereby challenges the assumed 'naturalness' of the separation of household and labour market and prompts consideration of the production and socializing potential of civil (or 'co-operative') organizations situated between these two domains. Finally, the present employment crisis – which is not simultaneously a production crisis – offers the possibility of greater pluralism within civil society. It makes possible a radically different (post-social democratic) relationship between working time, income, and non-market social activities. It facilitates the equitable reduction and redistribution of paid employment through the gradual development of schemes which would allow the currently unemployed to engage in productive activity, legally guarantee individuals' rights to withdraw temporarily from employment, and thus enable *all* individuals to escape the compulsions presently experienced within both the private household and the labour market.

(b) *Political controversies* surrounding the failures of Keynesian welfare-state policies are also stimulating interest in the old distinction between the state and civil society. In the hands of its social democratic advocates, the welfare-state model supposed political power to be the most important condition of achieving more co-operative, democratic and egalitarian forms of life. In the field of domestic policy the welfare-state programme aimed to interject political, as opposed to market, priorities within the capitalist accumulation process. This was done by extending state planning mechanisms, expanding state social policy programmes which provided compensation for market-based inequalities, and (with the co-operation of trade unions and private firms) by utilizing macroeconomic policy to minimize (male) unemployment, even at the cost of accelerating inflation.

In Western Europe this social democratic programme has suffered serious political setbacks. During the past two decades its political effects have become evident. Among the most important are the decay of social solidarity, an increased level of scepticism about bureaucracy, professionalism and expertise, and a noticeable decline in the legitimacy of the ideals of socialism, with which social democratic programmes were strongly identified.[7] These political difficulties of the Keynesian welfare state have been exploited most successfully by neo-conservatism, which emphasizes the negative consequences of state intervention into the private markets of civil society.

Neo-conservatives typically argue that state intervention interferes with market mechanisms for determining wages, prices, investment and the distribution of jobs. The continual growth of government spending and the political difficulty of legislating higher taxes also produce sharp increases in the actual and anticipated rate of inflation. State-generated inflation produces uncertainty and confusion among capitalist investors. Their consequent reticence or outright unwillingness to expand and to enter into new ventures thus leads to rising unemployment and accelerating inflation.

Furthermore, the state's 'distortion' of the market's price system perpetuates the life of 'lame duck' enterprises. Their profitability and competitiveness are reduced, thereby increasing the long-term probability of redundancies and plant closures. Not only does the state's interference with market mechanisms tend to produce economic crisis; its social policy programmes and favourable policies towards trade unions also eat away at the basic ethical foundations of civil society. The willingness of capital to innovate and to take risks is weakened. Hard work and competitiveness in the labour market are discouraged. The foundations of individual freedom and equality of opportunity are threatened. Individuals become pawns in the hands of those who control and administer state power. Activities that are not regulated, financed or owned publicly are devalued. The whole political order becomes exposed to the dangers of totalitarianism.[8]

On the basis of this diagnosis neo-conservatives insist, against their social democratic rivals, that any crisis-management strategy based upon higher levels of government spending, expansive monetary policy, state assistance to declining firms and industries and protection against foreign competition is bound to *deepen* the present economic and social crisis. What is required is a radically different strategy for reducing those 'structural rigidities' which restrict the supply of goods and services within the economy – that is, altering its supply side. This means giving freer rein to market forces in areas such as health, education and communications policy. It also means privatizing or 'cutting back' the role of state-owned or state-supported firms and services, as well as curtailing the power of trade unions, so as to create a more 'flexible', co-operative and geographically mobile workforce.

Considered as an overall strategy for restructuring the Keynesian welfare state, these neo-conservative proposals amount to an attempt to synchronize state power with the new economic conditions prevailing in Western Europe. A *selective* withdrawal of state power from civil society and the gradual renewal of private competition and market ethics are envisaged. The state, in this view, should be biased more openly in favour of commodity production and exchange. Neo-conservatives do not normally call for limitations of the *power* of the state. State power is seen to be essential as a forum for determining and administering the rules of market competition, as well as for filling its gaps and limiting its malfunctions. Thus the main task is to render it more effective and legitimate by limiting its role as a provider of goods and services to civil society in favour of its role as the authoritative guardian of civil society. The state must become both more powerful and more limited in scope.

Neo-conservative proposals and initiatives are today hotly contested by social democratic defenders of the Keynesian welfare state, and – as Pierre Rosanvallon's essay indicates – by post-social democratic ideas and policies. Rosanvallon accepts that the present economic and political crisis of the welfare state raises fundamental questions about the desirable form and limits of state power in relation to civil society. But he argues that the currently dominant strategies for either 'privatizing' the welfare state or preserving it intact ('stop the cuts', or 'no privatization') remain trapped within the same unworkable and undesirable political paradigm. The fetish of market competition among private individuals and uncritical trust in the administrative state are in fact *complementary* perspectives. Both encourage the fragmentation of the social bonds of civil society. Conversely, neither perspective can imagine the possibility of increasing the scope and 'visibility' of these social bonds.

Rosanvallon's vision closely parallels the conclusions of Hinrichs, Offe and Wiesenthal. He argues that a key political task of the contemporary period is to bring into being a state-guaranteed civil society of greater density and to develop its scope for defining and satisfying social needs through networks of mutual support and exchange, instead of 'externalizing' these needs and abandoning their satisfaction to the twin poles of market or state. He rejects the inequitable, socially destructive and statist outcomes of neo-conservatism. He is equally critical of the narrow social democratic assumption that private services are synonymous with markets, profit-making and inequality and that public services are (or should be) identical with state provision, non-profit-making and equality. Instead Rosanvallon envisages a *variety* of mechanisms for publicly deciding and satisfying social needs. He sketches a three-pronged approach based on the reduced requirement for state intervention, a new (post-Keynesian) compromise between employers and workers, and the expansion of democratic forms of solidarity within civil society itself.

(c) The revival and reworking of old controversies about the relationship between civil society and the state is also linked with the rise of new *social movements*. During the past several decades in Western Europe there has been a vigorous growth of new forms of collective action. Among the most important examples are black and civil rights campaigns, feminism, student and youth movements, the peace movement and ecology. These social movements draw their support in novel ways from across class boundaries. As Alberto Melucci argues, they also place a high value upon grass-roots, informal and 'hidden' forms of organization and – notwithstanding their fundamentalist or authoritarian tendencies – consequently tend to be suspicious of business organizations, trade-union hierarchies, political parties and state bureaucracies. Since they develop largely outside and 'underneath' these dominant institutions of civil society and the state, social movements raise important questions about the distribution and legitimacy of macro power relations. But they do more than this: they also publicize grievances and uncertainties about everyday life and challenge the deep-rooted codes of social interaction within civil society.

For this reason Melucci doubts interpretations which emphasize the *political* dimension of social movements – their efficacy (or lack of it) within the political market. Melucci does not deny the significance of the new movements' involvement in established political processes, but he argues that political interpretations understate their *non-political* aspects. Today's movements tend to act at a distance from the world of official politics. They appear infrequently as publicly visible phenomena – for instance during public demonstrations in favour of black rights, or against nuclear power. Social movements *normally* consist – here Melucci's work is most original – of 'invisible' networks of small groups submerged in everyday life. From this 'subterranean' position these movements question and challenge the dominant codes of everyday life. They redefine its shared sense of time, space and interpersonal relations. They press home their conviction that it is possible to expand and democratize civil society in accordance with unconventional rules of space, time and interpersonal relations.

These social movements are, in this precise sense, the counterparts of the citizens' initiatives and social movements in Central and Eastern Europe. They are marked by a definite anti-political quality. Their activities are governed neither by the ultimate political fantasy of seizing and transforming state power, nor by the more humble desire to concentrate exclusively on party politics. Instead they concentrate on the undramatic task of publicizing and transforming the less visible fields of micro power relations within which they emerge and operate. Thereby they both deepen the division between the state and civil society and build new forms of solidarity, contributing to the pluralization of power relations within civil society itself.

Old Themes, New Confusions

Pressured by these various developments, political thinkers and social analysts in both halves of Europe have begun to recognize the potential importance of the old civil society–state distinction. In recent years this distinction has become something of a key word of intellectual discussion. This is an exciting, if controversial development, but it is hampered – and potentially threatened – by widespread confusion about the *several* meanings and *various* implications of the distinction.

On the political right in Western Europe, for instance, the term 'civil society' has been granted a kind of natural innocence and deployed as a poorly defined synonym for the market and other forms of 'private' life which are supposed to be good because of their opposition to state power.[9] Others, especially on the orthodox political left, display considerable hostility to the distinction (either because it is assumed to be the property of the right, or because it is said to fudge the crucial problems of property, class and class conflict – misleading claims, as several contributions to this volume show).

Yet others on the political left in Western Europe utilize the distinction as if it were invented (or developed most fully) by Antonio Gramsci in such writings as *Quaderni del Carcere* and *Note sul Machiavelli*.[10] Some writers see in the state–civil society distinction a way of conceptually analysing the empirical contours of past, present or emergent relationships between social and political institutions and forces. Others view the distinction normatively; still others cast it mainly in 'pragmatic' terms, as a means of formulating a social and political strategy or action programme.

Faced with this plethora of confused meanings and conflicting usages, it seems necessary to attempt some careful distinctions. The state–civil society schema can be understood in at least three different ways. Although these three approaches may – and usually do – crisscross and complement each other, they can also produce divergent types of claims and should therefore be distinguished carefully.

The aim of making such distinctions – summarized below, and evident throughout this volume – should not be to produce a new philosophical, sociological and political paradigm. Contemplating the formation of a grand theoretical explanation of the past, present and future relationships between states and civil societies would seem to be premature, if not wholly undesirable. A theoretical 'metadiscourse' of this kind would hypostatize the distinction, endowing it perhaps with anthropomorphic qualities. It would probably result in glib philosophical generalizations, oversimplified sociological observations and misguided or dogmatic political recommendations. Certainly it would trap usages of the distinction within a performative contradiction, by paralysing its radically *pluralist* or *democratic* potential.[11] Thus the purpose of clarifying the currently confused and overlapping usages of the state–civil society distinction should be altogether more modest: to develop an *interpretative standpoint* which can be of some utility in historical investigations, sociological inquiry, normative discussions and political action. While this more modest understanding of the distinction would be unlikely to overcome its deeply contested character (a fate it necessarily shares with all other major concepts in the human sciences), it would help to sort out its potential scope and strengths as well as its present *weaknesses* and *limits*.

(a) Analytic approaches

The state–civil society distinction can be used to analyse the origins, development and transformation of particular institutions or whole social systems. Analytic approaches selectively identify key institutions and actors, examine their complex patterns of interaction and attempt to reach some conclusions – based on theoretical distinctions, empirical research and informed judgements – concerning their origins, patterns of development and (unintended) outcomes. Their immediate (or avowed) aim is not to form normative judgements or to recommend courses of political action. Rather, they aim to develop an explanatory understanding of complex socio-political realities. Within such analyses, the distinction between civil society and the state operates as an ideal-type which may be directed at either the past or the present, or both past and present simultaneously.

Examples of the *contemporary* use of the distinction include

Alberto Melucci's investigations of the formation process of contemporary social movements and Hinrichs, Offe and Wiesenthal's examination of the relationship between households, labour markets and the welfare state (see part 2). New analyses of the interaction between civil society and the state under bureaucratic authoritarian regimes in Europe and Latin America provide another example. These analyses concentrate on the effects of the resistance by groups within civil society (for example the Human Rights Association in Turkey and the Assembleir de Civilidad in Paraguay) to repressive state rule and, reciprocally, on the ways in which the structures and strategies of authoritarian states have influenced the options and strategies of oppositional social groups.[12]

The distinction can also be used to examine *past* realities. Examples include Reinhart Koselleck's influential study of the series of deep-reaching (if self-contradictory) modernizing reforms initiated by the Prussian bureaucracy after the French Revolution[13] and Isser Woloch's examination of the bureaucratic destruction of popular draft resistance and the implementation of regular military conscription in Napoleonic France.[14] A similar usage of the distinction is evident in a massive recent comparative and interdisciplinary study of the nineteenth-century roots of the German 'divergence' from the Western path of modernization, encompassing such social and political factors as Germany's delayed process of nation-state building, the weakness of parliamentary-democratic institutions, the persistent strength of non-bourgeois power groups such as the landed aristocracy, the officer corps and the bureaucracy, and the considerable grip of *obrigkeitsstaatlich* and pre-modern cultural traditions, all of which played a crucial role as possibility conditions of Nazism.[15]

Several contributions to this volume expand the time frame of this type of historical analysis. Norbert Elias and Helmut Kuzmics discuss some key features of the European civilizing process, whose close connection with the origins of modern civil societies is suggested by the simultaneous appearance of the term 'civilization' and the state–civil society distinction during the second half of the eighteenth century. Kuzmics examines the central themes of Elias's classic work *Über den Prozess der Zivilisation*, which sketches a 'prehistory' of key aspects of the formation of modern civil societies. It concentrates mainly on French absolutism in order to highlight a complex two-stage process of historical development: the moulding of a class of autonomous, landowning warlords into a court elite under the patriarchal control of a centralized monarchy; and the gradual decomposition of this courtly elite by the encroachment of professional, bourgeois administrators within the state apparatus. Elias suggests that the wave of civilization attending this double transformation subjected certain groups to fundamentally new codes of conduct. It made men who fought, ate and slept on horseback into 'individuals' who were prone to 'polish' and 'cultivate' themselves in accordance with the ideal of 'refinement of manners, worldly wisdom and politeness, and the spreading of knowledge and good behaviour' (Mirabeau). The courtly etiquette of civilized behaviour left a powerful imprint on the bourgeoisie, whose character structure developed neither from scratch nor (as Weber implied) from Protestantism alone.

Compared with the uncivilized, who experiences savage pleasure and unfettered hatred in destroying and tormenting everything hostile, the civilized bourgois citizen is capable of suppressing impulses of pain and pleasure and transforming them into prolonged sequences of action. The degree of self-restraint in bourgeois social interactions increases. Restraint becomes guided by an interior voice, and the social space between individuals tends to become a passionless void. According to Elias this type of pacification has far-reaching effects, among which is its facilitation of the birth of civilized societies operating under the shadow of the nation-state, with its monopolization of the means of violence. Under the impact of the civilizing process, violence tends to become depersonalized and invested in the state's repressive apparatuses. A civil society free of immediate physical violence becomes possible. Yet as Kuzmics emphasizes, Elias is aware of a double standard in the European civilizing process. Even though violence within civil societies is strictly regulated by states, citizens are still called on periodically to kill external enemies because the interaction among heavily armed nation-states remains fundamentally uncivilized. This double standard weighs heavily on civil societies, as Elias's case study of the pre-Fascist radicalization in the Weimar Republic shows. It constantly threatens them from within, through the militarization of civil society, and from without, by means of acts of war and (threatened) invasion.

Jenö Szücs's contribution also examines some aspects of the birth of modern civil societies. It aims to clarify the extent to which the modern European division between society and the state did not arise *ex nihilo* but was conditioned by prior historical developments which varied geographically. He proposes, for example, that three European regions – Western, East-Central and Eastern – each experienced forms of absolutism. Each form sought in different ways to preserve certain elements of the feudal heritage, to protect the system of production and exchange, and to develop the state apparatus. But the methods, goals and degree of coherence of these absolutist states – as well as the level of resistance of civil society to their power – varied greatly from region to region. All this depended on the dynamism of these regions, their geopolitical situations, and – here Szücs boldly projects the modern civil society–state distinction 'backwards' – their inherited medieval infrastructures of political and social power.

In Western Europe, for example, the feudal components of the medieval *corpus politicum* relinquished their struggle only gradually and unwillingly. There were frequent rebellions by the nobility, bourgeoisie and peasantry against state-builders, so that absolute states appeared only in the seventeenth century. All European absolutist states strove to subordinate and homogenize their subjects, but in practice nowhere in the West were various local autonomies and 'freedoms' eliminated. Not surprisingly, in this region the lifespan of absolutist states was comparatively short. They were overthrown relatively early (as in the Netherlands and England) and survived the eighteenth century only in 'semi-peripheral' areas (Spain, Portugal, Southern Italy) produced by the relocation of the centre of the world economy to the Atlantic region.

In Eastern Europe, by contrast, absolutism developed earlier, lasted much longer and served as the fundamental framework for all subsequent developments. Western absolutism subordinated society to the state, whereas Eastern absolutism 'nationalized' it. In contrast to this Eastern model – here Szücs's analysis directly complements Vajda's – the states of East-Central Europe (the Polish-Lithuanian kingdom, Brandenburg-Prussia, the Habsburg dynasty) displayed a peculiar and uneven mixture of both Western and Eastern characteristics during the era of abolutism. Structures of the West European type were widely evident, even if shallower and deformed to some degree. State-builders therefore had to reckon with pre-existing networks of social power. The various methods they invoked resulted in hybrid state structures of the above-mentioned three varieties. These state structures of East-Central Europe were shaped by the strength of social power groupings and the impact of the waves of historical events pounding this sector from the two expansive regions of Western and Eastern Europe as well as the thousand years of threatened invasion from Asia Minor.

Macrosociological attempts to synthesize analyses of the past and present contours of the modernization process can also be guided by the civil society–state distinction. A recent example is Jürgen Habermas's interpretation of modernity. This distinguishes between the logics of the political and economic systems, regulated respectively by administrative power and money, and the life-world of self-organized public spheres based on solidarity and communication. From this standpoint European modernization is viewed as a process of differentiation and interaction of these three domains of reality:

> Capitalism and the modern state, guided by the media of money and power, become differentiated from the social mechanisms of the life-world, which reacts in a characteristic way. Socially integrated spheres of action within civil society crystallize into a private and public sphere, in opposition to the system-integrated and complementary domains of the economy and state.[16]

Habermas observes that the uncoupling of these systems from the life-world (or civil society) is the precondition of its genuine pluralization, but he also emphasizes that civil society is threatened constantly by the expansionist logics of the political economy.

Although such reinterpretations of modernity in terms of the state–civil society distinction appear to be only in their infancy, they provide a welcome corrective to 'capitalism-centred' perspectives. These latter approaches emphasize that the emergence of an independent capitalist economy – based on the wage-labour–capital relationship, the reinvestment of surplus and constantly expanding accumulation – is the essential element in the massive transformations of modern times. In all traditional societies, the economic system was submerged in general social relations. The emergence in modern times of an independent, self-regulating economy independent of the political and household spheres constituted a dramatic reversal of this rule. This exceptional development is captured in Marx's analysis of capitalism as a self-referential system of commodity production by means of commodities. Capitalism is understood as a permanent revolution. It

> drives beyond national barriers and prejudices as much as beyond nature worship, as well as all traditional, confined, complacent, encrusted satisfactions of present needs, and reproductions of old

ways of life. It is destructive of all this, and permanently revolutionary, tearing down all obstacles that impede the development of productive forces, the expansion of needs, the diversity of production and the exploitation and exchange of natural and intellectual forces.[17]

The standard objection to this view is that modern capitalism rests upon (in the sense that it presupposes for its functioning) institutions which are not capitalist *per se*. As Luhmann has pointed out, nearly all macrosociological accounts of modernity can be seen as criticisms of monistic attempts to found a theory of the modern world upon explanations of its economic dynamism.[18] A central theme in Weberian sociology exemplifies this trend: the one-sided 'economism' of the classical Marxian approach is rejected in favour of a more complex understanding of states as (potentially) independent structures which are often capable of shaping, even sometimes determining, their economic environment. This heuristic approach fruitfully asserts both that states are potentially autonomous agents and, conversely, that economic (class) power relations shape and limit state structures and policies. The separation of the economic from the political is still viewed as a characteristic feature of modernity, but their interaction is seen to be a permanent problem of modern times. Attempts are therefore made to formulate hypotheses about the conditions which hinder or promote state autonomy, its effectiveness, its unintended consequences and its impact upon the economic sphere.

Sociological approaches which attempt to synthesize economy- and state-centred perspectives (nowadays evident in the convergence of neo-Weberian and neo-Marxian approaches[19]) are important. But they require correction with a more generous (that is to say, more complex) view of the organizing principles of the non-state sphere. The 'rise and maturation of capitalism' has not been synonymous with the *universal* influence of commodity production and exchange, the irreversible destruction of 'community life', the general spread of crass materialism and possessive individualism, or the growth of class conflict as *the* central social conflict. At one time or another, modern civil societies have comprised not only capitalist economies but an eclectic variety of *non-economic* organizations.[20] Modern civil societies have comprised a constellation of juxtaposed and changing elements that resist reduction to a common denominator, an essential core or generative first principle. They have included capitalist economies and households; social movements and voluntary public spheres (churches, organizations of professionals and independent communications media and cultural institutions); political parties, electoral associations and other 'gatekeepers' of the state–civil society division; as well as 'disciplinary' institutions such as schools, hospitals, asylums and prisons.

These non-market, non-state organizations have always been related, in complex and often contradictory ways, to capitalist economies. Their survival and growth has undoubtedly contributed to the inner contestation and restlessness which is a distinctive feature of modern civil societies. These societies have resembled what Adorno once called a force-field – a domain marked by the complex interplay of attractions and aversions, and thus by dynamic, transmutational structures. They have been marked by 'the despotism of the factory' (Marx) as well as by struggles for the right to organize against economic despotism. They have developed elaborate networks of prisons, schools, hospitals and other 'cruel ingenious cages' (Foucault). But they have also given birth to prison reform leagues and campaigns against capital punishment, excesssive police powers and unlawful detention; and attempts have been made to counter their institutions of compulsory schooling and medicalization through voluntary reading circles, adult education schemes, childcare networks, student movements, public-sector trade unions and alternative forms of medicine.

To point in this way to the *complexity* of the arrangements of modern civil societies is not to suppose that they are havens of democratic pluralism in a heartless world of capitalist enterprises and bureaucratic states. To this point in modern times, civil society cannot be thought of accurately as an inclusive domain in which every citizen can hope to attain freedom, individuality and social justice within a state-guaranteed framework of legal equality, plurality (access to a variety of voluntary associations) and unrestricted public spheres in which social interests and political norms can be communicated and tested.[21] Carole Pateman indicates an important reason why this view is flawed. She argues that there is one fundamental sense in which all descriptions and analyses of modern civil society as a sphere of complex freedom and equality must be rejected as apologetic or, at least, as highly idealized. Modern civil societies, past and present, tend to be *male-dominated.*[22] Today this domination extends from discrepancies and explicit biases within civil law and social policy arrangements, through discrimination against women within the sphere of commodity production and exchange (evidenced in the gendered division of labour and in sexual harassment), to the compulsive prejudice that women are naturally fit for the (unpaid) household tasks of shopping, washing, cleaning, and rearing children.

Pateman also argues that descriptions of civil society as a domain of universal freedom and equality are unconvincing even in terms of their chosen categories of analysis. She demonstrates that the early modern discussion of civil society and the state always supposed the *exclusion* of women from civil society and their confinement to the privacy of the household. The revolutionary slogan of the late-eighteenth-century defenders of civil society – 'Liberty, Equality, Fraternity' – expresses this literally. Certainly, the household is conceived in a variety of ways: Hobbes, for instance, understands patriarchal family life to be absent in the natural condition and yet assumes that it will be the foundation of Civill Society. According to Locke, the male-dominated household is intrinsic to the natural sociability on which civil society is founded. For Hegel, the patriarchal family is an ethical realm which is dependent upon both civil society and the state. But common to all these various interpretations, Pateman shows, is their representation of the household as the proper domain of the socially and politically dependent wife. Within this sphere, women's functions of child-bearing, child-rearing and maintaining the household are deemed to correspond to their unreason, disorderliness and 'closeness' to nature. Women and the domestic sphere are viewed as inferior to the male-dominated 'public' world of civil society and its culture, property, social power, reason and freedom. In short, civil society is established after the image of the civilized male individual: it rests on a foundation of excluded women, who are expected to live under conditions of household despotism.

(b) Political calculation

The state–civil society schema can also be used primarily as an aid to strategic political calculation. In this second approach the dichotomy between civil society and the state serves as a criterion to establish what must be done (and what must not be done) in order to reach a goal whose desirability is taken for granted. In contrast to analytic approaches, which are concerned less directly with political questions, the state–civil society distinction is developed mainly with an eye to the (potential) political gains of oppositional social movements or power groups against their (potential) opponents – or, conversely, to the stabilization of political power against (potential) challenges from movements or power groups operating within civil society itself. The normative considerations underpinning 'tactical' approaches of this kind are usually assumed or stated as a given. The main concern is with the calculation of the *means* of achieving or stabilizing certain ends.

Tactical usages of the distinction between civil society and the state date from the end of the eighteenth century, when the protagonists of this novel distinction turned their backs on overextended ('despotic') state power. The late-eighteenth- and early-nineteenth-century debate about civil society and the limits of state action – surveyed in the next essay – resonated primarily among social groups who greatly feared concentrations of political power. Their confidence in the justice of existing power arrangements plummeted. As their old loyalties faded social obligations and legal codes were felt as impositions, as a form of continual humiliation. Most members of these groups, who had at least a little property and some education, found that their scientific, literary, artistic and religious pursuits placed them at odds with existing state power and the corporate privileges it secured. These groups constituted (potential) discussing and reading public spheres. They sought to construct a 'public opinion' on political matters and to direct this opinion, in the name of the emerging civil society, at the arcane and often repressive actions of the state.

From the mid nineteenth century onwards a quite different tactical use of the state–civil society distinction is evident within the European socialist tradition.[23] Attempts were made to instrumentalize it – to develop political strategies for *abolishing* the division between civil society and the state, which was viewed, negatively, as synonymous with 'capitalism'. Gramsci's development of a theory of civil society during the period of Italian Fascism is a case in point. His approach, as Norberto Bobbio points out, remains faithful to the classical Marxian goal of a communist society without class divisions, and thus without the division between the state and civil society. This future society without a state, which Gramsci calls 'regulated society', is the ultimate goal of working-class struggles, guided by the Party and its intellectuals, to establish an anti-bourgeois hegemony within civil society, itself conceived as the mediating link between the class-structured economy and state institutions based on coercion.

Gramsci supposed that in Western bourgeois systems civil society comprises a variety of 'cultural' institutions which function to reproduce or to transform the dominant bourgeois sense of reality, which tends to be shared by the dominated classes and groups. He further supposed – against the trade-unionist preoccupation with struggles at the point of production – that the grip of the bourgeoisie is most vulnerable in this domain. Civil society resembles the trench systems of modern warfare. Its labyrinthine structure normally resists the 'incursions' of economic crises and protects the state apparatus, but it is precisely this complexity which allows well-organized assailants to infiltrate.

Gramsci reasoned that a protracted 'war of position' for control over civil society would be the most effective way of politically undermining the domination of the bourgeoisie in its 'home territory' of the economy and the coercive state. The empowerment of the subordinate classes – their transition from the realm of necessity to the realm of freedom – depends vitally upon the prior transformation of conditions within civil society itself. A proletarian 'war of position', if conducted with tact and dedication, could develop a *communist* civil society, whose enlargement to the point of universalization – here Gramsci implicitly challenges the Bolshevik strategy of seizing political power violently – would obviate the dangers of illegitimate political dictatorship resulting from a 'war of movement' or sudden frontal assault upon the state apparatus.[24]

What can reasonably be expected from strategic uses of the state–civil society dichotomy today? And does the Gramscian variant remain relevant? For the purposes of political action, the distinction between civil society and the state is clearly of considerable use in thinking in *generalizing* terms about the problem of Soviet-type totalitarianism and, in Western Europe, about a constellation of novel developments ranging from transformations in the structure of contemporary capitalist economies to the growth of social movements and political debates concerning the future of the Keynesian welfare state. However, beyond such generalizations not much can or should be said about the efficacy of the distinction in specific social and political contexts. Efforts to maximize the level of 'concreteness' of the idea of civil society for political purposes should be resisted, precisely because social and political action ultimately thrives best upon *judgements*.[25]

Judgements do not involve identifying particular events or contexts as instances of one or another general rule or formula.

Nor should they consist in arbitrary decision-making based on particular, private preferences. Properly speaking, political and social judgements – those made within the context of the state or civil society – stand between these two extremes. They are, in Kant's terms, a variety of reflective rather than of determinant judgement. They thrive upon reflections on the relationship between the wider context of social and political action and the individual event, novel predicament or unexpected crisis embedded within that wider context. Good judgement, whether in the sphere of the state, civil society or its mediating institutions, is not a technique or set of general rules that can be memorized from books filled with general theories. It is a practice improved only by experience within those domains themselves.

Concerning Gramsci, Pelczynski argues that developments in Central and Eastern Europe, especially in Poland, have given the Gramscian approach – albeit in a radically modified shape – a fresh lease of life. One key theme within the Gramscian political strategy – the tactical importance of non-market, non-state institutions – is also hinted at in Melucci's defence of public spheres for the development of certain 'rights of everyday life' and in Rosanvallon's call for a civil society of greater density and scope. In each case, however, the similarities with Gramsci's approach are at best limited. Each contribution raises serious doubts about the adequacy of the Gramscian schema for contemporary political strategy. They point to the need for a *post-Gramscian* approach.

Three issues would seem to be especially important in making this transition. First, social and political conditions in Western Europe have changed dramatically since Gramsci's time. The more recent fragmentation of national labour movements, the decline in relative size of the 'core' working class, challenges to the work ethic and the growth of a plurality of new social movements – to mention just one cluster of contemporary empirical developments – cast doubt upon Gramsci's exaggerated belief that the industrial working class ('the fundamental class') would play the leading role in the anti-capitalist revolution. Post-Gramscian theories of civil society need to ponder such developments and, at a minimum, to reconsider the social and political potential of the organized working class in relation to other strata, groups and movements of civil society.[26]

Secondly, Gramsci's belief in the leading role of the Communist Party form is problematic. It evidently underestimates the totalitarian potential of monopolistic parties (outlined in part 3). It also understates the factors which work against the capacity of the mass political party to integrate civil society into its ranks and prompts consideration of other, less party-centred strategies for democratizing civil society and the state.[27]

Finally, Gramsci's reliance upon the Marxian postulate of the ultimate necessity of abolishing the state (and therefore civil society) is vulnerable to sociological objections, justified political anxieties and normative doubts. His interest in civil society is wholly opportunistic, driven by the reverie of abolishing civil society by means of civil society. Civil society is a temporary and dispensable arrangement. Gramsci's vision of a future 'regulated society' rested on a complex of deep assumptions – that capitalist society is characterized by a central contradiction and that there is a privileged subject capable of fulfilling the telos of history – which are contradicted by the growing differentiation and complexity of contemporary capitalist systems.

Twentieth-century attempts to reverse this differentiation process and to reunify civil society with the state through central-ized state power have had (and will in future have) totalitarian consequences. Conversely, attempts to undo social and political complexity by opting out of the political system and universaliz-ing civil society from below – the anarchist option – seem equally antiquated. They too rest on the nineteenth-century assumption of a single (class) standpoint from which the totality of society is both visible and transformable. Their actualization – through revolutionary self-management initiatives, for example – would also necessitate levels of collective unity, self-restraint and mutual surveillance that would probably result in a hellish form of 'terrorism from below'.[28] The abolition of 'external' political constraints and social obligations would necessitate their compul-sory internalization. The duty to love the collectivity would produce a new form of despotism, since all criticism would be deemed subversion, all debate a refusal to obey.

(c) The normative dimension

If neither the universalization of state power nor the universaliz-ation of civil society is viable or desirable under contemporary conditions, then the preservation of the institutional distinction between state and civil society would seem to be a *sine qua non* of democracy in complex societies. Here the normative dimension of the state–civil society distinction becomes prominent. Agnes Heller points out that if the utopia of the abolition of state power is abandoned, and if (at the other extreme) state tyranny is to be avoided, troubling questions are raised concerning the desirable relationship between the state and civil society.

In response to these questions Heller avoids substantive claims bearing on the desirable content of state policies, arguing instead that a fully modern political philosophy which welcomes diversity and pluralism must logically embrace the constitutive idea of formal political democracy. Formal political democracy – a special type of governing arrangement which guarantees the civil liberties of all citizens, political pluralism, the system of contracts and the principle of representation – is the only means through which state power can be kept flexible, open and responsive to the shifting needs and changing demands of civil society. Heller further argues that formal political democracy requires a complex of social institutions – a civil society – which is relatively (though never completely) independent of the state. It further requires a *particular type* of civil society: one whose economic structure, relations of contract and freedoms are not monopolized or choked by capitalist production and exchange.

In Heller's view the original Marxian critique of capitalism contains a fundamental (and still highly relevant) insight: in capitalist society every citizen has a formal right to own property, yet in practice the exercise of that right excludes *de facto* the majority of citizens from the enjoyment and disposition of all productive property, except for their abilities to exercise their own labour-power on the labour market. This exclusion of citizens from ownership and control of productive property diminishes their 'enjoyment ratio' and – despite the existence of political democracy, trade unionism and expanded consumer choice – deprives them of the possibility of determining the conditions and products of economic life within civil society. And because the economic power of private capitalist firms usually gives them privileged access to state power, citizens are further disadvantaged in a political sense.

These points seemed obvious to the nineteenth- and early-twentieth-century Marxian tradition. Yet according to Heller, the fundamental flaw in its criticism of capitalism is the assumption that the injustice and unfreedom generated by capitalist private property must be overcome (either temporarily or permanently) through state control of productive property.[29] In practice, as the earliest case of Bolshevism indicates, this assumption encouraged attempts to integrate the whole of civil society forcibly into the state, and thus to solve the property question not through the

abolition of property but through the state monopoly of disposition over the productive forces, including labour-power itself.
Heller argues that the state's elimination of the right of property
necessarily destroys political democracy. Citizens *qua* citizens no
longer have independent social soil on which to plant their feet
firmly. She reasons that the *positive* abolition of private property –
the generalization of property ownership – is the only way in
which formal political democracy could be combined with a post-
capitalist property system which guarantees every citizen the
ability to dispose of the forces of production and to enjoy the
fruits of productive activity.

In contrast to Pateman, Heller does not discuss the implications of her revised understanding of democracy for the
position of women and for the relationship between households
and other organs of civil society.[30] Nor does she analyse in detail
how the development of a self-regulating civil society within the
framework of formal democracy could be effected politically.
Justifiably this task is left to more strategically inclined
approaches, represented here by Rosanvallon and Hinrichs, Offe
and Wiesenthal. The importance of Heller's philosophical
defence of the state–civil society distinction arguably lies
elsewhere. It suggests, paradoxically, that normative usages of
this distinction can avoid becoming trapped within monistic
normative claims, which in practice always have dogmatic implications and consequences. By concentrating instead on the
implied socio-political conditions necessary for the institutionaliz-
ation and preservation of a genuine *variety* of forms of life, Heller's
reflections help to clarify the intimate connection between
normative pluralism and the institutional division between civil
society and the state.[31] Her contribution indicates that normative
pluralism implies the need for formal political democracy, for
institutional arrangements which ensure that protagonists of
similar or different forms of life can openly and continuously
articulate their respective points of view. Further, she shows how
normative pluralism implies the necessity of political, administrative and legal mechanisms for managing conflict, for restricting
and actively reducing the bitter conflicts and paralysing consequences that frequently issue from struggles among incompatible
forms of life.

In this respect, normative pluralism is incompatible with the
nineteenth-century utopia of abolishing the state; active and
strong political institutions are indispensable conditions of
preserving political pluralism. But this also means, finally, that

normative pluralism implies the need for mechanisms for preventing the 'overpoliticization' of life: for ensuring a genuinely pluralistic and actively self-organizing civil society which is independent of state power and capable of questioning and – from time to time – resisting its expansionist claims.

Understood in this way, the distinction between civil society and the state has two complementary normative functions. The distinction can be used – as it is in the discussion of totalitarianism in part 3 – to warn of the undesirable or unworkable consequences of practical attempts to annul the separation of state and civil society. This *precautionary* function of the distinction normally supplements its *advocacy* function – prominent in the contributions to part 2 – which consists in normative efforts to highlight the need for (greater) pluralism in the distribution of social and political power.

No doubt much hard work needs to be done to elaborate theoretically these normative dimensions of the state–civil society distinction. Such elaboration would have to be precise, but not too precise, so as to give full recognition to possible institutional change. The normative dimensions of the civil society–state distinction need to be elaborated sufficiently to show their relevance for thinking about concrete institutional procedures and struggles without, however, becoming too closely identified with specific institutions and thereby sharing their contingency.

This task of elaborating the normative dimensions of the distinction between civil society and the state could be facilitated by addressing the wide range of issues raised by analytic and strategic-political usages of the state–civil society schema. As well, a normative theory of civil society and the state could benefit from critical encounters with the pluralist trends within contemporary philosophy.[32] It could also profit from critical dialogues with early modern political thought, particularly its preoccupation with civil society and the limits of state action (to recall the surprisingly familiar title of an essay by Wilhelm von Humboldt of the early 1790s[33]). This period of political thinking was deeply sensitive to questions concerning how to control and limit the exercise of political power. It has a remarkable capacity to force us, often against our intentions, to think more deeply about these questions. Its condescension by posterity should therefore be regarded with deep suspicion. Early modern political thought can teach us, its heirs, much about the 'perennial problems' of the modern state and civil society. For that reason alone, the contemporary viability of a forward-looking normative theory of civil society and the state arguably depends in part upon its ability to look backwards, so as to build upon and imaginatively transform a heritage which becomes more precious the more it is half-forgotten, or abolished outright.

Notes

1. Alexander Solzhenitsyn, 'The Smatterers', in Alexander Solzhenitsyn *et al.*, *From Under the Rubble*, London 1976, p. 275 (translation modified).

2. Erich Angermann, 'Das "Auseinandertreten von Staat und Gesellschaft" im Denken des 18. Jahrhunderts', *Zeitschrift für Politik*, vol. 10, no. 2, 1963, p. 101; Franz-Xaver Kaufmann, 'The Blurring of the Distinction "State versus Society" in the Idea and Practice of the Welfare State', in F.-X. Kaufmann *et al.*, eds, *Guidance, Control, and Evaluation in the Public Sector*, Berlin and New York 1986, pp. 127-38; Anthony Giddens, *Social Theory and Modern Sociology*, Cambridge 1987, pp. 275-96; Salvador Giner, 'The Withering Away of Civil Society?', *Praxis International*, vol. 5, no. 3, October 1985, pp. 247-67.

3. E. Pankoke, *Soziale Bewegung-Soziale Frage-Soziale Politik*, Stuttgart 1970.

4. Karl Polanyi, *Origins of Our Time. The Great Transformation*, London 1944.

5. Claus Offe, *Contradictions of the Welfare State*, ed. John Keane, London and Cambridge, MA 1984.

6. See Alain Lipietz, *Mirages and Miracles. The Crises of Global Fordism*, London 1987; Christopher Freeman, 'Keynes or Kondratiev? How can we get back to full employment?', in P. Marstrand, ed., *New Technology and the Future of Work and Skills*, London 1983; Michael U. Piore and Charles F. Sabel, *The Second Industrial Divide*, New York 1985; and John Keane and John Owens, *After Full Employment*, London 1986.

7. See my *Democracy and Civil Society*, London 1988, especially essay 1.

8. Ernst-Wolfgang Böckenförde, 'Die Bedeutung der Unterscheidung von Staat und Gesellschaft im demokratischen Sozialstaat der Gegenwart', in Ernst-Wolfgang Böckenförde, ed., *Staat und Gesellschaft*, Darmstadt 1976, pp. 395-431. A similar concern is expressed in Jean-François Revel, *How Democracies Perish*, Brighton 1985, and in Antony de Jasay, *The State*, Oxford 1985.

9. See for example the argument for a 'neo-Copernican revolution' in favour of civil society against the state in Jean-Marie Benoist, *Les Outils de la liberté*, Paris 1985.

10. Examples include Anne Showstack-Sassoon, 'Civil Society', in Tom Bottomore, ed., *A Dictionary of Marxist Thought*, Oxford 1983, pp. 72-4, and John Urry, *The Anatomy of Capitalist Societies. The Economy, Civil Society and the State*, London and Basingstoke 1981.

11. Cf. my 'Democracy, Ideology, Relativism', in *Democracy and Civil Society*. A contrary view is defended in Frane Adam and Darka Podmenik's introduction to *Socialistična Civilna Družba?*, Ljubljana 1985, pp. 13-16.

12. For the case of Turkey, see Mehmet Ali Dikerdem, 'A Turkish Tug-of-War', *Index on Censorship*, vol. 16, no. 6, June 1987, pp. 15-19. Some Latin American examples include 'Etat et société en Amerique latine', special issue of *Revue de l'Institut de Sociologie*, Brussels 1981, vols 1-2; Alfred Stepan, *The State and Society: Peru in Comparative Perspective*, Princeton, NJ 1978, and 'State Power and the Strength of Civil Society in the Southern Cone of Latin America', in Peter B.

Evans *et al.*, eds, *Bringing the State Back In*, Cambridge 1985, pp. 317-43; Guillermo O'Donnell, 'Tensions in the Bureaucratic-Authoritarian State and the Question of Democracy', in David Collier ed., *The New Authoritarianism in Latin American*, Princeton, NJ 1979, and 'Y A Mi, Que Mierda Me Importa? Notes on Social Interaction and Politics in Argentina and Brazil', paper prepared for the Helen Kellogg Institute, University of Notre Dame, May 1984; 'Sociedad Civil y Autoritarismo', *Critica y Utopia*, vol. 6, March 1982; and Bernardo Sorj and Maria Herminia Tavares de Almeida, eds, *Sociedade e Politica no Brasil Pós-64*, São Paulo 1983.

13. Reinhart Koselleck, *Preussen zwischen Reform und Revolution: Allgemeines Landrecht, Verwaltung und soziale Bewegung von 1791 bis 1848*, third edn, Stuttgart 1981. A short introduction to the argument is provided in 'Staat und Gesellschaft in Preussen 1815-1848', in Werner Conze, ed, *Staat und Gesellschaft im deutschen Vormärz 1815-1848*, Stuttgart 1962, pp. 79-112.

14. Isser Woloch, 'Napoleonic Conscription: State Power and Civil Society', *Past and Present*, no. 111, May 1986, pp. 101-29.

15. The first findings of the Bielefeld research group are published in Jürgen Kocka, ed. *Bürger und Bürgerlichkeit im 19. Jahrhundert*, Göttingen 1987; and in the forthcoming three-volume study edited by Jürgen Kocka, *Bürger und bürgerliche Gesellschaft im 19. Jahrhundert. Deutschland im europäischen Vergleich*.

16. Jürgen Habermas, *Theorie des kommunikativen Handelns*, Frankfurt am Main 1982, vol. 2, p. 471. A parallel attempt to develop the state–civil society distinction in terms of modernization theory is evident in Frane Adam, 'O treh pristopih k pojmu "civilne družbe"', *Katedra*, no. 10/11, May 1987.

17. Karl Marx, *Grundrisse*, Harmondsworth 1973, p. 410 (translation modified).

18. Niklas Luhmann, 'Kapital und Arbeit. Probleme einer Unterscheidung', in Johannes Berger, ed, *Di Moderne – Kontinuitäten und Zäsuren*, special issue of *Soziale Welt*, no. 4, Göttingen 1986; cf. Alvin W. Gouldner, 'Civil Society in Capitalism and Socialism', in *The Two Marxisms. Contradictions and Anomalies in the Development of Theory*, London and Basingstoke 1980.

19. Examples include Theda Skocpol, *States and Social Revolutions: A Comparative Analysis of France, Russia and China*, Cambridge and New York 1979; Anthony Giddens, *The Nation-State and Violence*, Cambridge 1985; Claus Offe, *Contradictions of the Welfare State*; and Bob Jessop, *The Capitalist State: Marxist Theories and Methods*, New York 1982.

20. There has been considerable theoretical awareness of the survival and growth of non-capitalist organizations within modern civil societies, as has been shown by Antony Black, *Guilds and Civil Society in European Political Thought from the Twelfth Century to the Present*, London 1984. Unfortunately, Black's important observations are liable to be misunderstood, especially because his definition of the term civil society is altogether unhistorical – it takes no account of the semantic transformation of the term at the end of the eighteenth century, for instance – as well as too narrowly defined, as a system of market exchange and competitive individualism.

21. The failure to distinguish between the hitherto dominant (less than pluralist) reality of modern civil societies and the *idea* of a fully open and democratic civil society weakens the analysis of Jean Cohen, *Class and Civil Society. The Limits of Marxian Critical Theory*, Amherst 1982.

22. Similar interpretations of the male bias in early arguments for a civil society independent of the state are evident in Anna Yeatman, 'Despotism and Civil Society: The Limits of Patriarchal Citizenship', unpublished paper, Adelaide, 1983;

and Ute Frevert, *Frauen-Geschichte. Zwischen bürgerliche Verbesserung und neuer Weiblichkeit*, Frankfurt am Main 1986, p. 16: 'The enlightenment idea of autonomy, self-determined personality, talents and interests ... is applied only to men.' Some male writers already spotted this self-contradiction. For example Theodor von Hippel, *Über die bürgerliche Verbesserung der Weiber* (1792), appeals to the reason and humanity of men and encourages them to examine their despotic power over women with the same critical eye with which they view absolute states; and according to Chamfort, *Products of the Perfected Civilization* (1794): 'Society, which greatly shrinks men, reduces women to almost nothing.'

23. See my 'Remembering the Dead. Civil Society and the State from Hobbes to Marx and Beyond', in *Democracy and Civil Society*.

24. Antonio Gramsci, *Selections from the Prison Notebooks*, ed. and trans. Q. Hoare and G. Nowell Smith, London 1971, pp. 235, 268.

25. Christopher Pierson's stimulating contributions to a democratic theory of civil society and the state are sometimes seduced by this will to 'concreteness'. His criticism of the abstractness of recent theoretical contributions to the state–civil society discussion tends to blur the *variety* of usages of the distinction sketched here. It also rests on a call for 'concretizing the general advocacy of legally guaranteed social institutions in a socialist civil society to show just what institutions and what guarantees are intended' ('New Theories of State and Civil Society. Recent Developments in Post-Marxist Analysis of the State', *Sociology*, vol. 18, no. 4, November 1984, p. 570).

26. This is a key theme of neo-Gramscian writings such as Ernesto Laclau and Chantal Mouffe, *Hegemony and Socialist Strategy. Towards a Radical Democratic Politics*, London 1985, especially chapter 4.

27. See 'Party-Centred Socialism? Reflections on Contemporary European Socialism and its Party Forms', in *Democracy and Civil Society*.

28. Cf. Michael Walzer, 'The Revolutionary Uses of Repression', in Melvin Richter, ed, *Essays in Theory and History*, Cambridge, Mass. 1970, pp. 122-36.

29. Similar perspectives are developed in 'Remembering the Dead: Civil Society and the State from Hobbes to Marx and Beyond', in *Democracy and Civil Society*, and in Leszek Kolakowski, 'The Myth of Human Self-Identity. The Unity of Civil and Political Society in Socialist Thought', in Leszek Kolakowski and Stuart Hampshire, eds, *The Socialist Idea. A Reappraisal*, London 1977.

30. See Maria Márkus, 'Women, Success, and Civil Society. Submission to, or Subversion of, The Achievement Principle', *Praxis International*, vol. 5, no. 4, January 1986, pp. 430-42.

31. This connection is elaborated in 'Democracy, Ideology, Relativism', in *Democracy and Civil Society*.

32. One example is the theory of 'democratic relativism' defended in Paul K. Feyerabend, *Erkenntnis für freie Menschen*, second edn, Frankfurt am Main 1980, part 2, chapter 3, and his *Problems of Empiricism. Philosophical Papers*, Cambridge 1985, vol. 2. Compare my critiques of Jürgen Habermas's theory of truth and politics in *Public Life and Late Capitalism*, Cambridge and New York 1984.

33. *Ideen zu einem Versuch die Grenzen der Wirksamkeit des Staats zu bestimmen*, Stuttgart 1982 (1972).

PART ONE

The Modern Philosophical Tradition Reconsidered

Despotism and Democracy

The Origins and Development of the Distinction Between Civil Society and the State 1750–1850*

John Keane

Under one despot, I need only stand up against a wall when I see him coming by; or prostrate myself, or knock my forehead against the ground, according to the custom of the country. But under a body of perhaps a hundred despots, I may be obliged to repeat this ceremony a hundred times a day; which is not a little troublesome to those who are not very nimble.

Voltaire

Introduction

Until the middle of the eighteenth century, European political thinkers without exception used the term civil society to describe a type of political association which places its members under the influence of its laws and thereby ensures peaceful order and good government. The term formed part of an old European tradition traceable from modern natural law back through Cicero's idea of *societas civilis* to classical political philosophy – above all to Aristotle, for whom civil society [*koinōnia politiké*] is that society, the *polis*, which contains and dominates all others.[1] In this old European tradition, civil society was coterminous with the state. Civil society [*koinōnia politiké, societas civilis, société civile, bürgerliche*

*For their stimulating comments on an early draft of this essay, I should like to thank Jürgen Kocka, Hans Medick and Ursula Vogel.

Gesellschaft, Civill Society, societá civile] and the state [*polis, civitas, état, Staat, state, stato*] were interchangeable terms. To be a member of a civil society was to be a citizen – a member of the state – and, thus, obligated to act in accordance with its laws and without engaging in acts harmful to other citizens.

Well into the eighteenth century the influence of this classical understanding of civil society remained unchallenged in Britain, France and the German states. It is evident in Hume's observation that 'liberty is the perfection of civil society, but still authority must be acknowledged essential to its very existence.'[2] Rousseau also speaks in this vein:

> Look into the motives which have induced men, once united by their common needs in a general society, to unite themselves still more intimately by means of civil societies [*sociétés civiles*]: you will find no other motive than that of assuring the property, life, and liberty of each member by the protection of all.[3]

Kant repeats this theme: the greatest problem facing the human species is that of establishing a civil society [*societas civilis*] 'in which freedom under external laws is combined to the greatest possible extent with irresistible force, in other words, of establishing a perfectly just civil constitution.'[4]

This traditional concept of civil society began to implode during the second half of the eighteenth century. Sharing the fate of many other concepts in the terminological upheavals of this *Sattelzeit* (Koselleck), it becomes fragile and polysemic, an object of intensive discussion and controversy. The term civil society certainly remained a key word of European political thought throughout the period 1750-1850. By the middle of this period, however, civil society and the state, traditionally linked by the relational concept of *societas civilis*, were seen as *different* entities.[5] Viewed retrospectively, this century-long process of 'disordering' and 'subdividing' the old concept of civil society was highly complex and uneven, geographically, temporally and semantically. The geographic boundaries of this process are most difficult to specify. The distinction between civil society and the state (or 'government', as it was called) almost certainly originated in the Anglo-American world, where, in contrast to continental European thought, 'the state' was rarely seen as an impersonal institution which acts, and therefore (periodically) requires the complete obedience of its subjects.[6] From there its dissemination was geographically restricted, at least initially, to the western and middle regions of Europe.[7] While this much can be observed safely, the rapid circulation of the state–civil society distinction within these regions makes it extremely difficult to pinpoint national differences in terms of either its (relative) presence or absence in political discourse.

In diachronic and semantic terms, the transformation process of the term civil society was no less uneven and complex. During the period 1750-1850 it becomes marked by a deeply protean, even confused quality. The traditional, increasingly moribund meaning coexists and overlaps with the new, incompatible distinction between the state and civil society, whose meaning becomes subject in turn to pluralization through interpretation and disputation.

In the face of such complexities, generalizations about the origins, development and regional significance of the state–civil society distinction are fraught with difficulties, even hazardous. Such simplifying generalizations about the life and times of the concept of civil society, however preliminary and tentative, are nevertheless highly important, since by helping to clarify aspects of the concept's complex history they also help to specify its significance for historical research, as well as for contemporary political thinking orientated to current political controversies and social struggles.[8] Guided by this premiss, this essay suggests one possible generalization about the origins and development of the state–civil society distinction after 1750 in Britain, France and the German states. It reconstructs four temporally and geographically *overlapping* 'phases' of the subdivision and pluralization of the traditional concept of *societas civilis.*[9]

In the early years of the transition period, it is argued, the traditional concept reaches breaking point and becomes impregnated with its future meaning. The attempt is made simultaneously to justify a specifically modern form of civil society – a sovereign, centralized constitutional state standing over its subjects as a *societas civilis cum imperio oder Imperium* – and to emphasize the strategic importance of guarding against its authoritarian potential by fostering the growth of independent 'societies' within civil society. This internal rupturing of the classical concept of civil society developed earliest and most vigorously in Britain and France. The opposition of *société naturelle*, meaning the sphere of economic relations, to *société politique*, for example, is a prominent theme within Physiocratic doctrine. In the German states the traditional concept of *societas civilis* remained intact and dominant somewhat longer.[10] Nevertheless, the decay of the traditional concept is evident in works from all three regions. Examples include Joseph Priestley's *An Essay on the First Principles of Government, and on the Nature of Political, Civil, and Religious Liberty* (1768), Voltaire's *Traité sur la Tolérance* (1763), and Kant's *Idee zu einer allgemeinen Geschichte in weltbürgerlicher Absicht* (1784). This first phase in the 'modernization' of the concept of civil society is illustrated below with one randomly chosen (although highly influential) example: Adam Ferguson's *An Essay on the History of Civil Society* (1767).

The pathbreaking suggestion that the independent 'societies' of a civil society can legitimately defend themselves against the state is consolidated during a second phase of development, in which the novel distinction between civil society and the state becomes contemptuous of the status quo and impregnated by utopian hopes for a future marked by social equality, civil liberties and limited constitutional government. This revolutionary theme of 'civil society against the state' is virtually absent in German political thought – Johann Georg Adam Forster's *Über die Beziehung der Staatskunst auf das Glück der Menschheit* (1794) is a notable exception to the widespread faith of late-eighteenth-century German intellectuals in enlightened reforms from above.[11] This theme first appeared in the 'American and French revolution controversies' in Britain and France, and is prominent in Thomas Spence's *The restorer of society to its natural state in a series of letters to a fellow citizen* (1801), Thomas Hodgskin's *Travels in the North of Germany* (1820) and Emmanuel Joseph Sieyès's *Qu'est-ce que le Tiers-État?* (1789) and the *Déclaration des droits de l'homme et du citoyen* (1791). It is illustrated below by Thomas Paine's *Rights of Man* (1791-92).

During a third phase of development, the anti-statist impulse of the distinction between civil society and the state is weakened. The distinction is preserved, but its predecessors' trust in a free, independent civil society is reversed in favour of sovereign state action. The freedom of civil society is seen to be self-paralysing and conflict-producing, and therefore in need of stricter state regulation and control. This theme of 'the state against civil society' is evident in Jeremy Bentham's *Anarchical Fallacies, being an Examination of the Declaration of Rights issued during the French Revolution* (1796? [1824]), Jean-Charles-Leonard Sismondi's *Nouveaux principes d'économie politique* (1819), and Paul Pfizer's *Briefwechsel zweier Deutschen* (1831, 1832). It is most vigorous and prominent in German political thought, where it appears – simultaneously with phase two – as a defensive reaction against late-eighteenth-century arguments for the separation of civil society from the state. From the time of the French Revolution, what is characteristic of German discussions of *bürgerliche Gesellschaft* is not the fundamental importance of its separation from the state, as Manfred Riedel and others have implied, but rather the necessity of its regulation, restriction and (partial) integration by means of legal, administrative and political controls. The state is viewed as the progenitor of *bürgerliche Gesellshaft*, its guardian, educator and punisher.[12] This characteristic trend culminates in Lorenz von Stein's apology for a state-dominated society in *Geschichte der sozialen Bewegung in Frankreich von 1789 bis auf unsere Tage* (1850) and is exemplified below by G.W.F. Hegel's *Grundlinien der Philosophie des Rechts* (1821).

A fourth contribution to the 'modernization' of the concept of civil society conducts something of a rearguard action against this third view. It fears that civil society is being suffocated gradually by new forms of regulatory state power. Accordingly, it urges the importance of protecting and renewing a pluralistic, self-organizing civil society independent of the state. Before 1850 this fourth viewpoint is least developed in German political thought, although it can be detected, for instance, in Robert von Mohl's writings, such as *Die Polizei-Wissenschaft nach den Grundsätzen des Rechtsstaates* (1832) and *Über Bureaukratie* (1846). It develops more vigorously and influentially in British and French writings, such as J.S. Mill's essays *Civilization* (1836) and *De Tocqueville on Democracy in America* (1835, 1840) and Anne Louise Germaine de Staël's *Considérations sur les principaux événements de la Révolution française* (1818). The theme of protecting society against state sovereignty is especially strong in the post-1814 period of Restoration in France. Liberal thought of this period attempted to understand 'that inexplicable vertigo called the Reign of Terror' (Constant) and to create a political system guaranteeing stable representative government and social liberties. This trend is illustrated here by Alexis de Tocqueville's *De la démocratie en Amérique* (1835-40).

Despotism and Civil Society

The first signs of the breakdown of the classical concept of civil society are evident in Adam Ferguson's remarkable Scottish Enlightenment work, *An Essay on the History of Civil Society* (1767).[13] This essay sketches a 'natural history' of the human species in its transition from 'rude' forms of life to a 'polished' or civilized society, understood in its classical sense. Civil society is not yet perceived as a sphere of life distinct from the state – in Ferguson's view the two are, or should be, identical. A civil society is a type of political order which protects and 'polishes' its mechanical and commercial arts, as well as its cultural achievements and sense of public spirit, by means of regular government, the rule of law and strong military defences.[14]

Past examples of civil society in this sense include the smaller citizen states of classical Greece and the Roman republic. These older civil societies serve as a counterpoint for Ferguson's critical analysis of modern civil societies such as Britain. The latter display certain unique – and self-paralysing – features. In Ferguson's view, 'civilizing' trends are strongly evident in modern societies. Commerce and manufacturing expand by leaps and bounds. Sources of natural wealth are tapped on an unprecedented scale. The mechanical arts are constantly perfected. The division of labour principle is applied increasingly to producers by entrepreneurs, whose costs diminish and profits increase. This principle is also extended to the modern state, which begins to resemble a large and complex machine whose individual parts conform blindly to the purposes of the government of the day:

> The soldier is relieved from every care but that of his service; statesmen divide the business of civil government into shares; and the servants of the public, in every office, without being skilful in the affairs of state, may succeed, by observing forms which are already established on the experience of others. (pp. 181-2)

Regular and orderly government of this type reduces social conflict and quickens the progress of commerce and manufacturing. Commodities of every kind are consequently produced in abundance. This stimulates new desires for wealth, as well as a shared sense that the so-called 'necessaries of life' are neither naturally given nor fixed in their limits (pp. 142, 217, 244-7). In all, the establishment of regular government and the progress of commerce and manufatures fills modern civil societies with hustle and bustle. In this 'age of separations' there is a lively 'air of superior ingenuity' (pp. 183-84) unknown to earlier 'savage' (hunting and fishing) and 'barbarian' (pastoral and agricultural) ages.

Ferguson is by no means an apologist of modern progress. He emphasizes that the success of modern civil societies in establishing regular government and promoting commerce and manufacturing does not immunize them automatically against self-paralysing dangers. Modern civil societies are civilized to an insufficient – and reversible – degree. They may be called 'civilized' or 'polished', but they are subject none the less to various powerful forms of corruption and decline. Ferguson emphasizes that such decay is not primarily the result of 'the fickleness and inconstancy of mankind' (p. 210). Rather, it is an unintended product of the arrangements of moden civil society itself. Of particular concern to Ferguson – his indebtedness to the older tradition of civic humanism is evident here[15] – is the matter in which civil society induces a loss of 'public spirit' among its (male, property-owning) citizens. Their 'disinterested love of the public' withers away; public life is considered 'a scene for the gratification of mere vanity, avarice, and ambition; never as furnishing the best opportunity for a just and a happy engagement of the mind and the heart' (p. 258).

Chief among the causes of this corruption of public spirit is the modern division of labour. Ferguson argues that corruption was relatively absent in more simply organized 'rude' (hunting and fishing) societies and in the smaller citizen states of classical Greece and the Roman republic. In modern civil societies, by contrast, the deepening division of labour – between public administration and private citizens and politicians, between entrepreneurs and workers, soldiers and civilians – corrodes the bonds of civil association. Even the sense of interdependence among groups of individuals dissolves. Civil society 'is made to consist of parts, of which none is animated with the spirit of society itself' (p. 218). Thus, the single-minded pursuit of commerce and manufacturing by the propertied classes embroils every class in the competitive struggle for private gain, luxury and fame.

The struggle for wealth and its display greatly increases social inequality. The lowest ranks, envious of others' wealth and vanity, are driven into sycophancy or criminality and debauchery (pp. 186, 254, 259-60). Meanwhile the higher ranks channel their energies into material or mechanical activities at the expense of literature and higher learning. Under the mask of politeness and moderation, they blindly pursue luxuries and frivolous honours. They also become jealous and possessive. As individual members of civil society, they consider the political community only in so far as it serves their personal advancement or profit (pp. 19, 199, 201, 238, 247, 252, 256-7). Paradoxically, this mercenariness of the propertied classes makes them deceitful and rapacious –

always ready to trespass on the rights of others – as well as 'servile' and 'effeminate' – always ready to adapt for the sake of some future advantage. Their capacity for public-spirited citizenship and political leadership accordingly declines. It is weakened further by the growth of public administration (which requires their subordination in public affairs) and by their cession of military duties to professionalized armies (pp. 220, 230, 255). According to Ferguson, modern civil societies are seriously endangered by this corruption of public spirit. Not only is the advance of corruption camouflaged by the establishment of regular government and the vigorous progress of commerce and manufacturing, but the loss of public spirit neutralizes (male, property-owning) citizens' suspicion of power and thus prepares the way for despotic government.

The dialectic between civil society and political despotism is basic to Ferguson's argument. Despotism is seen as a form of oligarchic state which pacifies its subjects and divests them of their traditional civil rights, if necessary by bureaucratic regulation, fraud and military force. It dispenses with public discussion and encourages jealousy and mutual mistrust among the governed. Despotism greatly fears man's natural 'spirit of dissension' (p. 269), and for that reason thrives on the corruption of public spirit. For that reason also, despotism has a deep affinity with modern civil society. Ferguson warns that the path to despotism is *prepared* by civil society: 'The rules of despotism are made for the government of corrupted men' (p. 240). Civil society destroys public spirit. It strengthens the scope and power of state administration and accustoms its subjects to the civil order and tranquillity it secures. Civil society also institutes a professional army, thus exposing itself to the dangers of government by military force.

While Ferguson does not consider despotism to be the 'fate' of modern civil society, his argument certainly poses some difficult political questions. How can the advance of despotism be prevented? Is modern civil society capable of reforming itself? Or is political corruption an ineradicable feature of modern times? In response to such questions, Ferguson is straightforward enough: despotism is preventable, but only in so far as the privileged (male, property-owning) citizens of civil society strive to raise their level of public-spiritedness and capacity for civil association and leadership of the lower ranks under a sovereign constitutional monarchy.

Admittedly, this proposal for a *more* civil society guided by a

constitutional monarchy bears the marks of Ferguson's classical
fear of the 'effeminacy' of 'the fair sex' (p. 201) and the underclasses[16] and his dislike of republican government. Apart from
vague references to the resilience of the 'human spirit' (pp. 278-
80), it also fails to specify how the corrupted citizens of civil
society can shake off their corruption – or even an entrenched
despotism – and learn to 'love the public, and respect ... its laws'
(p. 267). Ferguson insists that 'liberty is a right which every
individual must be ready to vindicate for himself' (p. 266), but
whether this right is to be enforced through honourable or heroic
individual acts or peacefully organized civil action remains
wholly unclear. Ferguson's defence of a public-spirited constitutional monarchy is none the less extremely interesting. It poses
with great clarity a thoroughly modern political dilemma, which
in turn very nearly bursts the seams of his classical concept of civil
society.

Ferguson recognizes that the public spirit typical of the savage
tribe, the barbarian clan or small states such as classical Greece
cannot be re-created in the large-scale, complex civil societies of
modern times (or at least not without sacrificing the achieved
benefits of regular constitutional government, commerce and
manufacturing). But Ferguson also recognizes that large-scale
modern civil societies breed political despotism. The centralized
political-legal arrangements of civil society – the 'government of
laws' (p. 263) – can help to restrict political abuses and secure
citizens' civil liberties and 'rights of property and station' (p. 156).
But centralized government based on the rule of law cannot alone
guarantee the civil freedoms of citizens, since those who exercise
power directly are apt constantly to abuse it.[17] Hence the
dilemma: modern civil society requires for its survival a sovereign, centralized constitutional state which, together with
commerce and manufacturing, breaks 'the bands of society' (p.
218) and threatens citizens' civil liberties and capacity for
independent association, thus undermining a *sine qua non* of life in
a civil society.

Ferguson's attempted resolution of this dilemma is brief and
tentative, but nevertheless of great interest to a contemporary
history of the modernization of the concept of civil society. His
key normative principle is the creation and strengthening of citizens' associations – whether in courts of law (juries), the military
(citizens' militias) or in civil society at large. According to
Ferguson, man, in contrast to the animals, has an innate capacity
'to consult, to persuade, to oppose, to kindle in the society of his

fellow-creatures' (p. 218). He acts best when in social groups. His life is therefore happiest and freest when under the influence of the 'animated spirit of society' (p.30).

It follows that governments become illegitimate – despotic – whenever they stifle the public spirit so engendered by association in social groups (p. 64). The unity of civil society must not be achieved at the expense of social solidarity:

> The great object of policy ... is, to secure to the family its means of subsistence and settlement; to protect the industrious in the pursuit of his occupation; to reconcile the restrictions of police, and the social affections of mankind, with their separate and interested pursuit. (p. 144)

Here Ferguson comes close to saying that the survival and progress of modern civil society require the development of independent social associations – the development of a civil society within a civil society. Not surprisingly, his classical train of thought never allowed this paradoxical conclusion. To have taken that step would have made no sense either to his classically minded contemporaries or to future thinkers, for whom civil society and the state would no longer be coterminous entities.

Civil Society versus the State

Ferguson's cautious suggestion that the 'animated spirit of society' may need to be defended against political power is developed explicitly during a second phase of the modernization of the concept of civil society. This transition is evident in Thomas Paine's polemic against Edmund Burke in the *Rights of Man* (1791-2).[18] This work throbs with the immediacy and drama of the French Revolution.[19] Its exuberant optimism also reflects the innovations of the American Revolution: the declaration of the natural rights of man and of popular sovereignty as fundamental constitutional principles; the establishment of the right to resist unlawful government as a basic legal principle; and the implementation of a republican and altogether new federal political structure. According to Paine, the power of the state must be restricted in favour of civil society because within all individuals there is a natural propensity for society: existing before the formation of states, this natural sociability predisposes individuals to establish peaceful and happy relations of competition and solidarity based only on reciprocal self-interest and a shared sense of mutual aid. The state is deemed a necessary evil and civil society an unqualified good. The legitimate state is nothing more than a delegation of power for the common benefit of society. The more perfect civil society is, the more it regulates its own affairs and the less occasion it has for government. There is an inverse relationship between *société libre, gouvernement simple* and *société contrainte, gouvernement compliqué.*

The possibility of a naturally self-regulating society administered by a limited state is contrasted with the present age of despotism. With the notable exception of America, Paine complains, states everywhere crush and barbarize their populations. Global despotism – the constitutional monarchy of Britain as much as the Bourbon absolutism of France – makes individuals fearful of thinking. Reason becomes considered as treasonable, and individuals' natural rights to freedom are hounded to every corner of the earth. The modern world is 'uncivilized' (p. 105) because it is overgoverned. Individuals consequently become caught in an endless labyrinth of political institutions which prevent them from scrutinizing the principles, good or bad, upon which existing laws are founded. Dependent upon the whims and fancies of political despots and their appointers, they are expected to be ignorant and submissive; they are tempted and cajoled constantly to pass, cash in hand, through 'a wilderness of turnpike gates' (p. 89). This makes them wretched, for the overwhelming force of despotic states and laws denatures individuals by tearing them away from themselves and from each other. They are degraded and victimized by a global system of *political* alienation. In this world turned upside down by despotic governments, (potentially) self-determining and sociable individuals become lost, causes and effects appear reversed, and states represent themselves as the real and proper source of property, power and prestige.

These inversions have highly negative consequences, or so Paine argues. He emphasizes that despotic states are responsible for maintaining the patriarchal form of power within households. Despotic states rest on and presuppose despotic households, in which the arbitrary exercise of power by fathers (bequeathing property to their first-born sons, for instance) reinforces 'family tyranny and injustice' (p. 105). Despotic states also institute class divisions within society by loading their subjects with excessive rates of taxation. Everywhere, the greedy hand of state thrusts itself into social life, seizing (the fruits of) its property and inventing further pretences for the collection of yet more taxation revenues. Such excesses of taxation throw parts of society into poverty and discontent. The propertyless are impoverished and oppressed, the rich become ever more privileged, and violent struggles beween classes ensue.

Self-aggrandizing, despotic governments also seek to extract power and revenue from their societies by cultivating bellicose national prejudices and preparing for armed conflict with other states. The age of despotism is also an age of war. States subjugate and plunder their populations in order to make war; conversely, they make war in order to extract revenues and support from their populations. Wars between states increase their power over their populations and this, in turn, further undermines the possibility of natural social harmony. War, says Paine, is 'the art of *conquering at home*' (p. 99).

Paine is convinced that this global subsumption of societies by despotic states is only temporary. The dissolution of arbitrary political power is merely a matter of time – despotic states are weak and unpopular by virtue of their 'artificiality'. The decisive question for him is only whether the approaching revolutions in modern government can be made to unfold by way of 'reason and accommodation' rather than through blind and dramatic 'convulsions' (p. 168). Pointing to the example of the American Revolution, Paine stresses repeatedly the need for deliberately resisting the excesses of state power. This conviction is nourished by two related but quite different types of argument which lead, as I shall show, to political conclusions very different from those of Ferguson.

In the first place, the legitimate state is that which is guided by the principles of natural right and active consent of the governed. Here Paine radicalizes the contractualist arguments of early modern political thought.[20] He emphasizes that the power of states is only ever delegated, on trust, by actively consenting individuals who can legitimately retrieve this power at any time by withdrawing their consent. No particular political group or institution is possessed of the right to bind and control how, and by whom, the world is to be governed. This follows from the principle that 'man has no property in man' (p. 64). All individuals are born equal, and with equal natural rights. (The textual evidence on this point suggests that Paine universalizes the contractualist thesis to include not only minorities but also women and the underclasses.)

These natural rights (to free speech, public assembly and

independent religious worship, for instance) are God-given and predispose individuals to act freely and reasonably for their own comfort and happiness, without injuring or trespassing the natural rights of others. In this sense, *natural* rights provide a *political* Archimedean point, a 'fixed and steady principle' (p. 151) for measuring the legitimacy of states. Natural rights, by definition, cannot be annihilated, transferred or divided, and – contrary to the conservatism of Burke and others – no generation is empowered to deny them to their heirs.

This rights-based argument – absent from Ferguson's discussion – indicates why Paine thinks that states cannot be understood as a compact between the governors and the governed. Rights-bearing, free and equal individuals naturally *precede* past, present and future states. Thus states can be considerd legitimate or 'civilized' only when they have been formed through the explicit consent of individuals and when this active consent is formulated constitutionally and articulated continuously through parliamentary, representative mechanisms. Civilized governments are constitutional governments empowered by the active consent of naturally free and equal individuals. These governments have no rights, but only duties before their citizens. They should be the product of contracting individuals and must always be considered as creatures of their constitutions, which specify such matters as the duration of parliaments, the frequency of elections, the mode of representation, the powers of the judiciary, the conditions under which war can be declared, and the levying and spending of public monies. Government without a constitution is equivalent to power without right:

> A constitution ... is to a government, what the laws made afterwards by that government are to a court of judicature. The court of judicature does not make the laws, neither can it alter them; it only asks in conformity to the laws made: and the government is in like manner governed by the constitution. (p. 93)

Particular governments cannot arbitrarily alter or expand their constitutions, nor can they legitimately violate the trust and consent of individual citizens. It is in the natural order of things, Paine concludes, that individual citizens are permanently sovereign. Any reversal of this natural order, and every attempt to preclude actively represented consent as the basis of law, is despotism: aggressive government accountable only to itself.

Paine proceeds from this first argument concerning the

natural rights of individuals to a second thesis which overthrows the classical understanding of the term civil society by distinguishing explicitly between civil society and the state. This thesis seeks to explain why free and equal individuals living together on earth actively desire peaceful and co-operative forms of social life which are self-reliant and independent of state institutions. According to Paine, there are two respects in which individuals are naturally disposed to co-operative forms of social life.

First, individuals' natural wants exceed their individual powers. This means that they are incapable of activating their powers and satisfying their diverse wants without the labours and assistance of others. Consequently, they are driven ('as naturally as gravitation acts to a centre' [p. 185]) to establish forms of commercial exchange based on reciprocal interest and the division of labour. Competitive market relations of this kind (as Paine says elsewhere) consist of 'distinct, unconnected individuals following various trades, employments and pursuits; continually meeting, crossing, uniting, opposing and separating from each other, as accident, interest, and circumstances shall direct.'[21]

The commercial dependence of individuals upon others for the satisfaction of their diverse wants is reinforced, Paine argues, by 'a system of social affections' (p. 185). This deep yearning for solidarity with others is a natural affection and, paradoxically, it is replenished continually by the motivating force of individuals' market interests. (Paine ignores Ferguson's fear of the loss of public spirit due to the growth of commerce and manufactures, apparently because he assumes the existence of a mainly pre-industrial economy based on perfect competition among small propertied worker-entrepreneurs.) This felicitous coincidence of market competition and the love of others, Paine concludes, predisposes individuals to live together harmoniously by exercising their natural rights to freedom and happiness within a civil society, unhindered by state institutions, which recognizes only the rules of mutual respect, the satisfaction of interest and the safety and freedom of all individuals.

Certainly Paine is aware that social life can be corrupted and deformed, and that this has political effects. In past times natural societies were always plundered and degraded by political conquerors armed with brutal weapons, exploitative laws and ideologies of 'political superstition' (p. 199). In the present age, social life continues to be encircled and suppressed by despotic states which rather than consolidating society seek to divide it, destroy its natural cohesion, and stir up discontent among its members.[22] Once individuals' desire for society is aroused, however, despotic states quickly begin to crumble into ruins. The desocialization of already free, equal and rational individuals is an impossibility (p. 140). Indeed, the more civil society develops confidence in its capacity for self-government, the less need there is for state institutions and laws. A confident, self-regulating society requires only a minimum of political mechanisms – what Paine calls 'government' – to ensure the natural interaction of the various parts of civil society upon each other.

Paine suggests also that the reduction of state power to a minimum would make possible the formation of an *international* confederation of nationally independent and peacefully interacting civil societies (pp. 147, 191-2). The nationally sovereign state would then be nothing more than the elected manager and guarantor of the 'universal peace, civilization and commerce' (p. 183) of civil society. This 'national association acting on the principles of society' (p. 189) is needed only to supply the few public services which civil society cannot conveniently supply for itself.

In contrast to the labyrinthine, spendthrift, secretive and bellicose operations of despotic states, the limited constitutional state would be qualitatively more simple and efficient, cheaper, and more open and peaceful. Its patterns of responsibility to society would be clear, well defined, and maintained through constitutionally guaranteed mechanisms of representation which protect society from the state. Individuals would understand clearly the origins and rationale of their political system. Nothing would be hidden from the eyes of civil society. The limited state would be as visible as it is near to its citizens, and its operations, as a consequence, would be widely supported.

Paine is certain that limited states guided by civil societies bonded together by reciprocal interest and mutual affection would make for a condition of global order and harmony. Freely interacting individuals thrive on the aid they receive from each other, and from other civil societies. Common interest is the 'law' of civil society, and it far outweighs the importance and steadying influence of positive laws enacted and administered by governments: 'The instant formal government is abolished, society begins to act. A general association takes place, and common interest produces common security' (p. 186). Paine conceives common security as a consequence of 'natural' forces, not as a *historical* achievement. Individuals tend to interact with others spontaneously; this leads them to form an interlocking, self-sufficient social whole emancipated from conflict. Hence, if states were everywhere constructed upon this natural social foundation, the present unfreedom, inequality and antagonisms among individuals and groups would wither away. Social divisions and (domestic and international) political unrest would be replaced by the 'cordial unison' (p. 189) of a civilized society.

The Universal State

The third phase of concern with civil society – illustrated here by G.W.F. Hegel's *Grundlinien der Philosophie des Rechts* (1821)[23] – can be understood as a reaction against its predecessor's unbridled enthusiasm for civil society. In Hegel's hands the term civil society assumes a less positive meaning; it is viewed as a self-crippling entity in constant need of state supervision and control. Hegel's interpretation nevertheless makes two novel contributions to the modernization of the idea of civil society, albeit at the price of a weakened sensitivity to political power and its authoritarian potential.

First, in striking contrast to Paine's account, civil society [*bürgerliche Gesellschaft*] is conceived not as a natural condition of freedom but as a *historically produced* sphere of ethical life [*Sittlichkeit*] 'positioned' between the simple world of the patriarchal household and the universal state. It includes the market economy, social classes, corporations, and institutions concerned with the administration of 'welfare' [*Polizei*] and civil law. Civil society is a mosaic of private individuals, classes, groups and institutions whose transactions are regulated by civil law and, as such, are not directly dependent upon the political state itself.

Hegel emphasizes that civil society in this sense is not a pre-given and invariable substratum of 'natural life' which exists beyond space and time. Rather, it is the outcome of a long and complex process of historical transformation: 'The creation of civil society is the achievement of the modern world' (p. 339). Moreover, the 'system of needs' it develops – here Ferguson's probable influence on Hegel is evident – represents a decisive and evident break with the natural environment (pp. 346-60).[24] The modern bourgeois-directed economy, for instance, is a dynamic system of commodity production by means of commodities. It greatly increases the level of specialization and mechanization of human labour. Nature is thereby transformed into an instrument for the satisfaction of human needs, which multiply and diversify and can therefore no longer be understood as 'natural' (pp. 341-3, 346-51).

Hegel's second novel contribution to modern theories of civil society follows from this critique of naturalism. In his view there is no necessary identity or harmony among the various elements of civil society. Harmony nourished by unadulterated love is an essential characteristic of the patriarchal family. Described by Hegel as the 'first ethical root of the state' (p. 396), the family is an immediate, unreflecting unity whose members (especially women, who are guided by intuition and feeling and therefore destined for love and marriage) understand themselves as 'accidents' (p. 313) and not as competitive individuals bound together by contract.

In civil society things are otherwise. Its multiple forms of interaction are often incommensurable, fragile, and subject to serious conflict. 'Nature', remarked Paine, 'is orderly in all her works', and this is why the manifold elements of civil society (its 'societies') merge spontaneously and harmoniously.[25] Hegel rejects this naturalistic assumption as well as its naive view of the sources of social equilibrium. Modern civil society, rather, resembles a restless battlefield where private (male) interest meets private (male) interest. It unfolds and develops in a blind, arbitrary, quasi-spontaneous manner. This means not only that it cannot overcome its own particularities but also that it tends to paralyse and undermine its own pluralism. As Hegel observes elsewhere, the exuberant development of one part of civil society may, and often does, impede or oppress its other parts.[26]

The subdivision of civil society into classes (or *Stände*) is a principal reason why it is divided against itself and therefore gripped by an inner restlessness. Hegel recognizes a variety of classes or class fragments – civil servants, landowners, peasantry, intellectuals, lawyers, doctors and clergymen – but he locates the moving principle of civil society primarily in the *Bürgerstand*. Much of his analysis is reminiscent of Ferguson's. Hegel argues that this class of burghers (in which he includes workers) is defined, paradoxically, by its selfish individualism. The burgher class certainly depends upon the corporations – municipal, trade, educational, religious, professional and other state-authorized forms of collective associations – which function as its 'second home', as a shelter which protects it from the vicissitudes of life in civil society and familiarizes it with a higher level of ethical (or public-sprited) form of life (pp. 394-5). The selfish actions of the burgher class and those of its unintended child, the 'rabble of paupers' (pp. 389, 395) are further restrained by the civil 'administration of justice' (pp. 360-82) and by the various regulations and moral improvements secured by the 'policing' agencies of civil society (pp. 382-93).[27]

Nevertheless, the burgher class tends to struggle against the restrictions imposed by the corporations, civil administration and police. It regards all these as the means of furthering its particular interests through commercial transactions (pp. 339-45). The burgher is less a public-spirited *citoyen* than a self-serving *bourgeois* who likes to keep others at arm's length. He is an apolitical man who likes to stand on his own two feet. He is impatient with traditional privileges, shows little genuine interest in public affairs, and is concerned only with his self-enrichment through the exercise of his private property. He views his freedom as abstract – as the freedom to act within the bounds of externally enforced laws which safeguard his property and enforce contracts. In this way – here Hegel agrees with Ferguson and Paine – modern civil society becomes a complex system of transacting individuals whose livelihoods, legal status and happiness are mutually interwoven. But it is precisely this universal selfishness – here Hegel rejects Paine's belief in natural sociability and Ferguson's trust in citizenship – which turns civil society into a blind and unstable field of economic competition among private non-citizens.[28]

This tendency is of great concern to Hegel and indicates why he emphasizes that modern civil society is incapable of overcoming its own particularity and resolving its inherent conflicts by itself. Civil society cannot remain 'civil' unless it is ordered politically, subjected to 'the higher surveillance of the state' (p. 397). Only a supreme public authority – a constitutional state managed by the monarchy, the civil service and the Estates – can effectively remedy its injustices and synthesize its particular interests into a universal political community. From this perspective Hegel criticizes modern natural law theory for confusing civil society and the state, for supposing the latter to be a mere partnership of its subjects (pp. 339-40, 415-31, 491-4) and thus for challenging the 'absolutely divine principle of the state, together with its majesty and absolute authority' (p. 400).

The ideal state is not a radical negation of a natural condition in perpetual war (Hobbes, Spinoza) nor an instrument for conserving and completing natural society (Locke, Pufendorf) nor a simple mechanism for administering a naturally given, automatically self-governing civil society (Paine). Rather, Hegel conceives the state as a new moment which contains, preserves and synthesizes the conflicting elements of civil society into a higher ethical entity. The state represents society in its unity. Civil society is *aufgehoben*: it is at the same time preserved and overcome as a necessary but subordinate aspect of a wider, more complex and higher community which is organized politically. These arguments lead Hegel to seek a path between Ferguson's and Paine's radically different theories of the state. According to Hegel, if the state demands from civil society only what is necessary for itself, and if it accordingly limits itself to guaranteeing this necessary minimum, then beyond this limit the state can and should permit considerable scope for the freedom of male individuals and groups acting within civil society. This means, on the one hand, that the state should not be considered as a central superintendant which direct the life of all other institutions (a type of state which Hegel identified in oriental despotism and in the Prussian state of Frederick the Great). On the other hand, against Paine and others, Hegel urges that the public authority cannot take the form of an administrative body which rarely interferes with the conduct of civil society (pp. 384-5, 406-11). He proposes that both points of view must and can be satisfied: the freedom of the members of civil society can be guaranteed and synthesized with the state's articulation and defence of the universal interest.

Although Hegel consequently recommends against dissolving the separation of civil society from the state, it is clear that the degree to which civil society is differentiated from the state cannot be fixed through hard and fast general rules. Ultimately, from his perspective, the relationship of state and society can be determined only by weighing up, *from the standpoint of political reason*, the advantages and disadvantages of restricting the independence, abstract freedom and competitive pluralism of civil society in favour of universal state prerogatives.

Hegel supposes two conditions under which state intervention (in his words, the state's 'purging of privileges and wrongs') is legitimate. First, the state may intervene in order to remedy injustices or inequalities within civil society – for instance, the domination of one or more classes by another, the pauperization of whole groups or the establishment of local oligarchies (within a region or municipality, for example). Secondly, the supreme public power is justified in intervening directly in the affairs of civil society to protect and further the universal interest of the population – which the state itself defines! The activity of the corporations is an important case in point: although they require autonomy to facilitate their members' development of *Sittlichkeit*, it is precisely because of their (potential) 'public' character that they require subjection to the 'higher surveillance' of the state, lest they degenerate into its rivals (p. 397). Thus, while Hegel defends the need for 'particularity ... to develop and expand in all directions' within civil society, he insists at the same time that the universal state has 'the right to prove itself as the ground and necessary form of particularity, as well as the power which stands over it as its final purpose' (p. 340; cf. pp. 384–5).

Considered together, these two conditions constitute a very broad licence indeed for state regulation and dominance of social life.[29] The fear of despotism which motivates Ferguson's and Paine's reflections on civil society is drastically weakened in favour of a deep trust in state regulation. Despotism is seen as a problem of earlier times,[30] and the problem of how, and under which conditions, male citizens can question, reconsider and resist state power falsely claiming to be universal – the problem of political democracy and active citizenship – falls into obscurity. Simply stated, if the requirements of the public good set limits upon the autonomy of civil society, and if the state itself – a monarchic one at that – is ultimately responsible for determining these requirements, how can its interventions possibly be identified and prevented as illegitimate?

Hegel's failure to deal adequately with this quintessentially modern problem of (democratic) checks and balances on the universal state – his assumption that the monarchic state is in the last instance sovereign *vis-à-vis* all relationships within the family and civil society – weakens, even contradicts, his claims on behalf of an independent civil society which guarantees the 'living freedom' of individuals and groups. From the perspective of Hegel's metaphysics, indeed, the ideal of the universal state is understood as 'absolutely rational' (pp. 399, 11-28). It is the highest and concluding moment of a process of historical development in which reason actively works itself into the existing world.

The universal state is the concrete human embodiment of the ethical Idea, of mind [*Geist*] developing from a stage of immediate, undifferentiated unity (the family), through that of explicit difference and particularity (civil society), to the concrete unity and synthesis of the particular in the state.[31] Given that the process of human history is in this sense 'the movement of God in the world' (p. 403), the universal state conceived by Hegel must be regarded as a secular deity whose claims upon its male citizens and female and other subjects are always for their benefit and, ultimately, unquestionable and irresistible.

The New Despotism

Tocqueville's *De la démocratie en Amérique* (1835-40)[32] – the fourth type of contribution to a modern theory of civil society considered here – provocatively attempts to draw attention to the political dangers implicit in such reasoning. According to Tocqueville, arguments in defence of a state which governs civil society in the name of the universal interest are implicated in a dangerous development: the growth of a new type of state despotism which is popularly elected. Drawing upon his study of American government and society (as well as his re-examination of the French Revolution in *L'Ancien Régime et la Révolution*), Tocqueville emphasizes that it is not conflict and disorder generated by particular interests but this new form of elected state despotism which is the principal hazard confronting modern nations. Paradoxically, an age which is committed ever more strongly to democratic mechanisms for resisting inequalities of power and wealth also favours, in the name of the sovereignty of the people, equality of treatment and uniform provision, the gradual concentration of power in the hands of a centralized administrative state which secures the well-being of civil society and robs it of its freedoms.

This state servitude is to be dreaded, Tocqueville explains, because its contours are so little examined and its negative consequences so poorly understood. The new despotism is without historical precedent. It is also difficult to detect inasmuch as modern democratic societies pride themselves on having shattered the despotism of aristocratic times. Modern nations no longer feel threatened by despotism because the stranglehold of that old form of power over its subjects is indeed in the process of being broken. According to Tocqueville's highly original thesis, a 'great democratic revolution' (vol. 1, p. 57), has begun to sweep through all spheres of modern life. In these post-aristocratic societies daily existence becomes agitated because democratic mechanisms awaken and foster a widespread passion for the equalization of power, property and status within the spheres of state and civil society.

Tocqueville observes that in the political realm [*société politique*] everything becomes disputed and uncertain. The convincing power of sentimental tradition, absolute morality and religious faith in otherworldly aims is shaken; in this sceptical, secular age of political democracy the stars of mythical belief fall to earth, the light of faith grows dim, and the horizons of political action become worldly and thus subject to argument, persuasion and practical judgement. Those who live in democratic nations consequently look upon political power with a jealous eye; they are prone to suspect or despise those who wield it and are thereby impatient with arbitrary state regulation. The state and its laws lose their divinity, coming to be regarded as necessary and/or expedient and as properly based on the voluntary consent of the citizens. The spell of absolute monarchic power is broken, political rights are extended gradually from the privileged political classes to the humblest citizens, and political regulations and laws are constantly subjected to redefinition and alteration.

Tocqueville emphasizes that distinctions and privileges are eroded gradually not only in the field of politics but also within the domain of civil society [*société civile*]. Modern democracies are subject to a permanent 'social revolution' (vol. 1, p. 69). Naturalistic definitions of social life – here Tocqueville agrees with Hegel – are replaced by avowed conventions. (Tocqueville notes, for instance, that democracy gradually destroys or modifies 'that great inequality of man and woman, which has appeared hitherto to be rooted eternally in nature' [vol. 2, p. 263], although this does not lead him to doubt that 'the sources of a ... woman's happiness are in the home of her husband'); (hereditary) property is parcelled out, social power is shared ever more widely, and the unequal capacities of classes tend to dissolve.

This is not to say that democracies are without concentrations of wealth. Such concentrations of property persist, but Tocqueville sees them as vulnerable, as subject constantly to redistribution through changes in fortune, competition, legal redefinition and social pressures from the propertyless. Having subverted the systems of feudalism and absolute monarchy, the democratic revolution refuses to bow before the social power of notables, merchants and industrial capitalists. The fear of losing their privileges strikes at the heart of these social groups – which is also why they have a hearty dislike of democratic mechanisms.

Tocqueville evidently exaggerates the momentum and extent of this levelling process, yet the logic of his explanation remains compelling: once certain social claims (for example rights to property) are defended by one group, the pressure is greater for extending them to other social groups; after each such concession

new demands from the socially less powerful force new concessions from the privileged, until the once restricted social claims
become universal in scope. The dilemma of modern civil societies
is that they must extend social rights to everybody or to nobody.
Since the latter option is an open embarrassment to democracy,
the process of social levelling tends to develop an irreversible
momentum of its own.

Democratic mechanisms, Tocqueville argues, stimulate a
passion for social equality which they can never quite satisfy:
'This complete equality slips from the hands of the people at the
very moment when they think they have grasped it and flies, as
Pascal says, an eternal flight' (vol. 1, p. 285). The less powerful
ranks of civil society are especially caught in the grip of this
dynamic. Agitated by the fact of their subordination and by the
possibility of overcoming it, they are also irritated by the uncertainty of achieving equality; their initial enthusiasm and hope
give way to disappointment and frustration and to renewed
commitment to the struggle for equality. This 'perpetual
movement of society' (vol. 1, p. 261) fills the new world of modern
democracy with radical scepticism and an impatient love of
novelty. In this democratic maelstrom, nothing seems any more
to be fixed or inviolable except the passionate, dizzying struggle
for social and political equality.

Tocqueville stresses that this struggle for equality is not synonymous with the securing of social and political liberties. Although
citizens cannot become equal unless their activities are also self-
determined, attempts to realize the ideals of equality and liberty
can contradict each other and should therefore be carefully
distinguished. Tocqueville sees this point as especially pertinent
in the contemporary period, in which the ideal of freedom from
despotism is being replaced by the goal of state-secured equality.[33] This 'democratic counter-revolution' is not primarily a
consciously willed process. Many are presently aiding and abet-
ting this counter-revolution without knowing it. Some of its
declared opponents are even happy to be driven along by its
peaceful currents:

> Day by day citizens fall constantly under the control of the public
> administration, to which they insensibly surrender ever greater
> portions of their individual independence. These very same citizens,
> who periodically upset a throne and trampled on the feet of kings,
> more and more submit themselves, without resistance, to the smallest
> dictate of a clerk. (vol. 2, p. 379)

The more this consensus about the need for centralized public regulation develops, and the more state institutions become practically involved in the provision of 'public utilities', the less civil society can cope without state direction, the need for which consequently grows. Trapped within this dynamic, individuals and social groups are drawn, willingly and without coercion, into relations of political dependence. The hands and eyes of the state intrude more and more into the minutiae of daily life. The democratic revolution loses momentum. In the name of democratic equality, government becomes regulator, inspector, adviser, educator, and punisher of social life. It functions as a kind of tutelary power which 'perpetuates in the social body a type of administrative drowsiness which the heads of the administration are inclined to call good order and public tranquillity' (vol. 1, p. 158).

This administrative suffocation of civil society is evident, Tocqueville argues, in the state's growing monopoly of public instruction, health care and the provision of support for the unemployed and destitute. Such state monopolies in the field of *polizei* are reinforced by the rise of capitalist manufacturing industry. Under capitalist conditions workers are degraded and subjected to a new social power group (an 'aristocracy', as Tocqueville calls them) of industrial manufacturers. This class springs from the heart of democratic society and potentially threatens its freedom and pluralism. It systematically applies the division of labour principle to manufacturing. This greatly increases the efficiency and volume of production. At the same time, the modern division of labour concentrates workers in crowded and putrid urban conditions, renders them more narrow-minded, brutish and impoverished, and disposes them to rebel against the existing social inequalities.

Tocqueville sees growing demands by the manufacturing class for state 'improvement' and surveillance of these rebellious urban poor as a likely consequence of the industrialization of civil society. In addition, he observes that the manufacturing class also expects the state to provide harbours, canals, roads and other large-scale infrastructural projects which facilitate the general acquisition of wealth. (Tocqueville evidently failed to consider the obstructive capacity of the manufacturing class – its self-interested propensity to resist state encroachments upon its 'private' power within civil society.) Finally, as the power and scope of the state increase, its consumption of manufactured goods grows larger. States even become directly involved in the manufacturing process, employing large numbers of engineers, architects, mechanics and skilled workers.

For each of these reasons, areas of civil life formerly beyond the control of state administration become subject to its inquisitive and directive powers. Tocqueville insists that this all-pervasive state administration is unlike any species of despotism which existed before. In former times, despotic states never attempted to monitor and control their subjects through strictly centralized, complex and meddlesome forms of power. Even at the height of the Roman Empire, Tocqueville claims, its cruel rulers did not seek directly to administer their populations down to the smallest detail; different nations within the Empire retained their diverse customs and powerful and active municipalities survived. The cruellest despotisms of past times never managed completely to eliminate forms of oppositional power.

The modern type of state despotism is in this sense qualitatively different. It stands guard over the whole of civil society as a power which is 'absolute, differentiated, regular, provident and mild' (vol. 2, p. 385). It is highly dangerous, because in the name of securing the welfare of the sovereign people it enslaves them in the minor (as well as the major) details of life. This type of tutelary power does not destroy life or tyrannize in the old ways. It rarely employs the coarse instruments of *autos-da-fé*, fetters and executioners. Modern state despotism perfects and 'civilizes' its techniques of control and is therefore rendered less odious and degrading in the eyes of its subjects. Peacefully, and by means of democratically formulated and administered laws, it transforms its (male) citizens into passive subjects who are expected to invest their trust in 'benevolent' power and busy themselves with family life, work and material consumption.

Tocqueville is appalled by this development. In his view it threatens to sabotage the decisive victories of the democratic revolution and its goals of equality and freedom for all citizens. Consequently, he reasons that the decisive political problem of modern times concerns how the equalizing tendencies triggered by this democratic revolution can be preserved without allowing the state to abuse its powers and rob its (male) citizens of their freedom. Tocqueville points out – against talk of the withering away or elimination of state power – that this problem of securing equality with freedom *cannot* be solved by abolishing political institutions. Active and strong state institutions are both necessary and desirable conditions of democratic freedom and equality.

Just as all speakers of a language must have recourse to definite grammatical forms in order to express themselves, so citizens living together in a democracy are obliged to submit themselves to a political authority, without which they would fall into confusion and disorder. This is especially so within large and complex democratic nations, whose common interests, such as the formulation and administration of positive law and the conduct of foreign policy, cannot be taken care of effectively without a powerful centralized governmental apparatus. However, in order to prevent the yoke of state despotism from descending on to the modern world and paralysing its revolutionary momentum, mechanisms of several kinds are required for preventing the build-up of power monopolies.

Within the realm of *state* institutions – here some key themes of the *Rights of Man* resurface – the paralysis of the democratic revolution can be minimized by ensuring that political power is distributed into many and various hands. A legislative power subject to periodic elections combined with a separate executive authority and an independent judiciary, for instance, minimize the risk of administrative despotism by ensuring that the political power which governs civil society frequently changes hands and adopts different courses of action and is thus prevented from becoming excessively centralized and all-embracing. Tocqueville also stresses the rich democratic consequences of citizens' action *within* state institutions. He sees the American jury system as exemplifying this principle of supplementing representative democratic mechanisms (for example, citizens' election of representatives to the legislature) with direct citizen participation. The jury system facilitates citizens' self-government as well as teaching them how to govern others prudently and fairly; they learn how to judge fellow-citizens as they would wish to be judged themselves. The jury system 'invests each citizen with a kind of magistracy; it makes them all feel the obligations which they are bound to discharge towards society and the part which they play in its government' (vol. 1, p. 376).

Tocqueville is certain that these kinds of *political* checks upon despotism must be reinforced by the growth and development of *civil* associations which lie beyond the control of state institutions. He no doubt underestimated the scope and democratic potential of workers' resistance to the grip of capitalist manufacturing industry upon civil society. (In *De la démocratie en Amerique* Tocqueville does not consider workers as a separate social class but rather as a menial fragment of *la classe industrielle*. This point of view, defended by Hegel and criticized by Marx, is also evident among other French writers such as Saint-Simon, for whom workers and entrepreneurs comprise a single social class: *les industriels*. This partly explains why Tocqueville reacted in contradictory ways to the events of 1848; as François Furet and others have pointed out, he interpreted these events both as a continuation of the democratic revolution and, spitefully, as a 'most terrible civil war' threatening the very basis of 'property, family and civilization'.[34]) Tocqueville failed to consider the possibility of a *socialist* civil society: a type of ultra-modern civil society no longer dominated by capitalist enterprises and patriarchal families.[35] He none the less saw correctly – as did Ferguson, Paine and Hegel before him – that forms of civil association such as scientific and literary circles, schools, publishers, inns, manufacturing enterprises, religious organizations, municipal associations and independent households are crucial barriers against both political despotism and social unfreedom and inequality.

Tocqueville never tired of repeating the point that the 'independent eye of society' (vol. 1, p. 236) – an eye comprising a plurality of interacting, self-organized and constantly vigilant civil assocations – is necessary for consolidating the democratic revolution. In contrast to political forms of involvement (such as participation in elections or jury service) which are concerned with the wider, more general community interests, civil associations consist of combinations of citizens preoccupied with 'small affairs' (vol. 2, p. 150). Civil associations no doubt enable citizens to negotiate wider undertakings of concern to the whole polity. But they do more than this: they also nurture the local and particular freedoms so necessary for maintaining democratic equality and preventing the tyranny of minorities by majorities. Tocqueville likens these civil associations to permanently open schools of public spirit within which citizens learn their rights and obligations, press their claims, and become acquainted with others. He probably underestimates the (likely) possibility of conflict among different civil associations and with the state itself (a consequence of his tendency to exaggerate the extent of democratization in modern societies). He none the less sees civil associations as arenas in which individuals can direct their attention to more than their selfish, conflictual, narrowly private goals; through their activities in civil associations, they come to perceive that they are not independent of their fellow-citizens and that in order to obtain others' support they must often lend them their co-operation.

Tocqueville acknowledges that civil associations in this sense always depend for their survival and co-ordination upon centralized state institutions. Yet he also insists – against Hegel – that freedom and equality among individuals and groups depend upon preserving types of organizations which nurture local freedoms and provide for the active expression of particular interests. The right of association within civil society is inalienable: 'No legislator can destroy it without attacking the foundations of society itself' (vol. 1, p. 279). A pluralistic and self-organizing civil society independent of the state is an indispensable condition of democracy. Tocqueville's pointed warning would have made no sense to the classical defenders of *societas civilis*: whoever promotes the unification of state and civil society endangers the democratic revolution. State power without social obstacles is always hazardous and undesirable, a licence for despotism.

Some Conclusions

When the development of the modern distinction between civil society and the state is considered in this way – as a complex and uneven process of overlapping semantic changes – several well-established misconceptions are dissolved. To begin with, it becomes clear that general references to civil society and the state as the 'two terms of a deep-lying antithesis of modern political consciousness'[36] are misleading, precisely because their unspecific, all-embracing character suppresses or eliminates important differences in the geographic distribution, temporal changes and semantic variation of the distinction.

The interpretation defended in this essay also casts doubt upon the commonplace assumption that it was German political thinkers, and Hegel in particular, who first (or most systematically) thematized the civil society–state distinction as a key organizing principle of the modern world. The most sophisticated version of this argument is expressed in the pathbreaking writings of Manfred Riedel, for whom Hegel's introduction of the concept of *bürgerliche Gesellschaft* constituted an innovation in political philosophy comparable to Bodin's concept of sovereignty and Rousseau's idea of the general will:

> Hegel drew together 'bürgerlich' and 'Gesellschaft' into one of the basic concepts of political philosophy. When viewed externally, this concept corresponds to the tradition of Aristotle's *koinōnia politikē*,

Bodin's, Melanchthon's or Wolff's *societas civilis*, and Kant's 'bürgerliche Gesellschaft'. In fact, it presupposes for its appearance a thoroughgoing break with this tradition. To this extent, one may well say that before Hegel the concept of civil society in the modern sense did not exist.[37]

This essay suggests otherwise. Hegel was neither the first nor necessarily the most important modern thinker to consider the subject of civil society. Between 1750 and 1850 literally hundreds of British, French and German political thinkers – the handful discussed above constitute only a limited sample of the most innovative and influential – concerned themselves with the subject of civil society and the limits of state action.

This essay further suggests that early modern German discussions of the scope and power of the state, at least when viewed comparatively, were the *least* receptive to the democratic political implications of the new distinction between civil society and the state. This characteristic German divergence from British and French political thought reflects some peculiarities of late-eighteenth- and nineteenth-century German historical development: the absence of a successful revolution from below; the belated construction (from above) of a viable nation-state framework; the slower development of commodity production and exchange; the weakness of parliamentary rule; a deeply rooted *Obrigkeitsstaat* tradition; and the fragility of a political culture of citizenship – expressed in the idea (which contrasts sharply with the British *citizen* and French *citoyen*) of the *Staatsbürger*, the passive subject whose egoism is restrained and liberty, property and spiritual identity guaranteed and defined from above through the state and its laws.[38]

The interpretation defended in this essay suggests, finally, that the principal catalyst in the semantic transformation of the traditional concept of *societas civilis* was *not* the passive or *ex post facto* recognition by political thinkers of the hard economic facts of early modernity: commodity production and exchange under capitalist direction. Since the mid nineteenth century, this view has been widely influential. It is traceable to Marx and Engels's famous but inaccurate account of the genesis and meaning of the term civil society:

Civil society [*bürgerliche Gesellschaft*] comprises the entire material interaction among individuals at a particular evolutionary stage of the productive forces. ... The term 'civil society' emerged in the eighteenth century when property relations had already evolved from the community of antiquity and medieval times. Civil society as such only develops with the bourgeoisie.[39]

Awareness of the importance of market competition, commodity production and exchange and the growth of the bourgeoisie – as even a cursory examination of the writings of Ferguson, Paine, Hegel and Tocqueville makes clear – was certainly an essential element in the modernization of the classical concept of civil society (which Marx and Engels here define out of existence). So too was hostility to the aristocracy and its inherited wealth, corrupt manners and political privileges. Yet property-centred interpretations of the origins and significance of this transformation are surely too simplistic. Like all monistic interpretations of the alteration of political language, they selectively – that is, one-sidedly – scrutinize and emphasize only *one* of the characteristic dimensions of the breakdown and subdivision of the classical concept of civil society. Other dimensions of the same process of conceptual transformation are suppressed arbitrarily or illegitimately judged to be of little or no 'relevance'.

Thus – to consider just several examples – property-centred interpretations fail to acknowledge early modern thinkers' deep awareness of the organizational *heterogeneity* and *complexity* of civil society. Analytically speaking, these thinkers rarely reduced the complex patterns of stratification, organization, conflicts and movements of civil society to the logic and contradictions of a mode of production – the emerging capitalist economy. More typically – the differences in meaning of the term civil society make it difficult to generalize – they usually noted the patterns of harmony or (potential) conflict between civil society's privately controlled commerce and manufacturing and its other organizations, including patriarchal households, churches, municipal governments, publishers, scientific and literary associations and such policing authorities as charitable relief organizations, schools and hospitals.

Property-centred interpretations also overlook the *anti-bourgeois* sentiments and normative implications of much early modern discussion of the state and civil society. Most early modern theorists of civil society – Ferguson, Paine, Hegel and Tocqueville among them – were not blind apologists of capitalism. They recognized and often feared the inequalities and possible losses of freedom caused by the growth of commodity production and exchange. Above all, these thinkers were deeply sensitive to the dangers generated by concentrations of political power. This is entirely understandable, although a mystery to property-centred approaches.

The late-eighteenth- and early-nineteenth-century debate about civil society and the limits of state action was energized primarily by *non-entrepreneurial* social groups whose scientific, literary, artistic and religious pursuits placed them at odds with the accumulation of state power and the corporate practices and elite privileges which it protected. These groups comprised rentiers, booksellers, journalists, academicians, schoolteachers and others of modest background. Their social position was no longer enmeshed deeply in the world of courts, communities, parishes and guilds. Although they were predominantly 'bourgeois' – in the loose sense that they had at least a little property and some education – these groups were not primarily entrepreneurial and they were often supported in their activities by elements of the nobility, state officialdom, lower churchmen and the artisanry. These non-entrepreneurial groups wanted change, which they typically viewed as creating a different set of political arrangements rather than simply altering the way power was exercised within the existing state apparatus. In this sense they constituted a (potential) discussing and reading public sphere which attempted to elaborate a 'public opinion' on political matters and to direct this opinion, in the name of the emerging civil society, at the secretive and arbitrary actions of the state.[40]

The fundamental point missed by property-centred accounts of modern civil society is that the transformation and subdivision of the idea of *societas civilis* was stimulated primarily by a specifically *political* development: the fear of state despotism and the hope (spawned by the defeat of the British in the American colonies, as well as by the earliest events of the French Revolution) of escaping its clutches.[41] The centrality and recurrence of the theme of despotism in the texts of Ferguson, Paine, Tocqueville and (to a considerably lesser degree) Hegel is neither fortuitous nor unrepresentative. The problem of political despotism and how to break its grip or prevent its growth played the decisive part in the late-eighteenth- and early-ninteenth-century intellectual unrest which resulted in the overthrow and modernization of the classical concept of civil society. Following Montesquieu's *De l'esprit des lois* (1748), many political thinkers during this period viewed despotic regimes with great trepidation. Despotism was seen as a type of political regime – founded originally among Orientals, but now threatening Europe from within – which ruthlessly crushes intermediate groups and classes within the state and forces its subjects to remain divided, ignorant and timid in spirit. Under despotism, Montesquieu remarked, mutual suspicion and fear are rampant. The lives, liberties and properties of citizens are always up in the air and at the mercy of the frightful maxim 'that a single person should rule according to his own will and caprice'.[42]

The image of despotism sketched by Montesquieu and other eighteenth-century writers no doubt contained highly 'fictional' elements.[43] It proved none the less to be a highly imaginative and politically fertile fiction in one vital respect. In Britain, France and (to a lesser extent) the German states, the fear of despotism – much more than the love of capitalism – induced a kind of intellectual flight from the status quo. This dynamic was particularly virulent at the time of the French Revolution. Despotism was viewed widely as a system of concentrated secular power without limits. It contained no guiding ideals. It was seen to feed upon its own expansion and to thrive upon the blind obedience of its anxious subjects. For this reason, despotism oversteps the limits of effective power. It crashes blindly through the world, leaving behind a trail of lawlessness, waste and confusion. Despotism thereby tends to destroy its own omnipotence and teaches its opponents to seek methods of blunting its impact on the world, encouraging them to seek refuge in a civil sphere which acts at a distance from political power.[44]

Through this typical pattern of reasoning the critics of despotism helped to exhaust the classical understanding of civil society and thereby prepared the way for its transformation into one of the distinctive concepts of nineteenth-century political thinking. In this way the fear of despotism contributed to the renewal of the old European spirit of liberty. It prompted a search for new ways of thinking about the modern state, stimulated calls for limiting its potentially dangerous power and led, unwittingly, to an entirely new understanding of civil society – a term which was itself capable of striking fear into the hearts of a good many political despots, old and new.

Notes

1. *Politics*, I, 1252a, 6-7.
2. 'Of the Origin of Government (1752)', in David Hume, *Political Essays*, ed. Charles W. Hendel, Indianapolis and New York 1953, p. 42.
3. *Discours sur l'oeconomie politique*, Paris 1763, p. 15.
4. *Idee zu einer allgemeinen Geschichte in weltbürgerlicher Absicht* (1784), fifth

thesis, in Immanuel Kant, *Schriften zur Anthropologie, Geschichtsphilosophie, Politik und Pädagogik*, Darmstadt 1975, p. 39.

5. Manfred Riedel's interpretations of this breakdown of the old *societas civilis* paradigm concentrate almost exclusively upon German political thought. They still provide fundamental hints for comparative attempts to understand the geographic and semantic complexity of this transition process in European thought as a whole. See especially 'Gesellschaft, bürgerliche', in O. Brunner *et al.*, eds, *Geschichtliche Grundbegriffe. Historisches Lexikon zur politisch-sozialen Sprache in Deutschland*, Stuttgart 1975, vol. 2, pp. 719-800; 'Der Begriff der "bürgerlichen Gesellschaft" und das Problem seines geschichtlichen Ursprungs', in *Studien zu Hegels Rechtsphilosophie*, Frankfurt am Main 1969, pp. 135-66; *Bürgerliche Gesellschaft und Staat. Grundproblem und Struktur der Hegelschen Rechtsphilosophie*, Neuwied and Berlin 1970; and 'Bürgerlichkeit und Humanität', in Rudolf Vierhaus, ed, *Bürger und Bürgerlichkeit im Zeitalter der Aufklärung*, Heidelberg 1981, pp. 13-34.

6. The first formulation of this distinction is probably to be found in the opening paragraph of Thomas Paine's *Common Sense* (Philadelphia 1776): 'Some writers have so confounded society with government, as to leave little or no distinction between them; whereas they are not only different, but have different origins. Society is produced by our wants, and government by our wickedness; the former promotes our happiness *positively* by uniting our affections, the latter *negatively* by restraining our vices. The one encourages intercourse, the other creates distinctions. The first is a patron, the last a punisher.'

7. Jenö Szücs, 'Three Historical Regions of Europe', in this volume.

8. Some important implications for social history of the modified *Begriffsgeschichte* approach adopted here are discussed in Reinhart Koselleck's *Vergangene Zukunft: zur Semantik geschichtlicher Zeiten*, Frankfurt am Main 1979, especially pp. 107-29. The special methodological difficulties attending the retrieval and development of past concepts for contemporary political thinking are analysed in my 'More Theses on the Philosophy of History', in James Tully, ed., *Meaning and Context. Quentin Skinner and His Critics*, Cambridge and New York 1987.

9. Untreated here is the proliferation of theoretical attempts to abandon or criticize the state–civil society distinction. During the course of the nineteenth century, and extending into the twentieth, most European thinkers turned their backs on the early modern controversies about the separation and interdependence of civil society and the state. See Manfred Riedel, 'Gesellschaft, bürgerliche', pp. 783ff; Alvin W. Gouldner, 'Civil Society in Capitalism and Socialism', in *The Two Marxisms. Contradictions and Anomalies in the Development of Theory*, London and Basingstoke 1986; and John Keane, 'Remembering the Dead. Civil Society and the State from Hobbes to Marx, and Beyond', in *Democracy and Civil Society*, London and New York 1988.

10. Utz Haltern, *Bürgerliche Gesellschaft. Sozialtheoretische und sozialhistorische Aspekte*, Darmstadt 1985, pp. 8-9. On the French case, see Lucien Febvre, '*Civilisation*: evolution of a word and a group of ideas', in *A New Kind of History*, ed. Peter Burke, London 1973, pp. 219-57. Unfortunately, equivalent studies of the transformation of the concept of civil society in British political thought are currently unavailable.

11. Horst Dippel, *Germany and the American Revolution 1770-1800. A Sociohistorical Investigation of Late Eighteenth-Century Political Thinking*, Wiesbaden 1978, especially part 4.

12. See Zwi Batscha and Hans Medick, 'Einleitung', in Adam Ferguson, *Versuch über die Geschichte der bürgerlichen Gesellschaft*, Frankfurt am Main 1986, pp. 30-33; James Sheehan, *German Liberalism in the Nineteenth Century*, London 1978, chapter 3; Lothar Gall, *Benjamin Constant. Seine politische Ideenwelt und der deutsche*

Vormärz, Wiesbaden 1963, especially pp. 107-8. The first generations of German liberal economists (such as Friedrich List) also expressed considerable reservations about *laissez faire*, as has been shown by Marie Elisabeth Vopelius, *Die altliberalen Ökonomen und die Reformzeit*, Stuttgart 1968.

13. All citations are drawn from *An Essay on the History of Civil Society*, ed. Duncan Forbes, Edinburgh 1966.

14. Compare Ferguson's later *Principles of Moral and Political Science*, Edinburgh 1792, vol. 1, p. 252: 'Civilization ... both in the nature of the thing and derivation of the word, belongs rather to the effects of law and political establishment, on the forms of society, than to any state merely of lucrative possession or wealth.'

15. The influence of civic humanism or classical republican politics upon the Scottish Enlightenment is discussed by John Robertson, 'The Scottish Enlightenment at the limits of the civic tradition', in Istvan Hont and Michael Ignatieff, eds, *Wealth and Virtue. The Shaping of Political Economy in the Scottish Enlightenment*, Cambridge 1983, pp. 137-78, and J.G.A. Pocock, 'Cambridge paradigms and Scotch philosophers: a study of the relations between the civic humanist and the civil jurisprudential interpretation of eighteenth-century social thought', in ibid. pp. 235-52.

16. Ferguson's discussion of commerce and manufacturing as an immanent feature of modern civil society (discussed above) is in tension with his thoroughly classical understanding of the necessary exclusion of women and labourers from civil society. From the classical perspective, those groups (domestic servants, slaves, labourers, women and artisans) who provide the necessaries of life are perforce unfree – they are situated in the *oikos*, the *societas domestica* – and therefore lack the political standing which confers civility.

17. *An Essay on the History of Civil Society*, pp. 69, 102, 125-41, 155, 166-7, 205, 266-89; compare the critical reference to Hume's defence of a 'government of laws' on pp. 263-4: 'the influence of laws, where they have any real effect in the preservation of liberty, is not any magic power descending from shelves that are loaded with books, but is, in reality, the influence of men resolved to be free.'

18. All citations are drawn from Thomas Paine, *Rights of Man*, ed. Henry Collins, Harmondsworth 1977.

19. On the highly politicized context of Paine's defence of the French Revolution, see Marilyn Butler, ed., *Burke, Paine, Godwin, and the Revolution Controversy*, Cambridge 1984.

20. On the historical origins and paths of development of contractualism, see John Keane, *Public Life and Late Capitalism*, Cambridge and New York 1984, essay 7.

21. 'Dissertations on Government, the Affairs of the Bank, and Paper Money', in *The Writings of Thomas Paine*, ed. M.D. Conway, New York 1967, vol. 3, p. 137.

22. This observation leads Paine to describe despotic government as a kind of fungus growing out of corrupted society (p. 126). Such imagery helps to clarify why Paine recommends caution in the overturning of old despotic governments. The principles of equal natural rights, active consent and respect for society, he argues, must be established sufficiently well within the population before revolution can successfully establish a limited constitutional state. Conversely, Paine's imagery implies that governments may have an important 'civilizing' function during the transition from despotism to civilized societies. If (parts of) civil society have been deformed by the operations of despotic states, then governments which have been established to protect the collective interests of society have a charter to 'explode ignorance and preclude imposition' (p. 206). He accordingly recommends an elaborate system of transfer payments to the elderly, the widowed, women, newly

married couples, the poor and the unemployed, disbanded soldiers and children, who would be schooled compulsorily. This kind of redistributive system, Paine argues, 'is not of the nature of a charity, but of a right' (p. 265). In *Agrarian Justice opposed to Agrarian Law, and to Agrarian Monopoly* (1797) Paine carried further these proposals for state provision, recommending retirement and physical disability pensions as well as a system of universal cash payments. He failed to address the problem of whether such redistributive systems could be administered without a considerable expansion of the scope and power of the state.

23. All citations are drawn from G.W.F. Hegel, *Grundlinien der Philosophie des Rechts*, Frankfurt am Main 1976. Translations are my own.

24. On the relationship between the Scottish Enlightenment and Hegel, see Franz Rosenzweig, *Hegel und der Staat*, Munich and Berlin 1920, vol. 2, p. 118; Paul Chamley, *Économie politique et philosophie chez Steuart et Hegel*, Paris 1963, and 'Les origines de la pensée économique de Hegel', *Hegel-Studien*, no. 3, 1965; and Zwi Batscha and Hans Medick, 'Einleitung'.

25. *Rights of Man*, pp. 117, 126, 204.

26. *Die Verfassung Deutschlands*, in G.W.F. Hegel, *Politische Schriften*, Frankfurt am Main, 1966, p. 40.

27. Policing authorities protect individuals from themselves and from the 'wrongs' committed by one class of civil society against another (or against itself). These authorities are charged with the task of monitoring, regulating and polishing – civilizing – civil society, by means of public health care, schooling of children, bridge-building and street-lighting, setting prices of basic commodities and providing relief for the poor and encouraging them to labour. Hegel considers these agencies of civil society, and not the state (which co-funds them), although he continues to speak of *Polizei* in the pre-nineteenth-century sense also evident (although in a more limited way) in Ferguson's writings. See Kurt Wolzendorff, *Der Polizeigedanke des modernen Staats*, Breslau 1918, especially chapters 1-3, and Franz-Ludwig Knemeyer, 'Polizei', in O. Brunner *et al.*, eds, *Geschichtliche Grundbegriffe*, Stuttgart 1978, vol. 4, pp. 875-97.

28. Cf. the earlier remark in *Jenenser Realphilosophie*, ed. J. Hoffmeister, Leipzig 1931, vol. 1, p. 239: 'Society becomes a huge system of mutual interdependence, a moving life of the dead. In a blind and elemental fashion, the system moves this way and that like a wild animal calling for permanent regulation and restriction.'

29. This licence becomes more prominent in Hegel's later political writings, as is evident in his changing views on the scope of state action. In *Die Verfassung Deutschlands* (1799-1802), for example, he specifically criticizes contemporary theories of the state, including Fichte's *Grundlege des Naturrechts*, which suppose that the 'state is a machine consisting of a single spring which imparts motion to the remainder of the infinite wheelwork, and that all institutions arising from the nature of a society must be conducted, regulated, ordered and watched over by the supreme public power' (*Politische Schriften*, p. 40). He speaks of the functions of the state as limited to those of 'organizing and maintaining its power and hence, its security at home and abroad' (pp. 40-41). At the close of the Napoleonic era (see his *Verhandlungen in der Versammlung der Landstände des Königreichs Württemberg im Jahre 1815 und 1816* [1817], in *Politische Schriften*, pp. 140-276), he expands this conception of the role of the state to include education, the administration of justice, the support of religious institutions, and maintenance of the poor. His last writings (e.g. *Über die englische Reformbill* [1831], in *Politische Schriften*, pp. 284-98) recommend state interference with property relations in order to provide work and subsistence for the downtrodden.

30. In the *Philosophy of History*, trans. J. Sibree, London 1905, pp. 109-10, Hegel

placed the concept of despotism within a teleological framework of historical development culminating in modern Europe. Despotism, a type of arbitrary political regime in which one rules and the rest succumb to laws external to them, is understood as an oriental phenomenon: 'The history of the World travels from East to West, for Europe is absolutely the end of history.... The East knows, and to the present day knows only, that *One* is free; the Greek and Roman world, that *some* are free; the German world knows that *all* are free. The first political form therefore we observe in history, is *Despotism*, the second *Democracy and Aristocracy*, the third *Monarchy.*'

31. This interpretation may be disputed on the ground that in Hegel's view the properly political state is only the ultimate *human* institution (i.e. the culmination of 'objective mind') and, as such, remains subordinate to 'Absolute Mind', whose three forms are philosophy, religion and art. (See *Grundlinien der Philosophie des Rechts*, pp. 415-31, and the concluding section on Absolute Mind in the *Encyclopädie der philosophischen Wissenschaften im Grundrisse*, third edn, Leiden 1906, paras 377-577.) This type of objection would not affect the point that Hegel conceives the universal state as unchallengeable – even by religion. For the relationship of Absolute Mind (eternal truth as reason) and 'objective mind' (the universal state) is teleological – genuine truth is the prodigious transfer of the 'inner into the outer, the building of reason into the real world' – hence, in principle, a non-antagonistic relationship in which the earthly state is the external embodiment of truth as ultimate reason.

32. All citations are drawn from Alexis de Tocqueville, *De la démocratie en Amérique*, preface by François Furet, Paris 1981, two vols. All translations are my own.

33. Tocqueville's argument is inspired directly by his American experiences and by the events of the French Revolution. It is also pitted against the statist Liberalism of Guizot and others, whose suspicion of associations coming between the individual citizen and the state was based on the simplistic equation of liberty with (legal and political) equality. On the problem of *étatisme* in nineteenth-century French political thought, see Dominique Bagge, *Le Conflit des idées politiques en France sous la Restauration*, Paris 1952; Henri Michel, *L'idée de l'État: essai critique sur l'histoire des théories sociales et politique en France depuis la Revolution*, third edn, Aalen 1973; Roger Soltau, *French Political Thought in the Nineteenth Century*, New York 1959; James T. Schleifer, *The Making of Tocqueville's Democracy in America*, Chapel Hill 1980, part 4; and Pierre Rosanvallon, *Le moment Guizot*, Paris 1985.

34. François Furet, 'The Passions of Tocqueville', *The New York Review of Books*, 27 June 1985, pp. 23-7.

35. See my *Democracy and Civil Society.*

36. R.N. Berki, 'State and Society: An Antithesis of Modern Political Thought', in Jack Hayward and R.N. Berki, eds, *State and Society in Contemporary Europe*, Oxford 1979, p. 2. Other writers remain unaware of the late-eighteenth-century breakdown and pluralization of the classical civil society concept. See, for example, Immanuel Wallerstein, *The Politics of the World Economy. The States, the movements and the civilizations*, Cambridge and Paris 1984, pp. 1-2, and John B. Thompson, 'Editor's Introduction', in Claude Lefort, *The Political Forms of Modern Society. Bureaucracy, Democracy, Totalitarianism*, Cambridge 1986, p. 321, note 10: 'The term "civil society" refers, in its classical sense, to all those spheres of social life which are organized independently of the political action of the state.'

37. 'Hegels Begriff der >bürgerlichen Gesellschaft< und das Problem seines geschichtlichen Ursprungs', in Manfred Riedel, ed., *Materialien zu Hegels Rechtsphilosophie*, Frankfurt am Main 1975, vol. 2, p. 262; cf. pp. 263, 269.

38. See P.L. Weihnacht, 'Staatsbürger. Zur Geschichte und Kritik eines politschen Begriffs', *Der Staat*, no. 8. 1969, pp. 41-63, especially p. 58; and Michael Stolleis, 'Untertan-Bürger-Staatsbürger. Bemerkungen zur juristischen Terminologie im späten 18. Jahrhundert', in Rudolf Vierhaus, ed., *Bürger und Bürgerlichkeit im Zeitalter der Aufklärung*, Heidelberg 1981, pp. 65-99.

39. Karl Marx, Friedrich Engels, *Die deutsche Ideologie*, in *Werke*, Berlin 1969, vol. 3, p. 36. The analogous (non-Marxian) view that the eighteenth-century defence of *laissez faire* was synonymous with the recognition of the essential difference and separability of the terms civil society and the state is defended in E. Halévy, *La Formation du radicalisme philosophique*, 3 vols, Paris 1901-4, vol. 1, p. 237.

40. See Jürgen Habermas, *Strukturwandel der Öffentlichkeit. Untersuchungen zu einer Kategorie der bürgerlichen Gesellschaft*, Neuwied 1962; John Keane, *Public Life and Late Capitalism*, chapters 2, 7; Günther Lottes, *Politische Aufklärung und plebejisches Publikum: zur Theorie und Praxis des englischen Radikalismus im späten 18. Jahrhundert*, Munich 1979; and James J. Sheehan, 'Wie bürgerlich war der deutsche Liberalismus?', mimeographed lecture, Bielefeld 1987.

41. Among the most pertinent contributions are: Robert R. Palmer, *The Age of the Democratic Revolution: A Political History of Europe and America 1760-1800*, Princeton, NJ 1959-64, 2 vols; Ernst Fraenkel, *Amerika im Spiegel des deutschen politischen Denkens. Äusserungen deutscher Staatsmänner und Staatsdenker über Staat und Gesellschaft in den Vereinigten Staaten*, Cologne and Opladen 1959; Horst Dippel, *Germany and the American Revolution 1770-1800*, especially part 4; Durand Echeverria, *Mirage in the West: A History of the French Image of American Society to 1815*, Princeton, NJ 1957, reprinted 1968; Brian Singer, *Society, theory and the French revolution: studies in the revolutionary imaginary*, London 1986, chapters 7, 11; Gianfranco Poggi, *The Development of the Modern State*, Stanford 1978, chapter 4; and Erich Angermann, 'Das "Auseinandertreten von Staat und Gesellschaft" im Denken des 18. Jahrhunderts', *Zeitschrift für Politik*, no. 10, 1963, pp. 89-101.

42. *De l'esprit des lois*, ed. Victor Goldschmidt, Paris 1979, Book 3, chapter 2, pp. 143-4. No comprehensive reconstruction of the eighteenth- and nineteenth-century theoretical controversies aroused by despotism is yet available. These controversies include Montesquieu's transformation of the classical Greek understanding of despotism [*despótēs*] as a form of kingship exercised legitimately by a master over slaves; his indebtedness to the medieval discussion of despotism as a variety of illegitimate kingship; his rejection of Bodin's and Hobbes's positive rendering of despotism as a form of political rule justified by victory in war or civil war; the eighteenth-century French controversies prompted by the Physiocratic defence of *despotisme légal*; the explicit criticism of Montesquieu's Eurocentric views of oriental despotism in Anquetil-Duperron's *Législation orientale* (1778); the prominence of despotism as a category within the American and French Revolutions and their aftermath; the utilitarian theory of 'vigorous despotism'; and the withering away or transformation of the concept of despotism during the nineteenth century. The origins and development of the concept of despotism before the mid eighteenth century are discussed in R. Koebner, 'Despot and Despotism: Vicissitudes of a Political Term', *Journal of the Warburg and Courtauld Institutes*, vol. 13, 1950, pp. 275-302. More generally, see Alexander Yanov, *The Origins of Autocracy*, Los Angeles 1980, and Norberto Bobbio, 'Grandeur et Décadence de l'idéologie Européenne', *Lettre internationale*, no. 12, Spring 1987, pp. 8-11.

43. Alain Grosrichard, *Structure du sérail: la fiction du despotisme asiatique dans l'Occident classique*, Paris 1979.

44. On the idea of the paradoxical weakness of despotic states, see Leonard Krieger, *An Essay on the Theory of Enlightened Despotism*, Chicago 1975, pp. 37-9.

Gramsci and the Concept of Civil Society*[1]

Norberto Bobbio

From Society to the State and from the State to Society

Modern political thought from Hobbes to Hegel is marked by a constant tendency — though expressed in contrasting ways — to consider the state or political society, in relation to the state of nature (or natural society), as the supreme and definitive stage in the common and collective life of humanity perceived as a rational entity, as the most perfect or least imperfect result of that process of rationalization of the instincts or passions or interests via which the rule of uncoordinated force is transformed into one of co-ordinated liberty. The state is conceived as a product of reason, or as a rational society, the only one in which human beings can lead a life which conforms to reason: that is, which conforms to their nature. This conception merges and fuses both the realist theories, which describe the state as it is (from Machiavelli to the theorists of the 'reason of state'), and the theories of natural law (from Hobbes to Rousseau and Kant) which propose ideal models of the state, defining how a state should be in order to realize its true purpose. The process of rationalization of the state (the state as rational society), which is characteristic of theories of natural law, merges with the process of 'statization' of reasons, which is characteristic of theories of the reason of state. In Hegel, who represents the decisive break with this tradition of

*Translated by Carroll Mortera.

73

political thought as well as its culmination, the two processes are synthesized, so that in the *Philosophy of Right* the rationalization of the state achieves its ultimate expression and is at the same time represented not simply as a proposal for an ideal model, but as the key to understanding the real movement of history: the rationality of the state is no longer just a necessity but a reality, not just an ideal but a historical event.[2] The young Marx showed a deep insight into this feature of Hegel's philosophy of right when he wrote in an early comment: 'Hegel is not to be blamed for depicting the nature of the modern state as it is, but for presenting that which exists as the *essence of the state.*'[3]

The rationalization of the state came about through the constant use of a dichotomic model, where the state is conceived as a positive moment in contrast to a pre-state or anti-state society, which is relegated to a negative moment. One can distinguish, even if in a rather schematic way, three principal variants of this model: the political state as a radical negation which therefore eliminates and overthrows the state of nature, that is as a renewal, or *restauratio ab imis*, compared to the phase of human development which precedes the state (Hobbes–Rousseau); the state as a conservation–*regulation* of natural society and therefore no longer seen as an alternative to the phase which precedes it, but as something which actualizes or *perfects* it (Locke–Kant); the state as the conservation and *transcendence* of pre-state society (Hegel), in the sense that the state is a *new* moment and does not only perfect the earlier phase (which differs from the model of Locke–Kant), yet is one without constituting an absolute negation and therefore an alternative (which differs from the model of Hobbes and Rousseau). While the state of Hobbes and Rousseau definitively excludes the state of nature, Hegel's state *contains* civil society (which is the historicization of the state of nature or the natural society of the philosophers of natural law). Hegel's state contains civil society and transcends it, transforming a merely formal universality [*eine formelle Allgemeinheit*] into an organic reality [*organische Wirklichkeit*], thus differing from Locke's state which contains civil society (still conceived by Locke as a natural society) not to transcend it, but to legitimate its existence and its aims.

With Hegel the process of rationalization of the state reaches the highest point of the parabola. In those same years, with the works of Saint-Simon – which took account of the profound transformation of society resulting not from political revolution but from the Industrial Revolution and predicted the coming of a new order which would be regulated by scientists and industrialists as opposed to the traditional order upheld by metaphysicians and the military[4] – the parabola had begun its decline and the theory, or simply the belief (the myth), of the inevitable withering away of the state began to be formulated. This theory or belief was to become a characteristic feature of the political ideologies prevalent in the nineteenth century. Marx and Engels would use it as one of the central ideas of their system: the state is no longer the reality of the ethical idea, the rational *in se et per se*, but according to the famous definition in *Capital* it is the 'concentrated and organized violence of society'.[5] The antithesis to the tradition of the philosophy of natural law which culminated in Hegel could not be more complete. In contrast to the first model, the state is no longer conceived as an elimination of the state of nature but rather as its conservation, prolongation and stabilization. In the state the reign of force has not been suppressed but perpetuated, with the only difference that the war of all against all has now been replaced by a way of one side against the other (class struggle, of which the state is the expression and instrument). In contrast with the second model, the society in which the state is the supreme ruler is not a natural society which conforms to the eternal nature of humanity but a historically determined society characterized by certain forms of production and certain social relations. Therefore the state, as an institution of the dominant class, instead of being the expression of a universal and rational need is both the repetition and reinforcement of particularistic interests. Finally, in contrast to the third model, the state is no longer presented as the transcendence of civil society but merely as its reflection: as civil society is, so is the state. The state incorporates civil society not in order to transform it into something else but to keep it as it is; civil society, which is historically determined, does not disappear into the state but reappears in the state in all its concrete manifestations.

From this threefold antithesis one can derive the three basic elements of Marx and Engels's doctrine of the state:

1. The state as a coercive apparatus or as the 'concentrated and organized violence of society': an instrumental conception of the state which is the opposite of the ethical or finalistic one.

2. The state as an instrument of class domination, where 'the executive of the modern State is but a committee for managing the common affairs of the whole bourgeoisie': a particu-

laristic conception of the state as opposed to the universalistic conception characteristic of all the theories of natural law including Hegel's.

3. The state as a secondary or subordinate phenomenon in relation to civil society where 'it is not the State which conditions and regulates civil society, but it is civil society which conditions and regulates the State':[7] a negative conception of the state which is in complete opposition to the positive conception found in rationalistic thought.

As a coercive, particularistic and subordinate apparatus, the state is not the final phase of the historical process: it is a transitory institution destined to be transcended. As a consequence of the inversion of the relation between civil society and political society, the conception of historical process has been completely turned on its head: progress no longer moves from society to the state, but on the contrary, from the state to society. The line of thought, beginning with the conception that the state abolishes the state of nature, ends with the appearance and consolidation of the theory that the state itself must in turn be abolished.

Antonio Gramsci's theory of the state – I am referring particularly to the Gramsci of the *Prison Notebooks* – belongs to this new stage of political thought where the state is not an end in itself but an apparatus, an instrument. It does not represent universal interests but particular ones; it is not a separate and sovereign entity set above the underlying society but is conditioned by and thus subordinated to society. It is not a permanent institution but a transitory one which is bound to disappear with the transformation of the underlying society. It would not be difficult to find, among the many thousands of pages of the *Prison Notebooks*, extracts which reflect the four fundamental themes of the state as an instrumental, particular, subordinate and transitory entity.

Even so, anyone who has acquired a certain familiarity with Gramsci's works knows that his thought has original and personal features which do not admit facile categorizations – almost always inspired by polemical political motives – such as 'Gramsci is Marxist-Leninist'; or 'he is more of a Leninist than a Marxist'; or 'he is more of a Marxist than a Leninist'; or 'he is neither Marxist nor Leninist' – as if 'Marxist', 'Leninism', 'Marxism-Leninism' were clear and distinct classified concepts which allowed this or that theory or group of theories to be without leaving any margin of uncertainty whatsoever, able to be used like a ruler to measure the length of a wall. When undertaking research into Gramsci's thought, the first task is to look for and analyse these personal and original features with no other concern than to reconstruct the outlines of a theory which seems fragmentary, diffuse, unsystematic, with some terminological vagaries, but which is, however, given coherence (especially in his writings from prison) by a deep unity of inspiration. The sometimes overzealous claims made for his orthodoxy with respect to a given party line has provoked a strong reaction which has led many to seek out any sign of heterodoxy, or even of apostasy; the impassioned apologetics on his behalf are, if I am not mistaken, provoking an iconoclastic reaction, one which has still not come into the open but can be detected in certain signs of exasperation. But just as orthodoxy and heterodoxy are not valid criteria for a philosophical critique, so exaltation and irreverence are deceptive and misleading states of mind in which to gain understanding of a particular phase in the history of thought.

Civil Society in Hegel and Marx

To reconstruct Gramsci's political thought the key concept – the one which forms the necessary starting point – is that of *civil society*. One must begin with the concept of civil society rather than with that of the state, because it is his use of the former rather than the latter which differs significantly from that of not only Hegel but also Marx and Engels.

From the time when the problem of the relationship between Hegel and Marx moved from the comparison of methods (the use of the dialectic method and the so-called 'standing Hegel on his head') to the comparison of *contents* as well – for this new point of view the works of Lukács on the young Hegel have been fundamental – the paragraphs where Hegel analysed civil society have been studied with greater attention. The larger or smaller quantity of Hegelianism in Marx is now *also* assessed according to the extent to which Hegel's description of civil society (more precisely of the first part on the system of needs) can be considered as a prefiguration of Marx's analysis and critique of capitalist society. An insight into the connection between Marx's analysis of capitalist society and Hegel's analysis of civil society was provided by Marx himself in a famous passage from his 'Preface to *A Contribution to the Critique of Political Economy*', where he writes that in his critical analysis of Hegel's philosophy of right:

I was led by my studies to the conclusion that legal relations as well as forms of state could be neither understood by themselves nor explained by the so-called general progress of the human mind, but that they are rooted in the material conditions of life, which are summed up by Hegel after the fashion of the English and French of the eighteenth century under the name 'Civil Society'; the anatomy of that civil society is to be sought in political economy.[8]

But as it turned out, on the one hand, interpreters of Hegel's philosophy of right had a tendency to focus their attention on his theory of the state and to neglect his analysis of civil society, which became important in Hegelian studies only around 1920. On the other hand the Marxist scholars had, for a long time, a tendency to consider the problem of the connections with Hegel exclusively from the viewpoint of Marx's acceptance of the dialectical method. It is well known that in the works of the most important Italian Marxist scholars such as Labriola, Croce, Gentile and Mondolfo, some of whom were Hegelians or Hegelian scholars, there is no reference to Hegel's concept of civil society (even though we find it in Sorel). Gramsci is the first Marxist writer who uses the concept of civil society for his analysis of society with a textual reference, as we shall see, to Hegel as well.

Yet unlike the concept of state, which has a long tradition behind it, the concept of civil society, which derives from Hegel and comes up again and again especially in the language of the Marxist theory of society, is used also in philosophical language, not in a rigorous or technical way but with various shades of meaning which need to be carefully compared and clarified at the outset to avoid confusion. I think it is useful to establish certain points which would need a far more detailed analysis than I can give here or, indeed, am capable of providing.

1. In all the tradition of the philosophy of natural law, the expression *societas civilis* does not refer to the pre-state society as it will in the Hegelian-Marxist tradition but is a synonym, according to the Latin use, of political society and therefore of the state: Locke uses both terms as interchangeable; in Rousseau *état civil* means the state: also when Kant who, with Fichte, is the author nearest to Hegel, talks in his *Idee zu einer allgemeinen Geschichte in welt-bürgerlicher Absicht* of the irresistible tendency whereby nature pushes human beings towards the constitution of the state, he calls this supreme aim of nature concerning the human species *bürgerliche Gesellschaft*.[9]

2. In the tradition of natural law, it is well known that the two terms of the antithesis are not, as in the Hegelian-Marxist tradition, 'civil political society' but 'state of nature–civil state'. The idea of a pre-state stage of humanity is inspired not so much by the antithesis of 'society–state' but by that of 'nature–civilization'. Moreover, the philosophers of natural law increasingly recognized that the pre-state or natural state was not an asocial state – a condition of perpetual war – but an embryonic form of the social state characterized by the predominance of social relations which were regulated by natural laws, in the same way as family or economic ones were, or were believed to be. This transformation of the *status naturalis* into a *societas naturalis* is very clear in the transition from Hobbes–Spinoza to Pufendorf–Locke. Whatever Locke finds in the state of nature – before the state, together with family institutions, work relations, the establishment of property, the circulation of wealth, commerce, and so forth – shows that even if he calls *societas civilis* the state, the conception he has of the pre-state phase of humanity anticipates far more Hegel's *bürgerliche Gesellschaft* than it continues the *status naturae* of Hobbes–Spinoza. This way of understanding the state of nature as *societas naturalis* continues, both in France and in Germany, right up to the eve of Hegelian thought. The distinction between *société naturelle*, meaning the source of economic relations, and *société politique* is a constant theme of the Physiocratic doctrine. A passage in Kant's *Metaphysic of Morals*, the work which provided the starting point for Hegel's first critique of the doctrines of natural law, clearly asserts that the state of nature is also a social state and therefore 'it is not the social state that is in opposition to the state of nature, but the civil [*bürgerliche*] state, because there can very well be a society in the state of nature, but not a civil society', where the latter means political society, that is, the state – a society, as Kant explains, which guarantees what is mine and what is yours with public laws.[10]

3. With respect to the tradition of natural law, Hegel makes a radical innovation: in the definitive version of his monumental system of political and social philosophy as it appears in the 1821 edition of his *Philosophy of Right*, he decides to use the term civil society, which up to his immediate predecessors was applied to political society, to mean pre-political society: the phase of human society which had previously been called natural society. This is a radical innovation within the tradition of natural law, because Hegel, when characterizing the whole sphere of pre-state

relations, abandons the predominantly juridical analyses of philosophers of natural law, who had a tendency to discuss economic relations exclusively in terms of their juridical forms (theory of property and of contracts). This is because, unlike them, he had been drawn from his early years to the school of economic theory, especially the English one, for which economic relations constitute the fibre of pre-state society and where the distinction between pre-state and state is conceived increasingly as a distinction between the sphere of economic relations and that of political institutions. The *locus classicus* for this concept is Adam Ferguson's *An Essay on the History of Civil Society* (1767; translated into German the following year and known to Hegel), where the expression *civil society* (translated into German as *bürgerliche Gesellschaft*) is the antithesis of primitive society rather than the antithesis of political society (as for Hegel) or of natural society (as for the philosophers of natural law), and it would soon be replaced by Adam Smith in a similar context by the term *civilized society*.[11] While the adjective 'civil' in English (as in French and Italian) also has a meaning of non-barbaric – 'civilized' – in the translation to the German *bürgerliche* (and not *zivilisierte*) the ambiguity between the meaning of non-barbaric and non-state is eliminated, though it leaves the other more serious ambiguity to which Hegel's use of the term gives rise: between pre-state (as antithesis of 'political') and state (as antithesis of 'natural').

4. Hegel's terminological innovation has often concealed the true significance of his substantial innovation, which does not consist, as has often been claimed, in the discovery and analysis of pre-state society, because this discovery and analysis had already been introduced at least since Locke, albeit under the name of state of nature or natural society. Instead it consists in the interpretation of the concept provided by the *Philosophy of Right*: Hegel's civil society. In contrast to the conception of society from Locke to the Physiocrats, it is no longer the reign of a natural order which must be freed from the restrictions and distortions which bad positive laws imposed on it but, on the contrary, the reign 'of dissoluteness, misery and physical and ethical corruption',[12] which must be regulated, controlled and superseded in the superior order of the state. In this sense, and only this sense, Hegel's civil society – not the natural society of natural jurists from Locke to Rousseau to the Physiocrats – is a pre-Marxist concept. Nevertheless, one must still point out that Hegel's concept of civil society is in a certain respect wider and in another more restricted than the concept of civil society as it would later

be taken up in the terminology of Marx and Engels, from which it passed into general currency. Wider, because civil society for Hegel includes not only the sphere of economic relations and the formation of classes but also judicial machinery and administrative and corporative structures: two domains of traditional public law. More restricted, because in Hegel's trichotomic system (not the dichotomic one of natural jurists) civil society constitutes the intermediate sphere between the family and the state, and therefore does not include all pre-state relations and institutions (including the family), as is the case with the natural society of Locke and with the term civil society in its most common use today. Civil society in Hegel is the sphere of economic relations together with their external regulation according to the principles of the liberal state, and it simultaneously comprises bourgeois society and the bourgeois state. It is in civil society that Hegel concentrates his critique of political economy and of political science, inspired respectively by the principles of natural liberty and the state of law.

5. The meaning of 'civil society', extended to the whole of pre-state social life as a stage in the development of economic relations which precedes and determines the political stage – and constituting therefore one of the two terms of the antithesis 'society–state' – is established by Marx. Civil society becomes one of the elements of the conceptual system of Marx and Engels, from Marx's early studies such as 'The Jewish Problem', where the invocation of Hegel's distinction between *bürgerliche Gesellschaft* and *politischer Staat* constitutes the premiss for Marx's criticism of the solution given by Bauer to the Jewish question,[13] to Engels's later works such as the essay on Feuerbach, where we can find a passage frequently quoted, and rightly so, for its incisiveness and simplicity: 'The State, the political order, is the subordinate, and civil society, the realm of economic relations, the decisive element.'[14] The importance of the antithesis 'civil society–state' must also be related to the fact that it is one of the forms through which the fundamental antithesis of the system is expressed, that between a base and superstructure: if it is true that political society does not constitute the whole of the superstructure, it is also true that civil society is coterminous with — meaning that it extends just as far as – the base. In the same passage from the 'Critique of Political Economy' where Marx refers to Hegel's analysis of civil society, he specifies that 'the anatomy of civil society is to be sought in political economy', and then immediately formulates the thesis of the relationship

between base and super-structure in one of his most famous passages.[15] In this context, it is important to bear in mind another of Marx's most important pronouncements on the subject:

> The form of relations determined by the existing productive forces at all previous historical stages, and in its turn determining these, is *civil society*. ... Already here we see how this civil society is the true focal point and theatre of all history, and how absurd is the conception of history held hitherto, which neglects the real relationships and confines itself to the actions of princes and states. ... Civil Society embraces all the material relations of individuals within a definite stage of the development of productive forces. It embraces the whole commercial and industrial life of a given stage and, hence, transcends the State and the nation, though, on the other hand again, it must assert itself in its foreign relations as nationality and inwardly must organize itself as state.[16]

Civil Society in Gramsci

Our brief analysis of the concept of civil society from the philsophers of natural law to Marx[17] led up to the identification, first introduced by Marx, of civil society with the structural sphere or 'base'. Well, this identification can be considered as the starting point for the analysis of the concept of civil society in Gramsci, because – precisely in the characterization of the nature of civil society and its location within the system – Gramsci's theory introduces a profound innovation with respect to the whole Marxist tradition. *Civil society* in Gramsci *does not belong to the structural sphere, but to the superstructural sphere.* In spite of the many analyses that have been made in the last few years of Gramsci's concept of civil society, it seems to me that this fundamental point, upon which the whole of his conceptual system hinges, has not been sufficiently stressed, even if there has been no lack of scholars to highlight the significance of the superstructural dimension in this system.[18] It will be sufficient to quote a fundamental passage from one of the most important texts in the *Prison Notebooks*:

> What we can do, for the moment, is to fix two major superstructural 'levels': the one that can be called 'civil society', that is the ensemble of organisms commonly called 'private', and that of 'political society' or 'the State'. These two levels correspond on the one hand to the function of 'hegemony' which the dominant group exercises through-

out society, and on the other hand to that of 'direct domination' or rule exercised through the State and the juridical government.[19]

For good measure he cites a major historical example: for Gramsci, civil society in the Middle Ages is the Church understood as 'the hegemonic apparatus of the ruling group, which did not have its own apparatus, i.e. did not have its own cultural and intellectual organization, but regarded the universal, ecclesiastical organization as being that.'[20] To paraphrase the passage of Marx quoted above, it would be tempting to say that for Gramsci civil society comprises not 'all material relationships', but all ideological–cultural relations; not 'the whole of commercial and industrial life', but the whole of spiritual and intellectual life. Now, if it is true that civil society is, as Marx says, 'the focal point, the theatre of all history', does not this shift in the meaning of civil society in Gramsci induce us to ask the question if, by any chance, he has not located 'the focal point, the theatre of all history' elsewhere? We can present the problem of the relations between Marx (and Engels) and Gramsci in the following more succinct manner: both in Marx and in Gramsci civil society, and not the state as in Hegel, represents the active and positive stage of historical development. However, in Marx this active and positive stage is a structural phenomenon, while in Gramsci it is superstructural. In other words, what they both stress is no longer the state, as Hegel had done – thus bringing to a close the tradition of natural jurisprudence – but civil society, so that in a sense they entirely reversed Hegel's conception. The difference is that Marx's reversal implies the transition from the superstructural or conditioned moment to the structural or conditioning one, while Gramsci's happens within the superstructure itself. In saying that Gramsci's Marxism consists in the revaluation of civil society *vis-à-vis* the state, one obscures the difference between what civil society means for Marx and Gramsci respectively. Let me make myself clear: I do not wish to deny Gramsci's Marxism, but I want to point out that the revaluation of civil society is not what associates him with Marx, as a casual reader might think, but what distinguishes him from Marx.

In fact, contrary to what is commonly believed, Gramsci does not derive his concept of civil society from Marx but is openly indebted to Hegel for it, though via a rather biased, or at least one-sided, interpretation of his thought. In a passage from *Past and Present*, Gramsci speaks of civil society 'as Hegel understands it, and in the way in which it is often used in these notes', and he immediately explains that he means by civil society 'the political and cultural hegemony which a social group exercises over the whole of society, as the ethical content of the State'.[21] This brief extract brings into focus two very important points: (1) Gramsci claims that his concept of civil society derives from Hegel's; (2) Hegel's concept of civil society, as understood by Gramsci, is superstructural.

A great difficulty arises from these two points: on the one side, Gramsci derives his thesis concerning civil society from Hegel and sees it as belonging to the superstructural sphere and not to the structural; on the other hand, as we have seen, Marx also involves Hegel's civil society when he identifies civil society with all economic relations: that is, with the structural sphere. How can we explain this contrast? I think the only possible explanation is to be found in Hegel's *Philosophy of Right*, where civil society includes not only the sphere of economic relations but also their spontaneous or voluntary forms of organization: the corporations and their first rudimentary rules in the juridical state. This interpretation is corroborated by a passage where Gramsci enunciates the problem of 'Hegel's doctrine of parties and associations as the private woof of the State'[22] and resolves it by observing that Hegel, stressing particularly the importance of political and trade-union associations – though still with a vague and primitive conception of association, which is historically inspired by a single example of organization (the corporative) – goes beyond pure constitutionalism (a state in which individuals and the government face each other directly with no intermediate society) and 'theorized the parliamentary State with its party system'.[23]

The assertion that Hegel anticipates the parliamentary state with its party regime is inexact:[24] in Hegel's constitutional system, which is limited only to the representation of interests and precludes political representation,[25] there is no room for a parliament composed of representatives of the parties, but only for a lower corporative house (alongside an upper hereditary house). But the brief annotation where Gramsci, referring to Hegel, speaks of civil society as of 'the ethical content of the State'[26] is almost literally exact. Literally exact, if we reognize that Hegel's civil society which Gramsci has in mind is not the system of needs – that is, of economic relations – which was Marx's starting point, but the institutions which regulate them, the corporations, which as Hegel says, along with the family, constitute 'the ethical root of the State, the one planted in civil society',[27] which he calls elsewhere 'the firm foundation of the State', 'the pillars of public freedom'.[28] In short, the civil society which Gramsci has in mind when he refers to Hegel is not that of the initial stage, of the explosion of contradictions which the state will have to overcome, but that of the final stage, when the organization and regulation of the various interests (the corporations) provide the basis for the transition towards the state.[29]

The Stage of Civil Society in the Dual Relation Base–Superstructure and Leadership–Dictatorship

It goes without saying that if Marx identifies civil society with the base, then Gramsci's transposition of civil society from the base to the superstructure necessarily has a decisive bearing on the Gramscian conception of the relations between base and superstructure. The problem of these relations in Gramsci has not up to now received the attention it deserves, bearing in mind the importance Gramsci himself gives to it. I believe that once we have correctly located the concept of civil society within his system we are in a position to adopt the right perspective for a deeper analysis. I consider that there are essentially two fundamental differences between Marx's and Gramsci's conceptions of the relations between base and superstructure.

First of all, of the two spheres – although still considered in their reciprocal relations to each other – for Marx the base is primary and subordinating, while the superstructure is secondary and subordinate. This at least is the case as long as one refers strictly to the text, which is relatively unambiguous on this point and does not put into question his underlying intentions. In Gramsci it is exactly the opposite. We must not forget Marx's famous thesis in the 'Preface to *A Contribution to the Critique of Political Economy*': 'The sum total of these relations of production constitutes the economic structure of society, the real foundation, on which rises a juridical and political superstructure, and to which correspond determinate forms of social consciousness'.[30]

Gramsci was quite aware of the complexity of the relations between base and superstructure and was always opposed to the reductionism of deterministic interpretations of Marxism. In an article of 1918 he wrote:

> Between the premise (economic structure) and the consequence (political organization), relations are by no means simple and direct; and it

is not only by economic facts that the history of a people can be documented. It is a complex and intricate task to unravel its causes and in order to do so, a deep and widely ranging study of all spiritual and practical activities is needed.[31]

And the following passage already anticipated the basic thesis of his *Prison Notebooks* that 'it is not the economic structure which directly determines political action, but it is the interpretation of it and of the so-called laws which govern the course it takes.'[32] In the *Prison Notebooks* this relation is represented by a series of antitheses, among which the following are the most important: economic sphere – ethico-political sphere; necessity – freedom; objective – subjective. The most important passage, in my opinion, is the following:

> The term 'catharsis' can be employed to indicate the passage from the purely economic (or egoistic-passional) to the ethico-political sphere, that is the higher elaboration of the structure into superstructure in the minds of men. This also means the passage from 'objective' to 'subjective' and from 'necessity' to 'freedom'.[33]

In each of these three antitheses, the second term always indicates the primary and subordinating moment. It should be observed that of the two superstructural phenomena, that of consent and that of force, one has a positive connotation while the other has a negative, and in this antithesis it is always the first phenomenon that is considered. The superstructure is the sphere of catharsis: the sphere in which necessity is resolved into liberty, understood in a Hegelian way as the consciousness of necessity. This transformation comes about as a consequence of the ethico-political dimension. Necessity, understood as the whole of material conditions which characterize a particular historical situation, is subsumed within the historical past, which is now considered as a part of the structure.[34] Both the historical past and the existing social relations constitute the objective conditions which must be recognized by the active historical subject which Gramsci identifies in the collective will. It is only through the recognition of these objective conditions that the active subject becomes free and is able to transform reality. Furthermore, at the very moment when the material conditions are recognized they become degraded to an instrument for a desired end: 'Structure ceases to be an external force which crushes man, assimilates him to himself and makes him passive, and is transformed into a means of freedom, an instrument to create a new ethical-political form, and into a source of new initiatives.'[35]

The relation between the structural base and the superstructure, when considered from a naturalistic point of view, is interpreted as a relationship of cause–effect and leads to historical fatalism.[36] But when considered from the viewpoint of the active subject of history and the collective will, it turns into a relationship of means and ends. It is the active subject of history who fulfils the task of recognizing and of pursuing an end and in so doing operates within the superstructural phase, using the base itself as an instrument. Therefore the base is no longer the subordinating moment of history, but becomes the subordinate one.

In simple terms this decisive shift in the conception of the base–superstructure antithesis can be summarized as follows. First the *ethical-political* sphere, being the sphere of *freedom* understood as consciousness of *necessity* (that is, of material conditions), dominates the *economic* sphere through the recognition of *objectivity* by the active subject of history. Through this recognition the *material conditions* can be resolved into an *instrument* of action so that the *desired aim* can be achieved. The second fundamental difference from Marx relates to the fact that Gramsci adds to the principal antithesis between base and superstructure a secondary one, which develops within the sphere of the superstructure between civil society and the state.[37] Of these two terms, the first is always the positive element and the second is always the negative. This is clearly shown in the list of opposites where Gramsci comments on Guicciardini's statement that arms and religion are indispensable to the state:

> Guicciardini's formula can be translated by various other, less drastic formulae: force and consent; coercion and persuasion; state and church; political society and civil society; politics and morality (Croce's ethical-political history); law and freedom; order and discipline; or (with an implicit judgement of somewhat libertarian flavour) violence and fraud.[38]

Gramsci was almost certainly referring to Marx's conception of the state when, in one of his letters from prison (that of 7 September 1931), on the subject of his research on intellectuals, he wrote:

> This study also leads to some refinements in the concept of the State, which is usually thought of as political society (i.e., a dictatorship or a coercive apparatus used to control the masses in conformity with a

given mode of production and economy) and not as a balance between political society and civil society.[39]

It is true that in Marx's thought, the state – albeit understood exclusively as a coercive force – does not constitute the super-structural sphere on its own, and that this sphere embraces ideologies as well. But it is also true that in the passage from the 'Preface to *A Contribution to the Critique of Political Economy*' quoted above (which was well known to Gramsci and which he could have found fully corroborated by the first part of the *German Ideology*, if he could ever have known it),[40] ideologies *always* come *after* institutions, as a secondary phenomenon within the same secondary sphere, because they are considered in terms of posthumous and mystified–mystifying justifications of class domination. This thesis of Marx had had an authoritative interpretation, at least in Italian Marxist theory, in the work of Labriola. Labriola had explained that the economic base determines *primarily and directly* the rules and forms of subjection between human beings: that is the law (ethics) and the state; and *only subsequently and indirectly* the objects of imagination and thought, in the production of religion and of science.[41] In Gramsci the relation between institutions and ideologies, though remaining within a framework of a reciprocal action, is inverted: the ideologies become the primary agent of history and the institutions the secondary one. Once the sphere of civil society is considered as the one in which the transition from necessity to freedom takes place, ideologies, which have their historical roots in civil society, are no longer seen merely as a posthumous justification of a power whose historical formation is dependent on material conditions, not merely as rationaliz-ations of a power which already exists, but as forces capable of shaping and creating a new history and contributing to the formation of a new power which will progressively emerge.

Historiographical and Practico-Political Applications of the Concept of Civil Society

The unique position that civil society occupies in Gramsci's conceptual system causes not one but two reversals as regards the traditional, scholastic interpretation of the thought of Marx and Engels: the first consists in his according primacy to the super-structure over the base; the second in the primacy given, within the superstructure itself, to the ideological factor over the institutional factor. As regards the simple dichotomy that was our starting point, namely 'civil society–state', which became the prevalent conceptual scheme for historical interpetations quoting the authority of Marx, Gramsci's scheme is more complex. In fact, it makes use – although the reader might not always realize it – of two dichotomies which only partly overlap: between necessity and freedom, which corresponds to the dichotomy between base and superstructure; and between force and consent, which corresponds to the dichotomy between institutions and ideologies. In this more complex scheme, civil society is both the active object (as opposed to the passive) of the first dichotomy, and the positive object (as opposed to the negative) of the second. It seems to me that this is the whole of his system.

This interpretation can be substantiated by consulting those passages in his writings where Gramsci draws consequences from his frequent and varied use of the two dichotomies in his prison writings. I think it would be useful, and would give a clearer understanding, if we were to distinguish two different uses of the dichotomies: a merely historiographic one, where they are used as canons of historical interpretation–explanation; and a more pragmatically political one, where the same dichotomies are used as criteria to distinguish what must be done from what must not be done.

In general I think we can say that in Gramsci's historiographical use the first dichotomy – the one between the economic factor and the ethico-political factor – serves to identify the essential elements of the historical process; the second – the one between the ethical factor and the political factor – serves to distinguish the phases of ascent and the phases of decline in the process of history, according to the prevalence of the positive or negative element. In other words, moving from the central concept of Gramsci's thought, that of 'historical bloc – by which Gramsci means the totality of a historical situation, which includes both the structural and the superstructural element – the first dichotomy serves to define and to delimit a determinate historical bloc, while the second serves to distinguish a progressive historical bloc from a regressive one.

Let me give some examples: the first dichotomy is the conceptual instrument with which Gramsci singles out the Moderate Party and not the Action Party as the movement which led to the unification of Italy (this is one of the fundamental themes of the notes on the Risorgimento); the second dichotomy explains the crisis of Italian society after the First World War, where the dominant class had ceased to be the ruling class; a crisis which, because of the split between rulers and ruled, could be resolved 'only by the pure exercise of force'.[42] The major symptom of the crisis – that is, of the dissolution of a historical bloc – consists in the fact that it is no longer able to attract the intellectuals, who are the protagonists of civil society: the traditional intellectuals preach morals and the un-traditional ones construct utopias; in other words, neither group has any link with reality.[43]

Moving from the historiographical to the pragmatic aspect – that is, to the question of political action – the use Gramsci makes of the first dichotomy constitutes the grounds for his continued polemics against economism – against the claim to resolve the historical problem which the oppressed class has to face operating exclusively within the sphere of economic relations and the antagonistic forces they generate (the trade unions). The use of the second dichotomy is one of the greater, if not the greatest, source of original observations in the *Prison Notebooks*, where the stable conquest of power by the subordinate classes is always considered as a function of the transformation which must first be operated in civil society. Only by taking into account the way these two dichotomies continuously overlap is it possible to explain the twin front on which Gramsci's criticism advances: against exclusive concentration on the base, because this leads the working class towards a sterile and indecisive class struggle; and against exclusive concentration on the negative aspect of the superstructure, because this too leads to a short-lived and indecisive victory. This battle on two fronts takes place once again in civil society. One front is concerned with transcending the material conditions which operate within the base; the other is set against a false way of transcending these conditions (one which would be pure domination without consent). The failure to apply, or to apply correctly, one or other dichotomy leads to two opposite errors in theory: the confusion between civil society and base generates the error of trade unionism; the confusion between civil society and political society generates that of idolatry of the state.[44]

Political Leadership and Cultural Leadership

While the first polemic against economism centres on the theme of the *party*, the second focuses on dictatorship not accompanied by a reform of civil society and gives prominence to the theme of *hegemony*. The analyses which have just been made put us in an excellent position to realize why the themes of the party and of hegemony occupy a central place in Gramsci's conception of society and of the political struggle. They are, in fact, two elements of civil society opposed both to the base, inasmuch as they represent a superstructural phenomenon, and to the negative aspect of the coercive state, inasmuch as they represent a positive aspect of the superstructure. Party and hegemony – along with the theme of intellectuals which is connected to both – are the two major themes of the *Prison Notebooks* and, at the same time, those which allow a comparison between Gramsci and Lenin.

During the elaboration of the concept of hegemony, which Gramsci carried out in his reflections in prison, he frequently paid homage to Lenin specifically for his achievements as a theorist of hegemony.[45] But it is not generally realized that the term 'hegemony' does not belong to Lenin's usual terminology, while it is typical of Stalin's who, in a manner of speaking, canonized it. Lenin preferred to speak of *leadership* [*rukovodstvo*] and of *leader* [*rukovoditel*]. In one of the rare passages where the expression *holder of hegemony* [*gegemon*] appears, it is clearly used as a synonym for leader.[46] The term hegemony and the words derived from it appeared quite late in Gramsci's terminology too, in the two works of 1926 ('Letter to the Central Committee of the Soviet Communist Party' and the unfinished essay 'Alcuni temi della questione meridionale'[47]) – that is, in his last works before the *Prison Notebooks* – whereas it is used very seldom in the works directly inspired by Lenin, those from 1917 to 1924.[48]

However, we are mostly interested in the conceptual problem, not the terminological one. From the conceptual point of view the same term, 'hegemony', no longer has the same meaning in the *Prison Notebooks* (and in the *Letters*) as in the two works of 1926. In the latter the term is used – and conforms to the official meaning still prevalent in Soviet texts – to indicate the alliance between the workers and the peasants. That is, with the meaning of *political leadership*;[49] while in the subsequent writings it is frequently used to denote 'cultural leadership'.[50] It is in this significant change of meaning – generally insufficiently appreciated – that the originality of Gramsci's thought lies. In fact, in spite of the homage paid by Gramsci to Lenin as the theorist of hegemony, in the current debate over Marxism it is not Lenin who is the pre-eminent theorist of hegemony, but Gramsci himself. Put simply, he owes this achievement to a possibly unconscious and yet important distinction introduced between a narrower meaning, where hegemony means *political leadership*, and a wider meaning, according to which it also means *cultural leadership*. I have said 'also', because in the *Prison Notebooks* the second meaning does not exclude but includes and subsumes the first.

In the pages which deal in a programmatic way with the modern Prince (first published at the beginning of the *Notes on Machiavelli*), Gramsci proposes two fundamental themes for studying the modern party: one on the formation of the 'collective will' (which is the theme of political leadership); the other on 'moral and intellectual reform' (which is the theme of cultural leadership).[51] I insist on these two different meanings of hegemony because in my opinion a comparison between Lenin and official Leninism on the one hand, and Gramsci on the other, can be fruitful only if we understand that the concept of hegemony, in the passage from one author to the other, has become wider, so that it includes the moment of cultural leadership. It is also necessary to recognize that by 'cultural leadership' Gramsci means the introduction of a 'reform', in the *strong* meaning of this term when it refers to a transformation of customs and culture, as opposed to the *weak* meaning the term has acquired in the political use (hence the difference between 'reformer' and 'reformist').

We could say that in Lenin the prevalent meaning of hegemony is political leadership, while in Gramsci it is cultural leadership; but we should add that this prevalence has two different aspects:

1. For Gramsci the factor of force is instrumental and therefore subordinate to the moment of hegemony; while for Lenin, in the works he wrote during the Revolution, dictatorship and hegemony go hand in hand, and in any case the factor of force is the primary and decisive one.

2. For Gramsci the conquest of hegemony precedes the conquest of power, while for Lenin the former accompanies the latter, or actually follows it.[52]

But even though these two differences are important and based on their texts, they are not essential. Both can be explained by the great diversity of the historical situations in which the two theories were elaborated: Lenin's at the height of the conflict; Gramsci's during the withdrawal which followed the defeat. The essential difference, in my opinion, is another: not a difference of more or less, before or after, but a qualitative difference. By this I mean that the difference does not lie in the contrasting way the two writers conceive the relation between the moments of hegemony and dictatorship, but – independently of their different conceptions of this relation, which can be explained historically – in the *extension*, and therefore in the *function*, of this concept in their two systems of thought.

As regards its extension, Gramsci's hegemony, as we have seen, includes both the factor of political leadership and the factor of cultural leadership. The hegemonic forces therefore include not only the party but all the other institutions of civil society (in Gramsci's meaning of the term) which have some connection with the elaboration and diffusion of culture.[53] As regards its function, hegemony aims not only at the formation of a collective will capable of creating a new state apparatus and transforming society but also at elaborating and propagating a new conception of the world. To be precise, Gramsci's theory of hegemony not only relates to a theory of the party and the state, or to a new conception of the party and the state, and involves political education, but also includes all the manifestations of civil society in the new and wider sense explored earlier, now conceived as a superstructural, primary historical force.

This underlines once again the importance of civil society in Gramsci's system. The function Gramsci assigns to hegemony in transcending mere domination forcefully reveals the pre-eminent position he attributes to civil society, which is the mediating factor between the base and secondary superstructural phenomena. Hegemony is the intermediary force which welds together determinate objective conditions and the actual domination of the ruling group: this conjunction comes about within civil society. As we have seen, in Gramsci only, and not in Marx, this intermediary force is accorded an autonomous space in the system, namely in civil society. By the same token it is only in Gramsci, and not in Lenin, that the factor of hegemony enlarged to occupy the autonomous space of civil society acquires a new dimension and a broader content.[54]

Civil Society and the End of the State

The last of Gramsci's themes where the concept of civil society plays a major role is the end of the state. The withering away of the state in a classless society is a constant theme in the works Lenin wrote during the Revolution; at the same time it is an ideal upper limit to social evolution within orthodox Marxism. In the *Prison Notebooks*, which were written when the new state had already been given solid foundations, this theme does appear, but only in a marginal way. In most of the rare passages which mention the end of the state it is conceived as a 'reabsorption of political society in civil society'.[55] The society without a state, which Gramsci calls 'regulated society', results from the enlarging of civil society, and therefore of the hegemonic forces, until all the space occupied by political society has been eliminated. The states which have existed until now are a dialectical unity of civil society and political society, of hegemony and dominion. The social class, which will succeed in making its own hegemony so universal that the factor of coercion will become superfluous, will have achieved the conditions for the transition to a regulated society. In one passage 'regulated society' is even used as synonymous with civil society (and also with ethical state),[56] that is, as civil society freed from political society.

Even if it is only a matter of a different *stress* and not of *contrast*, we could say that in the theory of Marx and Engels, adopted and popularized by Lenin, the movement which leads to the withering away of the state is essentially a structural one (transcendence of the antagonism between classes until the classes themselves are suppressed); while in Gramsci it is principally a superstructural process (enlargement of civil society until its universalization). In Marx and Engels, the two terms of the antithesis are: society *with* classes – society *without* classes; in Gramsci they are civil society *with* political society – civil society *without* political society. The fact (which I have constantly stressed) that civil society is a mediating element between the structure and the negative aspect of the superstructure has an important consequence for the dialectical process which leads to the withering away of the state: where there are only two terms – civil society–state – the final stage (that is, the society without classes) is the third term of the dialectical process: the negation of the negation. Where there are already three terms, the final stage is attained by a strengthening of the intermediate term. It is significant that Gramsci does not speak of transcendence (or of suppression) but of *reabsorption*.

As we have seen, the beginning of the nineteenth century saw the first reflections on the Industrial Revolution, leading to a reversal in the way in which the relation between society and state was traditionally conceived. It is a cliché that in the works of the philosophers of natural law the theory of the state is directly influenced by a pessimistic or optimistic conception of the state of nature: whoever considers the state of nature as evil sees the state as an innovation; whoever considers the state of nature as fundamentally good sees the state more as a restoration. This interpretative scheme can be applied to the political writers of the nineteenth century, who invert the relation 'society–state' by seeing, in concrete terms, the pre-state society in industrial (bourgeois) society. There are some, like Saint-Simon, whose starting point is an optimistic conception of industrial (bourgeois) society; and others, like Marx, who start out from a pessimistic conception. For the first group the withering away of the state will be a natural and peaceful consequence of the development of the society of producers; for the others an absolute reversal will be necessary and society without the state will be the effect of a true and real qualitative leap. Saint-Simon's scheme of evolution envisages the transition from a military society to an industrial one; Marx's scheme, on the other hand, envisages the transition from capitalist (industrial) society to socialist (industrial) society.

Gramsci's scheme undoubtedly fits into the second of these two conceptions. But here civil society appears as a third term because it is no longer identified with the state of nature, nor with industrial society, nor generally with pre-state society, but with the factor of hegemony: with one of the two components of the superstructure (the factor of consent as opposed to the factor of force). By conceiving civil society as a third element Gramsci's scheme seems to approximate more closely to the first conception, because here the state disappears following the withering away of civil society: through a process of reabsorption rather than transcendence. Yet the new and different meaning Gramsci gives to civil society prevents us from interpreting it too simplistically. Breaking with the tradition which translated the old antithesis 'state of nature–civil state' into the antithesis 'civil society–state', Gramsci translates another great historical antithesis, between the Church (broadly speaking, the modern Church is the party) and the state, into the antithesis 'civil society–political society'. So when Gramsci speaks of the absorption of political society in civil society he does not intend to refer to the whole historical process but only to the process that takes place within the superstructure, which in turn and in the last instance is conditioned by changes in the base. So it is the absorption of political society in civil society, but simultaneously the transformation of the economic structure, which is dialectically connected to the transformation of civil society.

In this case too, the key to an accurate interpretation of

Gramsci's conceptual system is to understand that 'civil society' is one of the two terms, not only of one antithesis but of two different antitheses, which are interwoven and only partially overlap. If we look at civil society as a term of the base–superstructure antithesis, the end of the state is the transcendence of the superstructural stage in which civil society and political society are in reciprocal equilibrium; if we look at civil society as an aspect of the superstructure, the end of the state is a reabsorption of political society in civil society. The apparent ambiguity is due to the real complexity of the historical bloc, as Gramsci conceived it. That is, it is due to the fact that civil society is a constitutive factor of two different processes which happen interdependently but without fully overlapping: the process which moves from the base to the superstructure, and the one which takes place within the superstructure itself. The new historical bloc will be the one where this ambiguity also will be resolved by the elimination of dualism in the superstructural sphere. In Gramsci's thought, the end of the state consists precisely in this elimination.

Notes

1. This essay was originally published in *Gramsci e la cultura contemporarea: Atti del Convegno Internazionale di Studi Gramsciani*, Rome 1968. The text published here differs from the one presented at the Congress of Cagliari only in that it has had a few formal corrections. I particularly wanted to clarify or strengthen several sentences which had led some critics, especially Jacques Texier, to infer that my intention was to see Gramsci as anti-Marx. I stress, however, that the content has remained the same. [We should point out that Bobbio uses the Hegelian term 'moment' extensively in this essay. Since this is less current in English than in Italian social thought we have tended to paraphrase with terms such as 'factor', 'stage' or 'phase'. Trans. and Ed.]

2. For more details refer to my essay 'Hegel e il giusnaturalismo', *Rivista di filosofia*, no. 57 (1966), p. 397.

3. Marx and Engels, 'Critique of Hegel's Philosophy of Right', *Collected Works*, Moscow and London 1975, vol. 3, p.63.

4. See for example the chapter, 'L'Organisateur', in *Œuvres de Claude-Henri de Saint-Simon*, 1966, vol. 2, pp. 17 ff. English trans. in *The Political Thought of Saint-Simon*, ed. G. Ionescu, Oxford 1976, pp. 138-42.

5. Karl Marx, *Capital*, London 1970, vol. 1, p. 703.

6. *Manifesto of the Communist Party*, in Marx and Engels, *Selected Works*, 3 vols., Moscow, 1973, vol. 1, pp. 110-11.

7. Frederick Engels, 'On the history of the Communist League', *Selected Works*, vol. 3, p. 178.

8. In Marx and Engels, *Basic Writings on Politics and Philosophy*, ed. Lewis S. Feuer, London 1969, p. 84.

9. In *Metaphysik der Sitten, bürgerliche Gesellschaft* stands for *status civilis*, that is, for state in the traditional meaning of the word. English trans. in I. Kant, *The Metaphysical Elements of Justics*, trans. J. Ladd, New York 1964, p. 75.

10. Ibid., pp. 75-7.

11. Adam Smith, *An Inquiry into the Nature and Causes of the Wealth of Nations*, London 1920, p. 249.

12. G.W.F. Hegel, *Hegel's Philosophy of Right*, trans. Knox, Oxford 1965, pp. 123-4.

13. 'The perfected political state is by its nature the *species-life* of man in *opposition* to his material life. All the presuppositions of this egoistic life continue to exist *outside* the sphere of the state in *civil* society, but as qualities of civil society.' Marx, *Early Writings*, trans. R. Livingstone and Ge. Benton, Harmondsworth 1975, p. 220. See also *Economic and Philosophical Manuscripts (1844)*, *'Society*, as it appears to the political economist, is *civil society'*, in *Early Writings*, p. 369.

14. Engels, 'Ludwig Feuerbach and the end of classical German philosophy', in Marx and Engels, *Selected Works*, vol. 3, p. 369.

15. 'The sum total of these relations of production constitutes the economic structure of society, the real foundation, on which rises a legal and political superstructure and to which correspond definite forms of social consciousness.' (*Selected Works*, vol. 1, p. 503.)

16. *The German Ideology*, in *Selected Works*, vol. 1, pp. 38, 76.

17. For more detailed indications see my article 'Sulla nozione di societa civile', *De homine*, no. 24-5, pp. 19-36.

18. In particular, to my knowledge, G. Tamburrano, *Antonio Gramsci*, Manduria 1963, pp. 220, 223-4.

19. *Quaderni del Carcere*, ed. V. Gerratana, Turin 1975, p. 9. English trans. in *Selections from the Prison Notebooks*, ed. and trans. Q. Hoare and G. Nowell Smith, London 1971, p. 12. There are even some passages where, as is well known, civil society is considered, broadly speaking, as an aspect of the state. See also *Lettere dal Carcere*, Turin 1948, p. 481; *Note sul Machiavelli*, Turin 1966, p. 130, *Prison Notebooks*, p. 261; *Passato e Presente*, Turin 1966, p. 72, *Prison Notebooks*, p. 239.

20. *Machiavelli*, p. 121; *Prison Notebooks*, p. 170 n.

21. *Passato e Presente*, p. 164.

22. *Machiavelli*, p. 128; *Prison Notebooks*, p. 259.

23. Ibid.

24. For a biased interpretation of Hegel, which has already been commented on by Sichirollo, see the passage on the importance of the intellectuals in Hegel's philosophy (*Quaderni del Carcere*, pp. 46-7).

25. G.W.F. Hegel, *Philosophie des Rechts*, para. 308. English trans. *Hegel's Philosophy of Right*.

26. *Passato e Presente*, p. 164.

27. Hegel, *Philosophie*, para. 255.

28. Ibid., para. 265.

29. Ibid., para. 256, which states that it is through the corporation that 'the transit from the sphere of civil society into the State takes place'.

30. Marx, 'Preface to *A Contribution to the Critique of Political Economy'*, *Selected Works*, vol. 1, p. 503.

31. *Studi Gramsciani*, Rome 1958. pp. 280-81.

32. Ibid., p. 281.

33. *Il Materialismo Storico e la filosofia di Benedetto Croce*, Turin 1948, p. 40; *Prison Notebooks*, p. 366.

34. 'The structure is actually the real past, because it is the testimony, the

indisputable document of what has been done and continues to exist as a condition of the present and of what is to come.' (*Il Materialismo Storico*, p. 222.)

35. Ibid., p. 40; *Prison Notebooks*, p. 367.

36. For an interpretation and a criticism of fatalism, see *Passato e Presente*, p. 203.

37. Tamburrano has pointed out to me that as regards the relation between civil society and state, it is more a matter of distinction than of antithesis. This remark is preceptive, but I am tempted to answer that it is a characteristic of dialectic thought to resolve the distinctions into antitheses, so that one can then proceed to transcend them.

38. *Machiavelli*, p. 121; *Prison Notebooks*, p. 170 n.

39. *Lettere dal Carcere*, p. 481.

40. 'The ideas of the ruling class are in every epoch the ruling ideas: i.e., the class which is the ruling *material* force of society, is at the same time its ruling *intellectual* force.' Immediately afterwards he gives the example of the doctrine of the division of powers as an ideological reflection of a society where power is truly – that is, in reality – divided (see *The German Ideology*, in *Selected Works*, p. 47).

41. A. Labriola, *Saggi sul materialismo storico*, Rome 1964, pp. 136-7.

42. *Passato e Presente*, p.38; *Prison Notebooks*, p. 276.

43. *Machiavelli*, pp. 150-1.

44. *Passato e Presente*, p. 38; *Prison Notebooks*, p. 268.

45. *Il Materialismo Storico*, pp. 32, 39, 75, 189, 201; *Prison Notebooks*, pp. 55-6 n, 357, 381-2, 381 n; *Lettere dal Carcere*, p. 616.

46. 'As the only completely revolutionary class of contemporary society, it [the proletariat] must be the leader [*rukovoditolem*], the holder of hegemony [*gegemonon*] in the struggle of all workers and all the exploited against the oppressors and the exploiters. The proletariat is revolutionary inasmuch as it is conscious of this idea of hegemony [*etu ideu gegemonii*] and inasmuch as it puts it into practice' (vol. 2, p. 349). I am grateful for this and other linguistic information in the paragraph to the kindness of Vittorio Strada. In the only passage from Lenin which, to my knowledge, has been quoted by the scholars of Gramsci and where the term 'holder of hegemony' is supposed to appear (*Due tattiche della social-democrazia nella rivoluzione democratica*, in *Opere Scelte*, Rome 1965, p. 319; see the Preface to *Duemila pagine di Gramsci*, ed. G. Perrata and N. Gallo, Milan 1964, vol. 1, p. 96) the term which Lenin actually used is not 'holder of hegemony' but 'leader' [*rukovoditel*]. For Stalin's terminology, see *Dal colloquio con la prima delegazione operaia americana*, where, when enumerating the themes which Lenin had developed of Marx's doctrine, he says: 'In the fourth place, the theme of the hegemony of the proletariat in the revolution, etc.' (J.U. Stalin, *Opere Scelte*, Moscow 1947, vol. 1, p. 35).

47. *Duemila pagine di Gramsci*, vol. 1, pp. 799, 824-5.

48. Ferrata recalls the article 'La Russia Potenza Mondiale', 14 August 1920, where we can find the expression 'hegemonic capitalism' (*L'Ordine Nuovo (1919-20)*, Turin 1954, pp. 145-6). Ragionieri pointed out that the term 'hegemony' is used also in one of Gramsci's works written in 1924.

49. 'It is the principle and practice of hegemony of the proletariat that are brought into question; the fundamental relations of the alliance between workers and peasants that are disturbed and placed in danger' (*Duemila pagine di Gramsci*, vol. 1, p. 824); 'The proletariat can become the leading and dominant class to the extent that it succeeds in creating a system of class alliances, etc.' (ibid., p. 799). English trans. in Antonio Gramsci, *Selections from Political Writings 1921-26*, trans. and ed. Q. Hoare, London 1978, pp. 431, 443 respectively.

50. *Lettere dal Carcere*, p. 616: 'The moment of hegemony or of cultural leader-

ship'. Also 'intellectual and moral leadership' (*Il Risorgimento*, Turin 1949, p. 70; *Prison Notebooks*, p. 59).

51. *Machiavelli*, pp. 6-8.

52. I am referring to the well-known passages where Gramsci explains the success of the politics of the moderates during the Risorgimento (*Il Risorgimento*, pp. 70-2). For Lenin, the passage from the *Political Report* at the Eleventh Congress of the Party (1922) is very important; he complains about the inferiority of Communist culture compared to that of the opponents: 'If the conquerors have a higher cultural level than that of the defeated, they impose their own culture on them; if the contrary is true, the defeated ones impose their own culture onto the conquerors' (Lenin, *Collected Works*, vol. 33, London 1966, p. 262).

53. *Lettere dal Carcere*, p. 481, where he speaks of 'hegemony of a social group over the whole of national society, which is carried out through the so-called private organisms, such as the church, the trade unions, the schools, etc.'

54. We can find two decisive proofs of this new dimension and of this broader subject in the way in which Gramsci deals with the problem of the active subjects of hegemony (the intellectuals), and in the way he understands the content of the new hegemony (the theme of the *nazionale popolare*). But because these are two very broad subjects, I will restrict myself to these two observations:

1. Gramsci is certainly inspired by Lenin in his reflections on the new intellectual, who is to be identified with the leader of the party. Still, as regards the problem of the intellectuals, his thought cannot be understood if we miss its connection with the discussion on their function, which began very dramatically in about the 1930s during the years of the great political and economic crisis (Benda, 1927; Manheim, 1929; Ortega, 1930), even if Gramsci's constant interlocutor is Benedetto Croce alone.

2. With his reflections on the *nazionale popolare*, a characteristic theme of the historiography of opposition in the anti-history of Italy, Gramsci connects the problem of social revolution with that of Italian revolution. The problem of the intellectual and moral reform accompanies the reflections on the history of Italy from the Renaissance to the Risorgimento, and its principal interlocutor is Machiavelli, concerning the first problem, and Gioberti (the importance of whose influence on Gramsci has, to my knowledge, been stressed only by Asor Rosa in studies of Gramsci's sources) concerning the second.

The Fraternal Social Contract[1]

Carole Pateman

The sons form a conspiracy to overthrow the despot, and in the end substitute a social contract with equal rights for all ... Liberty means equality among the brothers (sons) ... Locke suggests that the fraternity is formed not by birth but by election, by contract ... Rousseau would say it is based on will.

Norman O. Brown, *Love's Body*

The stories of the origins of civil society found in the classic social contract theories of the seventeenth and eighteenth centuries have been repeated many times. More recently, John Rawls and his followers have given new lease of life to the story of the contract that generates political right. But in all the telling of the tales, and in the discussion and argument about the social contract, we are told only half the story. Political theorists present the familiar account of the creation of civil society as a universal realm that (at least potentially) includes everyone and of the origins of political right in the sense of the authority of government in the liberal state, or Rousseau's participatory polity. But this is not the 'original' political right. There is silence about the part of the story which reveals that the social contract is a fraternal pact that constitutes civil society as a patriachal or masculine order. To uncover the latter it is necessary to begin to tell the repressed story of the genesis of patriarchal political right which men exercise over women.

Most discussions of contract theory accept uncritically the

claim that the stories successfully show why the authority of the state is legitimate; but the critical failure to recognize the social contract as fraternal pact is of a different kind. Only half the story appears in commentaries on the classic texts or in contemporary Rawlsian arguments, because modern political theory is so thoroughly patriarchal that one aspect of its origins lies outside the analytical reach of most theorists. Political theorists argue about the individual, and take it for granted that their subject matter concerns the public world, without investigating the way in which the 'individual', 'civil society' and 'the public' have been constituted as patriarchal categories in opposition to womanly nature and the 'private' sphere. The civil body politic created through the fraternal social contract is fashioned after only one of the two bodies of humankind.

The patriarchal character of civil society is quite explicit in the classic texts – if they are read from a feminist perspective. In this essay, I can draw attention to only a few of the implications of such a reading and to some of most obvious omissions in standard discussions of contract theory.[2] For instance, civil society is public society, but it is not usually appreciated that feminist arguments refer to a different sense of the separation of 'public' and 'private' from that typically found in discussions of civil society.

The meaning of 'civil society' in the contract stories, and as I am using it here, is constituted through the 'original' separation and opposition between the modern, public – civil – world and the modern, private or conjugal and familial sphere: that is, in the new social world created through contract, everything that lies beyond the domestic (private) sphere is public, or 'civil' society. Feminists are concerned with *this* division. In contrast, most discussions of civil society and such formulations as 'public' regulation versus 'private' enterprise presuppose that the politically relevant separation between public and private is drawn *within* 'civil society' as constructed in the social contract stories. That is to say, 'civil society' has come to be used in a meaning closer to that of Hegel, the social contract theorists' greatest critic, who contrasts the universal, public state with the market, classes and corporations of private, civil society.

Hegel, of course, presents a threefold division between family, civil society, state – but the separation between the family and the rest of social life is invariably 'forgotten' in arguments about civil society. The shift in meaning of 'civil', 'public' and 'private' goes unnoticed because the 'original' creation of civil society through the social contract is a patriarchal construction which is also a separation of the sexes. Political theorists have repressed this part of the story from their theoretical consciousness – though it is implicit in the assumption that civil life requires a national foundation – and thus liberals and (non-feminist) radicals alike deal only with the liberal understanding of civil society, in which 'civil' life becomes private in opposition to the public state.

Perhaps the most striking feature of accounts of the contract story is the lack of attention paid to fraternity, when liberty and equality are so much discussed. One reason for the neglect is that most discussions pass over the insights about fraternity found in Freud's versions of the contract story. Fraternity is central to socialism, and nineteenth- and twentieth-century liberalism, as a recent study has shown, relies heavily on fraternity as a crucial bond integrating individual and community. However, discussions of fraternity do not touch upon the constitution of the 'individual' through the patriarchal separation of private and public, nor upon how the division within the (masculine) 'individual' includes an opposition between fraternity and reason. Fraternity comes to the fore in liberals' attempts to formulate a more sociologically adequate account of the individual than is found in the abstract conceptions of classic liberal contract theory. But for feminists explicit recourse to liberal or socialist fraternal bonds merely exposes the patriarchal character of ostensibly universal categories and calls attention to the fundamental problem of whether and how women could be fully incorporated into a patriarchal civil world.

A feminist reading of the contract stories is also important for another reason. The contemporary feminist movement has brought the idea of patriarchy into popular and academic currency, but confusion abounds about its meaning and implications and recently some feminists have argued that the term is best avoided. 'Patriarchy' is, to my knowledge, the only term with which to capture the specificities of the subjection and oppression of *women* and to distinguish this from other forms of domination. If we abandon the concept of patriarchy the problem of the subjection of women and sexual domination will again vanish from view within individualist and class theories. The crucial question, therefore, is the sense in which it can be said that our own society is patriarchal.

Two popular feminist claims about patriarchy add to the confusion. The first is that the literal meaning of 'patriarchy', rule by fathers, is still relevant. To insist that patriarchy is nothing more than paternal rule is itself a patriarchal interpretation, as an examination of the classic texts reveals. The second claim is that patriarchy is a timeless, human universal, which obviously rules out the possibility that men's domination of women takes different forms in different historical periods and cultures. More precisely, neither claim about patriarchy can acknowledge that our own momentous transition from the traditional to the modern world – a transition which the contract stories encapsulate theoretically – involved a change from a traditional (paternal) form of patriarchy to a new *specifically modern* (or fraternal) form: patriarchal civil society.

Few of the participants in recent feminist debates about patriarchy seem aware of the significance of patriarchal political theory in the classic sense: that is, the patriarchalism of Sir Robert Filmer and other less well-known writers of three centuries ago. Nor have they taken account of the theoretical and practical significance of the battle waged between the patriarchalists and the social contract theorists. Zillah Eisenstein has done so, but on the other hand Jean Elshtain's references to patriarchal theory merely reiterate the standard view in political theory that patriarchalism had suffered a fatal defeat by the end of the seventeenth century.[3] This is far from the case, and an understanding of the exact sense in which, and the limits within which, the contract theorists emerged victorious over the patriarchalists is central to an appreciation of how a specifically modern form of patriarchy was brought into being.

Patriarchal political theory had little in common with the ancient tradition of patriarchalism that took the family as the general model for social order and made claims about the emergence of political society from the family, or the coming together of many families. In *Patriarchalism in Political Thought*, Schochet emphasizes that patriarchal theory was formulated explicitly as a justification for political authority and political obedience, and – as he also stresses – it was systematized in opposition to the social contract theories that were developing at the same time and challenging (one half of) the patriarchalists' most fundamental assumptions.[4] Patriarchalism developed, and was 'defeated', in a specific historical and theoretical context.

The standard interpretation of the conflict between the patriarchalists and the contract theorists treats it as a battle over paternal rule and focuses on the irreconcilable differences between the two doctrines over the political right of fathers and the natural liberty of sons. The patriarchalists claimed that kings and fathers ruled in exactly the same way (king were fathers and vice versa); that family and polity were homologous; that sons were born naturally subject to their fathers; and that political authority and obedience and a hierarchy of inequality were natural. The contract theorists rejected all these claims: they argued that paternal and political rule were distinct; that family and polity were two different and separate forms of association; that sons were born free and equal and, as adults, were as free as their fathers before them; that political authority and obligation were conventional and political subjects were civil equals.[5] It is true that in this particular controversy the patriarchalists were defeated. The theoretical assumptions of the contract theorists were an essential part of the transformation of the traditional order and the world of father-kings into capitalist society, liberal, representative government and the modern family.

However, this familiar version of the story in which the sons gain their natural liberty, make the contract and create liberal civil society, or Rousseau's participatory civil order, is only half the tale. It is a patriarchal reading of the texts which identifies patriarchy with paternal rule; it therefore omits the story of the real origin of political right. Patriarchalism has two dimensions: the paternal (father/son) and the masculine (husband/wife). Political theorists can represent the outcome of the theoretical battle as a victory for contract theory because they are silent about the sexual or conjugal aspect of patriarchy, which appears as non-political or natural and so of no theoretical consequence. But a feminist reading of the texts shows that patriarchalism was far from defeated. The contract theorists rejected paternal right, but they absorbed and simultaneously transformed conjugal, masculine patriarchal right.

To see how this came about – and hence to take a necessary first step towards elucidating some of the characteristics of modern patriarchy – it is necessary to begin with the patriarchal story of monarchical fatherhood exemplified in the writings of Sir Robert Filmer. Although Filmer's father is overthrown in the story of the social contract, his sons receive a vital inheritance that is, paradoxically, obscured by the doctrine of paternal right.

Filmer's aim was to show the awful error of the contract theorists' claim that men were by nature free and equal, a claim he saw as the 'main foundation of popular sedition'.[6] Filmer argued that all law was of necessity the product of the will of one man. All titles to rule devolved from the original Divine grant of kingly right to Adam, the first father. The ground was immediately swept from under the feet of the proponents of the doctrine of the natural freedom of mankind once it was recognized that 'the natural and private dominion of Adam [is] the fountain of all government and propriety.'[7] Filmer writes that 'the title comes from the fatherhood';[8] Adam's sons, and hence all succeeding generations of sons, were born into political subjection by virtue of Adam's 'right of fatherhood', his 'fatherly power', or the 'power of the fatherhood'.[9]

At the birth of his first son, Adam became the first monarch, and his political right passed to all subsequent fathers and kings. For Filmer, fathers and kings ruled by virtue of their fatherhood and all fathers were monarchs in their families: 'the Father of a family governs by no other law than by his own will.'[10] Filmer argued that no government could be a tyranny because the king's will was law; similarly, the will of the father was the absolute, arbitrary will of the *patria potestas* who, under Roman law, had the power of life and death over his children. Laslett comments that Filmer 'did not adopt the capital punishment of children by their fathers, but he quoted examples of it from Bodin with approval.'[11]

Filmer's view of the origin of political right seems, therefore, to be unmistakable: it derives from fatherhood. But patriarchy, even in its classical formulation, is more complex than its literal meaning suggests. Fatherly power is only one dimension of patriarchy, as Filmer himself reveals. Filmer's apparently straightforward statements obscure the foundation of patriarchal right. Paternal power is not the origin of political right. The genesis of political power lies in Adam's conjugal or sex right, not in his fatherhood. Adam's political title is granted *before* he becomes a father. Sons, as Filmer caustically reminds Hobbes, do not spring up like mushrooms. If Adam was to be a father, Eve had to become a mother and if Eve was to be a mother, then Adam must have sexual access to her body. In other words, sexual or conjugal right must *necessarily precede* the right of fatherhood.

Filmer makes it clear that Adam's political right is originally established in his right as a husband over Eve: 'God gave to Adam ... the dominion over the woman', and 'God ordained Adam to rule over his wife, and her desires were to be subject to his.'[12] However, sexual or conjugal right then fades from view in Filmer's writings. After proclaiming that Adam's first dominion or political right is over a woman, not another man (son), Filmer then subsumes conjugal right under the power of fatherhood. Eve and her desires are subject to Adam but, Filmer continues, 'here we have the original grant of government, and the fountain of all power placed in the Father of all mankind'. Recall that in the Bible story in the Book of Genesis, Eve is created only after Adam and the animals have been placed on earth. Moreover, she is not created *ab initio* but *from* Adam, who is thus in a sense her parent. Filmer is able to treat all political right as the right of a father because the patriarchal father has the creative powers of both a mother and a father. He is not just one of two parents; he is *the* parent.

The patriarchal image of political fathers (here in Locke's words) is that of 'nursing Fathers tender and careful of the publick weale'.[13] The patriarchal story is about the procreative power of a father who is complete in himself. His procreative power both gives and nurtures physical life and creates and maintains political right. Filmer is able to dismiss Adam's power over Eve so easily because, in the story, women are procreatively and politically irrelevant. The reason Adam has dominion over 'the woman' is, according to Filmer (here following a very ancient notion), that 'the man ... is the nobler and principal agent in generation.'[14] Women are merely empty vessels for the exercise of the father's sexual and procreative power. The original political right which God gives to Adam is, so to speak, the right to fill the empty vessel.

There is therefore no question to be asked, or error to be corrected, about women's natural freedom. Filmer invokes women merely to highlight the folly of the doctrine of the natural liberty of sons. The contract theorists' argument about natural freedom entails that 'there can be no superior power'. The full absurdity of that conclusion is revealed for Filmer in its corollary that 'women, especially virgins, [would] by birth have as much natural freedom as any other, and therefore ought not to lose their liberty without their own consent.'[15]

Filmer could present the natural freedom of women as the *reductio ad absurdum* of the contract argument becuase there was no controversy between the patriarchalists and contract theorists about women's subjection. The contract theorists' aim was theoretical parricide, not the overthrow of the sexual right of men and husbands. Both sides agreed, first, that women (wives), unlike sons, were born and remained naturally subject to men (husbands); and, second, that the right of men over women was *not political*. Locke, for example, concurred with Filmer's view that a wife's subjection has a 'Foundation in Nature'. The husband is naturally 'the abler and the stronger', so he must rule over his wife.[16] Rousseau, the vehement critic of the fraudulent liberal social contract that brings into being a corrupt civil society of inequality and domination, is no less insistent that women must be 'subjected either to a man or to the judgements of men and they are never permitted to put themselves above these judgements'. When a woman becomes a wife, she acknowledges her husband as 'a master for the whole of life'.[17]

The contract theorists' 'victory' hinged on the separation of paternal from political power, so they could not, like Filmer, subsume sexual under paternal – that is, political – rule. Instead, the social contract story hides original political right by proclaiming sexual or conjugal right as *natural*. Men's dominion over women is held to follow from the respective natures of the sexes, and Rousseau spells out this claim in detail in Book V of *Émile*. Locke has no quarrel with Filmer about the *legitimacy* of sexual, patriarchal right; rather, he insists that it is not political. Eve's subordination

> can be no other Subjection than what every Wife owes her Husband, ... Adam ['s] ... can only be a Conjugal Power, not Political, the Power that every Husband hath to order the things of private Concernment in his Family, as Proprietor of the Goods and Land there, and to have his Will take place before that of his wife in all things of their common Concernment.[18]

Both sides in the seventeenth-century controversy – unlike contemporary political theorists – were well aware that the new doctrine of natural freedom and equality had subversive implications for *all* relationships of power and subordination. The patriarchalists claimed that the doctrine was so absurd that the problems it raised of justifying, say, the power of a husband over his wife were immediately shown to be figments of the contract theorists' disordered imaginations. But if the contract theorists were content with conjugal patriarchy, the individualist language of their attack on paternal right meant that they had (as Sir Robert Filmer argued) opened the thin ends of numerous revolutionary wedges, including a feminist wedge. Women almost at once seized on the contradiction of an 'individualism' and a 'universalism' which insisted that women were born into subjection and that their subjection was natural and politically irrelevant. By the end of the seventeenth century, for example, Mary Astell was asking: 'If all Men are born Free, how is it that all Women are born Slaves?'[19]

The difficulty for the contract theorists was that given their premises, an answer to the question was impossible. Logically, there is no reason why a free and equal female individual should always (contract to) subordinate herself to another free and equal (male) individual upon marriage. The difficulty, however, was easily overcome. Political theorists, whether liberal or socialist, absorbed masculine right into their theories and 'forgot' the story of the origin of patriarchal power. Natural subjection was seen in terms of paternal power and three centuries of feminist criticism – whether written by women whose names never appear in political theory textbooks, by the co-operative or utopian socialists, or by the otherwise acceptable philosopher, John Stuart Mill – was suppressed and ignored.

The standard view that the rise of social contract theory and the development of civil society was also a defeat for patriarchalism has meant that some vital questions about the construction of the civil body politic have never been asked. One problem about the social contract that has received some attention is the question of exactly who makes the agreement. Many commentators talk uncritically of 'individuals' sealing the pact, but Schochet, for example, points out that in the seventeenth century it was taken for granted that fathers of families entered the social contract.

When I first began to think about these matters from a feminist perspective, I assumed that the social contract was a patriarchal contract because it was made by fathers whose agreement was taken to bind their families. Certainly, 'individuals', in the universal sense in which the category is usually used to mean anyone and everyone, do not make the social contract. Women have no part in it: as natural subjects they lack the requisite capacities and abilities. The 'individuals' of the stories are *men*, but they do not act as fathers. After all, the stories tell of the defeat of the father's political power. Men no longer have a political place as fathers. But fathers are also husbands – Locke's friend Tyrrell wrote that wives were 'concluded by their Husbands'[20] – and, from yet another viewpoint, the participants in the social contract are sons or brothers. The contract is made by brothers, or a *fraternity*. It is no accident that fraternity appears historically hand in hand with liberty and equality, nor that it means exactly what it says: brotherhood.

If 'patriarchy' is all too often interpreted literally, 'fraternity' is usually treated as if its literal meaning had no relevance today and as if the terms in the revolutionary slogan, 'Liberty, Equality, Fraternity' unquestionably applied to us all, not only to men joined by fraternal bonds. Bernard Crick has recently pointed out that fraternity has been relatively little analysed, even though, he says, 'fraternity with liberty is humanity's greatest dream'.[21] When it is mentioned, fraternity is usually presented as an expression of community; it is seen as 'at bottom, a certain type of social co-operation ... a relation between a group of equals for the utmost mutual help and aid'.[22] Or as Crick argues, addressing his fellow-socialists, fraternity is an ethic and social practice that

> goes with simplicity, lack of ostentation, friendliness, helpfulness, kindliness, openness, lack of restraint between individuals in everyday life and a willingness to work together in common tasks.[23]

The general acceptance that 'fraternity' is no more than a way of talking about the bonds of community illustrates how deeply patriarchal conceptions structure our political theory and practice. Feminists have long appreciated the extent to which socialist solidarity and community has meant that women are little more than auxiliaries to the comrades and that women's political demands must wait until after the revolution. But the problems women have in finding a language in which to make their demands is illustrated by the final words of Simone de Beauvoir's *The Second Sex*, where she states that 'men and women [must] unequivocally affirm their brotherhood.'[24]

The fact that the social contract is not an agreement between individuals, fathers, or husbands, but a fraternal pact becomes particularly clear in Freud's versions of the social contract story. Freud's account of the murder of the primal father by his sons is not usually considered in discussions of the social contract. Yet, as Brown states, 'the battle of books re-enacts Freud's primal crime.'[25] And Rieff treats Freud's myth of the parricide as a version of the social contract, to be considered as part of the same tradition as the theories of Hobbes, Locke or Rousseau.[26] The best warrant of all is available for this interpretation. In *Moses and Monotheism* Freud refers to the pact made by the brothers after their dreadful deed as 'a sort of social contract'.[27]

But, it could be objected, Freud's myth is about the origins of society itself. Freud claims – and this is taken at face value by Juliet Mitchell's *Psychoanalysis and Feminism*, which has been very influential among feminists – that the parricide ushers in 'civilization': that is, human society. However, the classic society contract theorists are also sometimes read in the same way; the passage from 'the state of nature' can be seen as the transition from nature or savagery to the first human social order. In neither case is there good reason to accept a universal reading that identifies 'civilization' or 'civil society' with society itself. When the form of the laws instituted by the brothers is examined, it is clear that the stories are about the origin of a culturally and historically specific form of social life. The close connection between 'civil society' and 'civilization' is suggested too by the fact that the term civilization came into general use only towards the end of the eighteenth century, 'to express a particular stage of European history, sometimes the final or ultimate stage'.[28] 'Civilization' expressed the 'sense of modernity: an achieved condition of refinement and order'.[29]

In her interpretation of Freud, Mitchell claims that the 'law of the father' is established after the parricide. On the contrary: the law of the father, the absolute rule of one father-king, holds sway before his murder. The crucial point about the contract is that it takes place after the death of the father and abolishes his arbitrary right. Instead, the brothers (sons), prompted by remorse for their dreadful deed, by love and hatred, and by a desire to prevent parricide in future, establish their *own* law. They establish justice, 'the first "right" or "law"'[30] – or civil society. The law, or arbitrary will, of the father is overthrown by the combined action of the brothers, who then place mutual restrictions on themselves, establishing an equality which, Freud states, 'saved the organization which had made them strong'.[31] A contract between free and equal brothers replaces the 'law of the father' with public rules which bind all equally. As Locke makes clear, the rule of one man (father) is incompatible with civil society, which requires an impartial, impersonal set of rules promulgated by a collective body of men who stand to the law and each other as free equals, as a fraternity.

At this point the objection might be raised that even if brothers enter the contract, they cease to be brothers once the pact is concluded. In the act of contracting they constitute themselves as equal, civil 'individuals' and thus cast off familial and, hence, fraternal ties. The fundamental distinction between the traditional patriarchy of the father and modern patriarchy is precisely that the latter is created in separation from, and opposition to, the familial sphere.

However, it does not follow that all ascriptive ties are therefore abandoned and that the term 'fraternal' ceases to be appropriate. Brown claims that there is an 'inner contradiction' in the trilogy of liberty, equality, fraternity: 'without a father there can be no sons or brothers.'[32] However, as recent accounts of fraternity make clear, the concept covers much more than bonds of kinship. 'Individuals' can be part of a fraternity or a brotherhood – a 'community' – even though they are not brothers (sons of a father or kin). The father is dead and the participants in civil society have left kinship behind them, but as civil individuals they still share an ascriptive bond – a bond *as men*.

Freud's story of the parricide is important because he makes explicit what the classic tales of theoretical murder leave obscure: the motive for the brothers' collective act is not merely to claim their natural liberty and right of self-government, but *to gain access to women*. In the classic theorists' state of nature, the 'family' already exists and men's conjugal right is deemed a natural right.[33] Freud's primal father, his *patria potestas*, keeps all the women of the horde for himself. The parricide eliminates the father's political right, and also his *exclusive* sexual right. The brothers inherit his patriarchal, masculine right and share the women among themselves. No man can be a primal father ever again, but by setting up rules that give all men equal access to women (compare their equality before the laws of the state) they exercise the 'original' political right of dominion over women that was once the prerogative of the father.

Freud writes of the brothers' 'renunciation of the passionately desired mothers and sisters of the horde'.[34] This is misleading. The fraternity do not renounce the women, but each gives up the desire to put himself in the place of the father. As part of the fraternal social contract, the brothers institute what Freud calls the law of exogamy or kinship. In historically specific terms, the brothers create the modern system of marriage law and family and establish the modern order of conjugal or sexual right. The 'natural foundation' of civil society has been brought into being through the fraternal social contract.

The separation of 'paternal' from political rule, or the family from the public sphere, is also the separation of women from men through the subjection of women to men. The brothers establish their own law and their own form of sexual or conjugal dominion. The fraternal social contract creates a new, modern patriarchal order that is presented as divided into two spheres: civil society or the universal sphere of freedom, equality, individualism, reason, contract and impartial law – the realm of men or 'individuals'; and the private world of particularity, natural subjection, ties of blood, emotion, love and sexual passion – the world of women, in which men also rule.

In short, the contract constitutes patriarchal civil society and the modern, ascriptive rule of men over women. Ascription and contract are usually seen as standing at opposite poles, but the social contract is sexually ascriptive in both form (it is made by brothers) and content (the patriarchal right of a fraternity is established). Civil individuals have a fraternal bond because, *as men*, they share a common interest in upholding the contract which legitimizes their masculine patriarchal right and allows them to gain material and psychological benefit from women's subjection.

One important question raised by the contract stories is exactly how the 'foundation in nature', which upholds the subjection of women, should be characterized. Locke tells us that the strength and ability of the man (husband) is the natural basis of the wife's subordination: a view which becomes absorbed into patriarchal liberalism, but also opens the way for liberal feminism. Feminists began to criticize the argument from strength long ago,[35] and although the claim is still heard today, historically it has become less and less plausible to rely on strength as the criterion for masculine political right. Contemporary liberal feminists, following the lead of much earlier writers like Mary Astell and Mary Wollstonecraft, have attacked the alleged lesser ability and capacity of women as an artifact of defective education, as a matter of deliberate social contrivance, not a fact of nature.

The difficulty for the liberal feminist argument is that education cannot be equal while men and women remain differentially positioned within their 'separate spheres', but the patriarchal division between the private family and public, civil society is a central structural principle of liberalism. Moreover, the problem runs deeper than a liberal perspective suggests. Liberal feminism assumes that the relevant political problem is to show that women possess the capacities men possess and can do what men can do. However, this also assumes that there is no political significance to the fact that women have one natural ability which men lack: women, but not men, are able to give birth.

Now, it may be claimed that this provides no 'foundation in nature' for women's subjection because birth (unlike child-rearing) is ultimately irrelevant to the development of the capacities of civil beings. The difficulty with this argument is that it, too, ignores the story of the 'origin' of patriarchal political right, and thus the importance of birth for patriarchal civil society. The ability to give birth, both actually and metaphorically, is central to patriarchal theory.

Filmer's argument shows that Adam's right of domination over Eve is the right to become a father: a right to demand sexual access to Eve's body and to insist that she give birth. Eve's procreative, creative capacity is then denied and appropriated by *men* as the ability to give *political birth*, to be the 'originators' of a new form of political order. Adam and the participants in the fraternal social contract gain an amazing patriarchal ability and become the 'principal agents' in political generation. Moreover, in patriarchal argument birth also symbolizes and encapsulates all the reasons why it has been claimed that women must be bodily removed from civil society.[36]

Some of the murky depths become clearer in the stories told by Rousseau and Freud. Women, they insist, are unable to transcend their bodily natures in the manner required of 'individuals' who are to participate in civil life and uphold the universal laws of civil society. The female body, subject to uncontrollable natural processes and passions, deprives women of the reason and moral character which can be educated for civil society. (In another essay I began to explore one aspect of this perception of women and its corollary that we pose a permanent threat to civil life.[37])

Rousseau's solution is that the sexes must be segregated to the greatest possible extent, even in domestic life. Significantly, in *Émile* Rousseau allows the tutor to give only one direct command, in which he sends Émile away from Sophie for an extended period to learn about politics and citizenship before he is permitted to claim her body as a husband. Freud offers no solution but states explicitly that from the 'beginning' – from the original parricide in which women are at stake, and which is endlessly reproduced through the Oedipus complex – women continue to have 'a hostile attitude towards' civil society.[38] Or, as Mitchell interprets Freud, a woman 'cannot receive the "touch" of the law, her submission to it must be in establishing herself as its opposite.'[39]

Women are 'opposite' to and outside the fraternal social contract and its civil law in two senses. First, they are 'originally', necessarily, excluded from an agreement through which the brothers inherit their legacy of patriarchal sex right and legitimize their claim over women's bodies and ability to give birth. Secondly, the civil law encapsulates all that women lack. The civil law stems from a reasoned agreement that it is to the rational mutual advantage of the participants to the contract to constrain their interactions and desires through a law equally applicable to all. Women's passions render them incapable of making such a reasoned agreement or of upholding it if made. In other words, the patriarchal claim that there is a 'foundation in nature' for women's subjection to men, is a claim that women's bodies must be governed by men's reason. The separation of civil society from the familial sphere is also a division between men's reason and women's bodies.

Feminist scholars are now showing how, from ancient times, political life has been conceptualized in opposition to the mundane world of necessity, the body, the sexual passions and birth: in short, in opposition to women and the disorders and creativity they symbolize.[40] In Filmer's classic patriarchalism the father is both mother and father and creates political right through his fatherhood, but Filmer's account is only one version of a long Western tradition in which the creation of political life has been seen as a masculine act of birth: as a male replica of the ability which only women possess.

The fraternal social contract is a specifically modern reformulation of this patriarchal tradition. The father is dead, but the brothers appropriate the ability specific to women; they, too, can generate new political life and political right. The social contract is the point of origin, or birth, of civil society, and simultaneously its separation from the (private) sphere of real birth and the disorder of women. The brothers give birth to an artificial body, the body politic of civil society; they create Hobbes's 'Artificial Man, we call a Commonwealth', or Rousseau's 'artificial and collective body', or the 'one Body' of Locke's 'Body Politick'.

The 'birth' of the civil body politic, however, is an act of reason; there is no analogue to a bodily act of procreation. The social contract, as we are all taught, is not an actual event. The natural paternal body of Filmer's patriarchy is metaphorically put to death by the contract theorists, but the 'artificial' body that replaces it is a construct of the mind, not the creation of a political community by real people. Whereas the birth of a human child can produce a new male or female, the creation of civil society produces a social body fashioned after the image of only one of the two bodies of humankind. Or, more exactly, the civil body politic is fashioned after the image of the male 'individual' who is constituted through the separation of civil society from women. This individual has some singular – and largely unrecognized –

aspects precisely because his defining characteristics are thrown into relief only through the contrast with the womanly nature that has been excluded from civil society.

The abstract character of the individual in liberal contract theory has been criticized from the left ever since Rousseau's initial attack. But because the critiques invariably pass silently over the separation of male reason from female body in the original creation of the civil individual, one of his most notable features has also silently been incorporated by the critics. The 'individual' is disembodied. For three centuries the figure of the individual has been presented as universal, as the embodiment of all, but it is only because he is disembodied that the 'individual' can appear universal. Like the new body politic he, too, is 'artificial': he is nothing more than a 'man of reason'.[41]

In the most recent rewriting of the liberal contract story in *A Theory of Justice*, Rawls claims that his parties in their original position know none of the essential facts about themselves. Thus it might seem that Rawls's parties are truly universal and that the original choices include a choice between the two bodies (sexes) of humankind. The fact that Rawls ignores this possibility, and writes that the parties can be seen as heads of families,[42] shows how deeply entrenched are patriarchal assumptions about the proper characteristics of the 'individual'. Moreover, the attributes of the parties and their original position illustrate the fact that Rawls stands at the logical conclusion of the fraternal contract tradition. The original position and its choices are explicitly hypothetical (logical) and the parties are nothing more than disembodied entities of reason; otherwise they could not help but know the natural facts about themselves, inseparable from their bodies, such as the facts of sex, age and colour.[43]

Ironically, the disembodiment necessary to maintain the political fiction of the universal civil individual poses profound problems for fraternity. For individualist liberals the problems are part of their wider difficulties over the self, and involve an opposition within the individual between fraternity and reason. The opposition between reason and fraternity is an opposition between the public and the private. But this is not the patriarchal opposition between 'private' and 'public', between family (women) and civil society (men); instead, the relevant division between public and private is the other opposition to which I referred earlier: the opposition located within 'civil society' as I am using the term.[44] For liberals relying on a social view of the self or for socialist critics of liberalism the problems arise because in the 1980s an emphasis on fraternity begins to reveal the patriarchal character of their theories. To preserve universality, '*the* individual' must be abstracted even from his masculinity and fraternity, so that the individual has no body and, hence, no sex.

The creation of the 'individual' presupposes the division of rational civil order from the disorder of womanly nature. It might thus seem that the civil individual and the body politic made in his image would be unified. Indeed, they are so presented in liberal theory, but its critics from Rousseau onward argue that the individual and civil society are inherently divided, one from the other and within themselves. The individual is torn between *bourgeois* and *citoyen*, or between *Homo economicus* and *Homo civicus*, and civil society is divided between private interest and the public universal interest, or between 'civil' society and state. The point about such critiques, however, is exactly that they are concerned with extrafamilial social life and with the individual as an inhabitant of the public world.

The liberal opposition between private and public (like the patriarchal opposition between the sexes) appears in a variety of guises: for example, society, economy and freedom stand against state, public and coercion. Liberals see these dualities as posing important problems of freedom, since the private sphere of civil society must be protected from the coercive intrusions of the state, and they now spend a good deal of time and effort trying to sort out where the dividing line plausibly can be drawn. Their critics, on the other hand, argue that the opposition between private and public poses an insoluble problem; that it is an unbridgeable structural fissure at the centre of liberalism. I agree with the critics; but the criticism does not go far enough because it takes no account of the 'original' patriarchal division and thus leaves the critics' own conception of the 'individual' and 'civil society' untouched.

In *Knowledge and Politics* Robert Unger presents a comprehensive discussion and critique of the liberal dichotomies, but even his analysis of the division between fact and theory, values and rules, desire and reason, ignores the fact that it also represents the opposition between the sexes. The 'self' is implicitly taken to be masculine. The reference to 'men' must be taken literally when he writes:

> the dichotomy of the public and private life is still another corollary of the separation of understanding and desire. ... When reasoning,

[men] belong to a public world. ... When desiring, however, men are private beings.[45]

In Unger's account, the 'desire' and associated disorder represented by women and their private world has been 'forgotten'. The 'self' has become that of the male individual in civil society, an individual torn between the claims of public interest ('reason') and private or subjective interest ('desire'). The opposition between women, bodies, passion, and men, reason, rational advantage, is repressed and replaced by the dichotomy between the individual's private interest and the claims of the public interest or universal law.

In this form, the dichotomy is also expressed as an opposition between the fraternity and reason of civil individuals. The only ties between the individuals of liberal contract theory are those of self-interest. The individual is, as it were, a collection of pieces of property that can, through rational calculation of the mind, be made the subject of contract. The individual thus enters into only certain kinds of relationship and this limitation gives rise to another familiar difficulty within liberal theory: that of presenting a coherent conception of citizenship or the political. The liberal individual's political bonds with other citizens are merely another expression of the pursuit of self-interest; *Homo civicus* is absorbed into, or is nothing more than one face of, the 'private' *Homo economicus*. However, this view of the individual as citizen – as public or civil individual – systematically undermines one of the most significant expressions of fraternity.

Liberal individuals interact in a benign public world. They compete one with the other, but the competition is regulated and the rules are fair; the only coercion required is to enforce the rules. Hence the division between private and public as an opposition between society and state is often presented as between freedom and coercion. Currently this position is associated with the New Right, but in the past *le doux commerce* could be offered as the antithesis of violence and the idealist liberals, claiming to have reconciled the oppositions, could assert that will, not force, is the basis of the state.

On the other hand, it is also clear that the individual can be required to protect his protection (as Hobbes put it) by something more than mere obedience to the law. He may have to surrender his body in defence of the state. Indeed, this has always been seen as the ultimate act of loyalty and allegiance, the truly exemplary act of citizenship. However, it is also an act which will never be to the rational advantage of a liberal individual, as Hobbes's logical working out of radical individualism reveals. In the clash between private and public interest, the private claim always has the rational advantage. It is not in the individual's self-interest to be a soldier; thus reason is torn apart from the fraternity on which citizenship, in the last analysis, depends. Of all the male clubs and associations, it is in the military and on the battlefield that fraternity finds its most complete expression.

The opposition between the figure of the soldier and the figure of the individual, or between fraternity and reason, is unique to liberal civil society. In many respects the fraternal contract story transforms ancient patriarchal themes into a specifically modern theory, but the conception of the liberal individual breaks with older traditions in which citizenship has involved a distinctive form of activity and has also been closely tied to the bearing of arms. Feminist scholars are now showing that from ancient times there has been an integral connection between the warrior and conceptions of self-identity, sexuality and masculinity, which have all been bound up with citizenship. The peculiarity of the liberal individual is that although he is male he is also defined – unlike either his predecessors in the traditional world or the 'individuals' that appear in social-liberal and socialist theory – in opposition to the political and the masculine passions that underlie the defence of the state by arms.

Although our consciousness is informed by the liberal individual's image, and many of our social practices and institutions presuppose that we are motivated by self-interest (the contemporary preoccupation with freeriders is no accident), the state has never relied on rational self-interest as the basis for sociopolitical order. Nor did most classical theorists, except Hobbes, have the courage of their theoretical convictions on this point. Hobbes's conclusion that Leviathan's sword was the only alternative to an inherently insecure 'artificial' ground for order was rejected in favour of such devices as natural law, sympathy, benevolence, or hidden hands – and socialists have appealed to solidarity, comradeship and community or, in a word, to *fraternity*. Historically, obedience and loyalty to the state have been fostered by appeals not to individual rational advantage but to ascriptive, psychological bonds, especially to nationalism, patriotism and fraternity. These are ties of a much more full-blooded character than, for example, Rawls's sense of justice and, most importantly, they appeal directly to the masculine self's sense of identity. However, the real and ideological basis for the motivating force of self-interest means that it is hard to eliminate the opposition between fraternity and reason.

When some liberals over the past century attempted to develop an adequately social and developmental conception of individuality, one that restored the affective ties of community that had been stripped away in liberal contract theory, they also turned to the idea of fraternity. In the eyes of these liberals, Gaus states, fraternity is the 'most powerful of communal bonds'.[46] The ideal of fraternity provides the 'pre-eminent conception of communal bonds in modern liberal theory', so that Dewey, for example, wrote of a 'fraternally associated public', and Rawls sees his difference principle as a 'natural meaning of fraternity'.[47]

The explicit use of 'fraternity' in both social-liberal and socialist attempts to reintegrate the civil individual and the community (or to reintegrate the liberal division between private and public) means that the patriarchal character of civil society begins to come to the surface. Moreover, the masculine attributes of the individual begin to be exposed. The universalism of the category of the 'individual' can be maintained only as long as the abstraction from the body is maintained. 'The individual' is a fiction: individuals have one of two bodies, masculine or feminine. But how can the feminine body become part of a (liberal or socialist) fraternal body politic?

Citizenship has now been extended formally to women, raising the substantive problem of how we can become civil 'individuals' made in the masculine image. The importance, in practice, of the intimate connection between masculinity, citizenship and bearing arms became explicit when women, taking the universalism of the principles of civil society at face value, demanded to be enfranchised. The 'jewel' in the armoury of the anti-suffragists was the argument from physical force.[48] Women, it was claimed, were naturally unable and unwilling to bear arms or use violence, so that if they became citizens, the state would inevitably be fatally weakened.

Now that women are enfranchised (and are even prime ministers) the same patriarchal view of citizenship is still found. In the British House of Commons in 1981, in a debate on the Nationality Bill, Enoch Powell argued that a woman should not pass on her citizenship to her child because 'nationality, in the last resort, is tested by fighting. A man's nation is the nation for which he will fight.' The difference between men and women, which must be expressed in citizenship, is that between 'fighting on the one hand and the creation and preservation of life on the other'.[49] It is true that women are now included as members of the armed forces but they are still excluded from combat units, which exemplify fraternities in action.[50]

'Men are born free': the rejection of (masculine) natural subjection generated the revolutionary claim that will, not force, is the basis of the state. One of the major successes of the fraternal contract story is the way it has helped to obscure coercion and violence in civil society and the manner in which 'will' is determined within relations of domination and subjection. Critics of contract theory have said a good deal about the inequality of parties to contracts and exploitation, but less about the consequences of contract and subordination. Only rarely have they discussed how contract gives the appearance of freedom to sexually ascriptive domination and subjection. Contract also hides the figure of the armed man in the shadows behind the civil individual. Foucault has counterposed a 'military dream' of society against the original contract (what is presented as the original pact in the familiar stories), but the two are not so far apart as they may seem.

Foucault writes that the military dream looked

> not to the state of nature, but to the meticulously subordinated cogs of a machine, not to the primal social contract, but to permanent coercions, not to fundamental rights, but to indefinitely progressive forms of training, not to the general will but to automatic docility.[51]

Automatic docility and the disciplines of the body portrayed by Foucault are part of the consequences of the fraternal social contract. Foucault states that 'the development and generalization of disciplinary mechanisms constituted the other, dark side' of the development of a 'formally egalitarian juridical framework'. However, it is less that the disciplines 'distort the contractual link systematically'[52] than that discipline in civil society, *which is also patriarchal discipline*, is typically established through contract. The forms of subjection specific to civil society are, as Foucault emphasizes, developed by the complicity of subordinates as well as by force – complicity made all the easier (as, importantly, is resistance) when consciousness is informed by patriarchal forms of liberty and equality. For example, when 'individuals' have a free choice of marriage partner, publicly recognized by a free contract, it is made harder to acknowledge that the marriage contract is a political fiction which ceremonially recognizes the patriarchal subjection of a wife and the masculine privileges of a husband.[33]

The modern discipline of the body is aided by political theory that has already separated reason from the body and the reason of men from the bodies of women. Foucault ignores the significant fact that the 'military dream' is a dream of men, whereas the fraternal social contract is also a dream of women. But the women's dream cannot be fulfilled, although the ostensibly universal categories of the contract make it always enticing. The history of liberal feminism is the history of attempts to generalise liberal liberties and rights to the whole adult population; but liberal feminism does not, and cannot, come to grips with the deeper problem of *how* women are to take an equal place in the patriarchal civil order.

Now that the feminist struggle has reached the point where women are almost formal civil equals, the opposition is highlighted between equality made after a male image and the real social position of women *as women*. Women have never, of course, been excluded entirely from civil life – the two spheres of the modern civil order are not separate in reality – but our inclusion has been singular. In a world presented as conventional, contractual and universal, women's civil position is ascriptive, defined by the natural particularity of being women; patriarchal subordination is socially and legally upheld throughout civil life, in production and citizenship as well as in the family. Thus to explore the subjection of women is also to explore the fraternity of men. Recent feminist research has begun to uncover – despite the important divisions between men of different classes and races (and associations and clubs where fraternity is given explicit expression are usually so divided) – how men, *as men*, maintain the power and privileges of their patriarchal right throughout the whole of sociopolitical life.

The fraternal social contract story shows that the categories and practices of civil society cannot simply be universalized to women. The social contract is a modern patriarchal pact that establishes men's sex right over women, and the civil individual has been constructed in opposition to women and all that our bodies symbolize, so how can we become full members of civil society or parties to the fraternal contract?

The contradictory answer is that women in civil society must disavow our bodies and act as part of the brotherhood – but since we are never regarded as other than women, we must simultaneously continue to affirm the patriarchal conception of femininity, or patriarchal subjection.[54] The peculiar relation between civil society and women and our bodies is illustrated by the fact that few legal jurisdictions have abolished the right of a husband to use his wife's body against her will; that coercive sexual relations ('sexual harassment') are part of everyday working life; that women's bodies are sold in the capitalist market;[55] that women, until 1934 in the USA and 1948 in Britain, lost their citizenship if they married foreigners; that only in 1983 did all British women citizens win the right to pass on their citizenship to their husbands and so enable them to live in Britain;[56] and that welfare policies still do not fully recognize women's status as individuals.

The theoretical and social transformation required if women and men are to be full members of a free, properly democratic (or properly 'civilized') society is as far-reaching as can be imagined. The meaning of 'civil society' (in both senses discussed here) has been constructed through the exclusion of women and all that we symbolize. To 'rediscover' a patriarchal conception of civil society will do little to challenge men's patriarchal right. To create a properly democratic society, which includes women as full citizens, it is necessary to deconstruct and reassemble our understanding of the body politic. This task extends from the dismantling of the patriarchal separation of private and public, to a transformation of our individuality and sexual identities as feminine and masculine beings. These identities now stand opposed, part of the multifaceted expression of the patriarchal dichotomy between reason and desire. The most profound and complex problem for political theory and practice is how the two bodies of humankind and feminine and masculine individuality can be fully incorporated into political life. How can the present of patriarchal domination, opposition and duality be transformed into a future of autonomous, democratic differentiation?

The traditional patriarchy of the fathers was long ago transformed into the fraternal, modern patriarchy of civil society. Perhaps there is hope, since these observations could be written only under the shadow of the owl of Minerva's wings. Alternatively, perhaps the time for optimism is past; feminism may have re-emerged at a point in the crisis of patriarchy in which the figure of the armed man – now armed not with the sword but with plastic bullets, cluster bombs, chemical, biological and nuclear weapons – has totally obliterated the figure of the civil individual. Perhaps, as Mary O'Brien suggests, 'the brotherhood have gone quite mad and lost control of their creations in some cosmic sorcerers' apprenticeship.'[57]

Notes

1. Earlier versions of this paper were presented to the Australian Women's Philosophy Conference, Adelaide, 1983, and the Annual Meeting of the American Political Science Association, Washington DC, 1984. I am grateful to participants in the discussions and to Ross Poole and Peter Breiner for comments on an earlier draft. Feminist conversations with Judith Allen, Moria Gatens and Elizabeth Gross helped me gather together my ideas on this and related topics.

2. A more extensive and detailed feminist reading of the contract stories and of their significance for the marriage contract and other contracts, such as that between prostitute and client, are presented in my *The Sexual Contract* (Cambridge, 1988).

3. Z. Eisenstein, *The Radical Future of Liberal Feminism*, New York 1981, chapter 3, but Eisenstein develops her argument in a different direction from my own; J. Elshtain, *Public Man, Private Woman: Women in Social and Political Thought*, Princeton 1981, chapter 3. More recently, see L. Nicholson, *Gender and History: The Limits of Social Theory in the Age of the Family*, New York 1986.

4. G. Schochet, *Patriarchalism in Political Thought: The Authoritarian Family and Political Speculation and Attitudes Especially in Seventeenth Century England*, Oxford, 1975.

5. This brief summary highlights the essential points of conflict between the protagonists, and thus glosses over the differences among theorists on both sides. Hobbes, for instance, saw paternal and political rule as homologous, but rejected patriarchal claims about paternity.

6. Sir R. Filmer, *Patriarchia and Other Political Works*, ed. P. Laslett, Oxford 1949, p. 54.

7. Ibid., p. 71.

8. Ibid., p. 188.

9. Ibid., p. 71; p. 57; p. 194.

10. Ibid., p. 96.

11. Laslett, 'Introduction', *Patriarchia*, p. 28. Filmer writes (p. 256): 'where there are only Father and sons, no sons can question the Father for the death of their brother.'

12. Filmer, pp. 241, 283.

13. John Locke, *Two Treatises, of Government*, ed. P. Laslett, second edn, Cambridge 1967, Book II, p. 110.

14. Filmer, p. 245.

15. Ibid., p. 287.

16. Locke, Book I, p. 47; Book II, 82.

17. Jean Jacques Rousseau, *Émile, or On Education*, trans. A. Bloom, New York 1979, pp. 370, 404.

18. Locke, Book I, p. 48.

19. Mary Astell, *Some Reflections Upon Marriage*, New York 1970, p. 107 (from the 1730 edition; first published 1700). On analogies drawn between the marriage contract and social contract and powers of husbands and kings, see M. Shanley, 'Marriage Contract and Social Contract in Seventeenth Century English Political Thought', *Western Political Quarterly*, vol. 32, no. 1, 1979, pp. 79–91.

20. Cited by Schochet, *Patriarchalism in Political Thought*, p. 202. I have discussed liberty, equality and the social contract in *The Problem of Political Obligation*, second edn, Oxford and Berkeley 1985.

21. B. Crick, *In Defence of Politics*, second edn, Harmondsworth 1982, p. 228.

22. E. Hobsbawm, 'The Idea of Fraternity', *New Society*, November 1975, cited

in M. Taylor, *Community, Anarchy and Liberty*, Cambridge 1982, p. 31.

23. Crick, *In Defence of Politics*, p. 233. Crick (p. 230) suggests that 'sisterhood' is 'in some ways truly a less ambiguous image of what I am trying to convey by "fraternity"'. Although he notes the relation between fraternity, the 'aggressive brothers' band' and 'stereotypes' of manliness, he argues that it is better to 'try to desex, even to feminize, old "fraternity", rather than to pause to rewrite most languages'; which exactly misses the point that language expresses and forms part of the patriarchal structure of our society ('language is a form of life').

24. Simone de Beauvoir, *The Second Sex*, trans. H.M. Parshley, New York 1953, p. 732. But of course we must remember that de Beauvoir was writing without the support of the organized feminist movement. Today, feminists have devoted a good deal of attention to language – and have provided some fascinating accounts of how, in practice, fraternity has shaped the working class and the labour movement, so that the 'worker' is a man and a member of the 'men's movement'; see especially C. Cockburn, *Brothers: Male Dominance and Technological Change*, London 1983; also B. Campbell, *The Road to Wigan Pier Revisited: Poverty and Politics in the 80s*, London 1984. (The term 'men's movement' is Beatrix Campbell's.)

25. N.O. Brown, *Love's Body*, New York 1966, p. 4. I am grateful to Peter Breiner for drawing my attention to Brown's interpretation in *Love's Body*. A similar point is made, though its implications for patriarchy are not pursued, by M. Hulliung, 'Patriarchalism and Its Early Enemies', *Political Theory*, no. 2, 1974, pp. 410–19. Hulliung (p. 416) notes that there is no reason why the parricide 'cannot just as well be turned into a morality play on behalf of ... democratic ideals' and that 'the assassins are "brothers" towards each other, and brothers are equal.'

26. P. Rieff, *Freud: The Mind of the Moralist*, London, n.d., chapter VII.

27. Sigmund Freud, *Moses and Monotheism*, trans. K. Jones, New York 1939, p. 104.

28. S. Rothblatt, *Tradition and Change in English Liberal Education*, London 1976, p. 18.

29. R. Williams, *Keywords: A Vocabulary of Culture and Society*, revised edn, New York 1985, p. 58. I am grateful to Ross Poole for drawing my attention to the emergence of 'civilization'.

30. Freud, *Civilization and its Discontents*, New York, n.d., p. 53.

31. Freud, *Totem and Taboo*, trans. A. Brill, New York, n.d., p. 186.

32. Brown, *Love's Body*, p. 5.

33. Again, Hobbes is an exception. There are no families in his radically individualist state of nature; women are as strong as men. However, he merely assumes that in civil society women will always enter a marriage contract that places them in subjection to their husbands.

34. Freud, *Moses and Monotheism*, p. 153.

35. For example, Mary Astell sarcastically remarks *(Reflections Upon Marriage*, p. 86) that if 'Strength of Mind goes along with Strength of Body, [then] 'tis only for some odd Accidents which Philosophers have not yet thought worthwhile to enquire into, that the Sturdiest Porter is not the wisest Man!' Or consider William Thompson, *Appeal of One Half of the Human Race, Women, Against the Pretensions of the Other Half, Men, to Retain them in Political, and Thence in Civil and Domestic, Slavery*, New York 1970, originally published 1825, p. 120: 'If strength be the superior title to happiness, let the knowledge and skill of man be employed in adding to the pleasurable sensations of horses, elephants, and all stronger animals. If strength be the title to happiness, let all such qualifications for voters as the capacity to read

and write, or any *indirect* means to insure intellectual aptitude be abolished; and let the simple test for the exercise of political rights, both by men and women, be the capacity of carrying 300lbs weight.'

36. This helps to explain why we do not have 'a philosophy of birth'; see M. O'Brien, *The Politics of Reproduction*, London 1981, especially chapter 1.

37. C. Pateman, '"The Disorder of Women": Women, Love and the Sense of Justice', *Ethics*, no. 91, 1980, pp. 20-34.

38. Freud, *Civilization and Its Discontents*, p. 56.

39. J. Mitchell, *Psychoanalysis and Feminism*, Harmondsworth 1975, p. 405.

40. See for example N. Hartsock, *Money, Sex and Power: Toward a Feminist Historical Materialism*, Boston, MA 1983, chapter 8; O'Brien, *The Politics of Reproduction*, chapters 3, 4; Elshtain, *Public Man, Private Woman*, chapter 1; H. Pitkin, *Fortune Is A Woman: Gender and Politics in the Thought of Niccolo Machiavelli*, Berkeley, CA 1984.

41. For his history, see G. Lloyd, *The Man of Reason*; '*Male*' and '*Female*' in *Western Philosophy*, London 1984. On the Cartesian 'drama of parturition', see S. Bordo, 'The Cartesian Masculinization of Thought', *Signs*, vol. 11, no. 3, 1986, pp. 439–56.

42. J. Rawls, *A Theory of Justice*, Cambridge, MA 1971, p. 128.

43. It will probably be objected that one can look younger or older than one's real age, or be convinced that one is in the 'wrong' body, or 'pass' as white. However, these examples all depend on the knowledge of age, sexual and colour differences and the specific meaning given to them in different cultures. One cannot, say, be a transsexual without already being fully aware of what 'masculine' and 'feminine' involve and how these are integrally connected to bodies. That Rawls's arguments, despite his apparently sexually undifferentiated 'parties', presuppose a sexually differentiated morality is shown in D. Kearns, '*A Theory of Justice* and Love: Rawls on the Family', *Politics*, vol. 18, no. 2, 1983, pp. 36-42.

44. This division between private and public is constituted in the second stage of the familiar story of the social contract (Locke's theory shows this clearly); see my *The Problem of Political Obligation*, chapter 4. See also my 'Feminist Critiques of the Private/Public Dichotomy', in S. Benn and G. Gaus, eds, *Private and Public in Social Life*, London and New York 1983.

45. R.M. Unger, *Knowledge and Politics*, New York 1976, p. 45. Unger has little to say about women or the family, but his comments (like those on the division of labour) illustrate that his critique is not the 'total critique' at which he aims. He notes, for example, that the family 'draws men back into an association that competes with loyalties to all other groups' (p. 264) – but it 'draws back' only those who go into civil society.

46. G.F. Gaus, *The Modern Liberal Theory of Man*, London 1983, p. 90.

47. Gaus, p. 94; he cites Dewey and Rawls on pp. 91 and 94.

48. The description comes from B. Harrison, *Separate Spheres: The Opposition to Women's Suffrage in Britain*, New York 1978, chapter 4. Women were once an essential part of armies, but by the First World War 'the once integral place of women in Western armies had faded from memory' (like so much else about women!); see B.C. Hacker, 'Women and Military Institutions in Early Modern Europe: A Reconnaissance', *Signs*, vol. 6, no. 4, 1981, pp. 643-71 (the quotation is from p. 671).

49. Cited in *Rights*, vol. 4, no. 5, 1981, p. 4.

50. On women, the military and combat, see J. Stiehm, 'The Protected, The Protector, The Defender', *Women's Studies International Forum*, no. 5, 1982, pp. 367-76; and 'Reflections on Women and Combat', Postscript to *Bring Me Men and*

Women: Mandated Change at the U.S. Air Force Academy, Berkeley, CA 1981.

51. M. Foucault, *Discipline and Punish: The Birth of the Prison*, trans. A. Sheridan, New York 1979, p. 169.

52. Foucault, *Discipline and Punish*, pp. 222-3.

53. See C. Pateman, 'The Shame of the Marriage Contract', in J. Stiehm, ed., *Women's View of the Political World of Men*, New York 1984.

54. Mrs Thatcher provides a fascinating illustration. On the one hand she is 'the best man in the Cabinet', the victor of the Falklands War, accomplice of Reagan's state terrorism against Libya, and is photographed with weapons. On the other hand she talks to the press about 'feminine' matters (such as having her hair tinted), draws headlines like 'Four Years on and looking Ten Years Younger', and uses the language of good housekeeping to talk about cuts in social welfare spending (see A. Carter, 'Masochism for the Masses', *New Statesman*, 3 June 1983, pp. 8-10).

55. For a critique of a contractarian defence of prostitution, see my 'Defending Prostitution: Charges Against Ericsson', *Ethics*, no. 93, 1983, pp. 561-5.

56. The right is still hedged with immigration restrictions that make it hard for black British women to exercise it; for an account of the interaction of sex and race in British law, see Women, Immigration and Nationality Group, *Worlds Apart: Women Under Immigration and Nationality Law*, London 1985. For the USA, see V. Sapiro, 'Women, Citizenship and Nationality: Immigration and Naturalization Policies in the United States', *Politics and Society*, vol. 13, no. 1, 1984, pp. 1-26.

57. O'Brien, *The Politics of Reproduction*, p. 205

On Formal Democracy

Agnes Heller

Democracy is by definition the rule of the people, a type of state in which it is both the right and duty of all citizens to create and enforce laws and to judge. Inseparable from this definition is the citizens' right and duty to obey the laws they have established.

It was on this basis, and also by taking in consideration the reality of huge state bodies, that Rousseau called in question the *raison d'être* of democracies. In huge nation-states, he argued, it is *ex principio* impossible for every citizen to participate in legislation, law enforcement, and jurisdiction. The future, in his estimation, belonged to the monarchies. Hardly had the ink dried upon the paper, however, when the Declaration of Independence, the model and fundamental text of all modern democracies, was formulated, the document of which one of the most eminent revolutionaries of the Third World, Ho Chi Minh, stated that it entails all the requirements and fundamental principles of socialism.

Formal Democracy

That modern democracy is 'formal' is commonplace knowledge. But we usually interpret the word 'formal' from different aspects. The rightist and partly also the leftist opponents of modern democracy identify the 'formal' character with being 'unreal', 'only apparent', 'fake'. They point back often in romantic nostalgia to the democracy of Antiquity as being 'real', 'substantial', and consequently 'authentic'. Such romantic nostalgia would do well to confront the facts of history, above all the primary one that the life span of non-formal democracies has been most limited. The statement of Aristotle, a highly realistic analyst, that all democracies are immediately transformed into anarchy, the latter into tyranny, was a statement of fact, not an aristocratic slandering by an anti-democrat. The Roman republic was not for a moment democratic. And I should like to add to all this that even if the degradation of modern democracies into tyrannies is far from being excluded (we were witness to it in the cases of German and Italian Fascism), the endurance of modern democracies is due precisely to their formal character. Moreover, it was this degradation into tyrannies that should have taught many leftist critics of modern democracy that 'formal' is not identical with 'unreal': that what they have considered to be a mere appearance was not apparent but 'authentic'.

What, then, does the 'formal' character of modern democracies entail? In the first instance, a relative (never complete) separation of state from society. Its democratic character is constituted by a fundamental document (mostly in the form of a constitution) which formulates the democratic civic liberties (the so-called 'human rights'), pluralism, the system of contract, and the principle of representation. Pluralism ensures the possibility of struggle among various power groups, including equilibrium and compromise, but it reveals nothing of how and by what factors the power groups are constituted. Human rights ensure the freedom of speech, association, organization, belief and property, but they do not guarantee the effectivity of their use; they do not stipulate anything with respect to the eventual collision of various civic liberties. The principle of contract ensures the possibility that the contracting partners will be able to modify their contrct and to sign their contracts (in the Declaration even the right of revolt is stated) but it does not guarantee any kind of support for the weaker contracting partner. So it builds violence into the constitution of the democratic state, the process through which one of the partners forces the other to conclude a new contract. The principle of representation ensures the legitimacy of governments through the participation of all citizens – further, the right of the representative organs to control those that are not elected. But it reveals nothing of what precedes and what follows the election of the representative organs.

As a result of all this, formal democracy leaves open and undecided the problem of the concrete structure of society. It is formal for precisely that reason. When Ho Chi Minh stated that socialism as a whole is comprised in the Declaration of Independence, he was right if we consider the democratic-ideal type of socialism. But those stating that in the Declaration capitalism is comprised just as well (considering again the 'ideal type' of capitalism) were similarly right. For the same democratic principles – since they are formal – can be the fundamental principles of both a capitalist and a socialist society incorporated in a constitution. However, this is not identical with the statement that formal democracy in itself is 'apparent', 'inauthentic'. Just the opposite: formal democracy is precisely the greater invention ensuring continuously the democratic character of a state. It is the indispensable presupposition of its democratic character. All those who want to replace formal democracy with so-called substantive democracy, and thereby reunify state and society in a totalizing way, surrender democracy as such.

As we know, in the small city-states of Antiquity the life span of such (no doubt glorious) attempts was very limited. In modern state bodies it cannot last more than a few months before it gives way to tyrannies. In her time, Rosa Luxemburg replied to the denouncers of formal democracy: there are no *bourgeois* civic liberties, only civic liberties as such. For formal democracy can indeed be transformed into a socialist democracy without being altered one iota. The principles of formal democracy do regulate our way of proceeding in social affairs, the manner of delivering our conflicts, but they do not impose any limitations on the content of our social objectives.

When stating that the Declaration of Independence gave birth to formal democracy, I do not mean to imply that it has in fact existed from that time on. The situation could, rather, be described correctly by contending that it existed as a *constitutive idea* which should be realized. The realization of all the fundamental principles (especially in Europe) was the work and deed of the workers' parties and the trade unions, but a tremendous role was played in it by the feminist movements too. The distinction between 'economic' and 'political' strikes was based, in the nineteenth century, on the very fact that the latter aimed directly at the realization of formal democracy. Political strikes were carried out incessantly in order to obtain universal suffrage – that is to say, to make it possible for workers and women to be represented in the legislative organs of the state. It was not capitalism that made formal democracy universal but the struggle against capitalism. At the same time, the struggle for formal democracy involved the striving for the new interpretation of certain civic liberties.

As already mentioned, formal civic liberties do not reveal anything of the hierarchy of these liberties. That is why 'freedom of property' and 'freedom of assembly' could collide with one another. The achievement of the free trade unions set limitations in a very long-lasting historical process on the previous interpretation of the 'freedom of property', even if not on the freedom of property itself. It is a historic fact that these struggles required enormous self-sacrifice and moral stamina, and it would be rather strange to assume that the European working class had committed itself to a mere 'appearance', to something 'inauthentic'. What people fight for is dear to them, and they are aware of why it is dear to them. The time has come when we must finally bear in mind that whenever people *could choose* between formal democracy and the limitation of democracy – or even the possibility of such a limitation – they constantly voted for democracy. Not even Hitler could seize power with a majority poll, even though he had supports like the world crisis and a lost war. All tyrannies obtained power by *coups d'état*. Even if the working class of a country fought with vehemence against capitalism, the majority of the workers never identified capitalism with formal democracy.

Who, then, identified capitalism with formal democracy? Who were the advocates of coupling dissatisfaction with capitalism and contempt for formal democracy? György Konrád and Ivan Szelényi were right to state that the identification was achieved by the ideology of the intelligentsia and that even now this ideology is the bearer of that identification.* Some of the best intellectuals coupled their overt contempt for capitalism with covert contempt for the empirically existing working class. The empirically given working class, they argued, is not aware of its real interests and real needs; theory should be brought in to the working class from outside. The intellectuals know what the workers ought to think, feel and act, for they are in possession of 'science', the only true science regarding the functioning of society. All institutional guarantees should give way to the establishment of that science; the society projected on the basis of that science will be the 'authentic' democracy.

---

*György Konrád and Ivan Szelényi. *The Intellectuals on the Road to Class Power*, New York 1978.

Rosa Luxemburg saw clearly that this was elitist thinking, and dangerous. When she said of Lenin that through his policy the Russian worker would be abandoned to a fistful of intellectuals, she was entirely right as far as the fundamental principles were concerned. Of course, it was impossible for her to foretell that as a result of the replacement of institutional guarantees by 'scientific social planning' not even the power of the intelligentsia could be ensured. When the only legitimacy is that of the 'only true science', the place of a fistful of intellectuals will be occupied by Genghis Khans. But even if we ignore this tragic inevitability, it still holds true that the errors of the masses are worth more than the wisdom of the Central Committee. In formal democracy error takes place in a learning process and a false step can in principle always be corrected, while the 'planning of the only true science' cannot (otherwise it would have to resign the legitimacy of the only true science). When the advocates of the 'only true science' engage in social experiments but retain the prerogative of absolute power, the masses in whose name they rule become not the subjects but the objects, the human rabbits of these experiments: they do not experiment, they are experimented with.

I do not want to deny that some of the objectives of the radical intelligentsia in question were exemplary, nor that some of them displayed a quite exceptional personal heroism. I ony want to state that their way of thinking entailed – and still entails – a dangerous 'short cut': the coupling of the millennial belief of social redemption with positivism. This attitude substitutes the reason of scientific planning for human common sense and reflection. But everyone is able to discuss and reflect on social goals and programmes. Special knowledge has the single – though highly important – task of objectifying these needs and reflections, of expressing them in one or another coherent theory. The 'only scientific truth', however, does not offer objectivations and alternatives for discussion and interpretation but expects that every one *should* acknowledge its 'scientific truth'; moreover, it suggests that its acceptance will be the panacea solving all problems instantaneously. As a consequence it suppresses common sense, excludes general reflection regarding goals and means.

This is why the concept of left radicalism should be reinterpreted now. One can be called radical if one wishes to transcend capitalism with all its implications, but one should be called a left radical only if one conceives of that task within the framework of formal democracy. A left radical is one who not merely fulfils the role of the enlightener (although she or he fulfils that too) but who also acknowledges the reality of all human needs (with the exception of those involving oppression and exploitation of others in the sense of the Kantian restrictive formula addressed against the use of the other as a 'mere means'), who knows that the knowledge of the intellectual is expertise and that in the selection of values all human beings are equally competent, and who admits that in deciding the problem 'what is to be done' no elite can play a crucial role. The left radical knows that the only true social objective is the one which is known as such by the majority of men and women and for which, as for the satisfaction of their own needs, they are ready to commit themselves. All this is true for the very simple reason that democracy is by definition the power of the people, and the power of the people is by definition democracy.

Democracy Besieged

Gunnar Myrdal writes, in a highly ingenious manner: 'Democracy is a most paradoxical form of government', and adds: democracy 'does not contain the certainty of its growth or even survival.'

Let us analyze first of all the question of 'survival'.

I have written that formal democracy (at least in the form of a constitutive idea) is already two hundred years old. I did not want thereby to deny its *fragility*. Its fragility originates from the same circumstance as its strength, endurance and plasticity: from its formal character. Briefly, the problem consists in the fact that the institutional system of formal democracy – precisely for being a democracy – renders possible the emergence and growth of anti-democratic institutions within the same democratic system. I am not referring here to anti-democratic parties, for *in themselves* they cannot endanger democracies; moreover, it is precisely their abolition which endangers democracy, an act of that sort being *ex principio* incompatible with the democratic system of institutions. I refer to institutions that can avoid the controls of the elected organs. All secret organizations belong to that type, as well as all kinds of organizations or enterprises that transcend the boundaries of *one* state, for both of them are in principle uncontrollable by the elected organs of a state.

The above fact has become a serious problem in the second half of the twentieth century. We have to face the fact that the struggle for formal democracy has not yet been completed.

There are three such institutions endangering or rendering doubtful the survival of democracy: multinational corporations, military establishments, and all secret police organizations, whether they serve the purposes of 'internal' or 'external' affairs.

Regarding multinational corporations, the government of one state cannot exert control, for the enterprise oversteps national boundaries. This is why all decrees intended to put limitations on them can be only partly, if at all effective. Freedom of organization cannot represent a counterbalance to freedom of enterprise in this respect. It cannot do so even in the form of trade unions, since that would presuppose that multinational corporations operate exclusively in countries where there is formal democracy, which is far from being so. The programme of self-management has still less of a chance in these concerns, for the very reason that it relies on the untenable assumption of a working class with relatively equal democratic traditions and relatively equal vocational training. As a result, a part of the economic power (even if not the overwhelming part, as maintained by some) is organized within the constitutional framework of formal democracy but operates outside that framework. All this involves not only the possibility of conflict but also the imminent danger that in case of a conflict the holders of economic power will limit the institutional system of formal democracy itself.

As a result of the development of military technique and the international situation, the national army becomes – or at least may become – in nearly all democratic countries an independent power. The army as an institution has, of course, never been democratic for any extended period. But its weight and influence were mostly limited, and it was always very far from challenging the fundamental institutions of formal democracy. It had 'secrets' only regarding strategy and tactics, and needed expertise only in that respect. The modern army is, however, a 'secret' one in its very essence, and requires expertise in all crucial problems. In the countries where conscription has been abolished, it is transformed into a 'separate state' within the body of the state. That separate state has its own objectives, values and, as it were, its own 'logic'. All this implies the possibility of conflict as well as the danger that in a conflict the army might simply eliminate the institutional system of formal democracy, especially in countries where the tradition of democracy is not deeply rooted enough or in which new social objectives were set within the framework of formal democracy and/or the democratic government temporarily became incapable of action.

The existence of both multinational corporations and powerful armies does not yet in itself contradict the institutions of formal democracy, even if they imply so much danger for the latter. The third-mentioned organization, however, the 'secret' police, is in contradiction *for reasons of principle* with formal democracy. Its very existence is anti-democratic. As a result it cannot be legitimated by the fundamental principles of formal democracy but only by some sort of 'emergency situation'. It is no doubt true that emergency situations do exist, and in them it may be legitimate to put temporary restrictions on formal democracy. Rationally speaking and taking into consideration the traditions of formal democracy, an 'emergency situation' of that sort can only be war. The extension of an 'emergency situation' beyond war conditions has always been regarded as a scandal in democracies. But this is the scandal that now characterizes nearly all democracies to some extent.

Within the body of the state an anti-democratic institution has come into being that not only threatens to restrict democracy but restricts it by its very existence. This institution operates a file system on what we think, what we believe, why we organize ourselves, although there is officially freedom of thought, of speech, and of organization. It reads our letters and taps our telephones, although the inviolability of the secrecy of private communications is set down in the constitution. This organization sets up and overthrows governments or at least exerts pressure on governments even though it is not an elected organ and cannot fulfil the assignment of the voters. Undoubtedly there are attempts (also on the part of the governments) to control or at least to restrict these secret organizations, sometimes even in the form of appealing to public opinion as well. However, such restriction can only be conditional and always limited in time, since there is no such elected organ or public protest that would compel the secret organizations to put their cards on the table. Whoever takes formal democracy seriously should insert into her or his programme the abolition of *all* secret organizations. For everything can always be legitimated by the slogan of the 'emergency situation' or the national interest. Spies and subversive elements have never threatened the existence of a democracy. However, should the emergence of anti-democratic organizations be allowed under the pretext of protection against spies and subversive elements, then we will be abolishing the same democracy in defence of which we created them.

One could object that organs of coercion have existed in all formal democracies: both police and army have been (and still are) deployed in defence of the social status quo. However, there is a difference of principle between police and secret (political) organs of investigation. At least theoretically, police can be mobilized only if some offence has already been committed, while secret (political) organs of investigation have a preventive function not only in practice but also in principle. Police have to work within a framework regulated by the law and in a way that is to be controlled by the government; accordingly, what the police can or cannot do depends on laws and governments. Further, the police can in principle be democratized. Police trade unions can come about in which the fact, the extent, and the manner of law enforcement can be disputed even in opposition to the government. Secret police and secret organs of investigation, however, cannot even in principle be democratized. Trade unions cannot come about in them, for their goals and *modi operandi* may be discussed only on the top echelons of the power structure (as a result of their secret character). Another reason for the impossibility of democratizing them is that democracy cannot, for reasons of principle, acknowledge them as organs belonging to the functioning of society; they can be legitimated, if at all, only by the slogan of the 'emergency situation'.

One manifestation of the anti-democratic character of various secret agencies and of the army becoming increasingly an independent power is that they represent the myth of 'authentic expertise' as against institutional guarantees. This is parallel to the ideologies whose advocates – having once seized power – set up and legitimate tyrannical social systems. Army commanders and senior intelligence officers are 'experts' too; being in possession of this or that type of knowledge, they supposedly know better than either the citizens or the government organs what is 'useful' for a state. They despise, with the haughtiness of intellectual 'experts', the elected leaders of the states whom they influence. There is no need to read espionage literature, only to grasp the logic of the situation in order to see that one branch of that 'specialized intelligentsia' feels a deeper understanding towards its opposite number than towards the citizen of its own state. Although the secret organs of investigation legitimate their own existence by the existence of the corresponding secret organizations of a state with which they are in a relation of tension, in the communication of the secret police organs there are considerable elements of a 'colleague-like' attitude.

These 'experts' consider the democratic framework of their

countries to be a burden to an ever-increasing extent and often feel envy for tyrannies where their opposite numbers are not bound – even relatively – by a burden of that sort. The secret organs of investigation (led by the logic of their own organization) always take pains to get rid of that 'burden'. This is why we have to see clearly that secret police organizations not only contradict democracy in themselves but will also constantly and consciously make efforts to reduce, even to eliminate, formal democracy. Tragic as it is, a world is not entirely inconceivable now in which formal democracy everywhere recedes. In fact formal democracies are now a minority in the world. They are, as it were, encircled. Encirclement on the outside, the rapid growth of anti-democratic powers in the inside: this is the threat in terms of which we can describe the situation of formal democracies. The greater a body of state, the heavier the pressure and power of inner anti-democratic forces (as in the case of the USA); the smaller it is, the heavier the pressure and power of outer anti-democratic forces. Formal democracy is nearly everywhere, all over the world, on the defensive.

As a result, the *survival* of formal democracy can be conceived now only in terms of *growth*. Growth can be projected in two processes: on the one hand as the transformation of formal democracy into an ever more socialist one; on the other hand as the gradual elimination of its external encirclement. I consider these two factors to be two aspects of the same process.

The Positive Abolition of Private Property

It is the paradox of formal democracy that it does not reveal anything of the economic structure of society, its relations of contract, and correspondingly its power relations. This is why formal democracy can coexist with capitalist society.

Let us repeat what the constituents of formal democracy are: the guarantee of civic liberties (human rights), pluralism, the system of contract, and the principle of representation.

Let us point out from among human rights the one that has bearing on the economic structure of society: the right to property. *Everyone* has a right to property.

In capitalist society, this meant – and means – the right of capitalist private property. Capitalist private property does not exclude the *right* of everyone to property (it would not then be the paradox of democracy) but as a result of the practice of that right it excludes *de facto* the majority of population from that property (with the exception of possessing one's own labour-power). That is to say, it eliminates the exercise of a right which is ensured as a right.

Property has two aspects: enjoyment and disposition. To deprive the majority of property means at the same time to deprive them of enjoyment (or to diminish the 'enjoyment ratio') and of the disposition over the conditions and products of economic life. Since, however, economic power always tends to control or influence political power (directly, or by corruption, or as a result of dominating the mass media and so on), those being excluded from economic power appear on the political scene as underprivileged as well. As a result of all this, equality turns into inequality and freedom into a mere potentiality – that is, freedom *from* something instead of freedom *for* something. The contract relationship will be the contract of the proprietors and those being deprived of propriety – as a consequence it will be formally equal, practically unequal.

It is not by chance that I repeat all these well-known facts. My purpose is to make manifest why it seemed to be plausible to resolve the paradox of formal democracy by way of *étatisation* – that is, by eliminating the right to property; why the temptation was so strong to reunify state and society, centralizing economic power in one hand (that of the state) simultaneously with the seizure of state power.

The above conception has been characterized by Marx himself as the *negative* abolition of private property, and is in fact negative in the sense that it replies to the paradox of formal democracy (the right of property leading to the exclusion of the majority from property) not by creating the actual ownership of the majority but by the abolition of the right to property: that is, by a negation. Of course, the abolition of the right to property – posited by formal democracy as one of the civic liberties, being attributed to society, not to the state – does not at all mean the abolition of property. Disposition over the productive forces and the produced goods of society has to be exercised further on. Disposition of that sort is, however, attributed now exclusively to *political* power.

It follows that political power will be the only organ of disposition, as a result of which it decides who and to what extent will participate in the enjoyment of property. By this very act the state deprives not only the former private proprietors of their properties but the whole society of the bare possibility of ownership.

Society as a whole becomes the conglomerate of wage-labourers. As a result, the contract can only be a contract between the individuals and the state. Since, however, the state concentrates all powers and it can dictate the terms of the contract, equality of contract is *formally* abolished. In so far as we conceive socialism as the negation of capitalism, the socialist character of that conception cannot be denied. However, this kind of interpretation of socialism does not grant either more freedom or more equality; moreover, it deprives people even more of formal freedom and equality; in this sense – and measured by the yardsticks of *socialist values* (realized freedom and equality) – it cannot be regarded as a socialist alternative.

The question is whether it is possible to resolve the paradox of formal democracy in a manner that does not abolish the right to property, that does not unify state and society. I believe that it is conceivable. This would be the process Marx called the *positive* abolition of private property. The abolition is positive when it does not abolish the right to property but *generalizes ownership*: that is, ensures for *all* members of society proprietorship, for *everyone* the ability to dispose of the production forces of society and to enjoy the fruits of productive activity. That is the conception of self-government in modern form. In so far as all members of institutions may equally participate in the determination of the way of functioning, the objectives, and the means of every social institution (be it productive, economic, scientific, social), then everyone disposes and at the same time takes part in the determination of what (and in what amount) should be turned into direct enjoyment, and to what kind of enjoyment.

In the case of collective ownership, the contract is a transaction of equals. A contract of that sort can always be modified (even cancelled), but the contractual character of society will not thereby be abolished. The paradox of formal freedom can gradually be resolved by the abolition of centralized economic power, including its privileged position over mass media and educational systems. If, however, privileged economic power no longer exists, the pluralistic representative system and its elected government can express the actual will of the citizens. As an embodiment of that will the state redistributes the produced goods, thereby eliminating or at least reducing the inequality being constituted in collective ownership *as well*. It goes without saying that self-governed society excludes not only in principle but *in fact too* the existence of all 'secret' organizations.

As mentioned, formal democracy does not exclude, but even

presupposes violence. As Marx said: where right confronts right, violence will decide. Only the one who has power is capable of coercion. The 'maturation' of formal democracy into a socialist one presupposes counterviolence for precisely that reason: as an ultimate consequence of the actual division of power. But counterviolence (just like violence) in formal democracy must be directed at the interpretation and reinterpretation of contracts and rights. It is precisely the substitution of new contracts for old ones that counterviolence has to achieve. But the system of contract itself cannot be made questionable in these struggles. If it does become questioned, if violence is not directed at concluding a new contract but at the abolition of the contractual system, it is democracy for whom the bell tolls.

I did not want to draw up a social model only to demonstrate that the fundamental principles of formal democracy not only do not exclude the realization of a socialist society which is the process of realization of freedom and equality (one which transcends and abolishes capitalism and at the same time is constituted by the values of socialism) but also to show that a society of that type can be conceived only as a consistent realiz-ation of the principles of formal democracy, as the practical solution of its paradox.

My reference to Marx's definition of the positive abolition of private property as counterposed to the mere negative abolition of the same through the '*étatisation*' of society does not yet solve the problem of Marxism and democracy. The socialist transform-ation of civil society into a self-regulating one within the frame-work of formal democracy is, however, very far from being identical with the model in which the positive abolition of private property was conceived in Marx's *œuvre* itself. That is why we have to raise the following questions simultaneously: whether we are justified at all in referring to his work in our theoretical propo-sal, and what kind of historical considerations permit us to abandon some features of the original idea that now seem vague indeed.

Marx assumed a communist society without a state. That is why, for the future, the relationship between state and civil society had for him no relevance at all. Where there is no state, there are no legal relations or institutions either; as a conse-quence, there are no rights. In the realm of *freedom* you cannot raise questions about *freedoms*. Although Marx presupposed that in the sphere of production humankind cannot overcome *necess-ity*, he also assumed the complete separation between administration of things and that of human beings to be possible. Necessity was attributed exclusively to the former. The system of contract is related to commodity production and to possibly conflicting, or at least differing, interests. Where there is no commodity production, there are no conflicting or differing interests – that is, there are no interests at all: there is no need for any contract whatsoever. Marx furthermore imagined a society not only without domination but also without power. Where there is no power, no one has to rule and the 'rule of the people' – democracy – becomes meaningless.

The utopia of the total abolition of the state was nothing but the acceptance of the conception of nineteenth-century liberalism from a socialist point of view. Although Karl Polanyi's analyses show that even the liberal *laissez faire* seems to have been nothing but a utopia and that state interventionism in some form was as old as capitalist society, nevertheless the function of the state was far from being of the same importance in the nineteenth century as in the twentieth. Nowadays no one can seriously conceive a social programme or perspective which would be based on the complete abolition of the state.

That is why we are obliged to reformulate the prospect of the future: if the state subsists, which type of state should it be, and which type of society should be related to this state? Where there is a state, there is power. If we are socialists, we have to consider the question: How is domination to be avoided? Where there is a state, there is no total freedom. Being socialists, we have to reconsider the question: How are human freedoms to be enlarged? Where there is a state, the public and private spheres can be unified only at the cost of tyranny. Whoever wants to avoid tyranny has to reconsider what kind of relations have to exist between state and society, the public and private spheres. If the administration of things and that of human beings cannot be isolated from one another, we are obliged to presuppose institutions which ensure the participation of everyone in the procedure of administration, in a direct and indirect way. If we cannot imagine a society expressing one homogeneous will, we have to assume the system of contracts which ensures that the will (and interest) of all has to be taken into consideration. Consequently, we have to presuppose democracy.

Democratic socialism is not therefore a random socialist model, somewhat embellished or supplemented with certain features of democracy, but a very definite model of socialism. It means the further development and transformation of civil society. Right as a legal category presupposes legal subjects and their autonomous possibilities the private and public spheres, guaranteed by the state. If the state swallows society, there are no spaces left where these rights could be applied or be realized in any way at all. They can be formulated only on a piece of paper, without any kind of relevance.

Marx incessantly related the positive abolition of private property to the value of freedom. If the abolition of the state – that is, the realization of an indivisible, total *freedom* – cannot serve any longer as a rational utopia, remaining faithful to Marx's spirit means formulating a possibility for the positive abolition of private property, together with a *possible maximum* of human freedom. And the realization of the principles of the Declaration of Independence would mean exactly this.

Growth and Survival

I have mentioned already that formal democracy is threatened from outside and inside. Its mere survival is dependent on its growth. Formal democracy can break through its encirclement only if it becomes socialist by resolving its paradox. If, however, the survival of formal democracy becomes a mere purpose in itself for the dominant political forces there will be a very slight chance for survival, especially in the countries where democratic traditions have no long record. And should formal democracy give way in those countries to some sort of despotic form of state, the encirclement of the more traditional democracies will be increased and we can even count on the increase of inner anti-democratic forces to an extent which leads ultimately to the abolition of formal democracy.

Bourgeois society is a dynamic society, characterized by the constant development of the forces of production and rapid changes in its relations of social contact. It means at the same time the constant growth of needs, both in quantitative and qualitative respects. Among these needs emerge radical ones directed at the solution of the paradox of formal democracy – that is, at transcending capitalism – which cannot therefore be satisfied by capitalist society. The above tension, of course, can be diminished in capitalist society too by channelling the growth of needs in a direction which is no obstacle to but rather a condition of the expansion of capitalist society. However, in order for that dissatisfaction actually to be channelled, the growth of production must be very rapid.

But 'production for production's sake' runs now against limits to an ever more increasing extent: it is delimited by the barriers of nature, directly and indirectly. It is pollution on the one hand, the planetary limits of natural resources on the other, that set limitations on that solution. It cannot be extrapolated for long, since all its difficulties with respect to inner and foreign policy are easily predictable. It should be added that welfare societies which increase the power of the state, but not that of society, may find themselves confronted with these barriers. But unsatisfied needs necessarily increase dissatisfaction and give greater chances to inner anti-democratic forces to restrict formal democracy, especially because the channelling of needs towards mere consumption transforms citizens into politically passive beings. And it is hardly believable that the citizen accustomed to political passivity could easily be mobilized in defence of his or her democratic civic liberties.

If, however, mobility is being initiated in the direction of the ownership of every citizen – that is, in the direction of solving the paradox of formal democracy – then it has a double meaning. In the first place it means the dynamic satisfaction of radical needs which presupposes the growth of production too (for radical needs are never isolated from other needs) but not according to a pace which would endanger the natural preconditions of mankind: the satisfaction of the needs for self-government in decisions determining our own fate, all these being not primarily problems of production but of property. Secondly, it means the increasing responsibility of everyone as producer, consumer and citizen; accordingly his or her activity in the further development and defence of democracy. A movement which takes off in the direction of such a formal socialist democracy could at the same time evoke confidence in peoples who have been acquainted until now only with the alternatives of tyrannies based on the dictatorship over needs and capitalism constituting inequality. All this would render possible the elimination of the gradual encirclement of democracies.

This possibility is all the more relevant since capitalist formal democracy has another paradox not yet mentioned: the guarantee of democratic coexistence *within* one country which does not exclude despotic oppression and inequality with respect to other countries. The unification of economic and state power – which does not even guarantee democratic coexistence within the boundaries of a single country – only increases that oppression based on inequality in the form of a total lack of independence within the oppressor and oppressed nation: that is, it resolves the paradox again in a negative form. The *positive* resolution of that paradox, too, can be conceived only in the perspective of a self-governed society. Decentralization of economic power and the demolition of 'secret' and uncontrollable organizations in themselves enhance the chances of a democratic foreign policy. True, they do not provide a guarantee. The successful solution of that second paradox is as dependent on the struggle of social forces as the first, but on a worldwide scale.

In this essay, I have attempted to delineate not the possibilities, but the alternatives offered by formal democracy. We all are aware of the limits of potentialities. The military predominance and privileged position of the superpowers is in itself a hard fact that forces us to become conscious of the difficulties facing us. There is no room for prophetic attitudes for every prophecy can turn into false predictions. Let us therefore put our hope in the hands of all those who practise their common sense. The future is their deed.

PART TWO

Western States and Civil Societies

The Civilizing Process*

Helmut Kuzmics

I   Civilization, Bourgeois and Courtly Society

The concept of 'civilization' usually brings to mind the 'Great Civilizations' of world history. Indeed, there is an inseparable conceptual link between the idea of the latter and that of 'development', which serves as an evaluative standard which is applied, explicitly or implicitly, to societies and their material and cultural achievements. It is in this sense that Parsons talks about the development towards Western modernity. By adopting an explicitly evolutionist perspective, he makes the West appear as one of a variety of great civilizations.[1] For Parsons, the central variable in the process of societal evolution is 'adaptive capacity', defined at the macro level.

This alleged capacity to adjust to changing environments (or should we speak of a capacity to *dominate the rest of the world?*) most often refers to the economically or politically productive dimension of societies, rather than to the behaviour of individuals[2] or to the consumptive dimension of individual lifestyles. Yet it does not seem very likely that the concept of 'adaptive capacity' would ever crop up in the self-description and self-characterization of individual agents' interpretations of their life-worlds. A similar problem is evident in the concept of 'modernization', which focuses on economic progress as either an explanans or an

---

*Translated by Hans Georg Zilian.

explanandum. Modernization is thought to be continuously self-reinforcing, and definitions of the concept usually contrast 'developed' and 'traditional' societies (or nations) mainly with reference to their respective adaptive capacities.[3] Such adaptation is said to be achieved by the creation of economic wealth as well as by the guaranteeing of political stability, perhaps by means of American-style 'democracy'.

Compared with this conventional conceptions of civilization, Norbert Elias's work – which is attracting an increasing amount of attention – develops a concept of civilization based on quite different premises. He asks how people experience something as 'civilized' or 'uncivilized'. He interrogates this self-perception by relating it to that of the Occident: how, he asks, would members of the Occident see medieval times, if a time machine were to take them there? According to Elias, the traveller's impression would be ambivalent: some features would be attractive, others repulsive, and the character of the observer would certainly make a difference. On the one hand, life in the past would seem free, unfettered and adventurous; on the other, barbaric, uncouth and squalid. According to Elias, the concept of 'civilization' can refer to a variety of phenomena, including those which Weber thought to be characteristic of occidental rationalism:[4] the state of technology, the type of manners, the stage of scientific development, religiosity, relations between men and women, forms of cooking, housing and punishment. Elias thereby points to social perceptions which consider 'civilizing' achievements to be those of a civilization: to be civilized is to have a standard of housing or a level of technological development consonant with the standpoint of the civilized, who are themselves Westerners and are anxious to distinguish themselves from those who are 'uncouth' or 'primitive'.[5]

Elias's starting point is a reconstruction of the semantic history of words for 'civilization' and similar phenomena. The medieval precursors of 'civilization' are *courtoisie* and *civilité*; a competitor can be found in the German concept *Kultur*, which marked a distinction between different social strata and even national characteristics: eventually, French and English 'civilization' were opposed to German *Kultur*. From the outset Elias avoids the danger of ethnocentric generalization, a danger which Western theorists of modernization found they had to heed long after they had succumbed to it.[6]

A genetic reconstruction of the concept of civilization within the framework of the sociology of knowledge eventually leads

Elias to consider the social modelling of affects in everyday life (initially with reference to the aristocratic upper classes between the ninth and the eighteenth centuries) to be the most important explanatory issue in the process of civilization. He asks: How did people's social standards for dealing with each other in everyday life develop? How did agents' conduct and experience change in the course of history? How does the civilized adult of today differ from that of medieval times? According to Elias – here his departure from both Weber's concept of *methodically rational conduct* and Adorno and Horkheimer's concept of instrumental reason is evident – the most important elements of 'civilized' behaviour are the degree of pacification, the refinement of customs, the degree of restraint in social interactions and in the (reflexive) relationship individuals have with themselves.

How, then, does Elias arrive at 'his' concept of civilization? According to him, it is through the analysis of changing linguistic usage that underlying forms of life become visible. In eighteenth-century Germany, for instance, there was a politically impotent and economically not very deeply rooted bourgeoisie; in France during the same era there was a bourgeoisie of steadily growing influence, striving increasingly for social reform: a bourgeoisie which sometimes even turned revolutionary and which, despite its struggle for political power, found the time to blend, as far as its outlook and lifestyle were concerned, with the aristocratic world. In the process, members of the aristocracy (such as Mirabeau) underwent to some extent what is now called 'embourgeoisement'.

Conversely, the French bourgeoisie managed to incorporate courtly elements into its concept of '*civilisation*' to a much larger extent than the regionally divided Germans, whose dichotomy of culture versus civilization contrasted the 'falsity' of formal, superficial courtly behaviour with true culture and virtue. For the latter, culture is the world of spiritual, artistic and religious achievement and is seen to be at odds with politics, the economy and society. The French notion of 'civilization', by contrast, refers to social qualities, furniture, clothes, language and manners. No stigma is attached to them, because they are conceived as purely 'external' as opposed to 'inner' values. (It is worth observing, however, that Rousseau's critique of civilization, as a counterpart of German Romanticism, was based on a similar contrast.[7]) Mirabeau's concept of civilization, on the other hand, distinguishes between true and false civilization and integrates concepts which are often incompatible with each other into the perspective of the Enlightenment. Thus, in his *Amy des Femmes ou Traité de la Civilisation* (1766), '*civilisation*' means the 'refinement of manners, worldly wisdom and politeness, and the spreading of knowledge and good behaviour'.[8]

Mirabeau, whom Elias invokes as the first literary source for the further development of the word '*civiliser*' into '*civilisation*', characterizes the latter intuitively in categories which are wholly courtly: '*adoucissement des mœurs*' and '*politesse*' play a central role; civilization appears not only as cognate to the Enlightenment but – being a bourgeois phenomenon – as rooted deeply in a courtly tradition of etiquette. Later, however, the concept of civilization attains ever-increasing prominence as a weapon of social reform. The Physiocrats added the idea of the free interplay of economic forces conceived after the model of natural science. Insight into the orderliness of these natural laws of society becomes constitutive of the new concept: 'true' civilization occupies a place between barbarism and 'false' civilization, which springs from too much money and too much intervention from the outside.

From there on, the French concept of civilization is wedded to the bourgeois notion of progress; knowledge turns into one of its central categories; the concept of 'being civilized' is transferred from the behaviour of individuals to the state,[9] the constitution, the educational system (and access to that system by the populace) and to a penitentiary system which is seen to be barbaric. Social inequality, anchored in feudal barriers, appears as barbaric and unreasonable. The same perspective is brought to bear on the lack of economic freedom imposed by government trade restrictions. The refinement of manners and the pacification of civil society are supposed to be the consequence of civilization in this wider sense.[10] In spite of all the differences between the face-to-face society of the courtly aristocracy and the world of the more abstractly interrelated, working bourgeois, there was – above all in France – an evolutionary continuity within the concept of civilization, a steady undercurrent which survived even the political ordeal of the bourgeois revolution.

It is upon these premisses that Elias develops the central elements of his concept of 'being civilized'. He focuses upon individual behaviour and its affective conditions (their transfer into the realm of macrophenomena is seen to be of secondary importance), while he gives greater emphasis to consumption than to production and lays more stress on politics than on economics. In acknowledgement of the courtly heritage, the refinement of manners, pacification[11] and an intensified inhibition of feelings are deemed to be central. Being civilized means that the emotions become rationalized and 'psychologized'. The image of others that we produce becomes deeper, psychologically speaking, due to the intensified interdependence of actions and to the necessity of making inferences from others' facial expressions to their strategic interests and involuntary motives. Emotions are also increasingly rationalized as the social space between individuals becomes a passionless void; to these individuals' rational image there corresponds a rational way of acting which transcends the logic of double-entry accounting since, as at the court, spontaneous feelings are subordinated to long-term strategic interests.

II The Development of the Apparatus of Self-Restraint

Elias's theoretical achievement is to have linked changes in agents' experience at a given level of civilization with both a psychological and macrosociological model of their joint development. He is concerned not with static comparisons but, rather, with tracing the social determination of emotional and instinctive life as a historical process.

This approach is guided by the decisive basic insight that 'spontaneity of bodily expression', 'self-control' (or 'self-restraint') and, in general, the idea of a self demarcated from its environment (a process called 'individualization') are the result of specific historical circumstances (or 'figurations'). The nature of the self changes with these figurations through a process which is not to be thought of as the unfolding of an immanent human spirit. The developmental process involving socially determined personality structures extends from the comparatively loosely regulated ways of dealing with one's own body and that of others before the age of the Crusades among the highest social strata, to the very complex differentiation of rules and patterns of behaviour in the age of the absolutist state.

Elias attempts to describe the sociogenesis of the civilized character structure by elaborating both the continuous and the novel elements in the intergenerational development of the 'apparatus of self-restraint'. In this process, the civilized person is sharply distinguished from the uncivilized person by the extent to which the former is capable of suppressing impulses of pleasure and pain and transforming and incorporating them into prolonged sequences of action. It is decisive that these 'self-restraints' can no longer be seen as 'restraints by others' (which they are), as restraints which are sociogenetically produced as 'self-restraints' in the first place. This phenomenon has often been labelled as 'reification' – as the man-made social rules which appear to be no more changeable than capricious nature or inanimate things. Thus Elias's approach also amounts to an historical sociology of knowledge which is concerned with 'recipe-knowledge', with knowledge of the rules of interaction in the intimacy of everyday performances, such as when people eat, drink, dance, play, have sexual intercourse, or behave aggressively.

His theoretical model is based on the assumption that the development of the ego and the superego is interwoven with the relevant parameters of macrosocial development. The transition from 'restraint by others to self-restraint' (which is accompanied by a higher threshold of shame and embarrassment) supposes that external restraints imposed on individuals become less direct: combined with a growing control over nature, this in turn fosters a more differentiated and rationalized perception of the psychological nature of human beings. According to Elias, growing demands from an increasingly complex social environment necessitate a more subtle tuning of behaviour: within such environments, individual civilization takes place and, as that becomes more common, societal civilization ensues.

This process is evident, for instance, in matters of table manners (concerning how people eat, which dishes – carved or uncarved – are served, what bodily utterances, such as smacking one's lips or belching, are permissible, and the changing use of cutlery or the shared or separate use of crockery). It is also evident in changing conventions of personal interaction: bodily utterances were suppressed and controlled and the relations between sexes, from conceptions of 'seemly' behaviour to sexual and erotic relations in the narrower sense, were regimented. But Elias is not concerned merely with 'peaceful' occupations and interactions. He also deals with the transformation of aggressiveness, pointing out, for instance, that it is a long way from the unchecked 'joy of killing' characteristic of the feudal anarchy of the European High Middle Ages[12] to the orderly martial conduct of 'civilized' armies subject to the Geneva Convention.

Elias illustrates these processes of change by analysing books of etiquette from various epochs. He thus renders visible the stages of affecting regulation. He also assumes that the ever-tightening net of regulations concerning the instincts and bodies of the secular upper classes, from the Middle Ages to the courtly absolutist era, indicates a historical process at the behavioural level. Many rules become transformed from obvious restraints by others (commands such as not spitting in front of superiors, not blowing one's nose without a handkerchief when at table, not belching) into self-restraints, due to the increasing interdependence of actions of an ever-increasing number of people. Eventually, people control themselves not only in front of persons of higher rank or strangers, but (as the example of daily hygiene shows) even when they are alone. In the books of etiquette, this kind of normative change is marked by a process of inverted trivialization: as the threshold of shame and embarrassment advances steadily, not only does the body become subject to ever-expanding taboos, but rules concerning the 'most natural' needs receive less and less mention. While one is embarrassed even to talk about 'it', it is not necessary to do so any more.

The macrostructural conditions of the civilizing process are the phenomena of the monopolization of power resources, centralization, and the creation of a 'monopoly of force', all of them set within the concrete historical con‛exts of Western feudalism.[13] Contemporaries experienced, but did not understand, these processes. The key social dynamics – the 'competition' for land, power and influence within the aristocratic anarchy of twelfth- and thirteenth-century Western feudalism – are beyond their cognitive grasp and even more beyond their control. Nevertheless, a form of 'rationalization' results: long-term perspectives are adopted and a detached stance is taken towards all kinds of mood changes, from darkest fear to ecstatic joy. This 'rationalization' is an unplanned result of blind forces which, according to Elias, can be studied and explained rationally.

From Elias's assumption of an 'affective household', partly amenable to individual planning and subject to historical change, the idea of 'planned economy of affects' can be derived. As sequences of action grow longer, there are gains (higher economic profits, greater security through an ego and superego in tune with reality) but also 'losses' for the economy of drives. When spontaneity is replaced by strategy, there is a trade-off between the uninhibited joy of the moment and the security of controlled planning. Prudence and its social preconditions are subtly rewarded: not only is spontaneous pleasure impossible or delayed, but unannounced and total terror is inhibited as well.

'Where Id was, Ego shall be' (Freud) means having a genuine chance of acting. As Elias says:

> Medieval conceptions of hell give us an idea of how strong this fear between man and man was. Both joy and pain were discharged more openly and freely. But the individual was their prisoner; he was hurled back and forth by his own feelings as by forces of nature. He had less control of his passions; he was more controlled by them.
>
> Later, as the conveyor belts running through his existence grow longer and more complex, the individual learns to control himself more steadily; he is now less a prisoner of his passions than before.[14]

Hence the shift from restraint by others to self-restraint is an irreducibly ambivalent process. Elias's variation on the theme of the 'Dialectics of Enlightenment' here centres on its agents and, in spite of a certain amount of tunnel vision, deals with the traditional topic of Western sociology and the allegedly permanent problem of modernity: the transition from *Gemeinschaft* (Community) to *Gesellschaft* (society) [Tönnies]. However, Elias tackles this theme in an empirical spirit and with reference to selected historical environments, which he attempts to conceptualize in terms of 'figurations'.[15]

It is at the level of 'figurations' that the social regulation of affects takes place. For example, at the feudal court of the High Middle Ages there developed a relative tightening of social relations. This coincided with a change in the balance of power between rulers and ruled and between men and women (evident, for instance, in the *courtoisie* of the minstrels). Between the period of the baronial court and that of the absolutist royal court there is a steady intensification of contacts, a continuous increase in the number of 'significant others' (G.H. Mead) and a proliferation of both restraints by others and self-restraints. During this period the balance of power shifts from those leading groups who comprise 'society' towards the central overlord. This transformation is independent of the personal attributes of the monarch, since it is in his – and the state's – interest to ban duelling among the members of the higher aristocracy and thus to interfere with the formerly sacrosanct prerogatives of the armed aristocracy.

These 'microenvironments', which successfully regulate affects, clearly cannot be understood in isolation from the economic and technological developments which produced them: the courts, after all, have to be financed. Yet the consequences of this rapid civilization of the previously independent warrior caste are striking: pacification, the refinement of manners, increased affective control, and mental reserve. In many situations in which the feudal lord would have used his fist or his sword the courtier remains quiet, pondering little schemes and counterschemes. Once developed the courtly code continues to be a formative force, partly filtering into the lower ranks of society. But this process is only partial: the courtier and the working bourgeois remain worlds apart.

III Industrial Civilization

Is there any purchase in a concept of civilization derived from face-to-face courtly society for an appreciation of the problems of modernity? In reply, some critics have spotted considerable difficulties in Elias's project. It is neither possible nor necessary to deal here with all the relevant arguments. I will instead discuss just one of these complex arguments, which runs as follows: if Elias's work is measured against the aspirations and achievements of Frankfurt Critical Theory it is inadequate, because it is incapable of capturing the specific nature of capitalism as a system of market forces and class domination, a system in constant danger of lapsing into barbarism.[16] The theory of civilization, in other words, is said to be unable to account for the permanent threat of barbarism in modern society: the Nazis were sticklers for table manners and SS officers listened to classical music, but this did not prevent them from committing gruesome acts of barbarism, which prompted Adorno to claim that no more poetry could be written after Auschwitz.

To begin with, there is a misunderstanding in this type of allegation. For its victims, mass-produced death means what death always means to its victims (and perhaps a bit more: when it is mass-produced it is difficult to die a dignified death, or to see others die with dignity). Nevertheless, the ritualized and bureaucratic character of this monstrous administration of murder makes clear that the motivation of those who *performed* the murders was comparatively irrelevant. This fact has been pointed out by many who survived and wrote about the camps, which usually had little in common with the spontaneity of knightly lords and their 'lust' for murder.

Elias can be criticized only if one ascribes to him a unilinear, evolutionary assumption of a correlation between individuals' affective control and structural peacefulness. However, the difference between aggressiveness within a limited field of interaction and structural, mechanized aggressiveness at a distance – for example, between nation-states – was perfectly clear to him. He argues only that the former has decreased since the days of the robber barons, that violence no longer concentrates on the body to the same extent, and that these changes are surely connected with the process of civilization. He does not deny the Janus-face character of the civilizing process, although – here he resembles Weber – he wants to eliminate a normative concept of progress from his descriptive analysis.

Calculated, unemotional barbarism has in the past been a feature of the 'dialectics of Enlightenment', and it is to be feared that we have not seen the last of it.[17] Elias's explanation of this phenomenon runs as follows. While a state-regulated society may be characterized internally by quite highly developed mechanisms for controlling violence, the relations among states may be very far indeed from having reached this stage. One state still represents a powerful threat to any other; states often battle for hegemony, while their relations are neither secured by a monopoly of force nor, consequently, governed always by the rule of law. The interaction among nation-states is less civilized than the exchanges among people within these states – there is a double standard of civilization. While violence within a society is taboo, its citizens are called upon to kill when conflict with an external enemy erupts. This line of reasoning is evident in Elias's essay 'Violence and Civilization' (see p. 177), which utilizes the example of pre-Fascist radicalization in the Weimar Republic to trace the drift into a type of physical violence which had macrostructural roots, which were nurtured in turn by authoritarian traditions and the career patterns of selected individuals.

Judged on its own terms, the theory of civilization and its double standards remain successful. But does not the theory have objective limitations? Some writers argue that Elias eliminates from his investigation of the regimentation of the body and domination within interpersonal relationships the kind of domination to be found in the sphere of *production*. This allegation raises the problem of which standards to apply to theories just as much as that of the criteria for judging their evaluator's pretensions. Is it possible to say something of interest about capitalism or 'labour' without engaging it directly? Might it not be that there are elements within this type of society which have their origin in more ancient historical formations? And is it not possible that a particular perspective might prove fruitful for understanding societies and their associated personality structures which are, or seem to be, wholly different?

Buck-Morss wants to answer all these questions in the negative. In her view, there is above all a discontinuity between the feudal and capitalist eras.[18] This rupture can be grasped only by introducing the concept of 'mode of production', thereby resorting to economic categories, in this case of the Marxian variety.[19]

Elias, however, wants to explain a specific thrust of civilization into absolutism and courtly society. In doing this he throws light upon the development of the state and the pacification resulting from the monopoly of force. Of course, these are institutional constraints which later brought about the well-known unfolding of the productive forces. The social character of the bourgeoisie does not develop from scratch (or from Protestantism alone) but incorporates courtly patterns. And Elias certainly does not neglect the economic processes which strengthened the bourgeoisie:

> The development of money and exchange, together with the social formations carrying them, stands in a permanent reciprocal relationship to the form and development of monopoly power within a particular area. These two series of developments, constantly intertwining, drive each other upwards.[20]

Many misunderstandings which have plagued the reception of Elias's work are the consequence of a theoretically ambitious project which is based on an empirical 'case' and combines social history, psychology and a macrosociological theoretical model. 'Historical interactionism' would be a suitable label for the micro aspects of Elias's project, which is most convincing in this area. The misunderstandings (for which occasionally Elias must take at least some blame) surrounding this project usually arise from illegitimate generalizations from its macrotheoretical model. His interpretation of history – a prehistory of modernization – is not, however, affected by this. Since Elias wants to explain only the thrust of civilization into absolutism and courtly society, he does not deal directly with the economic class struggle of the nineteenth century.

Of course, the economic and technical transformations of society which resulted in capitalism amounted to a qualitative and dramatic change. Although Elias adopts a conflict perspective throughout, he merely acknowledges the antagonistic interests and mutual interdependence of the different classes (as in modern war, when the victorious state must accept the severe disruption of its social system, because of its close entanglement with other nation-states in the contemporary world). The point is that the domination of capital is a form of domination less direct than the physical threat posed by the frenzied Lord of the Manor. In the final analysis it is a form of exploitation based on the monopoly of force, which appears to have vanished behind the veil of monetary exchange. Since the exercise of power has become less physical, Elias's analysis of civilized manners serves to remind us of their less civilized predecessors. To uncover what has been forgotten – a 'depth-history' of civilization – is Elias's achievement.

The claim that Elias has neglected the relevance of economic categories for a critical understanding of modern industrial civilization is sometimes specified in a different way. Granted, the ascetic capitalist has to delay a good deal of gratification for the sake of the unrestricted accumulation of capital (that is to say, restraints by others must be transformed into self-restraints); and the courtier also has to curtail his drives and emotions, either because he is engaged in scheming and plotting or because of aesthetic reasons embodied in the courtly code of morality. But in view of the dark satanic mills of industry, are such phenomena not wholly trivial? Do they not pale against the temporal discipline of the assembly line, which has no counterpart at the court? Is not a subtle analysis of the civilizing process, one which focuses on the problem of ever-expanding self-restraints, irrelevant in view of this massive form of restraint by others?[21] And, so the argument continues, is not modern marketing responsible for similar restraints based on a systematic distortion of needs? How do modern codes of behaviour develop in the face of industrialization and urbanization? What is the contribution of the lower classes?[22] What role did marginalization, the labelling of deviant behaviour as sick, mad or criminal, play in the development of occidental civilization?

In responding to these difficult questions, it makes sense to present the problem of rationalization at two different levels: rationalization as an increase of the subjective rationality of an agent, a process which unfolds at the level of individual consciousness and its corresponding affective economy; and rationalization as the establishment of objective rationality in the form of institutionalized norms.[23] The costs attached to the development of rationality have to be computed on *both* these levels. At the macro level these costs can be manifold. For example, they may arise when a degree of social complexity is created which turns out to be beyond the control of its agents. Thus the critique of the market system (or capitalism) and of bureaucracy is provoked continually by the remarkable paradox that within such complex systems small islands of extreme rationality coexist with a vast ocean of systemic problems. At the micro level the agents of the modern era have to face the consequences of this complexity and its problems, which are experienced in everyday life; these agents are no longer allowed to be flexible and autonomous but are *forced* to cope with normative conflict and to accept new responsibilities.

IV   The Scope and Limits of the Theory of Civilization

The claim that the 'evolutionary gradualism' of the theory of civilization renders it incapable of explaining the simultaneous appearance of civilization (in a narrower sense than is presupposed by the highest values of the Enlightenment) and 'barbarism' still needs to be confronted more thoroughly. The massive and unemotional barbarism produced by such novel reproduction mechanisms as the market or the nation-state – examples range from the merciless exploitation of workers in nineteenth-century high capitalism to the contemporary devastation of the Third World; from the workmanlike conduct of trench warfare during World War I to the cruel but impersonal bombing of cities as well as the mass slaughters of our century, which have sprung from abstract calculations performed in the name of various ideologies – is a much more important problem, it is claimed, than the courtly etiquette of Versailles, since this new type of barbarism – as Horkheimer and Adorno have shown – completely transcends the horizon of a face-to-face, affectively refined and repressed society.

This claim raises the question of the explanatory relevance of Elias's theory for the civilization of modern mass society. Faced with this question, it is necessary to examine closely the explanatory aspirations, the mode of explanation and intended range of the theory of civilization. To begin with, Elias has identified very acutely the differences between courtly and bourgeois society:

• The courtier entertains much more than the bourgeois; the working bourgeois spends much less time on social contact.[24]

- Courtly society comprises a much more tightly woven net of relationships; among the working bourgeois, by contrast, interactions mediated by *occupation*, *goods* and *money* predominate; such interactions are usually more matter-of-fact and abstract.

- There is a contrast between the bourgeois preoccupation with saving and the conspicuous consumption of the aristocracy. Both are shaped by social constraints. For instance, the aristocrat has to obey the imperatives of a rank in need of demonstration;[25] its high status creates the obligation of social generosity.

- The gap between the private and public domains is narrower in aristocratic society than in the world of the bourgeois. The privatization, intimacy and distinctive emotional culture of the latter has been emphasized frequently. Elias also spots this distinction by pointing to discontinuities in the respective developmental curves in the civilizing process. The aristocrat's house, for example, is so important because it is a direct symbol of his place within the structure of power and because the networks of communication impart a practical function to this symbol.

- In consequence bourgeois society, with its emphasis on privacy, facilitates a partial uncoupling of occupationally determined rank and social status from the sphere of leisure and consumption.

- The society of the working bourgeois adopts the rituals of courtly society – for example courtly patterns of speech – without, however, devoloping them further; these rituals are also incorporated more into leisure activities than into the occupational sphere.

- As industrial capitalism (a concept Elias does not use) develops, growing differentiation involves an increase in the standard of living, which in turn is a condition of a more stable superego; the social world becomes fragmented into the upper and lower classes (and within each stratum there is internal competition and continuous pressure from 'below').

- Special problems arise for the upwardly mobile, since they are beset by feelings of shame and embarrassment as soon as they adopt the norms and strategies of the upper classes.

- For the lower classes civilization frequently means coloniz- ation; the internalization of the norms of the upper classes becomes a strategy associated with the exercise of power.[26]

- In a later phase of upward mobility, bourgeois groups manage to distance themselves from these norms: they create their own signposts for indicating what is permitted and what is prohi- bited. Thus work is contrasted with idleness, virtue with frivo- lousness, nature with etiquette, and knowledge with manners.

- The rise of the bourgeoisie is completed when it gains control over the 'key monopolies' (the taxation system and the exercise of force). Eventually, the aristocracy and the bourgeoisie become amalgamated to a certain degree.

This list makes it perfectly clear that Elias self-consciously described and made intelligible only *part* of the prehistory of bourgeois man when analysing the civilized conduct of the court- ier. But he insists that the courtly etiquette of civilized behaviour left a powerful imprint on bourgeois man, and that this impact upon the bourgeoisie would be difficult to understand without his prehistory. Of course, the court is not the only mint where good manners and correct behaviour are coined. The working bourgeois is situated in a whole series of additionally relevant environments, including the city and the world of merchants and artisans. But the competences which the individual has to develop in the bourgeois era can be found, *in nuce*, in the rational- ity of the court.

It should also be clear from this list that Elias is familiar with the discontinuities, abstractness and coercive nature of the capitalist market system. And it should not be surprising that the modelling of the affects of workers, who appeared on the stage of this society relatively recently, obeys different laws from those found among the nineteenth-century bourgeoisie. There is no reason to assume, however, that the social character of workers on the assembly line could not be described within Elias's conceptual framework. Obviously this would involve a thorough investigation of their work situation and its biographical context in order to capture the more extrinsic virtues of the factory, such as punctuality, obedience and diligence. The result might strongly resemble the approach of E.P. Thompson.[28]

An evaluation of the interpretative standards usually applied to Elias's main works – *The Civilizing Process* and *The Court Society* – prompts the conclusion that much criticism of his work is misdirected because these criteria are inappropriate. Their inappropriateness stems from a conflation of and a failure to distinguish between a limited historical investigation and a general methodological approach for studying social reality. For instance, when Elias is taken to task for having neglected the Protestant ethic as a formative factor in the development of the civilized character,[29] the reply consists simply in pointing out that this would have amounted to a different undertaking, which nevertheless could have been accomplished on the basis of Elias's approach. Much the same applies to a whole range of objections concerning the need for more economics as well as more morality.[30]

Instead of all these misdirected criticisms, it should be acknowledged that Elias has added several interesting touches to our received picture of 'capitalism'. To the extent that the absolutist state and the bourgeoisie contribute to the development of industrial capitalism (thereby continuing the tradition of mercantilist 'courtly' capitalism, whose importance can hardly be overestimated, according to Sombart[31]), Elias manages to describe certain indirect features of capitalism. Rather than providing a history of capitalism he aims at a 'prehistory', recognizing all along that he is paying special attention to the non-economic dimensions of this process.

In another sense, Elias's 'theory' of civilization is more than simply a history of the civilizing process. His dynamic models of short-term historical changes (such as the monopoly mechanism, the royal mechanism [*Königsmechanismus*], competition) have to be distinguished from his model of long-term developments (such as the lengthening and increasing interdependence of chains of action and the integration of larger regional units) and their impact upon affective structures. When Elias's critics malign his conception as gradualist or evolutionist, they are presumably thinking of these longer-term processes. Yet as far as the transition to bourgeois society is concerned, such accusations are without foundation. Elias acknowledges that there are long-term discontinuities and also points to the fact that the shorter-term processes (which nevertheless may span decades, or even centuries) are unintended and, as such, produce disequilibria (such as monopolies of power) in which negotiation, and not a teleological pre-stabilized harmony, obviously plays an important role.

Only those who insist that a social theory has to be based exclusively upon economic categories will reject models which characteristically include the economic as a special case of a broader and more complex historical process. Such critics are guilty of a category mistake. They ignore Elias's self-imposed limits when dealing with his historical examples; and they misconstrue the a priori part of his 'theory' (its network of general concepts and models of phenomena on the micro and macro levels) as overly harmonizing and as glossing over a number of discontinuities because of his alleged failure to pay sufficient attention to the 'economic' – as if the 'economic' were the only instance pervaded by conflict and ruptures.

V The Civilization of Domination

What is the contemporary relevance of the theory of civilization? Does it have a critical potential even though it does not set out to explain, for example, assembly-line exploitation or the unkept promises of mass consumption?

Elias's thought weaves together several strands of social scientific discourse which are usually kept separate. It is *interpretative* – it focuses on agents' perceptions of their environments and of their 'selves'. It concentrates on the affects of the agent and avoids over-rationalization by taking into account the *unconscious* and the automatic. Moreover, Elias's method is *historical*[32] and process-orientated: on the one hand, agents find their actions constrained and pre-patterned by structures; in consequence, the study of existing mechanisms on their own will not suffice to provide an understanding of the whole situation (this brings in history, tradition, culture); on the other hand, the *process* is 'ontologically' pre-given: in social reality, all is becoming and decay – constancy is the puzzle, not change. The concepts developed in the context of this method mirror this emphasis on processes, but beyond this they reflect a pervasive *relationality*. The ruled leaves his imprint on the ruler, and vice versa; macro structures determine the affective structures of those sustaining them; thus there are no spheres of value which could be detached from the social structure, which would develop according to their own logic. And finally, in the *historical process* the intended is emphatically outweighed by the *unintended*: most of what there is is a blind entangled web.

This fruitful outlook can be brought to bear on the contours and problems of contemporary societies, including those to do with domination in the economy and the state.

For instance, if we compare Elias's work with the perspective of *Surveiller et punir: la naissance de la prison*, a parallel appears: both perspectives describe a development which starts with the body and ends with the soul. The differences are equally conspicuous. The clever courtier, bored to tears in the Versailles of Louis XIV (and to death under his successors) seems to have little in common with the criminologist, who wants to administer psychological treatment to the law-breaker. Nor is there an obvious route from the peasant who eats in an uncivilized manner to the soldier who becomes one with his rifle.

We have here two developmental series with different principles. The first is a face-to-face society subject – for whatever reasons – to a refinement of its table manners and rules of interaction, where aggressive behaviour becomes less and less physical, characterized by a privatization and intimization of needs, including 'natural activities', at the expense of the spontaneity of emotional expression and the satisfaction of drives. The complex 'etiquette' circumscribing all this can properly be called a 'code': it is structural knowledge which, in suitable environments, can be copied and applied again and again. For some aspects of this etiquette, an individual can be 'trained'; much of it, however, can be applied only if the reflexive 'self' of a person is engaged.

The second developmental series also incorporates a lengthening of sequences of action: the realm of the normative consists of all kinds of coercion, which becomes more and more serial, concentrated and subject to a division of labour. Monasteries, armies, factories, asylums – all these places of surveillance and regimentation are geared to a division of labour, function in accordance with it and are co-ordinated by force. Disciplinary measures range from the taming of the body to the control of activities through time budgeting, and the power of the administration relies on these methods to separate lepers, victims of the plague, beggars, madmen and criminals from society. The 'code', of course, is no longer that of etiquette: recipe-knowledge about discipline is handed down within armies, monasteries, asylums and factories, with many similarities. The code comprises techniques of punishment, rules of drill, plans for the construction of buildings and the allocation of time, thus enabling the authorities to 'manufacture'; but it is a code of power, of the restraint by others, as Elias would put it.

The two developmental series are not parallel, neither temporally nor as far as their object is concerned. Elias's 'restraints by others' are replaced in Foucault's thought by an economization of oppression.[33] To the extent that medicine, psychology, education and social work take over more and more powers of control and punishment, the legal machinery in turn can become more medical, psychological, pedagogical. This idea of Foucault's reflects a growing complexity which increasingly has to rely on the co-operation of the ruled. The religion of work is something quite different from taming somebody with the help of the whip; the morality of criminals, which becomes topical when the question is raised whether they can be reformed, matters only when the opportunities for control have become more comprehensive.

While it is clear that in order to understand certain modern 'civilized' relations of dependence we have to study the institutional characteristics of the present, there is still a host of lessons to be drawn from historical explanations. Relying on Elias, a problem can perhaps be solved that has vexed Foucault as well: to deal with power and violence, when they have become ever less visible and can be identified only through their action at a distance, obviously has to do with the way they have become rooted in the psyche and the body of the individual. In this context, Elias's approach – as exhibited in *The Civilizing Process* – proves helpful in two different ways: through the reconstruction of the *prehistory* of a society organized by the state on the one hand, and through a more adequate *method* on the other.

The kind of ethnographic detachment Foucault brings to bear on the Western tradition of punishment succeeds in highlighting its unbelievable brutality. But it is simply not possible to elucidate what is special about the developmental process of occidental civilization unless attention is paid to our *feudal legacy*, an inheritance from a period of anarchic competition in war slowly superseded by an unplanned *monopoly of force* wielded by the state. Later 'peaceable' forms of suppression were based on this monopoly of force. If this process is neglected, the more peaceful circumstances of a later age are misleadingly transformed into a matter of course – a charge that may well be levelled against economistic approaches.

On the other hand, Elias's *method* manages to throw light on several obscure aspects of Foucault's brand of structuralism. Foucault tries to develop a notion of decentralized power in order to contrast conceptions of a domination which is primarily 'manipulative' with a more plausible alternative. He fails, however, to provide a systematic link between history and social and affective structures, which is why his concept of power becomes diffuse: power is simultaneously everywhere and nowhere. Elias, by comparison, links structural changes of the soul to those of society, while conceiving of the latter as the unintended result of social actions; he does so in a more systematic way than most other social theoreticians.

The transformations of aggressiveness serve as a model of this kind of long-term process. Elias traces the developments leading from a society of warriors to bourgeois society. For the medieval knight, war means 'being stronger to get at the enemy, to cut down his vines, tear up his trees, ruin his land, storm his castle, fill in his well, capture and kill his people'.[35] In this world, a high level of individual aggressiveness was needed not only in wartime but at all times. Through his image of the 'affective household', Elias provides an explanation for the unadulterated aggressiveness of these strata:

> Much of what looks contradictory to us – the intensity of their devotion, their violent fear of hell, their feelings of guilt, their atonement, the immense outbursts of joy and mirth, the sudden flare-up and untamed force of their hatred and aggressiveness alternating with the utmost kindness and magnanimity – all these extremes of hatred and love, violence and repentance, are in fact symptoms of the same social and personality structure.[35]

But this spontaneity finds its counterpart in societal arrangements where ill-defined and dangerous situations prevail. A monopoly of force creates pacified spaces where rarefied manners can flourish. Within the courts, more subtle and more finely graded distributions of power emerge. Unabashed violence is replaced by intrigues, and even the powerful have to exercise restraints – their image of the world becomes increasingly psychological as well. Restraint becomes a matter of the interior voice. This applies to the less powerful, whose inner imperative more closely resembles restraint by others, just as much as to those of higher rank: the struggle between men turns into a struggle between man and himself, while everything reminiscent of violence becomes a matter of taboo and ostracism and is looked upon as uncouth and embarrassing. The price of an increased pacification is paid within the economy of drives. This is how Elias puts it:

> Even in this form as a control organization, however, physical violence and the threat emanating from it have a determining influence on individuals in society, whether they know it or not. It is, however, no longer a perpetual insecurity that it brings into the life of the individual, but a peculiar form of security. It no longer throws him, in the

swaying fortunes of battle, as the physical victor or vanquished, between mighty outbursts of pleasure and terror; a continuous, uniform pressure is exerted on individual life by the physical violence stored behind the scenes of everyday life, a pressure totally familiar and hardly perceived, conduct and drive economy having been adjusted from earliest youth to this social structure.[36]

In this perspective long-term changes acquire a general twofold dimension, as both uncontrolled developments at the macro level and internal changes of personality. In the study of the development of human societies, yesterday's unintended consequences turn into the unintended conditions of today's intentional action. As part of these conditions the dark mixture of passions, drives and contents of the superego is blended and shaped by blind, yet intelligible forces in 'figurations' characterized by balances of power which themselves slowly change. Through this, conspiracy theories fall by the wayside, as Foucault had envisaged. But it is Elias's work which shows much better that both the objectivity of power and the subjectivity of its occurrence can form part of the same analysis.

VI   Civilization and Civil Society

Among the broken promises of the Enlightenment are those to do with the development of democracy.[37] Modern societies may be entangled politically to a high degree; unfettered power may be relatively rare; and the structural necessity of considering many different interests may be inescapable. Nevertheless, it is well known that in the so-called Western democracies vast concentrations of uncontrolled power persist. The oligarchic principle has not been eliminated from political institutions, nor have pockets of power below the level of the territorial nation-state been dissolved. The business world and state administrations may have become acquainted with the notion that a citizen acting in a variety of different roles has certain basic rights, but we are still miles away from having effective forms of participation. Given the way technocratic and bureaucratic structures have pervaded market societies, it is unsurprising that invisible power has not become visible to a significant degree. The education of citizens has also fallen far short of the ideal of competent democratic participation. And in the societies of East-Central Europe, formally devoted to the idea of socialism, the problem of effectively controlling bureaucracy and of creating a critical public opinion is even more pressing.

In this situation, analogies with absolutist rule and the great reforming and revolutionary process which brought its downfall through an expansion of citizens' participation in the exercise of power do not seem very far-fetched. This revolutionary process, which produced the constitutional nation-state, has often attracted Elias's direct and indirect attention. Examples include his concern with the development of conceptions of 'being civilized' and their transfer to the political vocabulary of the Physiocratic reform movement in France; his attempt to explain the dramatic transformation of the courtly absolutist apparatus of power, with its ossified etiquette and ceremonies; and his concern, especially in more recent works,[38] with the peculiar German experience of having failed to create democratic rules of procedure. 'Civilization and Violence' is an example of the latter. It refutes those critics who have claimed that Elias failed to say anything about the possible relapse into barbarism by dealing with the prehistory of the Fascist withdrawal from bourgeois ideas and loyalties in favour of accepting political violence.

Each of these examples provides clues to Elias's view of the role of historically shaped structures of personality and mechanisms of self-control in political action. In his view, civilized political action presupposes a sense of proportion, tolerance, detachment *vis-à-vis* one's own affects, and the recognition of civil and liberal principles such as the obligation to behave decently in personal interactions with others.[39] These values, which are seen to complement a humanistic ethos of solidarity with the oppressed of all kinds, are learned as rules in power struggles free from violence; here Elias points to the example of England in the period from 1650 to 1750, when it underwent a transition from violence to parliamentary rule.

What can be learned politically from examples such as seventeenth- and eighteenth-century England or Weimar Germany? None of them derives from the combination of empirical and conceptual research so characteristic of Elias's best-known works. They are best seen as suggestions for further research, and it is abundantly clear that the specific historical features of different national situations are of great concern to Elias. If we add to these examples *The Civilizing Process*, a work dealing with the development of special skills for internalizing and transforming affects and for behaving in 'polished' and 'mild' ways, then it also becomes evident that distinctions must be drawn among different apparatuses of self-restraint and self-control – from manners in everyday life to the specific virtues of the politician, described by Max Weber, to the skilful art of the democratic power struggle free from violence. But it would be highly inconsistent with Elias's method to think that civilized 'values' could be developed outside the context of an existing power structure; just as the Physiocratic reform movement had a practical power basis, so democratic rules originated in a country which, at the time, was the richest in the world.

This link between the psyche and the structural conditions within a society is absent from Sennett's recent attempt to explain political apathy through reference to 'narcissism' and the illegitimate transfer of principles of intimacy to the public sphere.[40] Sennett criticizes political action guided by an ethic of conviction (especially that observable in recent years in the USA). He argues that instead of the consequences, only the subjective intentions of political actions are evaluated, and that formal, higher-level systems (such as the city and the state; in this context, Sennett does not mention the economy) are eliminated increasingly from political perception in favour of a particularistic concern with family, school and neighbourhood. Interpersonal narcissism, according to Sennett, is destructive enough within the small community, for it is uncivilized and tactless. In public life, however, it finds its counterpart in chummy 'charismatic' politicians and the increasingly destructive fraternity of a community whose boundaries have been drawn too tightly.

Sennett's view of an old problem is interesting inasmuch as it basically introduces the 'social character' of the citizen as a political agent in order to explain political apathy, a public sphere (in the political and the architectural sense) which is seen as no longer capable of functioning. It is also interesting because Sennett borrows examples from the civil society of the eighteenth-century capital cities. There, a balance between the 'private' and the 'public' was still evident – a balance, in Sennett's view, which is nowadays gravely disturbed. Despite all his weaknesses, Sennett argues, the citizen from the past seems today like a paragon of political virtue.

Sennett's analysis is deficient in several respects, especially when compared with Elias's approach. Sennett is convinced that the virtues of the actor facilitated public behaviour – in cafés, theatres and other public places – since they made possible easygoing contact with 'strangers'. The cities of the *ancien régime* thereby provided a better foundation for a 'public sphere' in the political sense, since authenticity has no place in political actions. According to Sennett, the desire for spontaneity can be satisfied better by those who hide behind masks and clichés than by those who torture themselves in a permanent quest for an improved self.

But Sennett's analysis contains certain errors, which arise from the scant consideration he gives to the social environments in which social characters are formed. (Occasionally, this consideration of social contexts is totally lacking: to the extent that he ignores the history of the USA, his procedure is even ahistorical.) Thus his analysis is one-sidedly idealistic, moralistic and insensitive to the facticity of societal power structures. No doubt unintentionally, Sennett's reversal of causality suggests that we can choose our selves in order to regain a better perpective on social reality. Alas, this does not make much sense. Elias has shown that – for the educated bourgeoisie of the eighteenth and early nineteenth century at least – romanticism, the search for authenticity, the pursuit of private happiness, the desire to distance one's self from deceptive appearances, and the emptiness of the powerful courtly aristocracy all went hand in hand with *political impotence*. The lack of political power led to the formulation of ideals out of touch with reality, not the reverse. Similarly, it makes more sense to assume that the twentieth-century 'marketing character' and the 'pseudo-ego' are the result, not the cause, of alienation in the world of modern bureaucracies and personality markets.

The actor-like agent of the eighteenth century described by Sennett is competent in many respects, in no small measure because his courtly predecessors invested a good deal of effort in their masks and manners. The sovereign eighteenth-century actor remains cool in his social interactions, masters the transition from the private to the public, avoids embarrassment and uses an elaborated code of verbal and non-verbal behaviour. The construction of such forms of self-restraint, which appear to be wholly natural, draws on many different resources and requires an intensive learning process as well as appropriate contexts of socialization. The skills of the courtier are mastered more easily by members of the *haute bourgeoisie*. Sennett's account of the fall of public man rests on an overly simplified account of the origins of this figure, suggesting that a homogeneous 'public sphere' stretched through the centuries. Yet public life was easy only so long as the town was still an appendage of the court.[41] It became more difficult as town life became anonymous and gained the upper hand. And public life in that form became impossible when it had to incorporate millions of inhabitants – members of the *petite bourgeoisie*, former peasants, small businessmen and workers – into its ranks. Public man did not simply fall: he would have had to be created afresh.

The resources required for this task were scarce at all levels. Manners 'degenerated' as a result of a situation – there were evident national differences, of course – where classes and strata which were lacking the relevant code of civilized behaviour and were comparatively powerless in most areas of life had to be integrated. A comparison of the social space of the aristocrat of the *ancien régime* with that of the dispossessed makes clear that the kinds of self-control involving dignity, tact and a splendidly polished public front requires a space in which these virtues can form and develop. Those who want to civilize the contemporary world should not forget this fact.

Notes

1. Talcott Parsons, *Societies. Evolutionary and Comparative Perspectives*, Englewood Cliffs, NJ 1966, p. 3.

2. Ibid., p. 21. Parsons thinks of himself as completing Weber's universal-historical interpretation of the development of 'occidental rationalism'.

3. Cf. Marion J. Levy, 'Social Patterns (Structures) and Problems of Modernization', in Wilbert E. Moore and Robert M. Cook, eds, *Readings on Social Change*, Englewood Cliffs, NJ 1967, p. 190.

4. Max Weber, *Gesammelte Aufsätze zur Religionssoziologie*, Tübingen 1972, vol. 1, pp. 1-16.

5. Cf. N. Elias, *The Civilizing Process. Sociogenetic and Psychogenetic Investigations. Vol. 1: The History of Manners*, Oxford 1978, p. 1.

6. Cf. Samuel N. Eisenstadt, *Tradition, Change, and Modernity*, New York, London, Sydney and Toronto 1973.

7. Honneth and Joas have emphasized this point concerning Rousseau as a shortcoming of Elias's analysis; see Axel Honneth, Hans Joas, *Soziales Handeln und menschliche Natur. Anthropologische Grundlagen der Sozialwissenschaften*, Frankfurt am Main and New York 1980, p. 117. See, however, the references to Rousseau in Elias, *The Civilizing Process*, vol. 1, p. 39.

8. Cf. Friedrich Jonas, *Geschichte der Soziologie*, 4 vols, Reinbek b. Hamburg 1976, vol. 1, p. 58.

9. Elias, *The Civilizing Process*, vol. 2: *State Formation and Civilization*, 1982, pp. 47–8.

10. Bauman cites the 'garden' (paradigm: Versailles) as an important element in the imagery of the civilizing process, whereby the wilderness of nature (including that of human nature) was supposed to be transformed. According to him the garden was an experience shared by the court, the salon, and the life-world of the *Philosophes*; see Zygmunt Bauman, 'On the Origins of Civilization: A Historical Note', in *Theory, Culture and Society*, vol. 2, no. 3, 1985, p. 78. See also the reference

to the strict regimentation of the landscape architects of Versailles as a symbol of the courtly structure of power in N. Elias, *The Court Society*, Oxford 1983, pp. 227-8.

11. This concept figures prominently in a whole series of other famous evolutionary theories: for example in Spencer's notion of a transition from militaristic to industrialized society, or in Buckle's theory of civilization.

12. Elias has often been criticized on this point. For a review of these criticisms, see N. Wilterdink, 'Die Zivilisationstheorie im Kreuzfeuer der Diskussion. Ein Bericht vom Kongreß über Zivilisationsprozesse in Amsterdam', in P. Gleichmann, J. Goudsblom and H. Korte, eds, *Macht und Zivilisation. Materialien zu Norbert Elias' Zivilisationstheorie 2*, Frankfurt am Main 1984, p. 285. Their main accusation concerns Elias's thesis that warlike aggressiveness in the earlier stages of societal development was 'spontaneous', in the sense of not being subject to rational control. They argue that even in those days violence was subject to a good deal of cognitive control and required a fair amount of foresight and self-monitoring (as in the knightly joust and the extensive practising it demanded). This accusation, however, does not penetrate to the heart of Elias's argument. He is concerned with the affective household as a whole, under conditions marked by the omnipresent threat of physical violence in everyday life, and in times when a monopoly of force was lacking. Conflicts between minor feudal lords and even between townsmen were resolved occasionally by resorting to extreme physical violence. Moreover, the interaction between the wider social world (in which feudal lords were at times as sovereign as contemporary states) and the social 'lifeworld' created a structurally determined high density of conflict, itself reflected within the psyche of the individual. The fact that calculated, cruel torture was even more intense in certain enclaves does not constitute a counter-argument against Elias's thesis. And as far as 'rationality' is concerned, it is Elias himself who insists, time and again, that the development of civilization does not begin from scratch – on the contrary, rationality is a process of rationalization.

13. According to one critic, Elias in fact produces a 'theoretically informed case study': that of France. See Samuel F. Sampson, 'The Formation of European National States, the Elaboration of Functional Interdependence Networks and the Genesis of Modern Self-Control', *Contemporary Sociology*, vol. 13, no. 1, 1984, p. 22.

14. Elias, *The Civilizing Process*, vol. 2, p. 241.

15. According to Elias, 'figurations' or 'configurations' are 'webs' of relations among interdependent human beings. Configurations often develop within the context of phenomena – the monetary economy, the division of labour, the formation of the state – which, although usually called macrosociological processes and structures, are better seen as lengthening chains of action and interdependence. He argues that figurations cannot be analysed by, say, examining the causal connections between macro and micro phenomena. Elias accepts the physicalist language of 'variables' as at best a necessary simplification, and would argue that such language is inappropriate for social life. Cf. his pertinent methodological observations in *Was ist Soziologie?* (Munich 1970, pp. 119-25; especially p. 124). This point is missed completely in the naive positivist criticisms of Henk Flap and Yme Kuiper, 'Figurationssoziologie als Forschungsprogramm', *Kölner Zeitschrift für Soziologie und Sozialpsychologie*, no. 33, pp. 273-301.

16. Cf. Susan Buck-Morss's review of Elias's *The Civilization Process*, *Telos*, no. 37, 1978, pp. 181-98, especially p. 188.

17. The fact that Elias did not exclude the possibility of such 're-lapses' is clear from the following passage, which refutes the charge that he defended a deterministic and evolutionary view of progress: 'We scarcely realize how quickly what we

call our "reason", this relatively farsighted and differentiated steering of our conduct, with its high degree of affect-control, would crumble or collapse if the anxiety-inducing tensions within and around us changed, if the fears affecting our lives suddenly became much stronger or much weaker or, as in many simpler societies, both at once, now stronger, now weaker.' (*The Civilizing Process*, vol. 2, p. 326.

18. Elias would dismiss such a polarization – feudalism versus capitalism – as an unrealistic simplification. He argues along these lines when indicating the changing composition over time of 'aristocratic' and 'bourgeois' groups; cf. *The Civilizing Process*, vol. 2, pp. 176-7 and, in general, the idea of a court society between feudalism and capitalism.

19. Some critics also take Elias to be an exponent of an 'evolutionary gradualism'. See Honneth and Joas, *Soziales Handeln und menschliche Natur*, p. 120. The charge of 'gradualism' is rather implausible. See *The Civilizing Process*, vol. 2, especially pp. 166-7, where the concept of the monopoly of power and force is explained, along with the role of conflicts, antagonisms of interest, and discontinuities.

20. Elias, ibid., vol. 2, p. 163. Compare Honneth's and Joas's claim (*Soziales Handeln und menschliche Natur*, pp. 120-21) that Elias's conception of the formation of the state is restricted to the political realm and lacks an economic materialist perspective.

21. Susan Buck-Morss's review of *The Civilizing Process*, p. 193.

22. Cf. Sampson, 'The Formation of European National States', p. 25; Honneth and Joas, *Soziales Handeln und menschliche Natur*, p. 121.

23. See Donald N. Levine, 'Rationality and Freedom: Weber and Beyond', *Sociological Inquiry*, vol. 51, no. 1, 1981, pp. 5-25, especially p. 10; cf. Joachim Israel, *Alienation: From Marx to Modern Sociology*, Boston, MA 1971, pp. 98-121.

24. For this and the following observations, see *The Court Society*, pp. 58-67; *The Civilizing Process*, vol. 2, pp. 305-19.

25. This was especially true of the members of the French aristocracy, whereas the English gentry differed in some respects (the position of the English aristocrat was based less on political factors than on economic conditions); see Barrington Moore, *Social Origins of Dictatorship and Democracy*, Boston, MA 1966, chapters 1.4 and 2.1.

26. Elias is well aware of the 'imperialist' and marginalizing character of civilization. He writes:

> The habituation to foresight, and the stricter control of behaviour and the affects to which the upper classes are inclined through their situation and functions, are important instruments of their dominance, as in the case of European colonialism, for example. They serve as marks of distinction and prestige. ... On the one hand they build, through institutions and by the strict regulation of their own behaviour, a wall between themselves and the groups they colonize and whom they consider their inferiors. On the other, with their social forms, they also spread their own style of conduct and institutions in these places. (*The Civilizing Process*, vol. 2, pp. 254-5.)

27. Elias has tried to deal with the issues of class struggle and workers' emancipation in *Was ist Soziologie?*, pp. 156-8, by drawing on the idea of 'multistoreyed models'.

28. E.P. Thompson, *The Making of the English Working Class*, Harmondsworth 1972, pp. 385-410.

176

29. A. Wehowsky, 'Making Ourselves More Flexible Than We Are – Reflections on Norbert Elias', *New German Critique*, no. 15, 1978, pp. 65-80.

30. Concerning the latter criticism, see R. Münch, *Die Struktur der Moderne*, 1984, pp. 282–4. The argument that Elias does not distinguish sharply enough between rules of etiquette and moral rules is made by Christian Lenhardt, 'Civilization and its Contents', *Canadian Journal of Political and Social Theory*, vol. 3, no. 1, 1979, p. 123.

31. Cf. W. Sombart, *Liebe, Luxus und Kapitalismus*, Munich 1967.

32. In his more recent works Elias more than once takes these developments into account, at least programmatically. For example, see 'Über den Rückzug der Soziologen auf die Gegenwart', *Kölner Zeitschrift für Soziologie und Sozialpsychologie*, vol. 35, no. 1, 1983, pp. 29-40, especially p. 35.

33. Here an analytic distinction has to be made between the liberalization of restraints by others and their transformation into self-restraints, even if as historical processes they frequently go hand in hand. What Elias insists on is the general widening of areas of regulation; the transformation of this regulation into self-restraints is, however, the most important aspect. Relevant in this context is Michel Foucault, *Surveiller et punir. La naissance de la prison*, Paris 1975.

34. Elias, 'On Transformation of Aggressiveness', *Theory and Society*, vol. 5, no. 2, 1978, pp. 229-42, especially p. 231.

35. Elias, 'On Transformation ...', p. 238.

36. Elias, *The Civilizing Process*, vol. 2, pp. 238-9.

37. For a list of these broken promises, see N. Bobbio, 'The Future of Democracy', *Telos*, no. 61, 1984, pp. 3-16.

38. See 'Einige Gedanken über die Bundesrepublik', *Merkur. Deutsche Zeitschrift für europäisches Denken*, no. 9-10, 1985, pp. 733-55, and the essay 'Civilization and Violence' in this volume.

39. 'Gedanken über die Bundesrepublik', p. 742.

40. R. Sennett, *The Fall of Public Man*, New York 1977.

41. *The Court Society*, p. 36.

Violence and Civilization: The State Monopoly of Physical Violence and its Infringement*

Norbert Elias

Civilization is never completed and constantly endangered. It is endangered because the maintenance of civilized standards of behaviour requires certain conditions, such as a relatively stable level of individual self-discipline. These are linked in turn to particular social structures, such as the provision of goods and services, the preservation of an accustomed standard of living and especially social pacification – the non-violent settling of conflicts through the state. But the internal pacification of society is always endangered by social and personal conflicts which are among the normal phenomena of social life and which the pacifying institutions serve to resolve. Due to hidden presuppositions, this problem of physical violence in social life – the problem of the tension between pacification and violence – is often examined in such a way that justice is not done to the observable contexts. Consider the following two approaches.

One false way of posing the problem is the currently widespread tendency to ascribe social conflicts and the resulting psychological conflicts to people's innate aggressiveness. The idea that people have an aggressive drive to attack others which resembles in its structure other innate drives, such as the sexual drive, is unfounded. People do have an innate potential automatically to shift their whole physical apparatus to a different gear if they feel

*Revised and edited translation of a lecture published originally in Joachim Matthes, ed., *Lebenswelt und Soziale Probleme*, Frankfurt 1981, pp. 98-122. Translated by John Keane.

endangered. The body reacts to the experience of anger by an automatic adjustment which prepares the way for intensive movement of the skeletal muscles, as in combat or flight. Human impulses that correspond to the model of a drive are released physiologically or, as is often said, 'from within', relatively independently of the actual situation. The shifting of the body's economy to combat-or-flight readiness is conditioned to a far greater extent by a specific situation, whether present or remembered.

The potential for aggressiveness can be activated by natural and social situations of a certain kind, above all by conflict. In conscious opposition to Lorenz and others, who ascribe an aggression drive to people on the model of the sexual drive, it is not aggressiveness that triggers conflicts but conflicts that trigger aggressiveness. Our habits of thought generate the expectation that everything we seek to explain about people can be explained in terms of isolated individuals. It is evidently difficult to adjust our thinking and, thus, the explanations of how people are interconnected in groups: that is, by means of social structures. Conflicts are an aspect of social structures. They are also an aspect of human life together with non-human nature: with the animals, plants, the moon and the sun. Human beings are by nature attuned to this life together with other humans, with nature, and with the conflicts all this entails.

The altered perspective suggested by this approach is manifested in a second, more significant respect. When the problem of physical violence is examined it is often asked how it is possible that people strike or kill others so that they become, for example, male or female terrorists. It would be more accurate, and thus more productive, if the question were posed differently. It should go: How is it possible that so many people can normally live together peacefully without fear of being struck or killed by stronger parties – as peacefully as is generally the case in the great state-regulated societies of contemporary Europe, America, China or Russia? It is often forgotten that never before in the development of humankind have so many millions of people lived together so peacefully – that is, with the considerable elimination of physical violence – as in the large states and cities of our time. This becomes evident only when one realizes how much more violent and how much higher in risk of physical attacks were earlier epochs of human development.

The primary behaviour, when one encounters conflict, gets angry at someone, or hates, is for people to attack each other or to strike or murder each other. The problem is how we can live together without all this – without fury, hatred, enmity, rivalry. All this remains, but attacks or even murders have generally fallen into the background. This problem is normally examined by asking how to explain acts of violence. Instead, we ought to ask how it can be explained that normally we live together peacefully within a state-regulated society. Only then would it be possible to understand and explain how people cannot submit to the standard of a quite peaceful social life, the standard of contemporary civilization.

The question of how we came to live together relatively peacefully in very large social groups is not difficult to answer. A particular form of organization has made it possible. One aspect of the problem was first observed by Max Weber. He pointed out that states are characterized by their rulers' claim to a monopoly upon physical violence. This means that we live within an organization whose rulers have at their disposal groups of specialists authorized to use physical violence if necessary to prevent all other citizens from using violence. This monopolization of violence (for whose development I have presented an explanatory model in the second part of *Über den Prozess der Zivilisation*[1]) is a sociotechnical invention of the human species. There are examples not only in the natural but also in the social field of the human species' sociotechnical inventions, which generally develop without planning in the course of many generations. The monopolization of physical violence is an invention of this type. It took shape very gradually over centuries until it reached the present state, which is by no means the final stage.

Such monopolies of physical violence – which at present are normally controlled and managed by governments and represented by the military and police as their executive organs – are, like so many human inventions, highly equivocal. Just as the taming of fire favoured civilized progress in the cooking of food as well as the barbarian burning down of huts and houses; just as atomic energy is both a plentiful source of energy and a frightening weapon, the social invention of the monopoly of physical violence is equally ambiguous. It is a dangerous instrument. From the ancient pharaohs down to present-day dictatorships, the power of disposal of the monopoly of violence is used for the benefit of certain small groups. But the function it has for its monopolists is not its sole function. The state monopoly of force also has a highly significant function for people living together within a state. Our pacification – the relatively peaceful collective life of large masses of people – is in good part based on this institution, which is closely connected with the state's fiscal monopoly.[2]

The crucial point is the balance beween the two functions of the monopoly of violence: the function for its controllers and for the members of the state-regulated society and, thus, the degree of internal pacification. In former times power was distributed so unevenly that the controllers of the monopoly of violence could give absolute priority to its function for themselves over its function for those they ruled. Louis XIV is reported to have said: 'I am the State.' He in fact felt himself to be its owner. Since then the balance of power in a few states has shifted in favour of the function of the monopoly of power for the whole state-regulated society.

Individual pacification – the fact that in a conflict the idea normally never enters our heads to rush at our opponent and initiate a brawl, however angry we may be – indicates a far-reaching civilizing transformation of the whole structure of our personality. Babies, regardless of which society they may belong to, protect themselves spontaneously by hand and foot. Children like to wrestle and box. The taboo against acts of violence, which is so deeply impressed upon adolescents in developed state-regulated societies, is closely linked with the growing effectiveness of the state monopoly of violence.

In the course of time the personality structures of individuals adjust to this. They develop a certain reluctance or even a deep loathing or disgust towards the use of physical violence. Thus in former times, as recently as the nineteenth century, it was quite acceptable in many strata for men to strike women in order to get their way. Today, the imperative that men may strike women under no circumstances – nor one another, even when they are stronger – or that even children may not be struck, is anchored far more deeply in individuals' feelings than in previous centuries. Only when this generally self-activated restraint of spontaneous impulses to act violently becomes conscious can the problem of intentional and reflected acts of violence in civilized societies be understood correctly.

Of course, within states legal and illegal violent groups remain. The situation is further complicated by the fact that there is no monopoly of violence on the international level. On this level we are living today just as our so-called primitive ancestors did. As tribes were earlier a danger to other tribes, so states today are still a constant danger to other states. Their representatives and members must always be on guard. They must always reckon with the possibility of being invaded by a stronger state and brought into dependency or even subjection. At the international level there is no overarching power to prevent a stronger state from invading a weaker state to demand taxes and obedience from its citizens and so *de facto* to annex the weaker state. Nobody can prevent a mighty state from doing this except another mighty state. And if such states exist they live in constant fear of each other, in the fear that their rivals could become stronger than themselves.

The inevitability of this double-bind process is often not seen clearly, because usually one takes sides. Yet in the field of international relations the strongest states are normally involved in hegemonic struggles with their rivals, in part because they live in constant fear of them. At this level there is no central monopoly of physical violence to restrain the participants from violent action if they believe themselves stronger and expect advantages from it. That is often how it was in *former* times, even within states. The stronger neighbour had to be feared. Those who were physically stronger could use their strength to threaten, extort, rob and enslave others.

The pacification and civilization of people living within a state has progressed. And yet a strange fault line runs through our civilization. When the word 'civilization' is used, it is often assumed that it refers to a firm entity. That is not the case. There is a very sharp distinction between the standard of civilized behaviour and experience in domestic as distinct from international relations. In domestic relations violence among people is taboo and, wherever possible, punished. In international relations a different standard prevails. Every larger state continuously prepares for acts of violence against other states. And when such acts of violence are carried out, those who carry them out are held in high esteem. They are often praised and rewarded.

If the reduction of mutual physical danger or increased pacification is considered a decisive criterion for determining the degree of civilization, then humankind can be said to have reached a higher level of civilization within domestic affairs than on the international plane. Within developed industrial states, which domestically are often almost fully pacified, the gap between domestic pacification and international threats is especially great. In international relations, human beings do not remain at a relatively low stage of the process of civilization because they are evil by nature or because they have innate aggressive desires. Rather, it is because they have developed certain social institutions within the state which can more or less effectively prevent every act of violence not authorized by that state, while such institutions are still wholly absent in international relations.

Domestically, there is a monopoly of violence by means of which it is normally possible to limit violent conflicts. On the international level, the monopolization of violence is still a very long way off. This deficiency is displayed all too clearly in the early efforts of the United Nations or of the International Court at the Hague for a non-violent settlement of conflicts at the international level. An army stronger than the states preparing for violent conflict or engaged in violent activities is required to prevent them from settling their conflicts militarily. If such an army existed, then the United Nations and other international institutions would exercise a global monopoly of physical violence. Since a monopoly of this kind does not exist, international relations in many ways do not match the relations of simpler groups of people living in the jungle. All larger and many smaller states constantly maintain specialists in violence who can be used whenever violent invasion by another state threatens, or whenever one's own state threatens to invade another.[3]

Although the formation of a monopoly of physical violence – the process of state-formation – is quite rudimentary at the international level, the development of a similar monopoly at the domestic level has progressed much further, but not everywhere at the same pace. Even where it is relatively effective, it remains vulnerable. In domestic crises, the state-authorized specialists in violence, the representatives of the state's monopoly on violence, become involved in a violent struggle with groups not authorized by the state. I should like to illustrate this type of development with a few examples from recent German history.

It would be a challenging task to write the biography of a state-regulated society such as Germany. For just as individuals' experiences of development from earlier times continue to affect their present, the same is true of nations. Thus, the experience that the German Reich was for a long time a weak state and occupied a relatively low position in the hierarchy of European states still lives on in Germany. When the Reich was weak, the self-esteem of its member nations suffered. Their sense of self-importance was damaged. One can still see, in the documents of seventeenth- and eighteenth-century Germany, how often people then recognized and experienced that Germany was weak compared with France, England, Sweden or Russia, because it was fragmented.

A biography of Germany would have to describe how this feeling of weakness and inferiority turned suddenly into its opposite when the formerly loose confederation was finally consolidated into an integrated state as the result of a victorious war. Its feeling of weakness turned into a feeling of unlimited strength and its inferiority complex into an unparalled self-esteem. The pendulum swung too much in the opposite direction. Germany, entering the magic circle of the European great powers, now became involved in their struggles for hegemony. In accord with the dynamics of the European configuration of states, in Germany – already under the second Kaiser and in an especially radical form, because this development came later – the idea also spread that it was not enough for this country, by its unification, to win a place as one of the great European powers. It had to become the major European and world power. In accord with this pendulum swing from extreme humiliation to extreme exaltation, more and more people in the ruling strata felt that Germany had to prepare for a struggle to dominate Europe, if not the whole world.

Of course, few great powers on this earth have ever resisted the temptation to win hegemony over their neighbours or over the whole known world if their ruling groups saw even the slightest chance of winning. Whether nowadays the USSR and the United States will resist the temptation remains to be seen. In Germany this situation was accompanied by something peculiar: a change in the relation between the privileged nobility, especially in Prussia, and the upper middle classes, particularly high officials and academicians. This change has not yet been fully clarified. Of course, in Germany under the Kaisers the nobility, with its strong military tradition, remained the leading stratum. The German bourgeoisie had to see that its own ideal, the unification of Germany, had been realized not through its own achievements and successes but from above through the successes of the military nobility.

In this situation a strange and significant (from the viewpoint of the civilizing process) thing happened. Parts of the bourgeoisie became assimilated into the higher stratum and internalized its military ethos. In the course of this appropriation, however, the military ethos became bourgeois. Traditional, taken for granted and mostly accepted unthinkingly by the nobility, the military ethos was appropriated deliberately, and advocated consciously with the zeal of a convert, by the upper strata of the bourgeoisie. Seldom before had so much been said and written in praise of power, including violence. Since the desired national unification had been achieved by winning wars under the nobility's military leadership, the upper bourgeoisie now concluded that war and violence were good and beautiful political instruments. Very important parts – although not the whole – of the German bourgeoisie developed this line of thinking into the heart of their ideology.

While for many nobles wars and diplomatic intrigues were a customary trade, a speciality with a long tradition, some parts of the peaceful bourgeoisie who had assimilated the military standards displayed a kind of romanticism of power and produced a literature which glorified power achieved through violence. Nietzsche, who served in the German army, provided a philosophical formulation for this ideology of the Wilhelminian bourgeoisie in his *Willen zur Macht*, though most certainly without realizing it. The books of the time, particularly Wilhelminian novels, depict bourgeois students duelling in conformity with the unified honour code of noble and bourgeois student associations. They also indicate the special status of bourgeois reserve officers and privy councillors in court uniform; and the process of adaptation of the higher bourgeois strata to nobility and court is easily recognized.

At the same time, one sees the peculiar and paradoxical social and psychological character of this upper bourgeoisie of academics and officials. Despite their mainly peaceful professional tradition and their relatively non-military cultural tradition, the members of the upper bourgeoisie sought to legitimate themselves as a second-rank, honourable profession and at the same time to adopt the bellicose outlook – often Machiavellian, especially in foreign policy – of the nobility, which remained more powerful and held the socially higher rank.

This aristocratic tradition changed when it was adopted by circles of the Wilhelminian bourgeoisie. Their efforts at assimilation reflected a hidden yearning to become nobility – something they never could achieve, at least not in one generation. Their emphasis upon violence can be illustrated briefly with an example.

In 1912 Walter Bloem, a popular bourgeois novelist, published a novel entitled *Volk wider Volk* in which he demonstrated the glorious experience of the victorious war of 1870–71. Consider the following description of an episode which indicates this explicitly positive evaluation of violence. It deals with the encounter of German troops with French resistance fighters, who were then called 'snipers' [*Franktireurs*]:

> The snipers were running for their lives. Then one stumbled ... a second later George's black horse shot past the prostrate man – only a brief stroke of his sword struck the upraised arm from behind which came a staring grimace filled with rage and mortal fear. It was a woman ... Now all three were harnessed together, the woman and the two peasants, and then off galloped the squadron. The prisoners had to run till their tongues hung out, unless they wanted to be dragged to death ... and the lancers did not spare their kicks and blows to the neck with lance-shafts ... even the woman received her fair share.... They had long since forgotten to distinguish between humans and brutes ... a captured enemy was nothing but a wild vicious beast.[4]

Feelings and corresponding acts such as these are certainly spontaneous everyday occurrences during the tumult of wars. What is typical of the German bourgeois situation of 1912 is the fact that here this kind of brutality is portrayed in an entertaining novel, quite explicitly and with a certain emphasis, as a sign of a positive and commendable standard of behaviour.

Such documents, of which there are many, clearly indicate that since the time of Schiller and other great German idealists, whose books in their time enjoyed great resonance among the educated German bourgeoisie, a fundamental transformation has taken place. The ultimate identification of human beings with each other, a goal which was perhaps excessively idealistic, is here denied intentionally and emphatically in favour of an exclusively national identification. During war, the common people on the enemy side need no longer be treated as people. These people are nothing but 'wild, vicious beasts'. The popular bourgeois authors obviously expected their readers to share and approve this attitude.

Then, in the year 1914, men and women went to war in a mood of certain victory. I myself, barely seventeen years of age, experienced it as something odd and not quite comprehensible. But I had fellow-students and acquaintances who shared the war mood. A characteristic quotation from the letter of a young law student who died one month later on the Marne exemplifies this mood:

> Hurrah, [he wrote home] finally we're going into the field. Of course,

we'll win. Nothing else is possible for a people who are so determined to win the war. My dear ones, be proud of living in such a time and in such a nation. And that you too have the privilege of sending those you love into such a glorious battle.

The war, as it developed, was actually murderous. The unplanned fighting ran contrary to the generals' preconceived plans. The military leaders on both sides had planned a bold military offensive, as short as possible; the French generals, especially yesterday's losers, expected a 'desperate offensive' and battles 'at a frenzied pace'. The Germans followed the modified Schlieffen plan, according to which the unexpected German invasion into Belgium and from there to France would be such a decisive blow against the French enemy that it might free German troops in the West for the war on the Eastern front. The planned offensives on both sides cancelled each other out. After tremendous losses, they degenerated into a grim trench warfare. This had been foreseen by a few outsiders, who had recognized that the development of weapons technology at that time favoured the defensive over the offensive. H.G. Wells, among others, had foreseen the stationary war.

When the United States (which, together with England, feared a continent ruled by Germany) entered the war, Germany's chances of victory disappeared completely. The inconceivable became a fact: Germany had exhausted its forces and lost the war. The Kaiser and the nobles lost their thrones. The courts, centres of Germany's good society, vanished. This same society which had been capable of rendering satisfaction – extending from the high nobility to the bourgeois student associations, from the field marshal to the bourgeois reserve officer, and united by a single distinctive code of honour – had been suddenly stopped in its race for European hegemony, like someone running with full force into a brick wall. A traumatic shock resulted.

Moreover, the international defeat of the Wilhelminian establishment was accompanied by an at least partial defeat on the domestic front. The end of the old regime and the country's resulting disarray magnified political opportunities for those who had previously been outsiders, especially organized labour. For the first time in German history, their representatives entered government. As usual in such cases, this rise of outsiders with a lower standing – a former saddler became successor to the Kaiser – was felt by many members of German good society to be an unbearable humiliation. The German case indicates in paradigmatic form the reaction of an establishment accustomed to ruling to structural development resulting in a power shift unfavourable to them. Not only revolutions, but also wars produce structural changes in power relations that were being prepared silently under the canopy of the traditional institutional framework. If the war had been won, the masses of people would probably have subordinated themselves to the victorious ruling groups. Instead, the lost war revealed the power shift that had been taking place in the course of Germany's rapid industrialization. In large numbers, soldiers and workers renounced their allegiance to the defeated leadership.

The development of both Germany and terrorism in Germany during the first republic can be better understood if one considers domestic and international power structures, as they were and as they were perceived. The Wilhelminian establishment, now enlarged by formerly excluded merchants and industrialist strata, had suffered a defeat. Clearly they were not willing to accept these international and domestic defeats. At first they did not know exactly how to reverse them. The way soon became very clear.

Similar situations, in which humiliation and the lust for revenge become predominant, have often been evident in the development of human societies. As far back as Antiquity there are documents showing clearly that established power groups perceive their powers over the lower orders as evidence of their higher human worth. The writer of a letter ascribed to Xenophon (probably from the later fifth century BC), who today is usually called 'the old oligarch', considered less powerful groups of people of lesser human value. The author was probably an Athenian aristocrat who had been expelled from Athens, along with other members of his estate, by the revolt of broader popular strata and the introduction of a democratic constitution. He speaks with considerable contempt for the democratic mob. Everyone knows, he writes, that these are undisciplined persons of bad character.[5]

A similar judgement is to be found in the report, dated 2 January 1920, of a Lieutenant Mayer, who had been sent to Würzburg as recruiter for the *Freikorps*, to his superior, Captain Berchthold:

> After not having failed on a single day ... to direct my attention to the people's present mood, my view was confirmed that everyone who stands above the mob longs for liberation from the pigsty, especially

from the Jewish yoke that burdens the people and, what is of
eminently progressive significance, is willing to lend a hand in the
coming work of liberation. The call 'Down with the Jews! Down with
the traitors of our nation!' resounds from the beer-hall. Posters and
slogans everywhere say the same thing. Erzberger is hanged repeatedly every evening.... Two gentlemen of the local *Reichswehr* are
joining us with their men. I hope to win over two more.[6]

This passage accurately describes the mood in' the more
respected circles of Würzburg at the beginning of 1920. At the
same time it describes the mentality of the *Freikorps*, who were
then the main agents of the extragovernmental political violence.
Their recruitment in wider circles prepared a putsch against the
hated parliamentary republic. As is well known, the first attempt
at such a putsch – the Kapp Putsch – failed. One of the *Freikorps*,
the Erhard Naval Brigade, was involved directly in this affair.
Later it gave rise to the undercover terrorist organization 'Consul'
which, among other things, attempted systematically to murder
undesirable prominent politicians.

Among the members of this organization were the murderers
of the parliamentary representative Erzberger, who was attacked
and shot to death on 26 August 1921, while walking in the Black
Forest. His companion, the representative Dietz, escaped with a
gunshot wound. The murderers, Heinrich Schulz and Heinrich
Tillessen, were former officers, belonged to the staff of the Erhard
Brigade, and were in the employ of a leading Bavarian politician,
Privy Councillor Heim. They were members of the German Fold
Protective League and other nationalist associations. After the
assassination the two men travelled to Munich, where the assassination had been planned. From there they fled, with false
passports issued by the Bavarian police, to Hungary, where they
were arrested briefly but then released after a telephone convers-
ation with a Bavarian authority. Their superior in 'Consul',
Captain-Lieutenant von Killinger, a former officer who had
fought against the Bavarian Council Republic and later participated in the Kapp Putsch, was accused of complicity in
Erzberger's murder but acquitted by the court in Offenburg.[7]

It is hard to estimate how many people were murdered as
political undesirables in the first years of the Weimar Republic by
members of the *Freikorps* and student associations close to them;
probably several hundred, perhaps more than a thousand.
Among them were prominent Communists such as Rosa Luxemburg and Karl Liebknecht, who after a fruitless working-class

uprising were dragged from a besieged house and, as far as can be determined, beaten to death with clubs on the way to prison. There were also lesser-known persons such as my schoolmate Bernhard Schottländer. With his thick glasses, he already looked like a young scholar in the first year of school. After reading Marx he leaned toward Communism and his body, if I remember correctly, was pulled out of the Breslau canal wrapped in barbed wire. There were liberal politicians such as Rathenau, and many whose names are forgotten.

Like most terrorists in the Bundesrepublik today, the terrorists of the Weimar Republic came mostly from bourgeois homes, with a minority coming from the nobility – mostly younger people. The younger cadres of Wilhelminian good society were either officers or students. From these two groups the terrorists of the Weimar Republic were recruited. Thus, a Bavarian pamphlet on the preparation of dictatorship contains a special section: 'Mobilization of the *Reichswehr* and the Student Body'.[8] Another pamphlet, also from the time of the Kapp Putsch, says under the heading 'Student Body':

> The mobilization committee must immediately establish contact with spokesmen of the student body, to ascertain to what degree students are organized and which of its parts are still uncommitted. Here it is especially important to establish who will become opponents due to their fanaticism, and who therefore must be eliminated. The principle must remain that the student body is organized in some campaigns or march groups, as a main reserve. For our main strength is in the student body.[9]

At that time the bulk of the students supported those who – together with the *Freikorps* and other military organizations – sought to put an end, if necessary through violence, to the younger parliamentary republic, replacing it with a strongly militaristic dictatorship. Of course, there were exceptions: students who did not support a 'revolt of the Fatherland' against the existing republic and were also against a military-bourgeois dictatorship. But then those were, as the terrorists at that time saw it, fanatics who had to be murdered. The idea that the murder of political opponents is acceptable seemed to be taken for granted.

It was not limited to one side. The war left considerable unrest and much bitterness in working-class circles. Perhaps they would have endured their often arrogant subordination if the Kaiser and his generals had won. But the defeat proved that they had been misled, that their leaders' promises had been empty, and that the hardship of the war had been in vain. The failed Kapp Putsch also stirred up bitterness among the workers. The hatred was mutual. When the Erhard Brigade withdrew from Berlin after the failure of the Putsch, it was jeered by the crowd. Some of the retreating troops simply turned around and fired into the crowd. About a dozen dead and many wounded were left on Pariser Platz.[10]

As always, mutual hatred and violence escalated on both sides. Thus in Schöneberg, on the day after the withdrawal of the Erhard Brigade, there was a clash between local inhabitants and the small military surveillance groups stationed there. Already at the time of the Kapp Putsch to the north and east of Berlin, as well as in parts of its suburbs, officers could not appear in uniform without running the danger of being attacked and roughed up by the inhabitants. The military leaders of the Kapp Putsch did organize troops primarily made up of former officers to keep order. But at the end of the Putsch these troops, who patrolled in relatively small groups, found themselves in the greatest danger from the mass of the local population. The officers stationed in Schöneberg received instructions to move out without weapons in order not to irritate the population. They were supposed to be taken to Lichterfelde in two waiting trucks. But after a hundred metres, the trucks were stopped by the pressing crowd. The agitated crowd threw stones and beer bottles at the officers. One of the trucks attempted to drive on. The crowds attacked the officers. In the ensuing brawl, nine officers were trampled to the ground and killed. The rest were pulled out, beaten and wounded, and taken to safety by the police, who had been called.[11] Similar scenes took place during the workers' uprising in the Ruhr region.

These events exemplify the previously mentioned double-bind process of violence. But compared with the Russian events – and especially with the organization of their predominantly agrarian masses for violent revolution – German industrial workers were at a disadvantage in mobilizing for violence. Apparently, the German Communist Party tried to transform workers' spontaneous excitement and local clashes and struggles with the *Freikorps* or *Reichswehr* into an organized military action. But the setting up of a high command in Mühlheim-Ruhr by a proclamation of the military leadership on 28 March 1920 did not have the desired effect. It failed to subordinate the local workers' associations to the military high command. Repeatedly, local leaders acted on their own initiative. It was easier at that time to change, at short notice, peasants accustomed to obedience into battle-ready troops rather than independent and self-confident industrial workers. At any rate, this seems to have been one of the experiences of the Ruhr uprising.

This experience, however, also throws light on the peculiar course of the double-bind process operating between the younger bourgeois officers and students and the workers. Both sides sought to realize their political goals through military force. It is unclear how intact the Russian officers' corps remained after the Czar's abdication. The German officers' corps remained fully operational as a unified cadre after the Kaiser's abdication. Its *esprit de corps* also remained intact. The army's supreme command was even partly responsible for the continuing integration of the state. The Allies, however, imposed severe restrictions on the German army. They had had enough of German militarism, yet they were no less afraid of the rise of Russian Communism in Germany. As a compromise they allowed Germany an army of 100,000 men rather than 400,000. This meant placing considerable numerical restrictions on the officers' corps. Many officers returning home from the field were relatively young. Most had no other ambition than to remain officers. They considered military service the only profession they understood and enjoyed. What were they to do? The voluntary units of the *Freikorps* provided the answer. There were many of them. They always formed around former officers with definite leadership qualities; for these for the most part young bourgeois groups there was a spectrum of clear enemies whom they attempted to fight with all available means when the opportunity arose.

On top of the list of these enemies were all groups labelled 'Bolsheviks'. These mainly comprised those parts of the working class who, whether under the influence of Communist cadres or spontaneously, participated in revolts and, consciously or not, tried to overthrow the parliamentary German republic in favour of a council republic. In addition, there was the parliamentary republic itself – especially those members of government or parliament who supported the signing of a peace treaty (the 'shameful peace') and the fulfilment of its conditions. The antipathy of the *Freikorps* for the republic (the 'pigsty'), parliament ('gossip shops') and especially the representatives of social democracy (the 'party bosses') who now occupied influential government positions was only marginally less intense than that directed against the Bolsheviks.

Nevertheless, the balance of power between the two sides was highly uneven. Despite their mercenary nature and unruliness, the *Freikorps* had military tradition in their bones. They were disciplined fighting troops as long as their sometimes charismatic leaders had their confidence. They were opposed by relatively undisciplined workers who at short notice and spontaneously were often to fight, but felt uneasy with the long-term military discipline necessary to carry out strategic struggles. Thus the *Freikorps* were able to gain the upper hand with relative ease, especially since they often received support from the *Reichswehr*. They were not only better trained but better armed than the fighting workers. Consequently, during the first years of the Weimar Republic the likelihood of successful workers' uprisings was very limited because the old officers' corps had remained essentially intact and because of the Allies' hostility to any spreading of the Russian Revolution.

But the Bolshevik danger was extremely important for the *Freikorps* and *Reichswehr*, since it legitimised their existence. By alluding to the Russian Revolution and the danger of its expansion, not only the *Freikorps* and the *Reichswehr* but many other 'fatherland' groups formed at the time (including the terrorist organizations) could count on the support of a broad circle of sympathizers within the bourgeoisie and the nobility. Hitler's subsequent success – especially in overcoming the Allies' opposition to German rearmament – can also be understood as a consequence of the Russian Revolution. It was the expression of the universal distaste of broad bourgeois circles, and even of considerable parts of the working class, for the 'spectre of Bolshevism' and the spreading of the Russian model of revolution to other countries.

Immediately after the war the realization of many dreams and wishes of the *Freikorps* was still far off. Thousands of officers were at the end of their careers because of the defeat and disarmament. Many had been fighting at the front for years. It was rarely possible to find a civilian position that matched their experience and status expectations. Many hoped to continue their officer careers in the regular army when Germany could again muster a larger *Wehrmacht*. This was reason enough for them to hate the republic, whose 'compliance politics' seemed to stifle these hopes. Others saw a new future in the Baltic provinces, where a German upper class had lived off the fat of the land. German Baltic large landowners and a few leaders of the Latvian national movement promised German freebooters land to settle on, if they helped emancipate them from Russian hegemony. So a whole group of *Freikorps* moved to the Baltic. There they could help fight against their most hated opponent, the Bolsheviks. They hoped, perhaps, that they could make up for the loss of Alsace-Lorraine by the annexation of the Baltic provinces to Germany. At the same time, by acquiring land they could expect a new livelihood appropriate to their class.

The slide of some of these groups into political terrorism against the new German state cannot be understood independently of this Baltic campaign. A few quotations from Ernst von Salomon's more or less autobiographical novel *Die Geächteten* (*The Outlawed*) can clarify the way people moved toward the systematic organization of murder and other forms of violence as a way of weakening and destroying a hated regime.[12]

Von Salomon, who was part of the circle of the murderers of Rathenau, indicated the direction of this development by the chapter headings of his novel. These included: I. The Dispersed; II. The Conspirators, and III. The Criminals. The stages individuals passed through in the 1920s were as follows: I. Officers in the Wilhelminian wartime army (or, if they were too young, cadets in the Prussian Cadet Corps); II. Members of one of the Freikorps, often participating in their unsuccessful Baltic campaign; and III. Members of a conspiratorial secret society of a terrorist kind. One could add entrance into the Nazi Party as the IV stage, which for many of the disbanded former members of the *Freikorps* meant at last the chance of securing a career and the ultimately illusory fulfilment of their political hopes. It has been claimed, not without justification, that the rise of Hitler would hardly have been possible without the organizational and military contribution of former *Freikorps* members.

As a young man just out of the cadet corps, von Salomon had ended up in a Hamburg *Freikorps* under the leadership of a Lieutenant Wuth. There he found himself in the company of somewhat wild and romantic adventurers with trooper-like customs. This is how the memory of a military advance appeared to him:

> For those of use who went to the Baltic, the word 'advance' had a mysterious, happy, dangerous sound ... the sound of a new togetherness ... the cutting of all ties to a sinking, rotten world, with which the real soldier no longer had anything in common.[13]

This clearly shows a characteristic stage of the process leading to terrorism. One feels like a detached outsider in relation to a society that appears to be completely rotten. This society seems to be dying and one hopes that it will die, even though it is not clear what will happen after it is dead. The irony here is that instead of the young and fragile German republic which seemed to be a rotten and dying world, it was precisely the old society, in which one had grown up, that was defeated. Imperial Germany had perished, but countless numbers of its representatives survived. Their mission in life had disappeared with the *Kaiserreich*. Education at the military academy had prepared Salomon for an officer's career in the Prussian army. The old army had disintegrated, while a new, much smaller one was just being formed. The top military leader had moved to Holland. Where in this republic, which originated from military defeat, was there still a meaningful place for men like him?

The Baltic campaign provided new hope. If the Baltic provinces, where for centuries German big landowners had played a leading role, could be detached from Russia by fighting the Red Army and annexed to Germany, then – this was the dream – the defeat and loss of territory in the west could be compensated for by gains in the east. Moreover, one could acquire a new position – perhaps even a landholding – adequate to one's class. At least, that was the promise made to those mercenaries who went to the Baltic. No one asked what the victorious enemies or the German government in Berlin would say to settlement of the Russian Baltic provinces. World politics seemed far away, and the dream was beautiful. However much this dream appeared as the new and better future which these men contrasted with a shabby republican Germany hated for its peace policy, what they were really dreaming of was a restoration of the old world: the restoration of a Germany Reich with a mighty army, in whose hierarchy officers and military values could again occupy the high position which was their due. Military discipline, toughness and guts would again win the high esteem they deserved. Bourgeois indolence and moral scruples deserved contempt, along with the civilians ruling in Berlin and the parliamentarians who talked a lot and did little.

For the freebooters in the Baltic, this parliamentary republic was an alien world. Unlike the old army, here their cohesion was no longer secured by either a state-sanctioned, bureaucratically elaborated set of military regulations or by an officer hierarchy whose crowning symbol was the sublime figure of the Kaiser. Basically, the men of the *Freikorps* felt obligated to no one except their own group. Just about every *Freikorps* had its own charismatic leader. His personal authority, his personal engagement in battle, his implicit promise of victory, booty and a better future held the group together and was decisive for its solidarity and fighting capacity.

Lieutenant Wuth, leader of the Hamburg *Freikorps*, was one of these charismatic leaders. As von Salomon describes him, he was a tall, tanned, rugged man. He used to rub a wild boar's tooth on his bristly beard, and before every battle he exchanged his field cap for a velvet beret of the kind worn by hikers. The Baltic battles were hard, the losses high, but hope persisted. And life was unconstrained and free, an alternative to the staid, stiff and cramped bourgeois life.

Then came the blow that destroyed their hopes. The unthinkable happened: the government reresentatives signed the terrible peace treaty that sealed the humiliating defeat. Von Salomon describes this traumatic experience:

> One day, at the beginning of the truce, we were sitting in Lieutenant Wuth's house. Schlageter had come to visit. We were discussing the possibility of a settlement in this country. Wuth wanted to buy a farm and a sawmill.... Then Lieutenant Kay entered the room and said hastily into the tobacco smoke: 'Germany has signed the peace treaty!' For a moment everyone was quiet, so quiet that the room almost shook as Schlageter stood up.... He paused, stared into space, and then said, with an angry tone in his voice: 'What concern is that of ours?' And he slammed the door.... We were shocked. We heard this and were astonished at how little all this really concerned us ...[14]

For a time they could actually believe that this far away event did not concern them. But the invisible threads linking them with the distant homeland were quickly felt. In reality, they were nothing but scattered German troops in remote Russian territories. The signing of the peace treaty by the newcomers who now represented Germany sealed their destiny, and they felt betrayed:

> We looked at one another, shivering. We suddenly felt the coldness of an unspeakable loneliness. We had believed that the country would never dismiss us, that it linked us with an indestructible stream, that it fed our secret wishes and justified our actions. Now everything was finished. The signature released us.[15]

This passage suggests the far-reaching emotional significance of the Berlin government's failure to say loudly and clearly in public: 'On the advice of the army's supreme command, our representatives have signed the peace treaty, just as it was presented to us.' Hindenburg's oft-praised peasant's craftiness had managed to shift the odium of signing the peace treaty and, hence, the military defeat on to the representatives of the parliamentary republic. This permitted those who felt disadvantaged by the republic to reject it.

The shock of signing so humiliating and burdensome a treaty may in other cases have had a somewhat different psychological effect, but the traumatic effect on the freebooters had exemplary significance. They knew nothing of the compelling circumstances that had caused the government to sign such a treaty. Perhaps they would have accepted it if the Kaiser or Hindenburg and Ludendorff had signed. But now men considered parvenus by the tradition of the old honourable society (and especially by those trained for the officer corps) seemed solely responsible for signing this peace treaty. Under pressure from *entente* and in accord with the peace treaty, the Berlin government finally ordered the withdrawal of German *Freikorps* out of the Baltic area. At this point many freebooters renounced their allegiance to the German government. They stayed and fought on not against the Red Army, which had retreated already, but against reorganized Latvian and Estonian troops supported by English warships.

Little by little, the *Freikorps* were pushed back. That was their second traumatic experience. Men who could not accept that Germany had been defeated in the west now personally experienced defeat in the east. The *Freikorps* position in the Baltic region gradually became untenable. When the first severe frosts of the Russian autumn came, lack of clothing supplies from the homeland slowly began to be felt. Many men lacked coats. Field jackets and trousers were tattered. Their boots had holes in them. And the locals constantly pressured the retreating troops, as the Russians had Napoleon's. Finally, rage erupted among the hard-pressed freebooters with their destroyed hopes. Salomon and others[16] have described what then happened. They struck back in rage and despair. Their last remnants of humanity were lost:

> We made the last thrusts. Yes, we got up once more and charged on a wide front. Once again, we drew the last man out of cover, poured over the snow-covered fields, and charged into the forests. We fired into surprised crowds, and raged and shot and struck and hunted. We drove the Latvians across the fields like rabbits and set fire to every house and blasted every bridge to dust and cut every telegraph pole. We threw the corpses into the wells and threw in hand grenades. We killed whoever we captured, we burned whatever would burn. We saw red, we no longer had any human feelings in our hearts. Wherever we

had camped, the ground groaned under our destruction. Where we had stormed, where formerly houses had stood, there now lay rubble, ashes, and glimmering beams, like abscesses in the bare fields. A huge trail of smoke marked our paths. We had ignited a huge pile of wood, which burned more than dead matter. On it burned our hopes, our desires: the bourgeois tablets, the laws and values of the civilised world, everything that we had dragged along with us as moth-eaten rubbish, the values and faith in the things and ideas of the time that had abandoned us. We pulled back, boasting, exhilarated, loaded with booty. The Latvians had never stood their ground. But the next day they returned.[17]

This account exemplifies a path towards barbarity and dehumanization which always takes considerable time to unfold in relatively civilized societies. Terror and horror hardly appear in such societies without a long process of social disintegration. All too often the act of naked violence as a group goal, with or without state legitmation, is analysed with the help of short-term, static explanations. That may be meaningful if one is not seeking explanations but only attempting to establish culpability. It is easy to see barbarism and de-civilization as the expression of a free personal decision, but that kind of voluntarist explanation is shallow and unhelpful.

If the *Freikorps* pattern of development is viewed as one of the routes to violent extragovernmental acts of terrorism during Weimar, as well as to state violence during Hitler's time, then one can better understand the extended, if less visible gestation period which precedes the more striking great acts of barbarism that otherwise seem to spring up out of nothing.

The men involved in the rage and madness in the Baltic – a few of whom, like Von Salomon himself, later sought to destroy the hated republic through terror – had set out with great expectations. Adventure attracted them. They dreamed of great successes. When signs of failure and defeat multiplied, they resisted. They wrapped themselves in their dream as if it were a protective garment. But when the grim reality finally caught up with them, they completely lost control. Their dream shattered under the growing pressure of a frustrating reality. In rage and despair they killed everyone who crossed their path. They pursued a course which some of them would later continue in secret organizations after their return to their homeland. They set out to destroy a world which refused them fulfilment and purpose and which therefore seemed meaningless.

In the preparations to destroy the Weimar government and to

set up a dictatorship, their hopes again revived. When the Kapp Putsch destroyed this hope, some members of the *Freikorps* saw no other way to undermine and crush the hatred regime than through terror. At the time, a group of former officers, mostly members of the Erhard Brigade, formed a secret organization. The murder of prominent politicians was to be a fanfare. With their help the rotten regime was supposed to become so undermined from within that it would collapse. Hitler then succeeded at what the *Freikorps* leaders failed to achieve: the actual destruction of the Weimar parliamentary regime. He succeeded largely because he concentrated on mobilizing the masses through extraparliamentary violence and extraparty propaganda. The *Freikorps* were among his most important forerunners. Their goals were in many ways identical with his. But despite the savageness of their attitude, they remained loyal to the officer tradition – the tradition of the old noble-bourgeois honourable society. Hitler, the lance corporal, broke through these elitist barriers, transferring the officers-and-students' movement into a broad populist movement without elitist restrictions.

Notes

1. *Über den Prozess der Zivilisation*, Basel 1939, trans. as *State Formation and Civilisation*, Oxford 1982.
2. Ibid.
3. But they can also be used in domestic conflicts to support one social stratum or a certain party in the struggle against others. The monopoly of violence has two faces.
4. Walter Bloem, *Volk wider Volk*, Berlin 1912, pp. 252 ff.
5. Quoted in a new introduction, 'A Theoretical Essay in Established-Outsiders Relations', in a Dutch translation, in *De gevestigden en de buitenstaanders*, Utrecht and Antwerp 1976.
6. E.J. Gumbel, *Verschwörer*, Vienna 1924, p. 14.
7. Ibid., p. 45.
8. Ibid., p. 29.
9. Ibid., p. 27.
10. Freidrich Wilhelm von Oertzen, *Kamerad, reich mir die Hände*, Berlin 1933, p. 156.
11. Ibid., pp. 158–9.
12. Ernst von Salomon, *Die Geächteten*, Berlin 1931.
13. Ibid., p. 69.
14. Ibid., p. 109.
15. Ibid., p. 110.
16. Von Oertzen, p. 131.
17. Von Salomon, pp. 144 ff.

The Decline of Social Visibility*

Pierre Rosanvallon

Overcoming the 'Nationalism or Privatization' Alternative

The present debate about the welfare state is trapped within the state control or privatization alternative. Economic arguments and ideological prejudice combine to polarize the issue along the lines of: *either* increased socialization *or* the pursuit of a new equilibrium based on an extension of private ownership. The future is conceived solely in terms of either the '*statist*' scenario or the '*liberal*' solution. And since the issue is presented solely in these terms, any middle way (such as advocating maintenance of the status quo) is a priori ruled out.

In view of the present discrepancy between the rates of growth and the 'natural' development rate of social spending, maintaining the present level of compulsory levies in relation to the GNP would effectively imply a reduction in social cover and, hence, increased privatization. This 'pincer effect' inevitably implies a choice. To deny it means automatically accepting a mechanical increase in the level of compulsory levies. Are we condemned, therefore, to having to choose between two unacceptable scenarios? The statist solution would result in serious financial difficulties in the present situation – but above all, it would be confronted by a diffuse social resistance that would be hard to overcome. Of course, one could point out that the level of compulsory levies in

---

*Translated by Gerald Turner.

Scandinavia far exceeds 50 per cent, and thereby infer that French society has yet to reach the limits of 'acceptable' socialization. However, in a period of low growth the point is scarcely relevant. Moreover, 'something' will have to happen before the welfare state can develop without engendering ever more resentment and opposition. That 'something', which would act as a spur to a collective will and give significance to stronger redistribution mechanisms, is one of the greatest challenges of the present period.

If there is no change in the relationship between the state and society, and if society itself fails to redefine the relationships among its individuals and groups, a further rise in taxation 'out of the blue' could create a condition of social paralysis or deadlock. We would remain trapped within the contradictions of the statist scenario. We would see a burgeoning of all the negative effects that accompanied the sharp rise in compulsory levies in the 1970s: growth in the underground economy and moonlighting and increased segmentation of the labour market. The creation of a dual society and dual economy are in fact a compensatory self-defence mechanism which society has developed to attenuate the extension of socialization and its implied costs. In this way, private firms and individuals seek to take back with one hand what they have to pay the state with the other. This gives rise to many instances of inequality: inequality engendered by dualism (for example between 'exposed' workers and 'protected' workers) and great discrepancies in the capacity of different individuals to benefit from it. Social effort, which in theory should generate greater equality, ends up multiplying the hidden inequalities and dislocating the scope for collective identity (of which regular working-class 'explosions' are an example).

The liberal scenario produces effects that are more immediately visible. It automatically means turning the clock back and reducing the process of equitable redistribution. It is a scenario of social regression. It presupposes a strong state prepared to confront any revolts that may arise. It also implies a deficit of legitimacy, which the intellectual reconstruction of neo-liberalism is in no position to furnish, however much it appeals to the middle classes. In the final analysis, this scenario is viable only in terms of a cynical decision to establish a social coalition to the sole detriment of the most deprived minority of the population.

Thus, in their different ways, both statist and liberal scenarios are unacceptable. Hence there can be no positive solution to the crisis of the welfare state if we remain locked into the nationalization/privatization dilemma. Furthermore, neither alternative offers a context within which to consider what 'social progress' will mean in the future. Both depend on the hypothesis that 'social development' has reached its limits (in a certain sense): the statist scenario behaves as if a sort of optional form of the state has been attained, a state that has only to be perfected, while the liberal scenario challenges it for reasons of economic equilibrium. Each case is argued solely in terms of social needs as expressed – and at least partly taken care of – at the present time. Neither imagines that new needs or demands might emerge in the coming years or decades. That will certainly not prevent them from emerging. The right to culture, environmental concerns, and other needs could become as costly in the future as the right to health. If these needs are regarded as rights, it will have to be recognized that a redistribution is required. The scope of demand for 'public services' could extend to new horizons. Neither of the two scenarios offers any prospect of tackling such a situation. They are both recipes for social paralysis, from which they offer no way forward.

It is therefore urgent to break out of the nationalization/privatization straitjacket. But how? Essentially, by redefining the frontiers and links between the state and society. The central issue raised by the crisis of the welfare state is simultaneously sociological and political. By reasoning solely in terms of 'nationalization or privatization' one mystifies the issue by restricting it to its financial aspects. 'Who is to foot the bill for social spending?' ignores the equally relevant question: 'What constitutes a public service?'

From this perspective there can be only one way forward for the welfare state, and it has to be pluralist. Somehow we have to overcome our misconception that public service = state control = non-profit-making = equality, and that private service = the market = profit-making = inequality. The way forward for the welfare state requires a new combination of these different components. The monopolistic logic of nationalization has to be abandoned in favour of a dynamic, triple combination of mechanisms of socialization, decentralization and greater autonomy:

- More flexible *socialization* by means of less bureaucracy and the rationalization of major amenities and public services; a lot more can be done in this sphere to simplify and improve administrative practices, but it is no longer a new approach *per se*.

- *Decentralization* by restructuring and converting certain public services to make them more accessible to their users; the aim would be to involve local communities far more in social and cultural questions and to encourage them to assume a greater share of responsibility for them.

- Greater *self-sufficiency*, achieved by handing over certain public-service responsibilities to non-state groups (associations, foundations, and so on). This approach promises to be the most innovatory and effective way of tackling the difficulties of the welfare state and confronting the questions of future social needs.

In broader terms, this alternative to the crisis of the welfare state makes sense only as part of a three-pronged approach of reducing the requirement for state intervention, reinstating mutual support as a function of society, and creating greater visibility for the social.

Reducing the State Intervention Requirement

The welfare state has expanded over the past hundred years or so as almost a natural response to the demand for social progress. Throughout that period liberal theorists and politicians have done nothing but deplore it, while proving incapable of halting its expansion. They have almost always had to play the role of spectators or even actors in a movement to which they have had fundamental objections. The 'liberal mind' has always found itself confronted by this paradox without ever really managing to cope with it. In the mid nineteenth century, for instance, Édouard Laboulaye asserted:

> In terms of actual practice, the omnipotence of the state has never been as openly acknowledged as now, whereas in terms of theory, its omnipotence is on the wane. Whilst administration makes greater and greater inroads, science resists this process and warns against this unwarranted and dangerous invasion.[1]

Present-day liberal theorists repeat this claim in practically the same terms. Meanwhile, the opponents of economic liberalism find themselves virtually in the same boat: they are incapable of envisaging social progress except in terms of an extension of the welfare state. They are incapable of regarding any curbs on the welfare state as being other than regressive, reactionary and antisocial.

What is lacking in each case is an analysis of the sociological mechanisms that give rise to the requirement for state intervention in the social sphere. The latter is regarded by each side as a fact of life – as either a positive or a negative given which is external to the economic and social system. Such an attitude reflects a purely instrumental concept of the state (whether of a minimal or a socially active variety). The demand for state intervention (in France, at least) is explained solely in terms of historical or psychological arguments, such as the awful weight of the Jacobin tradition, the influence of a fog-shrouded past ('the daughter of centuries', Laboulaye called it), the need for security, fear of responsibility, and so forth. What all such explanations have in common is their insensitivity to a concrete awareness or action, apart perhaps from the – necessarily gradual – transformation of *mentalités*.

It is precisely this demand for state intervention that we will have to analyse if the welfare state issue is to be considered from a new angle. We have to realize that it has sociological roots and that it is in fact no more than the other side of the coin of the extension of individualism. The liberal individual and the administrative state go hand in hand. The phenomenon of social massification always accompanies the trend towards social fragmentation; the two developments are not contradictory but complementary. In such circumstances the social bond is torn between two extremes, while the system for satisfying needs is itself bipolar: either the market or the state. No other scope exists for satisfying needs. The limits of the market, which result either from the structures for distributing primary incomes or the market's own dysfunctions, thereby serve mechanically to reinforce the state intervention requirement in all spheres. The satisfaction of social needs is governed completely by this dichotomy, which results in an extraordinary *inflexibility*. The crisis of the welfare state is in large measure an expression of the exponential social costs of this inflexibiity. The forms of solidarity currently secured by the state, as well as the way services and social provision develop, are no longer adequate to compensate for social fragmentation. Hypersocialization from above is incapable of coping with the demands induced by desocialization from below.

The state intervention requirement cannot therefore be regarded as an exogenous or autonomous variable. It is dependent on the *form of the social*, particularly its density and texture. If the social were no more than a network of independent and separate individuals, the state might eventually satisfy their needs. This would represent the only conceivable form of social solidarity, the only expression of collective life.[2] Reducing the state intervention requirement and promoting sociability therefore go hand in hand. The alternative to the welfare state is not primarily institutional, but societal. The task is to bring into being a civil society of greater density and to develop its scope for exchange and mutual support, instead of 'externalizing' these needs and abandoning their satisfaction to the twin poles of market or state. We will come back to this fundamental point later.

Clearly there is no way in which the state itself can be instrumental in bringing about such a reconstitution of society. The state cannot be employed to reduce state intervention. It would be inappropriate here to describe how this reduction should take place, as if it were programmable. What we must do instead is to define some of the necessary conditions that must be fulfilled if society is to carry out the task itself.

To begin with, the law must be adapted to the task. It too is bipolar and centred both on the individual (in the form of the *Code civil*, common law) and on the state. The 'sovereign, autonomous individual', as a particular and abstract representative of the human species, is the supreme purpose of the law, while at the same time the limitation of the individual's 'external' freedom is the law's sole function. In the eyes of the law the state merely embodies the supreme wills of individuals, conceived as their fusion into a single unit: Hobbes's 'multitude united in a single person'. As Gurvitch explains, this essentially individualistic view of the law means that the submission of a multitude of isolated and equalized individuals to the abstract generality of the law is 'the only possible manifestation of the legal community, whose members have no concrete links with each other'.[3]

Our own particular individualist-cum-statist legal framework provides no scope for the existence of any other form of grouping that may come into being within civil society, apart from those of enterprise or association. Yet neither enterprises nor associations have given rise to an independent law adapted to their particular social function. It was to fill this gap that Gurvitch developed the ideas pioneered by Duguit and Hauriou and spoke in terms of the establishment of a theory of social law. His aim was to overcome the discrepancy between social realities – which cannot be assessed solely in terms of the individual or the state – and the law, by recognizing the need for 'active communities' to become the normative points of reference capable of engendering a separate, autonomous law:

> The theory of social law aims to build a legal framework for a whole series of social realities which are usually excluded or disregarded by jurisprudence, such as the relationship between the organized and unorganized sections of social life; the link between 'Society' and 'the State'; the engendering of law within each individual cell of society; the spontaneous existence of law beyond preconceived bounds, etc.[4]

A legal effort of this kind is a precondition for any non-statist forms of socialization. I indicated in *L'Age de l'autogestion*[5] how such an approach could be adopted to enterprise and the consequences it would have in terms of ownership of the means of production, by pursuing the ideal of *dépropriation*. The definition of positive alternatives to the welfare state requires, on the one hand, that segments of civil society (neighbourhood groups, mutual aid networks, structures for running a community service, and so forth) be recognized as legal subjects and enjoy the right to establish laws independent of state law.[6] Such 'social institutions' are coming into being all the time. However, those which assume the official status of an 'association' are in an extremely precarious situation in that their every action is governed by the norms of state law. Progress towards a more 'flexible', less rigid society means that the law must become pluralist, that there should be a social law at least partly independent from state law (on the lines, perhaps, of the relationship between the law engendered by collective agreements on the one hand and the labour code on the other).

Such an immense revolution in our present forms of legal and political representation would mean moving beyond the welfare state as the sole expression and instrument of collective mutual support. This is not the only gain that would result from the abandonment of the costly confusion of 'public' and 'state'. It would also represent enormous progress were this problem to be considered intellectually from a new angle. And in practical terms, for instance, there is no reason why recognition should not be given to a *droit de substituabilité* (the right of private individuals to determine the use of a certain portion of their income tax) lying between the social sphere and the state sphere in matters of collective services (such as child playgroups). This would mean that when individuals come together to supply each other with a 'public service' usually provided by a specialized institution, the state would recognize – particularly in the form of a tax deduction – that their 'private' initiative fulfilled an essentially 'public' function. The only way to reduce the state intervention requirement in a non-regressive fashion is to encourage a multiplication of community self-help initiatives or locally organized, small-scale public services. So long as the boundaries between state and society, private and public remain rigid we will be condemned to paying more and more for a welfare state whose performance becomes relatively less and less efficient and effective.

Restoring Mutual Support to Society

The welfare state is a way of reintroducing an economic element into the sphere of the social by correcting and compensating for the effects of the market. The crisis afflicting this state derives principally from the way economic considerations were asserted, rather than from the economic principle *per se*. The machinery for engendering mutual support has become abstract, formal and diffuse. The development of bureaucratic practices and the growing burden of social regulation are fed by this abstraction and in turn reinforce it; hence the relative drop in their efficacy. As a means of reconciling social and economic factors, the welfare-state principle ends up operating in an excessively remote fashion. Increasingly, it towers above society; the gap it has created between the individual and the social sphere is now too great.

How can it be remedied? There is no other course possible but to bring society closer to itself. There must be an effort to fill out society, to increase its density by creating more and more intermediate locations fulfilling social functions, and by encouraging individual involvement in networks of direct mutual support. The welfare state derives essentially from an inadequate reading of social geography. It disregards its patterns of closeness or remoteness, dissemination or agglomeration. However, mechanisms of distribution and the supply of collective services are affected by the spatial structures of the social sphere. The situation of individuals cannot be understood independently of their location in social space. Poverty, for instance, cannot be defined entirely in terms of income. The degree of people's isolation and their location (town or country) can exacerbate the effects of low income. An individual who receives a minimum state pension but has a kitchen garden and enjoys close family and neighbourhood ties has a different standard of living from someone living cut off in a sixth-floor city flat.

What is meant here by 'filling out' society? At the outset, it is necessary to clear away a fundamental misconception. This concerns the utopia of 'community': the formation of small groups in which individuals would constitute a sort of extended family on a virtually self-sufficient basis. What is striking about this utopia is that it conceives the alternative to the society of market relations, individualism and desocialization in the nostalgic terms of a return to the community form.

The methodological distinction between the organic community and the individualistic society, considered as sociological ideal-types, is here transformed into a value judgement. The problem becomes that of rediscovering the 'good' community, as opposed to the 'bad' society. Logically associated with this value judgement is a veritable historical mythology concerning the evolution of family structures. From Bonald to Le Play, traditionalist 'sociology' sought to construct an imaginary object: the extended patriarchal family as a vast grouping of solidarity among the generations. Not until the research by Philippe Ariès did we discover that 'the often described theoretical evolution of the extended family into the nuclear family has no basis in reality.'[7] It is therefore impossible to *return* to a form of extended family. Although, broadly speaking, the accession of the individual has been the central characteristic of modernity, this does not mean it can be condemned as negative and made to serve as the basis for overhasty historical reconstructions. The transition from *Gemeinschaft* to *Gesellschaft* did not entail the transformation of generous mutual support into widespread egoism.

On the contrary, *Gesellschaft* evolved precisely because it seemed a formidable instrument of emancipation. The city always meant both the marketplace and a domain of freedom. It encouraged greater freedom by extending the bounds of the possible: deterritorializing individuals by making them independent of the land to which they had been previously assigned, thereby saving them from the repetitive and stifling circle of a circumscribed universe. Throughout the nineteenth century, the emancipatory nature of the town was asserted again and again.

This phenomenon still applies. It would be an illusion to think it is now finished. On the contrary, there is evidence everywhere that the demand for independence that typifies our culture is still a vital factor. Women's growing involvement in employment is a sign of this. Their entry into the labour market is the precondition for greater independence, despite the implicit exploitation. We are only just detecting the first signs of a new revolution: children's desire for independence from their parents. There is even a movement in Sweden that demands the right of children to 'divorce' their parents (financial independence being asserted as a right)!

The failure of the various communitarian experiments in the 1960s and 1970s is linked to the extraordinary power of this aspiration for autonomy and independence. It cannot be ignored when defining an alternative to the welfare state. The goal of closer relations within society cannot be achieved by means of nostalgic and backward-looking scenarios. It is pointless to dream of a renewed 'hearth and home' as a counterbalance to market-based socialization. How otherwise are we to reconcile the emergence of new non-state forms of mutual support with the desire for autonomy?

It is important to stress that there can be no *theoretical* response to this question. It is not necessary to define a sociological ideal-type that would be neither community nor society: to imagine a social 'model' between holism and individualism, as Louis Dumont puts it.[8] The formulation of a social policy is not something to be confused with the definition of a sociological concept. The 'sociohistorical' is never a pure expression of an ideal-type; it is always a complex and tangled reality which the sociologist seeks to unravel. In any event, the welfare state would have failed long ago if society were in fact as it is represented ideal-typically: merely a collection of individuals, forever fragmented in a radical way. The only reason our society functions is because it actually contradicts – albeit partially and to a limited degree – the individualist schema through which it is represented. For instance a number of sociologists, such as Agnès Pitrou, have demonstrated the existence of underground networks of family solidarity, whose economic importance would seem to be much greater than is often supposed.[9] The growth of the underground economy within the present crisis is also partly an expression of this capacity of the social fabric to engender within itself ways of resisting external shocks. While these various hidden 'shock absorbers' – all too rarely taken into account by economists or sociologists – no longer suffice, it is essential to recognize their existence, because without them the state intervention requirement would have been still greater. The alternative to the welfare state consists in appreciating their role and encouraging their extension.

It is precisely all these various forms of transversal socialism – from formal associations to informal co-operative initiatives for supplying services – that can help make mutual support once more the affair of society. The growth of such 'sociability' depends in the immediate term on increased free time. Lack of free time and social rigidity, in fact, go hand in hand. The less free time individuals enjoy, the greater are the demands they make on the state and the more they are dependent on the market. They can involve themselves in mutual support initiatives, extend their neighbourhood ties and establish various kinds of *ad hoc* solidarity only if they have the time to do so. From this perspective, reducing working hours is not just an economic argument for cutting unemployment; it is also a condition of learning new forms of life. Such promotion of closer ties within society should not, however, be viewed in the narrow sense of setting up stable, closed microcommunities. What is rather required is a multiplicity of temporary or limited associations – a type of multisocialization, whose pluralism of forms of sociability is by no means a constraint upon liberty, but instead an extension of each individual's freedom.

Increasing Social Visibility

Overcoming the 'privatization versus state control' alternative and reinstating mutual aid within the social domain: these two conditions of formulating an alternative to the traditional welfare state, particularly concerning the satisfaction of emerging social needs, should not lead us to forget that it is the latter that will continue to play the central role in promoting solidarity of various kinds. Their function consists essentially in ushering in a new phase of social development, without challenging the existence of nationwide systems in most of the chief areas of policy provision. But there is a growing call for conceiving the principal systems in terms of providing back-up for localized mutual support initiatives which need to become more widespread, comprehensive and definite through the establishment of more decentralized systems or small-scale initiatives emerging directly from concrete social relations.

But it is not enough to think only along these lines. There is also a need for the traditional welfare state to be revamped. While its administration must be improved and debureaucratized, attempts at simplification and rationalization carried out so far have almost always been thwarted or nullified due to the proliferation of regulations. This happens because of a concern not to ignore any unforeseen circumstance and to control every conceivable situation. Only decentralization of services, procedures and claims departments can hope to halt this costly inflation of regulations.

But there are still more important considerations. The crisis of the welfare state is as much the product of external blockages as of internal bureaucratic obstruction. Its mechanical and abstract expression of assistance, combined with doubts about its ultimate ends, engender a tendency to evade it. It functions as something of a black box or gigantic interface. The financial redistribution it operates comes to be viewed as almost entirely divorced from the social relations which are supposed to be its sphere of concern. The interface serves to blur the realm of the social. Actual social assistance is rendered by anonymous, impersonal mechanisms to such a degree that it is no longer perceived as social assistance as such.

Marxist critiques of market society have frequently indicated how the producers are concealed behind commodities. Marx maintained that in capitalist society relations between people take the bizarre form of relations between things. In a similar vein, one might say that in 'welfare' society relations of mutual support between people assume the form of reified relations between individuals and 'the system'. Wages, prices, profits, taxes and social contributions are all regarded as economic variables divorced from their real social context.

How can this problem be remedied? There is only one solution: increasing the degree of social visibility by allowing the sphere of the social greater freedom of movement. Intellectually speaking, this is not a very comforting prospect. It is much easier to conceive things in terms of the individual versus 'the system', and to consider society solely in the light of such theoretical oversimplifications as the 'opposition between rich and poor' or 'conflicts between the bourgeoisie and proletariat'. Such blinkered, black-and-white thinking is extremely costly. It serves to promote social rigidity and to justify selfish and corporatist behaviour, thereby impeding or actually blocking social change.

If the social sphere were to become more visible and capable of recognizing itself this would encourage the establishment of more genuine relations of mutual assistance, even if the procedures governing them would be more conflict-prone.[10] Today an opposite trend prevails, in which the entire machinery of social contributions is becoming increasingly invisible. The welfare state is operating within a fog, so to speak. Few wage-earners have any idea how much is deducted from their pay in real terms (the notion of gross wages meaning nothing either to the enterprise or to the employee). Value added tax, which accounts for about half of the revenues collected, is a 'painless' tax whose size is not appreciated by the consumer; only personal income tax allows those concerned to see clearly how much they are paying. It is no longer possible for individuals to discern the connection between individual deductions and the social uses to which they are put. The result is a universal lack of responsibility.

The only way for the welfare state to become better accepted is to make its machinery operate explicitly for everyone. Obviously there are risks involved in such greater truthfulness. It calls for recognition of the realities normal macrosociological concepts usually suppress or ignore: side benefits, the extreme heterogeneity of the wage system, and disparities in taxation. Greater visibility has its price. It can engender tensions and conflicts. The difficulties inherent in face-to-face encounters between individuals and groups are illustrated by the resistance in certain cases to experiments in publicizing salaries, wages or taxation contributions.

A totally visible society, in which everyone would live under the gaze of everyone else, would be intolerable. Girard (in *La Violence et le sacré*) has shown clearly how societies have a need to produce mechanisms for limiting the explosive effects produced by radically confrontational situations. But we run no risk of that at the present time – far from it, in fact. After all, what is more natural than the sort of tension created by living together, a tension of which class struggle is only one manifestation? Surely that is the function of democracy: to provide scope for the expression and treatment of this difficulty, of which the existence of opposing political parties is the sign? Conflict and society are inseparable terms. The acceptance of conflict lies at the heart of the process of the self-production of the social. Far from denying or ignoring conflict under the guise of an improbable 'consensus', the democratic ideal makes such conflict productive and constructive. In this sense, social visibility and the growth of democracy go hand in hand.

The supreme illusion fostered by the state is that everyone has a personal stake in keeping the social sphere a closed book, as if in the final analysis society could be nothing but a zero-sum game. In any event, the illusion boomerangs back on the state, because everyone is thereby justified in regarding it as the miraculous source of everything which exists. At a stroke it is the state which is suddenly the scapegoat, accused systematically of all possible evils while simultaneously being required to satisfy every possible demand on it. Thus, in the end, the interface turns out to be very costly.

Why then such great fear of visibility, to judge from all the evidence? Does it conceal a trap? Quite simply, because visibility cannot be understood in static terms. It establishes an infinite dynamic of social questioning. It forces society to face up radically to the question of what it is to become. The point is that we are used to giving stereotyped answers to this question by deferring to the pantheon of democratic values: liberty, equality, justice. However, when it comes to putting them into practice, these values turn out to be less obvious than they at first appeared. Equality? Very well, but what equality? And what, in fact, is equality? 'Equal pay' or the 'reduction' of inequalities? A 'just' distribution of the fruits of growth? Fine, but how does one define 'justice' in this case?

Here we come very close to the heart of democracy: the creation of a collective justification for collective existence, the production of negotiated standards.[11] Seen from this angle, the crisis of the welfare state is a sign of our society's deficit of cultural identity. Society remains silent, withdrawn; it is incapable of speaking for itself and conceiving its future. By freeing the welfare state we would also create public and democratic spaces for society to work on these basic issues in a lucid manner.[12] Bobbio provides a good illustration of how democracy can be conceived only as 'visible power' (and how the machinery of political representation makes sense only from this angle). In Bobbio's view the risk of a debasement of democracy is linked to the growth of invisible forms of power, such as the *cripto-governo* (the secret services, secret powers, and so on) and the *sotto-governo* (linked with the role of the underground economy). In this way he shows how economic and social decomposition goes hand in hand with the decomposition of democracy.

Increasing social visibility would also foster a more localized identification of needs and aspirations. It would enable forms of transversal socialization and small-scale mutual aid to come into being to deal with them. Mutual aid cannot be derived solely from rules and procedures; it must also have a *voluntary* dimension. 'Other people' are indissociably '*socius*' and 'neighbour' at one and the same time. I assist all other *socii* through the intermediary of the welfare state, but I render direct assistance only through one or two 'neighbourhood' networks. Justice cannot be solely a legal matter. 'Social morality' cannot be totally absorbed into and covered by the law. To suppose otherwise is a dangerous illusion, which is fostered whenever we represent the state as secular providence.[13]

The 'Post-Social-Democratic' Scenario

For almost thirty years now democratic industrial societies have developed, either implicitly or explicitly, within the framework of the Keynesian compromise which regulated relations between the economic and social spheres in the manner of a positive-sum game. The foundations for this model were the growth of the welfare state and collective bargaining. The welfare state governed relations between the state and the working class and reflected the latter's economic and political power, either in institutionalized form (as in the social democratic countries) or in the less stable form of a simple *de facto* balance of forces (as in other capitalist countries). Collective bargaining, for its part, provided the framework for relations bewteen employers and unions, and its significance clearly varied from country to country.

This model is currently bursting at the seams, due to the destabilization of these two basic foci of joint regulation. The fall in growth rates and the latest figures for economic activity tend to call into question the welfare state's previous trend of development. The conditions for social regulation and economic regulation no longer converge. Moreover, the nature of collective bargaining is being transformed with the increasing segmentation of the labour market and the phenomena associated with the break-up of the working class (mushrooming statutes, delocalization of production, the separation of the 'juridical enterprise' and the 'real enterprise' and so on).[14] The working class remained purposeful only within the context of a relatively homogeneous social sphere which could be apprehended in comprehensive terms. Nowadays, it is the dismantling of this relatively unified social sphere which is becoming the chief means whereby business firms economically regulate social costs. It is no longer the substance of social bargaining that is at stake, but its *scope*. The chief target of regulation is now the very *form* and *configuration* of the social sphere.

The Keynesian model is therefore caught in a double crisis. Alongside the exhaustion of the welfare state there is a weakening of the classic forms of collective bargaining. 'Logically', this should lead to a sharpening of the class struggle. For instance, the conditions governing the distribution of wages/profits are more brutal: they no longer form part of a general economic growth trend. Social relations are expressed increasingly in terms of a negative-sum game. Notwithstanding such trends, no sharpening of working-class struggle has occurred. It seems as if the Keynesian settlement, against all expectations, is being dismantled, without any great resistance. How is this possible? It is not enough to explain it solely in terms of falling trade-union membership or inadequate social mobilization resulting from some blindness towards the stakes involved (a blindness fostered – naturally! – by the evil power of 'the dominant ideology'). The chief reason for the 'acceptance' of the crisis of the Keynesian model resides essentially in the fact that the latter no longer appears to be a positive goal or a vector of social progress. The crisis of the welfare state is embedded within a context of diffuse scepticism about it by those very people who might have been expected to be its principal beneficiaries. This resistance has taken two forms.

At first, during the 1970s and before the economic crisis, diffuse criticism was voiced about the relations between the state and society. An almost universal, if vague, indictment of the state was levelled from both libertarian and liberal positions (which often overlapped). In the socialist political arena this development took the form of the demand for '*autogestion*', or self-managing socialism, with its critique of centralized management techniques, its advocacy of social change from below and its development of the theme of experimentation. This movement stimulated the emergence of a 'new political culture' which sought to give this rejection of 'statism' a positive strategic meaning.[15] In opposition to the Keynesian model, a self-management model was making headway.

Then the sociological base of the Keynesian model cracked. That model had been founded on a bipolar concept of social issues, perceived in class terms. Fresh areas of social conflict began to emerge which, for those involved, could not be described adequately in the traditional language of class struggle alone, such as relations between men and women, the 'leaders versus the led', and the state versus regions. Neither the welfare state nor collective bargaining was a suitable instrument for tackling these phenomena. But what was characteristic about the movements in question is that they retained a collective dimension. They established collective identities even though they lacked any organizational structure. The question therefore arose as to how they related to the traditional political formations (for example the political parties and the unions).

This question lay behind all Alain Touraine's efforts to analyse the emergence of the new social movements which both formed the structure of a *neo-Keynesian* arena and fulfilled a role equivalent to that of trade unionism within the classic Keynesian era.[16] His approach is similar to that adopted by the promoters of the self-management model, but the perspective is rather different. The latter were thinking essentially in terms of *correcting* the Keynesian model by developing more decentralized and autonomous social and political techniques. Touraine, on the other hand, looked at the question in rather more global terms and imagined a neo-Keynesian perspective in which one social movement would play a central role (and in this sense he remained a Marxist, in the strongest sense of the term).

At the turn of the 1980s, a new element emerged to undermine further the Keynesian model: social diffraction. This diffraction has several dimensions. It is an expression of the economic upheaval produced by both the segmentation of the market and the growth of the underground economy. It was accompanied by the phenomena of social withdrawal, the search for individual alternatives within the labyrinthine framework of the segmented labour market and the multitude of different statutes and regulations. A growing number of individuals came to the conclusion that the more advantageous course for them was to trace their own critical path within the overall social graph – to use the language of operational research – rather than improving their condition within the framework of collective advancement. This threw individual and collective relations into disarray and collective organizations, including trade unions, are increasingly feeling the effects in the shape of falling membership and a shrinking of their traditional areas of militancy. At present, the main feature of this diffraction of the social sphere is ambiguity. While it is a symptom of the reactionary withdrawal and an entropic lifestyle, it is also a sign of new social relations whose hallmark is the search for closer social ties and a critical approach to heavy-handed 'collectivism'. It marks a crisis in the form of the social, of the way in which individuals interact within a social system.

In this context, the very concept of economic or social regulation begins to lose its meaning. Notions of economic policy or social policy no longer fit this diffracted state of affairs, overlaid as it is by different networks and countless strata that resemble a veritable slice of flaky pastry. Regulatory social machinery is dispersed throughout the various layers of the social sphere.[17] This *intro-social* model of fractured regulation could prove positive if it gives rise to a more flexible and autonomous society. But it could also develop perversely into a dual society. The trend towards social diffraction, like the critique of the state, is largely indeterminate in terms of their outcome. They are just as likely to lead to individualism and classical liberalism as to usher in new social and political perspectives. And the ambivalent attitude of 'acceptance' towards the effects of the crisis of the Keynesian model needs to be viewed in the light of this indeterminacy.

The present crisis has therefore led to the emergence of two new models: self-management, which expresses a new conception of political forms, and the intro-social model, which seeks a new configuration of social forms. Three different modes of conceiving and regulating the social sphere are summarized in Table 1.

With the collapse of the Keynesian model as the one and only central mode of social regulation, the foundations of social democratic and socialist ideas have been challenged. Indeed, the chief symptom of the weakening of the social democratic perspective is its ability to think in any but defensive terms. However, there is no bringing back the past: the image of an energetic and inspirational social democracy cannot be restored. It is impossible to forget or erase the resistance to it and the social and cultural changes that imperil it. If the only goal it has to offer is a return to a Keynesian scenario, then it is on the road to collapse and will permit the neo-liberal forces to draw all the benefits from a situation in which the political and social forms of this Keynesian compromise are being unhinged. The most resilient features of the Keynesian model, paradoxically, will prove to be its most negative aspects.

Disparate coalitions – both inside and outside the state – will prevent the dismantling of the welfare state and in fact stand quite a good chance of maintaining its formal skeleton in order to

Table 1
Three Modes of Regulation in the Post-Social-Democratic Phase

	Keynesian approach	*Self-management approach*	*Intro-social approach*
Target of regulation	Class regulations (capital/labour)	State/civil society (base/summit)	Relations between Individual society/collective
Social agents involved	State, employers, unions (& appropriate political parties)	Social movement, grass-roots groups	Individuals, families, neighbourhood groups, etc.
Prime concern	Economic: sharing of growth (jobs, income, social facilities)	Sociopolitical: type of political forms (decentralization self-management, social experiments)	Societal: shape of society (structure, flexibility)
Area(s) of application	Discrete and homogeneous: the nation considered as a stable and restricted international division of labour	Dual: decentralized within civil society, centralized in political society (democratic public sphere)	Multiple and deterritorialized; visible and invisible
Mode of regulation	All-embracing: collective bargaining plus welfare state	Local (self-regulation) and comprehensive (democracy)	Dispersed and embedded in the social fabric

protect the jobs of state functionaries and preserve traditional regulations. It would then exist as just so much dead machinery. At the same time certain unions in a stronger strategic position could well continue to negotiate collective agreements in favourable conditions, but they would be transformed into powerful nuclei of corporatist privilege within a situation in which the structures of the balance of social forces had been thoroughly undermined. If those who derive the most benefit from the welfare state fail to propose a positive alternative to it, we shall find ourselves living in a bastard society in which ever stronger market mechanisms will coexist with rigid statist forms and the growth of a selective social corporatism. Such a society would be based on a multiplicity of dualisms, giving rise both to blockages and to new kinds of injustice. It would be socially intolerable and economically inefficient. Thus the alternative is not the nostalgic preservation of the Keynesian model or 'pure' neo-liberalism. In practical terms, the choice is between a rigid pseudo-liberal model and what I call a *post-social-democracy.*

Post-social-democracy is based on a reduction of the role of the Keynesian model in combination with self-managing and intro-social modes of regulation. This model is the only existing prospect of achieving a social compromise which has effects equivalent to those of the social democratic compromise within the Keynesian scenario. Its central objectives would be related to the forms of social and political life. It would consist in accepting the possibility of greater flexibility in economic activity and a measure of debureaucratization of the state in return for the recognition of greater autonomy for individuals and groups, an autonomy which would be guaranteed by collective action (including the unions) and by institutions. It would be a compromise that would require a reciprocal exchange of flexibility and rigidity. The unions, for instance, would accept greater mobility of the labour force in exchange for a greater role in the enterprise and economic policies; a loosening of trade-union practices in return for a loosening of employer practices; and greater flexibility of organizations in return for greater flexibility for individuals. No other scenario at the present time suits the current balance of forces within industrial societies. It is a scenario founded on compromise, in the sense that it is based on both reciprocal concessions and an exchange that is advantageous overall for the different parties involved. If such a compromise fails to materialize, employers will be free to tackle rigidities and to create new forms of flexibility on their own terms.

More generally speaking, the post-social-democratic compromise may be regarded as an overlapping threefold compromise:

• First there must be a new socioeconomic compromise with employers. A shortening and reorganization of working hours will be the first main bargaining counter. In France it is important that such a compromise should retain a classic Keynesian dimension, since collective-bargaining processes are particularly deficient in comparison with most other countries.

• Secondly, a new sociopolitical compromise with the state. The aim of this would be an acceptance of the stabilization of the welfare state at its present level in return for less state intervention in its classical form and greater scope for experiment and self-help initiatives in the sphere of collective services. This also implies an extension of civil liberties.

• Thirdly, society would have to compromise with itself in new ways. The goal would be to 'unblock' the welfare state and to encourage the expression of mutual aid based on negotiation rather than imposition – all within the framework of a more open society.

The post-social-democratic model would be a *democratic* compromise which gives a new and more concrete meaning to the idea of social contract. The development of a post-social-democratic scenario would help usher in a new era of genuine democratic public activity through which society could act more freely upon itself. This proposed compromise is not intended as a substitute for more ambitious projects such as self-managing socialism. But it must be admitted that in the short term the achievement of the latter is not on the agenda. However, the post-social-democratic scenario as I have defined it is the only one that does not conflict with such aims, even if only some of their respective institutional requirements coincide. The post-social-democratic compromise defines the optimum possible scenario within the limits imposed on French society at the present time.

Notes

1. Edouard Laboulaye, *L'Etat et ses limites*, Paris 1865, p. 7.

2. This is why the radical individualism that inspires the most vigorous condemnations of the welfare state is forced, logically, to exclude all 'social' or 'societal' considerations. See, for example, Robert Nozick, *Anarchy, State, and Utopia*, Oxford 1984.

3. G. Gurvitch, *L'idée du droit social*, Paris 1932; cf. his 'Essai d'une classification pluraliste des formes de sociabilité', (1938), reprinted in *La vocation actuelle de la sociologie*, vol. 1 of *Vers la sociologie differentielle*, Paris 1968.

4. Ibid, pp. 250-51.

5. *L'Age de l'autogestion*, Paris 1976.

6. See the important special issue of *Esprit* (March 1980) devoted to the theme of 'law and politics'.

7. See Philippe Ariès, *Histoire des populations françaises*, Paris 1971, and *L'Enfant et la vie familiale sous l'Ancien Régime*, Paris 1973.

8. Louis Dumont, *Homo aequalis*, Paris 1977.

9. Agnès Pitrou, *Vivre sans famille? Les solidarités familiales dans le monde d'aujourd'hui*, Toulouse 1978.

10. It is a well-known fact that in the matter of public-sector wage-bargaining a genuine contractual policy, whatever its limits, came into existence only after the

establishment of procedures for monitoring actual situations and their development.

11. Authors such as Rawls seek to halt this trend by imagining that it is possible to enact *definitive* rules concerning what is just. See John Rawls, *A Theory of Justice*, Oxford 1972.

12. Interesting evidence in this respect is provided by Noberto Bobbio. 'La democrazia et il potere invisible', *Rivista italiana de scienza politica*, no. 2, Bologna 1980.

13. The example of English society is particularly interesting when analysed from this angle. Even though the welfare state is much more developed than in France, the UK has some six million 'volunteer workers'. 'Good neighbour' schemes have created extremely dense networks of local exchanges, mutual assistance, reciprocal services, etc. Since 1977 an information body, the Mutual Aid Centre (MAC), has been operating as a focus for the exchange of experiences. In an interview for *Le Monde*, one of its organizers declared that those involved shared the conviction that there were many fields in which it was better to cope oneself and help one's neighbours than to rely on a remote and overburdened state. See Annie Battle, 'Inventer la vie en Grand-Bretagne', *Le Monde*, 7 April 1981. The MAC even launched a radio station devoted to information about these networks. The outcome is that whereas the economic situation in Great Britain is worse than almost anywhere else in Western Europe, the development of this sociability has meant that some parts of British society have managed to absorb the shock of the fall in purchasing power (almost 30 per cent in seven years!). Perhaps what has proved a means of social defence in this case might prove to be a vector of social development elsewhere?

14. See Jacques Julliard, Edmond Maire, Pierre Rosanvallon, Alain Touraine, Bruno Trentin, *Crise et avenir de la classe ouvrière*, Paris 1979 and André Gorz, *Farewell to the Working Class*, London 1982.

15. See Pierre Rosanvallon and Patrick Viveret, *Pour une nouvelle culture politique*, Paris 1977.

16. See the description of his research programme and methodology for analysing the new social movements in *The Voice and the Eye. An Analysis of Social Movements*, Cambridge 1981.

17. The attempt by economists to define and measure the informal economy is an expression of their efforts to bring this complex zone of activity within their usual categories and their desire to confine all the non-Keynesian areas within one single category of the 'underground' or 'black' economy.

Time, Money, and Welfare-State Capitalism*

Karl Hinrichs

Claus Offe

Helmut Wiesenthal

Any consideration of the present crisis and the future of the welfare state must begin with the conditions that prevail – and are likely to prevail in the foreseeable future – on the labour market. The functional relationships currently existing between the labour market and the welfare state's social security mechanisms are of a twofold nature. First, the fiscal *capacities* of most West European welfare states are determined basically by the volume of contributions and social security taxes that are extracted from employees' income and hence from the present level of employment and the dynamics of wage increases, the latter being partly determined by the former. Secondly – and conversely – the volume of *claims* made upon the welfare state is determined by the quantity of income needs that remain unsatisfied within the framework of the labour market and other institutions of civil society; these needs are supposed to be satisfied by the welfare state, most importantly through its schemes of unemployment insurance. Considered together, these two functional relationships constitute a well-known dilemma: the more the welfare state is made necessary by the shrinking employment opportunities provided by the economy, the less it is capable of playing that role because of the poor employment performance of the economy.

---

*The authors wish to thank John Keane for helpful suggestions and editorial assistance.

One type of resolution for this dilemma would be either to reduce the legal claims employees are allowed to make upon the redistributive and income-maintenance services of the welfare state, or to increase the share of individual employees' market incomes claimed by the social security system through increased contributions and taxations. However, such moves towards a downward adaptation of the welfare state appear to involve rather prohibitive political costs for both conservative-liberal and social democratic governments.

This essay therefore examines the range of available options for further developing the welfare state. It assumes that both the economic constraints of a long-term employment gap and the political constraints standing in the way of a complete abolition of major social security schemes will remain characteristic features of West European systems. After briefly reviewing some of the more commonly proposed (and less promising) public policy strategies (I), our discussion concentrates on working time as the most crucial strategic parameter of employment and social policies (II). We offer a sociological explanation for the striking fact that so little has been achieved by recent union demands for collective agreements involving worktime reductions. Finally we discuss a set of proposals whose introduction would allow the strategic parameter of working time to be used more effectively in the service of both full employment and social security policies (III). The empirical observations underlying this discussion are derived mainly from the major strike in the German metal industry in the early summer of 1984, in which the demand for the thirty-five-hour-week was central. The authors have also undertaken an extensive empirical study of the history and politics of working-time-related industrial conflicts.[1] However, the present essay refers to this research only in passing. We instead try to present the outlines of a theoretical argument that we believe is also valid for other 'disorganized' capitalist democracies and their differing types of industrial relations systems.

I   The Failure of Conventional Therapies

A given level of employment is seen conventionally as dependent upon three major economic variables. These are (a) the level of output and its rate of change: the rate of economic growth; (b) the level of productivity and its rate of increase; (c) the volume of labour supply and its demographic determinants. Each of these three variables can be considered as a parameter of strategic action; consequently anyone who advocates more far-reaching and less conventional policy options (as we do in the third part of this essay) must explain why efforts to work with any combination of these variables are likely to meet with little (if any) success. Fortunately, there is today a widespread consensus among experts and policy-makers about the insufficiency of these three strategies. We shall therefore restrict ourselves to a brief consideration of the main functional as well as normative arguments underlying this developing consensus.

(a) The first strategy for achieving full employment and restoring the fiscal equilibrium of the welfare state requires vigorous *economic growth* policies. Such economic growth rates would have to be enormous, far surpassing the growth rates of 2 to 3 per cent that many West European countries have experienced since about 1982 without, however, achieving a proportionate decline in the unemployment rate. The hard question, however, is what type of growth, and how could it be brought about? This question is difficult to answer convincingly for various reasons. First, Keynesian doctrines of 'global economic steering' have encountered increasing doubts and uncertainties during the last decade. On the one hand, autonomous demand increases and deficit spending affect various sectors of a highly heterogeneous economy in quite different ways: such measures may generate inflationary pressures in some sectors before becoming significant enough to generate more employment in other, more backward sectors, thus leading to a highly ambiguous overall net effect. On the other hand, it is plausible to assume that Keynesian modes of macroeconomic steering are effective only as long as major economic actors, particularly investors, do not anticipate them. The expectation that governments will adopt them tends to annihilate their desired effect. In other words, it seems likely that Keynesianism is most effective when it comes as a surprise, not as a predictable routine.

Secondly, it appears that a condition of market saturation prevails within the markets for many of the industrial goods which served (together with an increase of population, which has now come to an end) as the material basis of the post-war growth period. Thirdly, while it would certainly be mistaken to ignore ongoing processes of *product* innovation and the consequent opening up of markets for new (or, more typically, improved) products, one must also take into account the fact that *process* innovations seem to evolve more rapidly. Since the pattern of technological progress is biased in favour of the latter, this implies a bias towards capital goods rather than final consumption goods and towards productivity increases rather than output increases. Fourthly, environmental limits to further industrial growth have arisen; these have led to a widespread sense of doubt, if not hostility, concerning the technical and political desirability of continued industrial growth. This political and cultural climate of doubts, uncertainties and heightened risk awareness is giving rise, at least in some countries, to significant political objections and opposition to 'growth-through-industrialization' policies. Finally, a slowdown in the export of industrial goods can be expected. For example, although West German exports comprise an increasing share of the country's national product (18.5 per cent of GNP in 1970; 27.9 per cent in 1984), it is unlikely that this development will continue considering industrialized countries' moves towards protectionism and Third World countries' catastrophic foreign debts.

(b) The employment and fiscal problems of the welfare state might also be considered, secondly, from the perspective of changes in *productivity*. The idea of lowering productivity (or its rate of increase) is rarely advocated as such, but it is sometimes seen as the indirect and implicit side effect of measures designed to effect changes in the production process. For instance, proposals for workers' control or various forms of codetermination seem to imply that new patterns of decision-making regarding investment and technical change are likely to lower the rate of productivity increases. The same holds true of regulatory measures concerning work humanization and health and safety at work. The prevailing managerial standards and measurements of labour productivity are often (justifiably) criticized for systematically disregarding the long-term and external effects of productivity increases upon the health of workers, the environment, patterns of land use and other components of collective social welfare – none of which (sufficiently) enters into the accounting systems of capitalist firms. If such factors were taken into account, overall labour productivity would probably increase more slowly. Furthemore, it is often suggested that advanced industrial societies are currently transforming themselves into 'post-industrial' societies, in which the employment share of the service sector increases more rapidly than that of the secondary, or industrial sector; since services are considered generally to be less susceptible to productivity-increasing technical change, such post-industrial development would amount to an overall lowering of the rate of increase in labour productivity.

Although some of these arguments and observations may appear to be normatively attractive, it seems highly unlikely in practice that they would result in a significant reduction of the present unemployment levels. Such doubts apply particularly to the post-industrialism thesis, which underestimates the extent to which the required additional services will be performed through self-service, not in the form of employment.[2] The post-industrial thesis also neglects the fact that the growth of service employment (in both the private and public sectors) depends upon a growth of output within the industrial sector; it is not itself capable of compensating for a decline in industrial output and employment. As to the codetermination, work humanization and externalities arguments, their common defects have to do with the fact that the economies to which they are directed are themselves part of an international economic system characterized by fierce competition. Hence whatever measures one country undertakes to constrain the rate of increase of labour productivity (be it in the interest of employees and/or consumers or the general public) will soon risk undermining the international competitiveness – and *worsening* the employment level – of that country. Many people (including union officials) have been forced recently to recognize this painful dilemma that there is only one thing worse for workers and their employment security than the introduction of technical change: management's failure to introduce technical change.

(c) If neither economic growth rates can be increased nor productivity lowered without unacceptable side effects, the remaining variable within the conventional analysis of the unemployment problem is the *volume of labour supply*. Theoretically, the number of people seeking employment (the 'excessive' supply of labour) could be reduced by (1) changing the birth rate; (2) regulating international and interregional migration; and (3) influencing the labour-market participation rate. The problem with the first of these alternatives is the lack of clarity about the ways and (more importantly) the directions in which the present birth rate *should* be influenced, supposing that it *could* be. The problem of determining (let alone implementing) some 'optimal size of the population' is today as unresolved as it ever was.

More relevant is the second alternative, which has become one of the favourites among neo-conservative policy-makers. It consists of measures which make it either legally impossible or economically unattractive for foreigners to enter a given country or, alternatively, attractive for them to leave. The miscalculations and obvious irrationalities of this approach are by now common knowledge. Even when normative and political considerations are set aside, there is strong evidence suggesting that the jobs left by foreign workers would not be filled easily by domestic workers; that the loss of effective demand within the domestic economy that would follow a mass exodus of foreign workers would destroy more jobs than would be left vacant by the departing foreign employees; and that the effect of re-migration incentives is self-paralysing because the more people are induced to leave the country to return, say, to Turkey or Yugoslavia, the greater the rates of unemployment and general social insecurity in those countries and, hence, the greater the determination of the remaining foreign workers to stay.

The third of the above alternatives – reducing the labour supply – seems to be most suited to strategic attempts at reducing the fiscal and employment problems of the welfare state. Labour-market participation rates do indeed vary widely among OECD countries; hence it might appear worthwhile to reduce labour-market participation to the lowest conceivable level by appropriate regulations, incentives and disincentives. A sobering fact to be noted in this connection, however, is the absence of any significant statistical correlation between a country's labour-market participation rate and its rate of unemployment. High labour-market participation rates coexist with low unemployment (as in Sweden and Japan) and vice versa (as in the Netherlands and Italy).

Moreover, the institutional spaces of civil society within which it is considered normal and acceptable to live a life that is *not* centred on active labour-market participation are either scarce and already overcrowded or their conceivable expansion – in the form of schools and other educational institutions for the young, families for women, custodial institutions such as hospitals, prisons and welfare schemes for the deviant and poor, old age pension schemes for the old – would involve prohibitive costs for the state budget. As a consequence, measures to force workers (and particularly unemployed workers) to withdraw from the supply side of the labour market will meet either increasing resistance (from women, for example) or counterproductive and undesirable effects (as when the recipients of unemployment and welfare benefits join the ranks of the underground labour market and engage in illegal forms of employment and economic activity).

To be sure, the sense of ineffectiveness and failure produced by this brief review of the three conventional strategies for restoring equilibrium within the labour market does not imply that there is an automatic tendency for adopting more innovative and promising strategies. Should such strategies eventually be developed and implemented, they will be the result of social and political struggles which successfully overcome the philosophy of fatalism, inaction and cynicism that is currently gaining ground, and not only among those for whom the transformation of the labour market into a buyers' market is immediately profitable.

II   Rational Actors and Negotiated Working-Time Reductions

One such struggle which aims to develop new strategies for overcoming the unemployment problem is centred on the time dimension of the labour supply. The underlying idea is that the fewer hours, days, months or years the individual worker actually works, the more people can actually be absorbed and gainfully employed in the labour market. This idea of 'redistributing' employment more fairly inspired the major strike of the West German metalworkers' union (IGM) in 1984. On the basis of the above-mentioned case study, we have reached the conclusion that this strike and the terms of its settlement have failed to produce any significant impact upon the widespread unemployment it was intended to overcome, or at least alleviate. While this conclusion is hardly controversial, our explanation for this disappointing outcome suggests that the organizational and political means that can be mobilized within the framework of institutionalized industrial conflict are basically insufficient for success in any conceivable future round of industrial action. What are the facts and causal interpretations that lead us to this uncommonly negative assessment of the employment potential of conventional reforms in working-time policy?

The strongest argument in support of a view more confident than the one proposed here points to past industrial conflicts and collective agreements that have, in fact, resulted in quite substantial worktime reductions. Thus it must be asked why the present situation is so different, and why it renders inoperative those strategies that have worked so effectively in the past. In considering this question, three facts are important:

• In the past, the demand for worktime reduction was advocated and legitimized mainly in terms of increased *individual* welfare, such as the reduction of the stress and strain of the work process or the value of greater leisure time. When such individualistic demands predominated, unions' attempts to alter the quantity of worktime proved successful and durable. In contrast the *collective* effects of reducing the total volume of labour supply, hence relatively increasing collective employment security, were either ignored entirely or viewed simply as a welcome by-product. Where the improvement of the collective employment situation was the major objective (and individual welfare gains resulting from work-time reduction were only 'accessories'), the unions' efforts failed or yielded only marginal successes.

   In general, it can be said that within a capitalist economic structure there is little that workers – through collective action – can do to influence or determine the total volume of employment. If such effects occur at all, they tend to be the accidental result of strategies which are motivated by quite different considerations. The aggregate level of employment is simply not an item susceptible to negotiation between employers and unions; rather, it is a residual and indirectly determined variable. Even when they practise extreme forms of 'wage restraint', unions are neve able effectively to *oblige* employers to increase employment correspondingly. Knowing this, unions will be extremely reluctant to even consider wage restraints, not only because the intended gains are highly uncertain but also because disadvantages would definitely be incurred by such a strategy in terms of the union's loss of attractiveness among its members and thus a heightening of workers' rational motives to refrain from becoming, or even remaining, members of a union. It therefore appears highly unlikely that any union – even the most comprehensive, solidaristic and united – will be able to pursue strategies which aim solely at the *collective* (as opposed to the average individual) interest of wage-earners in a high aggregate level of employment.

• The capacity of unions to pursue effective strategies for overcoming the employment crisis is further diminished by the fact that workers' collective interest (the overall improvement of employment security and, consequently, the market-power position of labour) is by no means of *equal significance* for *all* union members, and that those workers who are most interested in improved employment prospects are typically the least unionized sectors of the working class. Recent research has demonstrated convincingly that as a consequence of the segmentation and fragmentation of the labour force, today's condition of mass unemployment is characterized by a highly unequal social distribution of unemployment risks. Some categories of workers (especially the young, the old, women and workers employed in certain industrial and regional sectors) are exposed much more heavily than others to the risk of losing their jobs and/or failing to find a job.[3]

In the Federal Republic of Germany it has been estimated that the experience of direct unemployment has affected no more than a third of the entire workforce over the last decade. Substantial groups of workers – particularly those represented most strongly by unions – have little or no reason to fear unemployment, even if it reaches much higher average levels. To suppose that all workers are equally and strongly interested in promoting their collective interest in full employment is to assume away sharp differences of unemployment risks among groups within the working class, or to invoke a sense of class solidarity which can be hardly be expected to prevail under conditions of a deep and lasting economic recession.

• It is true that unions' successful struggle for worktime reduction for the sake of improving the overall employment condition might also be valued for the individualized benefits it brings as a by-product and side effect of collective action. After all, even securely employed workers who support a union's worktime-reduction strategy because of a purely altruistic concern for their fellow-workers' collective welfare would also benefit in terms of reduced personal exhaustion from work or increased personal leisure time. Nevertheless, it remains unclear how highly such 'benefit' would be valued subjectively and hence whether that additional 'private' incentive to engage in the collectively beneficial struggle for worktime reduction would be sufficient to generate the degree of required mobilization and militancy among union members for pursuing a successful strategy under the unfavourable conditions of an acute employment crisis. And even if everybody were to agree that increased free time warrants attempts collectively to redistribute work, it is by no means certain that workers would agree on the *precise nature* of the worktime reductions. Should such reductions come in the form of hours, days, weeks or years? The pertinence of such questions is reinforced by the findings of an extensive survey, conducted in the Federal Republic of Germany, which indicates a wide and uneven variety of preferences among workers for various types of worktime reduction.[4]

To summarize: Worktime policies which aim to improve the overall employment situation seem highly unrealistic for three cumulative reasons. First, unions are collective actors whose struggle for collective improvements can easily be 'individual-ized'. No voluntary association can afford to strive purely for a collectively defined good (such as full employment); it must always make sure that the fruits of such collective effort can be perceived and enjoyed *individually*. Secondly, the restoration of full employment (in the conventional sense of reducing registered unemployment towards zero) could be enjoyed by individuals acting collectively only if they were affected equally by the risk of unemployment. This is clearly not the case with union members, due to the well known facts of labour-market segmentation and the unequal distribution of unemployment. Thirdly, the working-time situation and the patterns of workers' time needs are so dispersed that no *particular* measure of worktime reduction would respond to the felt needs and preferences of more than a small minority.

This discrepancy between *individual preferences* (which result in turn from highly diversified labour-market positions and working situations) and *'systemic' requirements* underlies the failure of exist-ing forms of collective action to produce worktime reductions capable of remedying the present critical employment situation. This discrepancy can be described in terms of a rationality trap: from the view-point of individual workers acting in a purposively rational way, it is undesirable to adopt strategies which are at the same time highly desirable when viewed from an aggregate or collective point of view. It follows that although the strategic choices of collective and individual actors may be at variance with the collective interest, they must in fact be considered as the outcome of 'rational', utility-maximizing calculations rather than as short-sighted, unenlightened, or amoral modes of action.

Let us explore further the reasons for this kind of rationality trap by examining the strategic choices and dilemmas of unions.

Within the West German system of industrial relations and collective bargaining, in which the formal practice of 'closed shops' is virtually unknown, the calculus of costs and benefits from the unions' point of view is roughly of the following types:

1. In the case of successful strikes or negotiations, the resulting benefits (for example wage increases) extend to both organized and non-organized employees, whereas the (potential) costs of such action are borne by the union members alone. This produces a strong tendency to freeriding, which is offset partly by 'selective incentives' reserved for union members only.

2. The temptation to freeride would become much more powerful, and potentially destructive of the very existence of unions, if union members paid the costs of collective action (by paying dues and engaging in strike action) while the *non*-organized were the major beneficiaries of such industrial action. In this second situation unions would subsidize the common good or welfare of *others*, while gaining few or no benefits (including self-respect) for their own members.

3. In a third problematic case, the union (and its members) incur substantial and definite costs, while the benefits (whatever their distribution) remain highly uncertain and at best marginal.

4. A fourth case is imaginable in which the costs of collective action are borne by all union members, while the benefits are restricted to a minority or to a few specific demands and needs of all members.

While the first of these scenarios presupposes a modest level of solidarity plus some selective incentives, the second case is much more demanding. For the sake of the continued existence of the union it requires a very high level of class *solidarity*, if not outright altruism. Similarly, the third case presupposes a degree of union *militancy* that borders on frivolous adventurism since it ignores the trade-off between present militancy and future strength, which would probably be exhausted by the present conflict. The fourth case, although easier, remains difficult enough since its solution presupposes a high level of intra-union solidarity *and* trust, the confident belief that the 'next round' will produce results favouring other categories of special groups and special needs.

The supreme goal of any collective actor is always to maintain and secure its own existence. As these four model scenarios illustrate, not all the substantive goals pursued by a union are equally compatible with this 'meta-goal'. A union becomes more vulnerable to the threats to its organizational integrity posed by the second, third and fourth types of strategic options the less it has already invested in the development of organizational features such as class solidarity, militancy and trust.[5] Given that non-partisan and largely depoliticized unions of the West German type fail to invest in organizational resources such as class solidarity, militancy and trust, it is hardly surprising that their working-time-reduction campaigns have been reluctant, badly prepared, uncoordinated and ultimately ineffective.

In order to compensate for the lack of such organizational resources they were forced to accept two compromises, which together negated the intended employment effect. One compromise consisted in a mixture of demands that included working-time reduction *plus* constant nominal weekly earnings. This altered set of demands was designed to minimize the costs of class solidarity for union members, and understandably so given that a series of recent wage settlements had already resulted in real income losses. The second compromise consisted in the unions' willingness to enter into a 'political exchange' with employers: in exchange for a small reduction of working hours, the unions granted employers the right to introduce more flexible work schedules which enable them to economize on labour. The consequence of this political exchange has been to reduce the employment effect to almost nil, precisely because it allows firms to adapt, within certain limits, the volume of employed labour at any particular point in time to (for example seasonal) fluctuations in demand and production schedules; thus it reduces the total labour input.[6]

If trade unions have few rational reasons for pursuing employment-effective worktime reductions as long as they remain conscious of the need to preserve themselves as *organizations*, what about their constituent members, the individual employees? For them – as for their unions considered as collective actors – there are quite a number of reasons, in terms of *individual* costs and benefits, why it is irrational for them to advocate and support employment-focused working-time strategies. To be sure, individual benefits – such as more leisure time, earlier retirement, or improved health and physical well-being – are not entirely absent from these strategies. Yet there are also costs, which must be weighed against such benefits.

The anticipated intensification and 'compression' of work that is likely to be among the managerial responses to the introduction of shorter hours arrangements is one type of perceived cost. A second type consists in the anticipated loss of real wages, which is viewed negatively as an individual sacrifice for the achievement of the collective good. Even in the (unlikely) case that hourly wages are increased by the same percentage as hours are decreased, nominal (monthly) earnings thereby remaining constant, the nominal wage increases that *would* have been possible – the opportunity costs incurred for the sake of shorter hours – would still result in individual losses. A third category of costs comprises the individual (and collective) losses of income incurred during strike action as well as the drain on the strike fund and material resources of the union, whose future ability to invest in strikes for higher wages may consequently be weakened.

The second and third categories of costs involve a conflict between the preference for free time and the preference for increased wages. If time and money are considered as alternative media of distributing welfare gains, it is evident that due to certain inherent characteristics of these two media, a rational actor will usually prefer extra money rather than more time. One reason for this is the asymmetrical relationship of convertibility between time and money: if one has lots of money, one can buy time, whereas lots of free time does not automatically provide the option of purchasing goods and services that otherwise have to be paid for with money.[7] Another reason is that in order to enjoy the use-value of free time one needs money to buy goods and services, in the absence of which free time often becomes worthless, if not marked by the negative use-value of boredom. A further difference between time and money, favouring the latter, derives from the fact that time is more 'fixed' than money. Time cannot be 'saved'. Today's free afternoon cannot be 'spent' next week, whereas today's wages can be combined subsequently with further units of money income and spent ten years from now.

The 'fixed' character of time compensations accounts for the difficulties of creating a collective consensus about which forms of working-time reduction are to be given priority. The reduction of night-shift workers' shift by, say, one hour would not greatly improve their working conditions and quality of life; thus they would be likely to give highest priority to early-retirement schemes for escaping completely from their 'unsocial hours'. Others, women with dependent children for instance, might instead be in favour of a four-day-week. However, there is no conceivable compromise between these two possibilities, since neither group would be likely to prefer (that is, be willing to give up any significant amount of monetary income for) an extra ten days' paid holiday per year – although all three solutions would reduce the total labour supply by exactly the same volume.[8]

Finally, while the possibility of a diminishing marginal utility of monetary income cannot be excluded, a decline in the marginal utlity of additional units of free time is bound to begin much earlier. There are various reasons for this. The more leisure time one already has, the less urgent is the need for even more, which is not necessarily so in the analogous case of money. Moreover, there is a hundred-per-cent ceiling in matters of time, whereas for all practical purposes there is no such ceiling when it comes to money.

The relatively low use-value of extra units of free time is also traceable to the structural constraints of 'modern' patterns of family life, household activities, and urban living conditions on its use. 'Productive' uses of time are monopolized by the workplace whereas – due to the lack of human and physical capital, space, and supportive institutional arrangements and traditions within civil society – free time tends to become a virtually empty 'space' to be filled with consumption activities, which of course require the spending of money. And since the location of 'time particles' within the time continuum can drastically affect their subjective value, the utility of additional units of leisure depends upon the degree of freedom of chronological choice. For instance, it is by no means clear how much individuals will value additional free time, especially if it is apportioned in small slices (as would occur in the reduction of the working week by one hour per day to thirty-five hours per week).

This host of difficulties facing trade-union attempts to ease the current critical employment situation by means of working-time reductions is further reinforced by (potential) employer resistance. The effectiveness of worktime policies depends upon employers' willingness to make major concessions, as well as upon unions' capacity to stand firm in the face of employer associations' arguments and propaganda concerning the likely counterproductiveness of union strategies. Employers are clearly unwilling to grant major concessions, for several rational reasons. They fear that a loss of competitiveness (and a possible rise in unemployment) would result from working-time reductions unless similar arrangements are developed simultaneously throughout the OECD countries, which is hardly likely. Employ-

ers and their associations also resist reductions in worktime
because they would severely undermine employers' economic
and socio-political power, which derives from the fact that within
a capitalist civil society in general – and *a fortiori* so under conditions of high unemployment – the labour market is a 'buyers'
market'. Consequently, they skilfully dramatize the likely
counterproductive effects of the working-time reduction strategy
and its consequent costs to *individual* workers.

III   Remaining Options and Emergent Opportunities

All these observations concerning unions, individual employees,
employers' associations and individual employers suggest that
there is a rationality gap between the levels of the 'systemic
requirements' of the welfare state, individuals' preferences and
collective strategies, and that the strategy of working-time reductions is unlikely to be successful within the industrial-relations
framework of capitalist democracies. It is therefore necessary to
consider institutional designs which could provide an integrated
solution for the present crisis of both the welfare state and the
labour market.

Most aspects of what is commonly described as the 'crisis of
the welfare state' are not generated at the level of welfare-state
institutions. Rather, they reflect a crisis that emerges on the level
of wage-labour, the core institution of capitalist societies. Wage-
labour is the channel through which income and the means of
subsistence are allocated to employees. Within this institutional
domain, between 70 and 92 per cent of the economically active
population of advanced capitalist societies are forced to perform
paid work and to win whatever social recognition they can
through this kind of work. For this overwhelming majority of the
population it is the labour contract and the labour market which
determine either directly or indirectly (via the household and its
'dependants') the basic conditions of work and life.

The crisis symptoms of the welfare state cannot therefore be
analysed adequately on the level of the state itself but must
instead be seen as deriving from malfunctions within the core
arrangements of civil society. The welfare state presupposes,
quite unrealistically, that within civil society most adult males are
employed most of the time and that the household is the main
agency of material and cultural reproduction. Civil society is
separated, according to this conventional view, into the two

sharply divided and complementary spheres of employment and consumption, workplace and household, the male and female domains. This dominant conception of civil society is currently being challenged for two reasons: first, because its two components, the labour market and the family, fail manifestly to perform the functions assigned to them; secondly, and more basically, because the prevailing view of civil society is analytically impoverished and normatively deficient because it ignores the (potential) importance of communal, co-operative and public spaces and functions lying *between* these two functionally differentiated spheres.

If we concentrate on the first of these two points, it is clear that the labour market's capacity to absorb all those who depend on it because they have no alternative mode of working and living is shrinking. The reasons for this have been mentioned in the first part of this essay. It is important to note here that the numerical disparity between those who *need* to be employed and those who *are* employed is not caused by a decline in total output of the economy, as was the case during the economic crisis of the early 1930s. This disparity is caused primarily by a divergence between the change rates of productivity and output.

Such divergence does not necessarily assume the form of rapid productivity increases combined with stagnant growth rates. It can also take the form of stagnant productivity levels combined with negative growth rates, or any combination between these two extremes possibilities. While we do not claim that there are trends towards strong productivity increases (which would be hard to measure anyway), we do make the more cautious claim that for the first time in modern times we are experiencing an employment crisis without a production crisis – an input crisis without an output crisis, as is were. Advanced capitalist societies remain globally wealthy in terms of their GNP, yet significant parts of their populations find themselves at or below the poverty threshold because their labour-power is neither utilized nor remunerated. This is the historically unique aspect of the present situation.

No doubt contingencies, risks, discontinuities and hazards have long been endemic features of a socioeconomic system whose dynamics are ruled by the logic of markets, including the labour market. Since the late nineteenth century, West European societies have developed numerous arrangements designed both to control the incidence of risks caused by the labour market and to minimize the consequences of these risks to the individual, should they occur. Education policies have been designed and expanded to facilitate the employment chances of labour-power. Keynesian economic policies have been used to maintain and to increase the economy's capacity to absorb the labour supply productively. And for those who cannot participate in the active labour force – for such reasons as youth, old age, unemployment, ill-health and disability – schemes of social insurance and transfer payments have been developed in order to protect them from poverty, as well as to prevent them from engaging in non-political or political types of conflict.

For a long period after the Second World War, the 'mixed economy' secured by the Keynesian welfare state seemed to be the ideal arrangement for allowing society to benefit from the evident gains in economic efficiency derived from the market in general and from the labour market in particular, while at the same time protecting society against the risks, externalities and injustices that an unregulated market system would necessarily entail.[9] Current developments suggest that this arrangement consisted of two components (market dynamics and state regulation; property rights and citizen rights) which could *coexist* only under a historically unique condition of economic growth which permitted a continuous, positive-sum economic game. But these components never really 'mixed' in the sense proclaimed by the theorists of the 'mixed economy', mainly because there was no formula for determining a viable combination of the two components.

This point is a common denominator of the New Right and the New Left critiques of the welfare state. The New Right complains, not without solid empirical evidence, that the welfare-state component of the political economy tends to suffocate the viability of the market by underming the incentives both to invest and to work. In the New Right's view, the welfare state has produced a growing avalanche of new demands which are bound eventually to destroy both the economy and the welfare system itself. The New Left critique of the welfare state is strictly reciprocal. It maintains, with equally strong supporting evidence, that there has never been a stable and organic coexistence of the two principles within capitalist societies. It insists that endemic economic and employment crises of the capitalist economy always destroy the seemingly well-entrenched compensatory mechanism of the welfare state, thus preventing it from functioning exactly when its functions are needed most urgently. According to this view, the constraints imposed by the welfare state upon the social power of capital are insufficient to resist the political repercussions of an economic and employment crisis.

One of the strongest empirical supports of this argument is the fact that the compensatory mechanisms of the welfare state (social insurance schemes and transfer payments) are neither insulated from the dynamics of the labour market nor insensitive to its malfunctioning. The welfare state can withstand relatively short periods of employment crisis affecting relatively small segments of the workforce. Beyond such recessions, which are strictly limited in time and scope, the welfare state's compensatory potential is undermined; the resources available for funding the 'social wage' to which citizens are legally entitled are diminished. This discrepancy leads necessarily to a redefinition and narrowing of both the welfare state's legal entitlements and the claims it grants, especially to those groups who are poorly organized and hence least likely to engage in collective conflict.[10]

If this functional dependency relationship of the welfare state upon the market-determined labour market is the key to understanding the present welfare-state crisis, then it follows that this crisis can be solved only 'outside' the welfare state: on the level of those societal institutions upon which the welfare state is itself dependent. This perspective, which views the wage–labour relationship as the main determinant of the present crisis, could lead to the formulation of a realistic, effective and integrated strategy for overcoming it. To be sure, this rules out schemes for abolishing the labour market and replacing it by either a primitive economy of self-employed small producers or a state-managed economy that would transform the whole of society into one huge factory.

In our view there are more piecemeal, more realistic and normatively more attractive options. These options take into account (a) the role and function of collective actors in the labour market; (b) the rights and options of individual employees; (c) the forms and spheres of activity outside the labour market; and (d) the mechanisms of income distribution. Their common denominator is the aim of emancipating human labour-power not only from the unequal power relationships deriving from the *functioning* of the labour market (which has been the traditional goal of the socialist project) but also from the negative effects of a *malfunctioning* labour market in a society that is nevertheless wealthy and highly productive.

How might this aim be achieved in practice? Trade unions, we argued above, are unable to reconcile the levels of systemic rationality and the rationality of individual actors. This weakness is relatively insignificant so long as their central focus is wages and the distribution of monetary income, and so long as general economic growth trends yield a sufficient surplus for distribution. However, as soon as low or zero growth rates prevail and the main interest of unions shifts towards 'qualitative' demands and employment issues, it becomes much harder to motivate individual union members to do what their collective interest requires – especially so in the absence of highly developed traditions of class politics. Under such conditions, the typical response of trade unions is to disregard both the collective interests of the working class as a whole and those specific demands and interests of groups within the unions which are not aggregated easily into an attractive package of demands that is worth fighting for.

If this is the case, then two new types of proposals are required for solving the welfare state/unemployment crisis. First, there is a need for greater decentralization of industrial-relations mechanisms in order to take into account local and specific interests and to exploit the particular opportunities that might offer themselves within particular branches of industry, regions, firms, or among certain groups of workers. Secondly, state legislation and state-administered programmes, such as legislation on working-time limitation, are necessary to compensate for the lack of comprehensiveness of unions and union strategies.

We have argued that while many individual employees are interested in a reduction of working time, and are even willing to make some wage sacrifices in exchange for such reductions, both the particular time patterns of work and the particular leisure-time needs of individual workers (which in turn result from particular household situations and other aspects of social life outside work) are so highly dispersed and differentiated that no single formula could serve the interests of each and every worker. If there no longer exists a 'modal worker'[11] whose individual interests the traditional collective-bargaining arrangements could still satisfy, then what is required is the *legal guarantee of individual rights to opt for 'temporary withdrawals' from employed work* according to their individual income and time needs.[12]

To avoid misunderstandings, it is important to emphasize that this proposal differs fundamentally from schemes for making working hours more 'flexible' simply by removing collective agreements on standard working hours. The problem with this type of 'deregulation' is that it implies significant losses of employees' power. Standardized working-hours arrangements have traditionally performed four highly important functions for workers:

(a) limiting disastrous competition among employees;
(b) serving as a 'ratchet' for further gains *vis-à-vis* capital within the exchange relationship;
(c) guaranteeing claims for a 'full income': that is, preventing employers from enforcing substandard working-time schedules and, thus, incomes below subsistence level;
(d) ensuring predictability and regularity of leisure hours for employees.[13]

Clearly, the abolition of standard working hours would remove these protective functions and thus make the asserted 'freedom of choice' for employees nominal and fictitious. In proposing a 'guaranteed individual option' in respect of working-time arrangements, we therefore suppose that these protective functions should remain effective legal entitlements.

The concept of a 'guaranteed individual option' to work less or not at all for certain periods (along the lines of sabbaticals) can be considered as an 'inverted' form of individuals' decisions to work longer hours (or employers' rights to demand overtime). It would have two clear advantages compared to standardized working-time procedures. First, the amount of voluntary non-employment and hence of additional employment required to satisfy employers' needs would probably be much higher than in any conceivable and realistic worktime-reduction scheme. Second, the total volume of temporary withdrawals from employed work could be finely tuned in response to both the actual use made by employees of these guaranteed options and the changing employment needs of the labour force as a whole.

The overall volume of time during which employees withdraw from employment will depend largely upon three factors: the range of uses to which they could put their extra free time; the status and recognition they derived from 'work' (or other worthwhile social activities) *outside* formal employment; and the amount of income (and future social benefits) they would have to forgo by withdrawing from employment. We have argued that 'modern' living conditions in industrialized and urbanized civil societies tend to devalue the usefulness of free time. However, its relative value, including marginal declines in its utility, is not something that must be accepted as given. It can be altered by means of institutional designs and political intervention. For example, it is well known that the 'usefulness' and efficiency of paid work depends very much upon economies of scale, and the same is probably true of work performed outside employment. As long as the basic unit of work outside employment remains households with limited physical and human capital, the productivity of non-employed and non-monetized work will remain hopelessly inferior to that of employed work. Yet co-operatives, clubs, private associations and voluntary networks of civil society demonstrate that work outside employment can be improved dramatically both in terms of productivity and in the quality of the goods and services it produces. This suggests the need for a political strategy which partially 'uncouples' work from employment – and thus maximizes individuals' ability temporarily to withdraw from paid work – by developing and subsidizing the physical and organizational infrastructures of 'non-employed' work.

The logical complement of this proposal partly to disconnect work from employment would be the partial uncoupling of income and employment. As we have argued above, the welfare state creates only the appearance, not the reality, of such a disjunction of income and employment. This is because (a) the income claims of recipients (such as the unemployed or old age pensioners) typically depend upon their former employment and/or their willingness to re-enter employment; and (b) the funds from which such claims are financed are tied directly, in most countries, to the volume of currently earned incomes through mechanisms such as social security tax. Both these links would need to be severed if individuals' income needs were to be satisfied in the form of a citizen's right to income financed through general taxation. This new mode of allocating income could be justified by the fact that income needs (a) cannot be satisfied fully through the labour market and (b) cannot be replaced fully by those new forms of work outside employment which generate non-monetary use-values.

Contrary to the negative-income-tax proposals of the New Right, the aim of a citizen's right to a basic income would not be to force people into employment; rather, it would aim to provide them with the adequate means of subsisting outside formal employment and hence of escaping the dictates of the labour market. In other words, it would seek not merely to prevent income poverty and 'poverty traps' but to create conditions under which voluntary non-participation in the labour market becomes a feasible and publicly recognized option, the exercise of which might even lead to the resurrection of communal forms of useful activity within civil society which would enable individuals to escape the dictates of both the private household and the labour market.

It is evident that this proposal for uncoupling employment and income could not be introduced immediately. It would need to be adapted to and co-ordinated with other parameters of social security.[14] Some first steps within this gradualistic approach might include reducing the losses of retirement benefits incurred by employees when they deviate from standard working hours; subsidizing time invested in socially useful activity outside the labour market (for example participation in voluntary associations which provide social services); supporting parental leaves of absence through grants whose value is calculated according to the average income of all employees; or promoting gradual retirement by compensating individuals for their earning losses when their working hours are reduced after a certain age.

Such innovations clearly do not amount to anything like a 'programme' for a guaranteed minimum-income scheme ready for implementation. Rather, they serve to shed some light upon the *possible* combination of fairer working-time arrangements, improved income-security mechanism and more widespread access to activities within – and outside – the labour market. It is evident that attempts to uncouple work and employment and sever the links between income and employment would by no means abolish the labour market entirely. Their purpose would be more limited and more realistic: to relieve both the suffering unemployed and the overloaded welfare-state system by reducing the scope of the overextended labour market to functions it is actually capable of performing.

Notes

1. This research project was funded by grants from the *Stiftung Volkswagenwerk*. The final reports were written by Helmut Wiesenthal ('Die Regulierung der Arbeitszeit. Regelungsdefizite im System der industriellen Beziehungen der Bundesrepublik Deutschland, untersucht am Beispiel er Arbeitszeitpolitik', Bielefeld 1985) and Karl Hinrichs ('Motive und Interessen im Arbeitszeitkonflikt. Eine historisch-systematische Analyse', Bielefeld 1986) respectively. Revised versions of these reports will be published in late 1987/early 1988 with Campus-Verlag (Frankfurt and New York).

2. See J. Gershuny, *Social Innovation and the Division of Labour*, Oxford 1983.

3. See Claus Offe, ed., *Opfer des Arbeitsmarktes. Zur Theorie der strukturierten Arbeitslosigkeit*, Neuwied and Darmstadt 1977; and C.F. Büchtemann, 'Der

Arbeitslosigkeitsprozeß. Theorie und Empirie strukturierter Arbeitslosigkeit in der Bundesrepublik Deutschland', in W. Bonß and R.G. Heinze, eds., *Arbeitslosigkeit in der Arbeitsgesellschaft*, Frankfurt am Main 1984, pp. 53-105.

4. U. Engfer, K. Hinrichs, C. Offe and H. Wiesenthal, 'Arbeitszeitsituation und Arbeitszeitverkürzung aus der Sicht der Beschäftigten', *Mitteilungen aus der Arbeitsmarkt- und Berufsforschung*, no. 16, 1983, pp. 91-105.

5. C. Offe and H. Wiesenthal, 'Two Logics of Collective Action', in C. Offe, *Disorganised Capitalism*, ed. John Keane, Cambridge 1986.

6. For a summary of the collective agreement on weekly worktime reduction reached by IG Metall, see K. Hinrichs *et al.*, 'Working Time Policy as Class-Oriented Strategy: Unions and Shorter Working Hours in Great Britain and West Germany', *European Sociological Review* no. 1, 1985, pp. 211-29.

7. Employees who strongly prefer leisure time are thus still likely to accept the option of a wage increase; conversely, employees who prefer the alternative of a wage increase are highly unlikely to opt for a working-time reduction. This point reinforces the conclusion that unions can aggregate income demands more easily than preferences for expanded free time. See the seminal contribution of L.N. Moses, 'Income, Leisure, and Wage Pressure', *Economic Journal*, no. 72, 1962, pp. 320-34.

8. For American survey results indicating variations in the subjective value of objectively equivalent volumes of working-time reduction, see F. Best, *Exchanging Earnings for Leisure. Findings of an Exploratory National Survey on Work Time Preferences*, Special Research Monograph No. 79, Office of Research and Development, Employment and Training Administration, US Department of Labor, Washington DC 1980. For results from the Netherlands, see T. Goedhart, 'De keuze tussen inkomen en vrije tijd', *Sociale Maandstatistiek*, vol. 25, no. 2, 1977, pp. 108-17; and H.H.B. Limberger, 'Arbeitstijdverkorting en de bouwvakarbeider', *Bouw/Werk 33. De bouw in feiten, cijfers en analyses*, no. 8, 1983, pp. 301-13.

9. See C. Offe, *Contradictions of the Welfare State*, ed. John Keane, London 1984.

10. R.G. Heinze, K. Hinrichs and T. Olk, 'The Institutional Crisis of a Welfare State. The Case of Germany', in E. Øen, ed., *Comparing Welfare States and Their Future*, Aldershot 1986, pp. 64-79.

11. H. Thierry, 'Arbeidstijdverkorting: modaal of in modaliteiten', *Beleid an Maatschappij*, vol. 8, no. 2, 1981, pp. 76-88.

12. This kind of individual legal entitlement would not preclude the possibility of employers exercising their powers of inducement and punishment in order to make workers' 'options' conform to their attempts to adapt 'flexibly' to market forces. However, the exercise of such power appears to be least effective when it is applied to individual workers rather than to collective and representative bodies such as works councils. See K. Hinrichs and H. Wiesenthal, 'Thesen zur Problematik nichstandardisierter Arbeitszeiten', *Sozialer Fortschrift*, no. 34, 1984, pp. 285-7; and H. Wiesenthal, 'Themenraub und falsche Allgemeinheiten', in T. Schmid, ed., *Das Ende der starren Zeit. Vorschläge zur flexiblen Arbeitszeit*, Berlin 1985, pp. 90-114.

13. For details see U. Engfer *et al.*, 'Arbeitszeitflexibilisierung und gewerkschaftliche Interessenvertretung – Regelungsprobleme und Risiken individualisierter Arbeitszeiten', *WSI-Mitteilungen*, no. 36, 1983, pp. 585-95.

14. Wetenschappelijke Raad vor het Regeringsbeleid: *Verniewingen in het arbeidsbestel*, Rapporten aan de Regering No. 21, The Hague 1981, p. 251.

Social Movements and the Democratization of Everyday Life

Alberto Melucci

I Conflict as Theatre: from Characters to Signs

In the tradition of both progressive and conservative social thought, conflict and its political representation is often viewed through the image of theatre. There is a stage on which the characters act; they follow a script which previses a happy ending, usually defined from the viewpoint of the author. In addition, there is a public which has to side with one or other of the play's main characters – the hero or the villain – since this choice determines the destiny of the society, its progress towards civilization or its descent into barbarism. This image may be too much of a caricature, yet there can be no doubt that the current view of social conflicts still belongs largely to this traditional representation of collective action. Such action is perceived as an event which takes place on a theatrical stage, acted out by characters defined by their dramatic role (and with intellectuals playing the part of authors of the script, prompters or even directors).

What I wish to argue in this essay is that social movements cannot be represented as characters, as subjects endowed with an essence and a purpose within a *pièce* whose finale is knowable. The reasons for the exhaustion of the traditional image of collective action are primarily historical. The conflicts which prompted the theoretical analysis of social movements – and, more generally, of collective class actors – were linked historically to forms of action in which social conflict was bound up with struggles for citizenship. During the phase of industrial capitalism, the action of the working class (the observation of which spawned the construction of theories about and methods of analysing collective action) comprised a number of interwoven struggles concerning, on the one hand, the class relationships inherent in the production system and, on the other, the demand for access to state power and the extension of political rights. Industrial class conflict was thus combined inextricably with the national question and, in the area of rights, with the task of including previously excluded social groups.

Older forms of collective action, such as those of the industrial working class, were viewed as characters, as 'objective' entities moving towards a destiny. This traditional model appeared plausible because the *historical* nature of collective actors was expressed through forms of action which were simultaneously social and political. I consider that this model of collective action under industrial capitalist conditions is now exhausted. This is neither because the struggle for citizenship is over, nor because there are no more areas of social life susceptible to democratization. Rather, it is because the social and political dimensions of collective conflicts have diverged. Social conflicts − in the strict sense of conflicts concerning social relationships constituting a given system and struggles for the extension of citizenship: that is, for the inclusion of excluded or underprivileged groups in the domain of rights and the rules of the political game − have become distinct and involve quite different actors and forms of action.[1]

There are also theoretical reasons for speaking of the end of movements as characters. These are linked more closely to the concerns of sociological analysis. Although the current manner of considering movements as unified entities − as homogeneous subjects moving towards ends − is influenced by that mythology of which I have spoken, it has virtually no analytical foundation. What is taken for granted − the existence of the collective actor − is in fact the product of highly differentiated social processes, action orientations, elements of structure and motivation. The problem to be faced in the analysis of movements is therefore primarily that of explaining how these different elements are synthesized, how a social actor is constituted and maintains itself as an empirical unit. Many analyses start from the implicit ontological assumption that the actor exists: in other words, that there is a 'workers' movement', a 'women's movement', a 'youth movement', an 'environmental movement', and so on. However, from an analytical viewpoint the problem is precisely that of explaining how that empirical unit which can be observed and called a 'movement' comes to be formed.

Even from a theoretical point of view, therefore, the image of a movement as character is inadequate and dissolves along with the metaphysical, essentialist idea of an actor endowed with its own spirit, with a soul that moves it and provides it with objectives. The progress of sociological thought and research has led collective actors to be viewed as the outcome of complex processes which favour or impede the formation and maintenance of solidarity, shared culture and organizational ties, all of which render possible common action. In other words, collective action is seen as a social product, as a set of social relationships, and not as a primary datum or given metaphysical entity.[2]

In the light of these considerations, I think it is easier to understand the contemporary empirical transformation of collective actors. Even though to a great extent we continue to refer to these actors within a traditional framework of analysis, empirical observation in fact indicates the plurality of elements that converge in those forms of action which – for the sake of convenience (or out of habit, or for lack of alternatives) – describe themselves, and continue to be described, as 'movements'. The over-use of the term 'movement' reveals its semantic inadequacy and conceptual fragility in explaining the *social* nature of collective action; at the same time it throws doubt upon the theoretical and linguistic universe of nineteenth-century industrial society, to which the term, along with many others (such as progress, revolution and classes) belonged. The inadequacy of the terms currently used to speak about contemporary conflicts is not a marginal issue: it is a sign that our theoretical – and not merely our semantic – universes have been exhausted.

The modern phenomena to which I refer (in particular the women's 'movement', the environmental 'movements', the forms of youth collective action and the mobilizations in favour of peace) are not concerned principally with citizenship. This is not to say that this theme has disappeared. In the collective action of women, for example, the problem of rights, inequality and exclusion constitute a large part of the mobilization process. But what women, along with other contemporary collective actors, have achieved is above all to practise alternative definitions of sense: in other words, they have created meanings and definitions of identity which contrast with the increasing determination of individual and collective life by impersonal technocratic power.

These 'movements' reveal conflicts concerning codes, the

formal regulators of knowledge, and the languages which organize our learning processes and our social relations. These conflicts
do not have a subject, at least not in the essentialist, quasi-
metaphysical sense in which one spoke in the past of 'subjects' of
conflicts. Contemporary collective action assumes the form of
networks submerged in everyday life. Within these networks
there is an experimentation with and direct practice of alternative
frameworks of sense, in consequence of a personal commitment
which is submerged and almost invisible.[3]

Such networks produce and process the same kind of information resources which lie at the basis of new forms of technocratic
power. The 'movements' emerge only in limited areas, for limited
phases, and by means of moments of mobilization which are the
other, complementary, face of the submerged networks. Thus for
example it is difficult to understand the massive peace mobilizations if one does not take into account the vitality of the
submerged networks of women, young people, environmentalists
and alternative cultures; these networks make possible such
mobilizations and render them visible in a punctual manner: that
is, at the moment when there emerges a confrontation or conflict
with a public policy.[4]

These two poles of collective action (latency and visibility) are
inseparable. Those who view collective action from a professional–political standpoint usually confine their observations to
the visible face of mobilization, overlooking the fact that what
nourishes it is the daily production of alternative frameworks of
sense, on which the networks themselves are founded and live
from day to day. From a political point of view, however, the
question arises as to whether it is possible to speak of the efficacy
of this type of latent action, and how to assess its success or
failure.

With reference to such action, concrete concepts such as
efficacy or success could be considered unimportant. This is
because conflict takes place principally on symbolic ground, by
means of the challenging and upsetting of the dominant codes
upon which social relationships are founded in high-density
informational systems. The mere existence of a symbolic
challenge is in itself a method of unmasking the dominant codes,
a different way of perceiving and naming the world. This
certainly does not mean that this type of action has no visible
effects. Contemporary forms of collective action produce 'measur-
able' effects on at least three levels.

First, they give rise to *modernization and institutional change*, by means of political reform or the redefinition of organizational cultures and practices. A second effect is the *selection of new elites*. In many Western countries during the 1970s, for example, collective action produced certain changes in the left-wing or progressive political organizations (such as political parties and trade unions) and, above all, resulted in the emergence of a new generation of skilled personnel in the key communications, media, advertising and marketing sectors of the 'information society'. (A survey of young managers within these sectors, especially in metropolitan areas, could throw significant light on the relationship between the new elites and the prior experiences of 'movements' or alternative cultures.) The third effect of collective action is *cultural innovation*: the production of models of behaviour and social relationships that enter into everyday life and the market, modifying the functioning of the social order by means of changes in language, sexual customs, affective relationships, dress and eating habits.

The significance of collective action is nevertheless not confined to these effects, even though attention is normally concentrated on them in order to measure the political efficacy or success of contemporary 'movements'. To confine social analysis to these aspects is to overlook a fundamental dimension of the contemporary conflicts: the 'movements' no longer operate as characters but as *signs*. They do this in the sense that they translate their action into symbolic challenges that upset the dominant cultural codes and reveal their irrationality and partiality by acting at the levels (of information and communication) at which the new forms of technocratic power also operate.

Empirical observation indicates three main forms of symbolic challenge. The first is *prophecy*: the act of announcing, based on experiences affecting the individual's life, that alternative frameworks of sense are possible and that the operational logic of power apparatuses is not the only possible 'rationality'. Prophecy, however, contains an insurmountable contradiction. Prophets announce something other than themselves, while at the same time holding themselves up as a model. Women speak of a right to differ which goes beyond the current female position, but they must also base themselves on the particularity of their biological and historical condition. Young people talk of possible alternatives in the definition and use of time, but they speak against the backdrop of their marginal and precarious condition. Environmentalists' call for a 'pure' nature depends upon a rich and developed society; and so on. Movement actors are very often torn between their prophetic role and their activity as *particular* social actors.

A second form of challenge is that of the *paradox*: the reversal of the dominant codes by means of their exaggeration, which in turn reveals their irrationality and the measures of silence and violence they contain. By exaggerating or pushing to the limit the dominant discourse of power, the 'movement' reveal the self-contradictory nature of its 'reasons' or, conversely, show that what is labelled as 'irrational' by the dominant apparatuses is perhaps dramatically true.

The third type of challenge is that of *representation*: collective actors' capacity to isolate form from content permits, by means of a play of mirrors, their retransmission to the system of its own contradictions. It is no accident that the use of expressive language, theatre, video and images of various kinds constitutes one of the central practices of the everyday networks of contemporary 'movements'.

These three forms of symbolic challenge produce systemic effects which ought not be confused with modernization and institutional changes, the circulation of elites or processes of cultural innovation. These effects consist mainly in *rendering power visible*. The function of contemporary conflicts is to render visible a power that hides behind the rationality of administrative or organizational procedures or the 'show-business' aspects of politics. Visible power disappears from modern societies; it multiplies and forms branches and is difficult to locate within figures or institutions, even though it comes to play a crucial role in shaping all social relationships.

Under these circumstances, not only the 'movements' but power itself ceases to be a 'character'. Power is transformed into a set of signs which are frequently concealed, interwoven with procedures, or crystallized in the undifferentiated consumption of the great media market. In complex systems, no one is responsible any longer for the goals of social life. Hence one of the fundamental roles of collective action is precisely that of rendering these ends explicit by creating spaces in which power becomes visible. Power which is recognizable is also negotiable, since it can be confronted and because it is forced to take differences into account.

Collective action makes possible the negotiation and establishment of public agreements which, although ever more transitory, nevertheless serve as a condition of a political democracy capable of protecting the community against the increasing risks of an arbitrary exercise of power or violence: since it is neutralized behind the formal rationality of procedures, power cannot be controlled unless it is rendered visible. It must be recognized, however, that in contemporary systems the available spaces for reaching agreements are limited and temporary. They have to be redefined continually and rapidly because the differences change, the conflicts shift, the agreements cease to satisfy and new forms of domination are constantly emerging.

II The End of Politics?

My argument so far certainly does not imply that in complex systems politics has become simply a residue of the past. On the contrary, 'political' relationships have never been so important as in complex systems. Never before has it been so necessary to regulate complexity by means of decisions, choices and 'policies', the frequency and diffusion of which must be ensured if the uncertainty of systems subject to exceptionally rapid change is to be reduced. Complexity and change produce the need for decisions and create a plurality of variable interests which cannot be compared to situtions of the past; the multiplicity and changeability of interests results in a multiplicity and changeability of problems to be solved. Hence the need for decisions: decisions which are continually subject to verification and exposed to the limitations and risks of consensus in conditions of rapid change.

I define a political relationship as one which permits the reduction of uncertainty and the mediation of opposing interests by means of decisions. I consider political relationships in this sense to be fundamental for the functioning of complex societies. In societies of this type, we are in fact witnessing a process of multiplication and diffusion of political instances. In different areas of social life and within institutions and organizations of many kinds authoritarian regulations are being transformed into political relationships. This process of 'transforming the authoritarian into the political' entails introducing systems of exchanges and procedures of negotiation which by means of confrontation and the mediation of interests produce decisions, whereas before there were only mechanisms for authoritatively transmitting regulations by means of power.

This 'political level' of relationships is to be found not only in national political systems but also within numerous productive, educational, administrative and regional institutions, as well as in areas of society in which – often after a struggle – new instances of political decisions, interest representation and negotiation are brought into being. This process of 'politicization' is linked to the complexity of the information systems, the need to cope with a changeable environment and the multiplying requirements of balance within the system itself. The importance of the 'political level' of relationships is evident not only within present-day Western parliamentary political systems. The problem of politics confronts every complex system, whatever type of political organization may be envisaged for it. Any project of democratization in an advanced society cannot ignore this problem, even though the intellectual and practical tradition of opposition movements is scarcely adequate for its resolution. For too long it was assumed that the specificity and autonomous logic of decision-making processes and mechanisms of representation could be annulled by means of the cathartic power of mass struggles. Today, it is evident instead that these problems remain entirely unresolved.

This does not mean that the quality of the interests entering into a decision-making process is irrelevant, nor that all these interests carry the same weight, nor that a given system automatically ensures equal access to each interest. It does, however, mean that the decision-making and representation processes are a specific and necessary condition of the functioning of complex systems.

This problem of decision-making processes, which function by means of representation, was underestimated or ignored outright by the Marxist intellectual tradition, which reduced representation to its 'bourgeois' forms and to parliamentary institutions and in so doing annulled the problem of how to mediate and represent a plurality of interests. The problem of representation is tied to complexity and therefore cannot be annulled, whatever model of political organization is envisaged. Representation involves an inevitable difference between representatives and those whom they represent; between the interests of each and between their concurrent or divergent logics of action.

Any process of democratic transformation must necessarily take into account this difference between the structures of representation and the demands or interests of the represented: a project of democratization intended to be 'progressive' or 'radical' is forced to imagine the social and political means of controlling this difference. A necessary condition of democratization is the refusal to deny this problem ideologically: only if and when it is acknowledged does it become possible to look for ways of controlling and reducing the distance separating power from social demands.

To return to the initial question of political relationships: these considerations serve to allocate politics its proper dimension, by both recognizing its specificity and defining its limits. A definition of politics as all-embracing is replaced by a recognition of its specificity and its 'functional necessity'. For the radical tradition, this recognition involves a difficult passage which entails – intellectually and practically speaking – all the depuration that always accompanies processes of desacralizing and laicizing social life. Politics guarantees the possibility of mediating interests in order to produce decisions. There are two reasons why politics in this sense is not the whole of social life:

1. There are structures and interests which precede, delimit and condition politics. Even if they are subsequently mediated by politics, these structures and interests exist irrespective of every ideological illusion of pluralism and official pretensions of representing society as if it were a spontaneous and open plurality of demands and needs. The political game never takes place on an open field with equal chances. In order to understand the unequal distribution of political chances and political power it is therefore necessary to consider the *limits* of the political game and, thus, the manner in which the social power underlying political institutions is formed.

2. There are dimensions of social phenomena – affective or symbolic relationships, for instance – which cannot be considered as political because they function according to a different logic, which it is therefore necessary to respect and not to violate.

These considerations suggest that we are not faced with the end of politics but, rather, with its radical redefinition. One – perhaps not unimportant – indication of this transformation of the significance and meaning of politics is the increasing difficulty of maintaining the classic distinction between 'right' and 'left' political traditions. The analytical vacuity of the term 'left' is now evident. While its sole function is that of empirically defining political agents linked to the Western historical tradition, it no longer reveals anything about either the new conflicts and actors or about the direction of contemporary social and political transformations.

Traditionally, the 'right' displayed an orientation towards the past, whereas the 'left' displayed an orientation towards the future. But the appearance of contemporary social 'movements' has impressed upon collective consciousness that we live in a society without a future, not only because the future is threatened by the possibility of a global catastrophe but because the central problem of complex systems is the maintenance of equilibrium. The allegedly 'anti-modern' character of 'movements' in fact consists in their proclamation of the end of linear progress and their affirmation of the sense of fighting for the present, upon which our future also depends.

Change in complex societies becomes discontinuous, articulated, differentiated. These systems never change at the same time and in the same way at their various levels. The political system, by means of decisions, can reduce the uncertainty and increase the transformation potential produced by conflicts, but this involves a separation of the agents of change from those who manage the transformation. The actors who produce the change and those who manage – that is, institutionalize – the transformation are not identical. In my view, the idea of a movement transforming itself into power while maintaining the transparency of its own expressed demands was revealed as an illusion the day after the October Revolution. But now we know the theoretical reasons why this idea was illusory from the beginning.

Changes within a complex system are always changes of an adaptive type; while they may also entail ruptures, these changes always pertain to the overall systemic balance. We know that power is necessary for the regulation of the complexity of any system and that it is structurally distinct from conflicts. The significance of conflicts is that they can prevent the system from closing in upon itself by obliging the ruling groups to innovate, to permit changes among elites, to admit what was previously excluded from the decision-making arena and to expose the shadowy zones of invisible power and silence which a system and its dominant interests inevitably tend to create. These possible consequences of conflict appear to be a fundamental (but not the only) function of social 'movements' and of a political opposition which resists the attempt to establish a new power on the ruins of the old or, at least, strives to prevent itself from reproducing such power.

III   The Dilemmas of 'Post-Industrial' Democracy

In recent years a considerable number of studies have been concerned with the crisis of the welfare state and with the problems of governability, pluralism and political exchange in neo-corporatist systems. At the same time, considerable attention has been given to the political effects of complexity.[5] In relation to the problems discussed above, this extensive debate has brought to light what can be called the dilemmas of post-industrial democracy.

The dilemma of *surplus variability* consists in the necessity of constant change while at the same time maintaining a stable normative and prescriptive nucleus. In complex systems it is necessary on the one hand to take into account changeable interests, a wide distribution of social actors and the variability of their aggregated interests, while on the other hand guaranteeing systems of rules and prescriptions which ensure a certain predictability to behaviour and procedures.

A second dilemma is that of the *undecidability of ultimate ends*. Complex systems display a great fragmentation of power. There is an increase in the number of groups capable of organizing themselves, representing their interests and extracting advantages from processes of political exchange; there is also a fragmentation of political decision-making structures, giving rise to numerous partial governments that are difficult to co-ordinate. At the same time there is a consolidation of uncontrolled and invisible organizations within which decisions about ends are made. The circles in which the sense of collective activity is determined become invisible and impermeable. Hence the dilemma of the undecidability of ultimate ends: while all too many decisions are made, it becomes increasingly difficult to decide what is essential.

Finally, there is the dilemma of *dependent participation*. In Western pluralist systems one observes an extension of citizenship and participation, together with an increasing need for the planning of society as a whole by means of bureaucratic-administrative organizations. The extension of the sphere of individual and collective rights necessitates planning, in order to co-ordinate the plurality of interests and decisions and to protect the corresponding rights of representation and decision-making. But each episode of planning spawns a technocratic decision-making centre, which inevitably curtails participation and effective rights.

These dilemmas are linked to profound transformations of the complex social systems. An exclusively political interpretation – one that is tied to the logic of decision-making and interest representation – fails to take into account the transformations of social production and the modification of social needs and interests: processes that precede the political system and subsequently enter it in the form of demands. Exclusively political interpretations of this kind are today prominent in the theories of 'rational choice' and political exchange, which evidently substitute for the economistic approaches of the past a new reduction of social relationships to political relationships. Politically reductionist approaches fail to appreciate that the understanding of the above-mentioned dilemmas, and possibly their solution, depends rather on the capacity to supplement what can be observed at the political level with an understanding of transformations in the structural logic and new structural contradictions of the complex systems.

These complex systems are forced to mobilize individual action resources in order to enable their high-density and highly differentiated organizational, informational and decision-making networks to function. At the same time, however, individual action acquires an 'elective' character, because individuals are attributed an increasing possibility of controlling and defining the conditions of their personal and social experience. The process of individualization – the attribution of a sense of social action to potentially every individual – is thus two-edged: while there is an extension of social control by means of an increase of 'socializing' pressures on individuals' motivational and cognitive structures, there is also a demand for the appropriation of the space-time-sense of life by these same individuals who are provided with broader possibilities of meaningful action.

The dilemmas of 'post-industrial' democracy are linked to this structural tension pervading the complex systems. If both the pressures for integration and the needs for identity-building are not taken into account, the essential components of the dilemmas mentioned above will escape analysis: variability and predictability, fragmentation and concentration, participation and planning represent, in the political sphere, two sides of a more general systemic problem. The attempt to resolve these dilemmas exclusively from within the political system can at best result in proposals and decisions of a (possibly innovative) technocratic-rationalizing kind.

However, both a careful consideration of the connection between the political dilemmas of contemporary Western societies and their constantly changing systemic logic and a recognition of the specificity and autonomy of political relationships are necessary if the problem of democracy is to be faced in its entirety. To believe that the essence of democracy still consists in securing the competition of interests and the rules that make their representation possible is to fail to appreciate the scope of the socio-political transformations taking place within complex systems. This conception of democracy corresponded to a capitalist system founded on the separation of the state from civil society, a system in which the state simply translated the 'private' interests formed in civil society into the terms of 'public' institutions.

Today, this distinction between the state and civil society, upon which the political experience of capitalism was based, has become unclear. As a unitary agent of intervention and action, the state has dissolved. It has been replaced from above by a tightly interdependent system of transnational relationships and subdivided from below into a multiplicity of partial governments, defined both by their own systems of representation and decision-making and by an ensemble of interwoven organizations which combine inextricably the public and private.

Even 'civil society' – at least as it was defined by the early modern tradition – appears to have lost its substance. The 'private' interests once belonging to it no longer have the permanence and visibility of stable social groups sharing a definite position in the hierarchy of power and influence. The former unity (and homogeneity) of social interests has exploded. Drawing upon a spatial image, and seen from above, it could be said that they assume the form of general cultural and symbolic orientations which cannot be attributed to specific social groups; seen from below, these interests are subdivided into a multiplicity of primary needs, including those which were once considered natural.

The simple distinction between state and civil society is replaced by a more complex situation. Processes of differentiating and 'laicizing' mass parties have transformed them increasingly into catch-all parties which are institutionally incorporated into the structures of government; at the same time, the parliamentary system tends to accentuate both its selective processing of demands and its merely formal decision-making functions. On another plane, there is an evident multiplication and increasing autonomy of systems of representation and decision-making; this process results in the pluralization of decision-making centres, but also carries with it the undoubted advantages associated with the diffusion of decision-making instances. Finally, on a further plane, there is an evident formation of collective demands and conflicts which assume the form of social 'movements' aiming at the reappropriation of the motivation and sense of action in everyday life.

Under the conditions, it would be illusory to think that democracy consists merely in the competition for access to governmental resources. Democracy in complex societies requires conditions which enable individuals and social groups to affirm themselves and to be recognized for what they are or wish to be. That is, it requires conditions for enhancing the recognition and autonomy of individual and collective signifying processes.

The formation, maintenance and alteration through time of a self-reflexive identity requires social spaces free from control or repression. These spaces are formed by processes (of organization, leadership, ideology) that consolidate collective actors, ensure the continuity of their demands, and permit their confrontation and negotiation with the outside world. Freedom to belong to an identity and to contribute to its definition thus presumes the freedom to be represented. But belonging is not identical with being represented – it is in a certain sense its opposite. Belonging is direct, representation is indirect; belonging means the immediate enjoyment of the benefits of an identity, whereas representation means deferred enjoyment; and so on.

Under pressure from this contradiction between belonging and representation democracy must entail the possibility of refusing or modifying the given conditions of representation, as well as the possibility of abandoning constituted signifying processes in order to produce new ones. A non-authoritarian democracy in complex societies presupposes the capacity of foreseeing and supporting this double possibility: the right to make one's voice heard by means of representation or by modifying the conditions of listening, as well as the right to belong or to withdraw from belonging in order to produce new meanings. These freedoms would facilitate the generation, for the first time, of certain 'rights of everyday life' such as those relating to space, time, birth and death, individuals' biological and affective dimensions, and the survival of the planet and the human species.

A necessary condition of such a democracy is public spaces independent of the institutions of government, the party system and state structures.[6] These spaces assume the form of an articulated system of decision-making, negotiation and representation in which the signifying practices developed in everyday life can be expressed and heard independently of formal political institutions. Public spaces of this kind should include some guarantees that individual and collective identities are able to exist; 'soft' institutionalized systems favouring the appropriation of knowledge and the production of symbolic resources; and open systems in which information can be circulated and controlled. Public spaces are characterized by a great fluidity, and their size may increase or diminish according to the independence they are accorded: they are by definition a mobile system of instances kept open only by creative confrontation between collective action and institutions. Inasmuch as public spaces are intermediate between the levels of political power and decision-making and networks of everyday life, they are structurally ambivalent: they express the double meaning of the terms representation and participation.

Representation means the possibility of presenting interests and demands; but it also means remaining different and never being heard entirely. Participation also has a double meaning. It means both taking part – that is, acting so as to promote the interests and the needs of an actor – and belonging to a system, identifying with the 'general interests' of the community. The public spaces which are beginning to develop in complex societies are points of connection between political institutions and collective demands, between the functions of government and the representation of conflicts. The contemporary 'movements' can act within these public spaces without losing their specificity.

The main function of public spaces is that of rendering visible and collective the questions raised by the 'movements'. They enable these 'movements' to avoid being institutionalized and, conversely, ensure that society as a whole is able to assume responsibility for (that is, institutionally process) the issues, demands and conflicts concerning the goals and meaning of social action raised by the 'movements'. In this sense, the consolidation of independent public spaces is a vital condition of maintaining – without seeking falsely to resolve – the dilemmas of 'post-industrial' democracy. For when society assumes responsibility for its own issues, demands and conflicts, it subjects them openly to negotiation and to decisions and transforms them into possibilities of change. It thereby makes possible a 'democracy of everyday life', without thereby either annulling the specificity and independence of the 'movements' or concealing the use of power behind allegedly neutral decision-making procedures.

Notes

1. This does not mean that social and political forms of action never combine empirically. On the contrary, feminist struggles are a typical example of the way movements combine the demand for inclusion and rights for an excluded social category (the struggle for *emancipation*) with the affirmation of a difference (the feminine difference) which challenges the dominant logic of the system (the *women's* movement). Another example of the intertwining of social and political demands is evident among the ethnic-national movements which have reappeared in the more advanced Western societies. These movements synthesize the heritage of concern with the national question and the new identity problems posed by the development of complex societies; see A. Melucci and M. Diani, *Nazioni senza Stato. I movimenti etnico-nazionali in Occidente*, Turin 1983.

2. The sociological contributions to the theory of 'movements', especially the European approaches and the resource mobilization theory of the 1970s, are discussed in A. Melucci, 'An End to Social Movements?', *Social Science Information*, no. 23, 1984, pp. 819-835. Resource mobilization theory is analysed in J.C. Jenkins, 'Resource Mobilization Theory and the Study of Social Movements', *Annual Review of Sociology*, no. 9, 1983, pp. 527-53; B. Klandermans, 'Mobilization and Participation: Social-Psychological Expansion of Resource Mobilization Theory', *American Sociological Review*, no. 49, 1984, pp. 583-600; and S. Tarrow, 'Struggling to Reform', *Cornell University Western Society Paper*, no. 15, 1983. On the European approaches, see A. Touraine, *Le retour de l'acteur*, Paris 1984 and J. Habermas, *The Theory of Communicative Action*, vol. 1, Boston, MA 1984. The interpretation of collective action as a 'constructed' reality is defended in A. Melucci, *Altri Codici*, Bologna 1984.

3. An empirical analysis of these networks is developed in A. Melucci, *Altri Codici*.

4. On peace mobilizations in particular, see A. Melucci, 'The Symbolic Challenge of Contemporary Movements', *Social Research*, no. 52, 1985, pp. 789-816; and G. Lodi, *Uniti e diversi. Le mobilitazioni per la pace nell' Italia degli anni '80*, Milan 1984. The role played by submerged networks in the mobilization process is also discussed by H. Kriesi, 'Local mobilization for the People's Petition of the Dutch peace movement', paper presented at the international workshop, 'Transformation of Structure into Action', Free University, Amsterdam, June 1986.

5. For a review of this literature, see especially C. Offe, *Contradictions of the Welfare State*, ed. J. Keane, London and Boston 1984, and P.C. Schmitter and G. Lehmbruch, eds, *Trends Towards Corporatist Intermediation*, London and Beverley Hills 1980.

6. The contemporary revival of the debate on civil society is moving towards this conclusion. See J. Cohen, *Class and Civil Society*, Amherst 1982; J. Cohen, 'Rethinking Social Movements', *Berkeley Journal of Sociology*, no. 28, 1983, pp. 97-113; J. Cohen and A. Arato, 'Social Movements, Civil Society and the Problem of Sovereignty', *Praxis International*, no. 4, October 1984, pp. 266-83; J. Keane, *Public Life and Late Capitalism*, New York and Cambridge 1984; and J. Keane, 'Despotism and Democracy', in this volume.

PART THREE

Eastern States and the Possibility of Civil Society

Totalitarianism Revisited*

Jacques Rupnik

> Imagine a pair of scales. On one is a gram, on the other a ton; 'I'
> on one, 'We', the One State, on the other. ... Hence the allocation:
> the rights to the ton, the duties to the gram, while the natural
> course from nullity to grandeur is to forget that you are a gram and
> to feel that you are a millionth part of a ton.
>
> Evgeny Zamyatin, *We* (1920)

A Paradoxical Journey

The journey taken by the concept of totalitarianism has been
fraught with paradox. It is a story of non-synchronization and
misunderstandings in East–West communication. At the time
when the Central-Eastern European countries were being incorporated into the Soviet bloc and experiencing the 'pure' totalitarianism of the Stalinist era, they were absent from the debate on
the concept then taking place in the West. The one explains the
other. Conversely, twenty years later, when the concept had been
virtually banished from Western Sovietology as an unscientific
Cold War product, it was reappropriated by the independent
political thinkers in Central-Eastern Europe. 1968 marked the
parting of the ways and was the catalyst which set the concept on
separate courses, East and West. For Western political scientists

---

*Translated by A.G. Brain.

détente provided the impulse, whose effects could be felt in the various interpretations of the nature of the Communist system. For the intellectuals of the 'other Europe', 1968 provided the final proof of the failure of reform and the existence of a permanent 'totalitarian' core at the heart of the Communist system. Consequently, if we are to trace the route taken by the concept of totalitarianism, we must not only look closely at the various attempts by the intelligentsia to find a way out of 'normalization' but also, indirectly, give some attention to the relationship between politics, political science, and the channels of East–West intellectual communication.

At a time when a large number of intellectuals were actively helping to provide the new Soviet-inspired political system with an intellectual legitimacy, others were being silenced in the Gulag or totally marginalized, as a result of which independent ideas about the new regime by 'eye-witnesses' were confined to the pages of their private diaries. In the circumstances, East European involvement in the debate could be only indirect, via such émigré authors as Czeslaw Milosz or Peter Meyer. The former made a vital contribution towards explaining the role of ideology in totalitarian systems with his penetrating study of the subjugation of intellectuals in Central-Eastern Europe by the 'new faith' from the East.[1] To Meyer we owe the first analyses of another of the specific features of totalitarian systems: Nazi and Stalinist anti-semitism.[2]

The poems of an Illyes or a Kolar do not only show clearly that Eastern European intellectuals had not all swallowed the 'murtibing' pill Milosz spoke about. They also provided – with a lucidity never since equalled – remarkable insights into the nature of what Western political scientists call 'totalitarianism'. These poems also point to another feature of attempts to define the concept: originally they tended to be literary and philosophical, rather than political. It is not inapposite in this connection to recall what happened to the concept in the West, where it first assumed literary form through Orwell's *Nineteen Eighty-Four*, whose publication was followed by a classic of political philosophy.[3] Only then was it systematized by political science.

Although the same sequence of literature–political philosophy–political science can be discerned in both West and East, in the former case it was condensed into the space of a few short years, whilst in the latter it has extended over three decades. There are a number of reasons for this. Firstly, as soon as it appeared,[4] and in spite of its clearly limited circulation, Orwell's

novel had a real impact in intellectual circles, whereas English
and American political science had a delayed effect. As a consequence, Eastern European philosophers and political scientists
were not to come across the concept until the period of 'de-Stalinization', which naturally meant that in intellectual and political
terms they were more preoccupied with change than with continuity. In other words, they tended to ignore the concept and in
those cases where someone bothered to tackle it, it was only to
reject it as outdated. Only at a later period, after the crushing of
the Prague Spring, did we begin to see the concept making a
fresh appearance among independent political thinkers. To a
certain extent (leaving aside the effects of intellectual fashion, in
which the media play a not inconsiderable role) developments in
the East recall the post-1968 course followed by 'anti-totalitarian'
left-wing intellectuals in France.

This reappropriation of the concept by non-official political
thinking in Central-Eastern Europe has taken place on three
levels. In the first place – and this is a relatively recent phenomenon – it has appeared at the level of public opinion. The word
'totalitarianism' (or, more frequently, the adjective 'totalitarian')
has become common parlance, so to speak. A recent sociological
survey of corruption in Poland (conducted by Kiciuski) revealed
that those questioned regarded the political system as the main
cause of that particular affliction. The most frequent responses
encountered were 'the concentration of power in the hands of a
few' and 'the lack of democracy, making social control impossible', but there was also 'totalitarianism', 'the system of totalitarian rule' and 'the *Nomenklatura*'.

Secondly, the term has become the 'common denominator' of
dissident political writings. The most recent instance – one which
reveals most clearly how much the concept has taken two separate paths in Eastern and Western Europe – is the way the
concept of totalitarianism is employed in the present discussions
about disarmament between Western peace movements and a
major section of East European dissident opinion. Their
disagreement could be summed up by saying that in the eyes of
the dissidents, Western pacifists tend to focus their attention on
the manifestations of war danger: the stockpiling of nuclear
weapons; for their part, the 'dissidents'[25] prefer to stress the roots
of conflict, which they see in the logic of a totalitarian system
which risks transforming the internal 'state of war' into an external one.

In the wake of 1968, a new approach to the Communist

system was pursued in the light of the concept of totalitarianism, but also in terms of the new realities of the Brezhnev era.[6] It came to be recognized that the failed or interrupted revolutions of Budapest 1956, the 1968 Prague Spring or Solidarity in Poland in 1980-81 forced a double conclusion: that totalitarianism is no longer what it used to be, and that the state-Party's hold over society has changed since the Stalin era. Those three great struggles (not to mention other minor ones) are proof that the system is far from static and that its stability is extremely precarious. On the other hand, those three very different attempts to confront, dissolve and then neutralize the 'totalitarian core' of the system all came to grief, which has prompted dissident political theorists to reconsider the concept in the light of both the new realities and the constants of the Communist system.

The way the concept of totalitarianism is employed in the other half of Europe also depends very much on circumstances and on what might be described as 'the possible future', as it is perceived at a given moment. Although this is a wild oversimplification, one is tempted to say that the concept of 'totalitarianism' does not feature prominently in political vocabulary when there is a hope of change on the horizon. Conversely, the expression makes a comeback when the prospect of overcoming the Yalta legacy seems to be postponed until doomsday. But here one should be careful not to over-generalize: Polish political discourse of the 1970s referred to 'totalitarianism', while focusing at the same time on the idea of transforming the relationship between state and civil society.

It is this interaction between the experiences and realities of Soviet-style Communisn and their treatment by intellectual critics of those particular countries that lies at the centre of the following effort to trace the course taken by the concept of totalitarianism in Eastern Europe. To simplify matters, it is possible to speak of two major phases which correspond to two kinds of attitude towards the concept of totalitarianism: the first, corresponding roughly to the period of 'de-Stalinization' (1956-68), could be called 'the East European contribution to efforts to demolish the concept'; the second, sparked off by the invasion of Czechoslovakia in August 1968 and 'consolidated' by the establishment, in December 1981, of the 'state of war' in Poland, has taken the form of an original effort to redefine the concept of totalitarianism, its sources, its means of social control, and its present crisis.

Totalitarianism Redefined: Images of Post-Stalinist Totalitarianism in Independent Political Thinking

1968 represented the zenith of both Communist 'reformism' and the challenge to the concept of totalitarianism. But the crushing of reform and, more generally, the ensuing Brezhnev period of conservative restoration throughout the Soviet bloc was perceived as the final defeat of the very idea of a fundamental reform of the system from within, and the ultimate proof of the impossibility of 'detotalizing totalitarianism'. It also meant, according to Kolakowski, the 'clinical death' of Marxist revisionism in Eastern Europe. From that moment, Communism 'ceased being an intellectual problem and became merely a question of power';[7] one is tempted to add: Communist ideology ceased being an intellectual problem, whereas power became one.

The second, related aspect of this evolution is the progressive jettisoning of the concept of 'Stalinism' so dear to the 'revisionist' Marxists of the 1960s in the East and the 'Eurocommunists' of the 1970s in the West. Solzhenitsyn is categorical on the subject:

> There never was any such thing as Stalinism (either as a doctrine, or as a path of national life, or as a state system) ... Stalin was a very consistent and faithful – if also very untalented – heir to the spirit of Lenin's teaching.[8]

The touchstone of Solzhenitsyn's argument is the Gulag, the concentration camp system whose origins unquestionably go back to Lenin's time and – most importantly – whose extent and central role in the system is what makes Communism akin to Nazism. Indeed, the bulk of writings by the survivors of the Gulag makes the concentration camp system and its close links with Marxist-Leninist ideology the pivot of Communist totalitarianism.

It was within this new intellectual framework that the concept of totalitarianism surfaced once more and subsequently became a common denominator of independent political thinking in Eastern Europe. This rediscovery of the concept (and realities) of totalitarianism was by no means a return to the American political science of the 1950s. It was a completely new attempt to redefine the concept in the light of the system's evolution and the new methods of Communist rule. It is possible to speak of two basic approaches, corresponding to two definitions of the concept of totalitarianism. The first – more literary and philosophical –

attempts to discern the 'essence' of totalitarian rule. The second adopts the methods of political science and seeks to lay bare the new workings of totalitarian or 'post-totalitarian' rule; both approaches are nevertheless concerned with exploring the origins of the totalitarian phenomenon.

The Orwellian Heritage: the 'Institutionalized Lie' and Totalitarian Languages

Many have read Koestler's *Darkness at Noon*, but few have a knowledge of Orwell's *Nineteen Eighty-Four*. Because of the difficulties in obtaining the book and the risk faced by anyone possessing it, it is only known to a handful of members of the 'inner Party'. These privileged individuals are fascinated by Orwell's Swiftian manner of observing details so familiar to them. It is impossible to employ such a style in the countries of the New Faith because allegory, being by nature capable of several interpretations, would run counter to the precepts of socialist realism and the requirements of the censor.[9]

This 1953 passage from Milosz deserves to be 'updated'. Firstly, it is difficult these days to overestimate the profound impact Orwell's novel has had on the intellectuals of Eastern Europe. It is one of the great post-war literary works to have marked a whole generation. The book escaped from the sanctum of the 'inner Party' to which Milosz refers and has been widely distributed in *samizdat* form. Secondly, they have recognized themselves in Orwell's book which, in the countries of 'existing socialism', is regarded not solely as a work of science fiction but as a description – often an incredibly precise and pertinent one at that – of the real nature of Communist rule. Eastern European intellectuals read *Nineteen Eighty-Four* with the same feelings that Winston Smith had on discovering the key to the system in Goldstein's book, in which, as Simecka says, they discover 'what they knew already'. And lastly, an 'Orwellian' or Swiftian literary genre, well suited to describing/interpreting the Communist system, has evolved over the past decade, the key examples being Zinoviev's *The Yawning Heights* and Tadeusz Konwicki's *A Minor Apocalypse*.

Whereas Amalrik posed the question whether the Soviet Union would survive until 1984, the Hungarian György Dalos, in *1985*, prefers to imagine a comic sequel to Orwell's novel. But if one were obliged to sum up in a single word what it is that constitutes the 'essence' of the totalitarian system in the view of the Eastern European intellectuals, it would be the supremacy of ideology as the institutionalized lie. The Orwellian theme of 'the lie' and resistance to the lie (or of 'living in the truth', as Havel put it) is the point of departure for the reconstitution of independent political thinking in Soviet-bloc countries.

Kolakowski provides the most lucid epistemological explanation of the lie's function in the totalitarian system. By systematically destroying historical memory and manipulating all information, the totalitarian regime destroys the very criterion of truth. Since truth alters in accordance with the needs of the rulers, a lie can become the truth, or rather, the very notion of truth disappears: 'This is the great cognitive triumph of totalitarianism. By managing to abrogate the very idea of truth, it can no longer be accused of lying.'[10]

In other words, we are not talking about the 'white lies' or half-truths in which politicans in all possible political systems indulge. We are talking about the Lie with a capital L which constitutes the foundations of a political system, what Kolakowski calls a 'new civilization'. This 'systemic' and 'existential' dimension of the lie is also examined by Solzhenitsyn:

> ... in our country the daily lie is not the whim of corrupt natures but a mode of existence, a condition of the daily welfare of each person. In our country the lie has been incorporated into the state system as the vital link holding everything together, with billions of tiny fasteners, several dozen to every individual.[11]

Defined in this way, the totalitarian lie rests on two pillars: the destruction of memory and totalitarian language. Consciousness is impossible without memory, and the destruction of the past and of historical memory is precisely at the heart of the totalitarian enterprise:

> A people whose memory – either individual or collective – has been nationalized and passed into State hands, and is therefore perfectly malleable and manipulable, are entirely at the mercy of their rulers; they have been robbed of their identity.[12]

Under the 'regime of oblivion' any attempt, however limited, to preserve one's memory, and hence one's freedom to think, represents, according to Simecka,

> an act of self-preservation, and self-defence in the face of total disintegration, as well as an assertion of human dignity. Nowhere in the world does history have such importance as in Eastern Europe.[13]

In Kundera's words: 'the struggle of man against power is the struggle of memory against forgetting.'

Czeslaw Milosz subtitled his *Captive Mind* 'an essay on the people's logocracies'. He emphasized that while the conquest of power could be achieved through 'the barrel of a gun', the maintenance of power is achieved through the 'muzzle of language'. This key idea of Orwell's *Nineteen Eighty-Four* – that totalitarian power cannot be maintained without a totalitarian language which is not solely the vehicle of the state ideology but, above all, intended to prevent the emergence of 'heretical' ideas – has been taken up again by dissident intellectuals in Russia and East-Central Europe alike. And rightly so. Indeed, the historian M. Heller has convincingly demonstrated this Orwellian heritage via official Soviet reference books displaying the concept of discourse and language current in the Soviet Union.

The aim, according to Heller, is to 'confer a political nuance on all words', in line with the regime's goal of 'politicizing all areas of life'. Viewed in this way, Soviet Communism would appear above all to be a 'linguistic dictatorship' by the McLuhan method ('the medium is the message'):

> The state has rationalized language and the means of information, it has become both the medium and the message; its subject of discourse is itself. It declares that the State is the most important thing of all, of which the citizens are no more than minuscule parts. Hence power must be maintained. Earlier ideologies admitted discussion. In contrast, this magnificent technology of power – the rationalization of the vocabulary – prevents any response.[14]

This is not solely a theoretical model but, as Simecka points out,

> a process which is already so far advanced in Eastern Europe that it truly threatens to destroy the capacity of a defenceless population freely to articulate a non-official evaluation of political, social and economic realities.[15]

How can this vision of a totalitarian 'logocracy' be reconciled with what has been said about the bankruptcy of the official ideology? The answer is to be found in the notion of the 'existential lie', which is quite distinct from conscious (or even enthusiastic) support for the ruling ideology. Indeed, in the present situation that the Czech writer Václav Havel describes as post-totalitarian, one need not believe all these mystifications, but one must behave as if one did, or at least put up with them tacitly, or get along with those who use them. But this means living within a lie. One is not required to believe the lie; it is enough to accept life with it and within it. In so doing one confirms the system, gives it meaning, creates it ... and merges with it.[16]

From this standpoint it is irrelevant whether, in terms of 'effectiveness', the official propaganda receives conscious support or merely arouses more or less cynical indifference. Most importantly, the institutionalized lie is an impersonal one. One can live in the lie without being taken for a 'liar': 'The impersonal lie and the impersonal murder are two forms of the political art that the totalitarian states have perfected.'[17]

From Social Control to 'Social Contract'

Western political science of the fifties (especially the classic work of Friedrich and Brzezinski) defined totalitarianism by a set of criteria such as the presence of a charismatic leader, mass terror, the 'permanent purge', and ideological mobilization. These criteria were superseded not only by Khrushchevian reformism but also by the conservatism of the Brezhnev era. Instead of rejecting out of hand the concept of totalitarianism in favour of others, borrowed either from the sociology of the Western political systems, or from theories of 'development' or modernization, independent political thinkers in Eastern Europe have redefined it in the light of the experience of the past twenty-five years. These analyses tend to stress the new machinery of social control: an evolution of the means of power, rather than of its nature. Among these studies one should also distinguish between the more theoretical approaches of Zinoviev and Mlynář, which seek to supply a coherent explanation of the relative non-violence of social control, and the more analytical approaches which try, by closely observing the realities of the 'normalization' process, to discern how a model of 'totalitarian normality' functions in practice, so as to bring out both the factors of its stability and its crisis tendencies.

Cybernetics to the concept's rescue?

The theoretical trajectory of Zdenek Mlynář (an 'official' political scientist turned Politburo member of a ruling Communist party in 1968, turned 'dissident' and forced into exile) provides a good illustration of the unsynchronized nature of East–West thinking on totalitarianism. At the very moment in the 1970s when Western Sovietology was coming to accept his ideas of the 1960s about how a 'limited pluralism' and the existence of interest groups could be institutionalized, Mlynář himself – by then a signatory of Charter 77 – was discovering the merits of the concept of totalitarianism, which he considers nowadays to be the most 'adequate' concept to form a political-science (as opposed to sociological) interpretation of the present Communist system. And irony of ironies, in order to (re)discover and reformulate the concept and rid it of certain outdated parameters, Mlynář invokes cybernetics and the concepts of power elaborated by another political scientist of Prague origins, Karl Deutsch.

It will be recalled that the latter – at the celebrated symposium organized in 1953 by the American Academy of Sciences – asserted the inevitability of the centrifugal dynamics which would eventually strike to the very heart of the Communist system. Now Mlynář has redefined totalitarianism precisely by taking as a starting point Deutsch's definition of power:

> By power we mean the ability of an individual or an organization to impose extrapolations or projections of their inner structure upon their environment. In simple language, to have power means not to have to give in, and to force the environment or the other person to do so. Power in this narrow sense is the priority of output over intake, the ability to talk instead of listen. In a sense, it is the ability to afford not to learn.[18]

In terms of this definition, says Mlynář, totalitarian power is able – in all spheres of activity and in relation to all 'subjects' (social groups, economic agents, citizens) – 'to impose the extrapolation or projection of its internal structure'. The chief characteristic of totalitarianism is the ongoing capacity to limit all scope for independent action in every possible sphere of social activity. In other words, it has nothing to do with the degree of violence or terror employed. Power remains 'totalitarian' even when the forms of repression are less visible (albeit still virtually present). One could go so far as to say that a system becomes truly totalitarian only when the 'terrorist' phase is completed – when all the subjects have lost their autonomy and capacity for self-government (the opportunity to change objectives, behaviour, and so on). Consequently, it is not a matter of interpreting the limitation of autonomy solely in terms of legal or penal constraints but always in the 'cybernetic' sense with which Deutsch invests it:

> A society or community that is to steer itself must continue to receive a full flow of three kinds of information: first, information about the world outside; second, information from the past, with a wide range of recall and recombination; and third, information about itself and its own parts. Let any one of these three streams be long interrupted, such as by oppression or secrecy, and the society becomes an automaton, a walking corpse.
>
> It loses control over its own behaviour, not only for some of its parts, but also eventually at its very top.[19]

Autonomy is thus limited by the fact that those in power tend to control all these sources and circuits of information. In Mlynar's view it is possible to talk of totalitarianism in those cases where the only contact the overwhelming majority of the population is able to have with other subjects or the outside world is through those circuits controlled by the regime (which is consequently able to determine the nature and extent of that information).

Through his reflections on the relationship between memory and autonomy, Mlynář renews the theme dear to Orwell (and Kundera) of the erosion of memory as the permanent goal of totalitarian power. In this respect ideology continues to be the mainstay of the 'real socialist' countries by creating a system out of the 'jamming' of information and memory. Hence all the talk of the revolutionary break with the past, the 'New Age', the 'new community of socialist nations', the 'new social forces' and last, but not least, the 'New Man'. The ultimate logic of totalitarianism would be the instrumentalization of all components of society as a consequence of its lost autonomy.

What Mlynář is proposing here is no more than a model, and he is the first to admit that in reality there is a whole range of situations as well as possibilities of future development. The main thing is to discover the 'threshold' at which autonomy is lost in order to provide a definition of a totalitarian situation. Thus, as soon as one moves from the theoretical model to the analysis of reality, the concept of totalitarianism gives way to notions such as 'totalitarian situations' or an 'underlying trend towards totalitarianism'.

Zinoviev, or 'totalitarianism from below'

Zinoviev has gone furthest towards constructing a theoretical model explaining the mechanisms of non-violent social control and the stability of the Soviet system. In fact, he rejects the very concept of totalitarianism because in his view it overstresses the similarities between the terrorist methods of wielding power employed by Nazism and Stalinism. He considers that such apparent similarities correspond solely to the installation phase of those regimes; consequently, the concept of totalitarianism ignores the specific features of the Communist phenomenon.

Zinoviev regards Nazism as essentially violence 'from above', whereas Communism, in its mature phase, is 'totalitarianism from below'. In contrast to Solzhenitsyn, who considers that the concentration camp system is the incarnation of Communism's true nature – a yoke foisted on people from outside – Zinoviev sees the camps at most as an epiphenomenon and regards Communist society as the culmination of 'humankind's natural, inherent' activity. Communism as a form of social organization corresponds, in his view, to a natural phenomenon in the history of humankind, which he calls the communal spirit; it is a system in which the usual counterbalances or safeguards of community life (law, morality, religion, and so forth – in a word 'civilization') are suppressed.

Taking up a position somewhere between Hobbes and Henri Laborit, Zinoviev sums up the essence of communalism in the phrase 'Man is wolfish towards Man'. The key component of the system is the 'cell', by means of which the individual is slotted into society. This cell (the factory, the state farm, the institute) constitutes the microstructure whose salient features are reproduced at the level of the state macrostructure. In other words – in contrast with the dominant theories in Central Europe which present totalitarianism as a conflict between state-Party and a fragmenting society – Zinoviev regards the Communist state as a reflection of a communalist society whose cell is the key productive link and the chosen place for the formation of 'the new man': *Homo sovieticus*. This view ultimately leads to the conclusion that every action, whether individual or collective, must necessarily be 'manipulated', even when it is directed against the regime. From such a standpoint resistance becomes meaningless, since everything is programmed or manipulated. Thus, however original Zinoviev's idea of regarding Communism as a social rather than a political system, and however much he puts his finger (even hyperbolically) on one of the major sources of the system's stability, his *Homo sovieticus* nevertheless borders on caricature and runs counter to the analyses of 'Communism as reality' coming to us from Central Europe.

The Contours of Totalitarian Power

What, then, are the contours of totalitarian power in its post-ideological and post-terrorist phase? The 'polymorphous Party' is the sole autonomous organization in a system in which all other institutions of state and society are subordinate. The Party ensures the monopoly of use of the state apparatus and thereby all organized forms of social life. This subordination of the state to the Party operates by means of the *Nomenklatura*, which ensures the Party's control over key posts in the state administration. This (unified/unifying) Party can occasionally diverge from the political line formulated in Moscow but may never abdicate its monopoly of power. Any failure on this point (as in Czechoslovakia in 1968) calls for a massive purge. There is always a 'vanguard' spare.

'Civilized violence', as Simecka calls it, has replaced the irrational terrorist violence of the Stalin era. It is harassment rather than physical terror, selective non-bloody terror. The police and judiciary make a show of respecting the regulations in force and prefer interrogations during office hours to those at three o'clock in the morning. This development is perfectly illustrated by the role of the 'confession' in the functioning of the Communist system, as analysed by Karel Bartosek. Defining the confession as the 'total submission of the individual to the lie and the agents of the lie', Bartosek traces the development from the 'big confessions' of the 1950s trials to the 'petty confessions' of 'normalization' in the 1970s. The 'big confessions' of the show trials had a deterrent function *vis-à-vis* the population, who assisted in institutionalizing the lie in the course of campaigns in which the media played an important part. By contrast, within the system of 'petty confessions' submission to the lie is exacted from the population by means of purges-cum-screening and other 'oaths of loyalty' (as in Poland). The goal is to create 'complicity' with the system and to smash the individual as the 'last step in the subjugation of civil society'.

Social Control and Social Contract

Although violent methods and the use of tanks prove necessary in situations of open crisis, the Communist regime disposes of other no less effective means of atomizing society. The system of 'petty confessions' is able to function only because the state is the sole employer of labour. Simecka provides a remarkable definition of this system:

> The totalitarian state has far more powerful weapons at its disposal [than violence]: all citizens are its employees and it is no problem to shift them up or down a scale of incentives – rewarding the good and punishing the bad. This capacity is a thoroughly modern weapon. It has worked well ... because it was brought into play only when existing socialism, in its infrastructures, most resembled a consumer society, i.e., when it had something to reward or punish with.[20]

Not only did this recipe prove particularly effective in the period of 'normalization', but in fact it represents the very basis of the Communist system in its post-terrorist and post-reformist phase. Since employment of labour is the pre-eminent instrument of social control, the workplace, as Kende points out, is 'the prime location for the regimentation of Sovietized societies'. Within this system police repression is replaced by the personnel office, the police officer by the personnel officer. Hungary, which enjoys the reputation of being 'different' from other Communist countries, is in fact a past master in the use of more sophisticated methods of repression and social control.

From social control it is a short step to an implicit 'social contract' between the state and the citizen: the citizens 'adapt themselves' by giving up their individual rights (civil liberties) and collective rights (freedom of association) and receive in exchange job security and a slowly – though fairly steadily – rising standard of living. The advent of the consumer society has perfected this 'contract', which has been in gestation since the 1960s. According to Simecka, the contract is

> a far more reliable guarantee of order to the state than all those expensive and ever-expanding organs of surveillance. The essential condition for the functioning of this contract is the level of enjoyment the state permits its citizens in their private lives.[21]

This system has been perfected since 1968 with the creation of a (small) army of unemployed – that is dissident – intellectuals. The 'new social contract' in fact requires the intellectuals to submit to censorship: in other words, to renounce their function as intellectuals. But even here, things have changed greatly since the 1950s. 'Under Stalin,' says György Konrád,

> censorship was both positive and aggressive, nowadays it is negative and defensive. Before, it used to tell you what to say. Now it advises you what not to say ... In a totalitarian situation, censorship cannot be formalized.[22]

In the same way that the transition has been made from mass terror to 'civilized violence', totalitarianism now prefers internalized self-censorship to institutionalized censorship. The relative isolation of dissident intellectuals (except at periods of open crisis) would seem, in a way, to confirm the effectiveness of these new techniques of totalitarian social control.

Totalitarianism or Authoritarianism?

Might not these new non-violent mechanisms of social control and the very emergence of the dissidence of the 1970s in fact 'prove' that it would be wrong to speak in terms of 'totalitarianism'? Ideology which was once – with terror – the other pillar of the system has been reduced to a ritual, and over the past fifteen years Communist regimes have tended to seek legitimacy either through nationalism (Romania) or economic measures (Hungary). This inevitably recalls the sort of values that Juan Linz tells us are espoused by 'authoritarian' regimes (nationalism, economic development, order). If one also takes into account the growing role of the military in the Soviet Union – and also, of course, in Poland – there is a temptation to follow Staniszkis and tend towards definitions usually employed in connection with authoritarian/bureaucratic regimes.

In Linz's view the latter display a 'very limited pluralism' and do not have a precise ideology but instead a typical 'mentality' in which 'a leader of a small group exercises power within formally ill-defined but perfectly predictable limits.' Interestingly the two political scientists of East-Central European origin who are closest to this position (and influenced by Linz) turn out to be Polish (one close to the regime, the other to the opposition). The first is Jerry Wiatr, who formulated his idea of Polish-style 'authoritarianism' (or Bonapartism) on the eye of the military *coup d'état* in 1981. He called for 'a new political system' in which the army and the Church (as institutions enjoying legitimacy, representing the state and civil society respectively) would take the place of the Party and Solidarity, which he saw as involved in a suicidal confrontation.[23] After the coup Wiatr was first promoted by Jaruzelski to head the Institute of Marxism-Leninism but was relieved of this post after the Soviets had publicly denounced his concept of the 'new political system'. It looks as if in Moscow there were no doubts about socialist regimes sliding hypothetically towards 'ordinary' authoritarianism.

The other theory of the slide from 'totalitarianism' into 'authoritarianism' came from a quite different standpoint. In her book *Poland's Self-Limiting Revolution*, Jadwiga Staniszkis analysed the dynamic of relations within a Communist regime, seeking 'a reduction from above of totalitarian domination' to prevent it happening 'from below'. It is in order better to absorb this pressure from society that 'post-totalitarianism' resorts to a 'bandy-legged pluralism'; Staniszkis compares this to the 'irresponsible pluralism' referred to by Linz in relation to authoritarian regimes, or to the 'fragmentation' (horizontal and vertical) of state structures and a sort of 'corporatism' whose apparent aim is that of 'borrowing from the catholic Church its legitimacy'. The aftermath of the 13 December coup would seem to put paid to the hypothesis of a slide towards an 'enlightened authoritarianism' having more in common with Pilsudski than with Marx and practising a corporatism legitimized by the *modus vivendi* with the Church. With the 'restoration of order' one also saw the re-emergence of the Party and its ideology. Perhaps we should therefore be talking of 'failed authoritarianism' rather than the 'failed totalitarianism' proposed by Michael Walzer.[24]

At the end of the day, all these debates about whether or not the Communist systems deserve the authoritarian label hinge on the status of ideology. Is the Soviet system still a 'Utopia in Power', as Heller and Nekritch maintain, or has it been transformed, as Castoriadis suggested, into a 'stratocracy', with nationalism taking the place of Marxism? Writers from East and Central Europe have made some very apposite contributions to this debate:

1. Whereas none of them seems to discern an incipient 'stratocracy' in Central-Eastern Europe, and although the plausibility of the phenomenon in respect of the Soviet Union is sometimes recognized, most writers concur in the view that the ideology is in

a state of decomposition. The 'radiant future' has given way to the 'cold utopia'.

2. In the 'post-totalitarian' phase, ideology none the less remains not only the sole discourse and means of communication between the state and the citizen but also – and perhaps above all – the chief means of homogenizing and integrating the ruling *apparat*. The upshot of this is a dichotomy in the system, which is 'totalitarian' inside the Party (itself clinging to an ideological legitimacy) and 'post-totalitarian' outside (where there is a mere ideological ritual).

3. No so-called 'totalitarian' system can achieve total control over society. It would be better, therefore, to talk of the system's totalitarian tendencies (anchored in ideology, with its own inherent self-perpetuating logic). What differentiates Communist totalitarianism from other so-called 'authoritarian' dictatorships is not the degree of violence but its intention.

The Sources of Totalitarianism: The State, Socialism and the Transformations of Modernity

The major contribution of authors from the 'other Europe' should not only permit a renewal of discussion about 'existing totalitarianism'. They are equally original concerning the sources of totalitarianism. For the Central-Eastern Europeans the chief source is, understandably, external. In Kuron's words:

> The totalitarian system was imposed on Poland thirty years ago by the armed forces of the Soviet Union with the approval of the Western powers, in particular the United States and Great Britain. The system's stability is assured by the Soviet Union's propensity – demonstrated on three occasions already – to reimpose itself by force on any nation which might attempt to liberate itself.[25]

Apart from this fact, which is as essential as it is elementary, one notes in the course of the past decade a new approach to the endogenous factors. This approach might help to reveal the more deep-seated sociocultural supports of the totalitarian system's hold over societies.

Jan Patočka, for instance, takes up Husserl's view of the crisis of the European conscience, a crisis whose origins he sees in the triumph of an impersonal rationality which he contrasts with the subjective universality of *das Lebenswelt*. Thus – in Patočka's view – in the same way that Galileo established the science of nature on a mathematization of the universe, so also – according to one of Patočka's most talented disciples, Bělohradský[26] – Machiavelli reduces politics to a technology of power. Viewed in this way, modern political theory from Machiavelli to Max Weber converges towards an autonomization of the state, whose functions obey a rationality divorced from conscience. From the moment legitimacy is founded on (or confused with) rational-bureaucratic legality, there is the risk that legitimacy and conscience will be absorbed by the institution or the *apparat*. This theme of 'law' devoid of 'human meaning' – and therefore, in the extreme, absurd – runs through the whole of early-twentieth-century Central European literature, and it is no accident that it is in Kafka, Musil, Broch or Roth (that is, somewhere between Prague and Vienna) that one discovers the most enlightening premonitions of the totalitarian potential within impersonal rationality. And for certain writers there is a great temptation to see in socialism – imaginary and then 'real socialism' – the culmination of modern state power's long march towards 'transparency' and 'innocence'.

From this point of view, the factor which transformed these potentialities into realities was Marxism and (for Kolakowski or Shafarevich) socialism as such. The 'Machiavellian' state may well be 'impersonal', but it remains circumscribed within the field of politics: it has no ambition to change 'human nature'. The Marxists (even Gramsci in his study of Machiavelli, no less) maintain that humankind is no more than a 'fixed ensemble of historically determined social relations'; consequently, by changing these conditions regimes can transform human nature. According to Karel Kosik, when interpreted in this way the theory of the 'New Man' risks drifting towards an 'insane utopia' legitimizing unlimited and irresponsible power.

Kolakowski and Shafarevich share the view that all socialist doctrines involving the central control of production and distribution inevitably engender the temptation to control minds. Starting with Plato's *Republic*, Shafarevich draws up the family tree of what he considers to be the 'kernel' of the 'socialist ideal' down to Marx, incorporating in passing the social doctrines of the medieval heresies (Cathars, Hussites, and so on) and the various types of utopia, not forgetting even the Enlightenment of the eighteenth century. These all bear, in his rendering, an uncanny resemblance to twentieth-century 'existing socialism', with its 'destruction of private property, religion and the family' and its corresponding 'demand for equality'. In short, when the socialist utopia is made into a science, the result is fairly predictable. ... Kolalowski, on the contrary, believes that the socialist utopia becomes totalitarian only when it is combined with a revolutionary will: in this sense Bolshevism and Fascism for him are closely related, incarnating respectively the internationalist and nationalist variants of socialist totalitarianism.

Intellectuals, the State and the Regime

Although, as we have seen, bureaucratic *étatisme* and Marxism are often perceived as the sources of totalitarianism, one should not forget the factor that links them: 'the intellectuals' march to power' (Konrád and Szelényi). Milosz and Kundera explored the particular reasons why the intellectuals are fascinated by membership of the 'magic circle of power' and its ideology. The contribution of the Hungarian school has been to investigate the motives of the intelligentsia as a social group.

The 'Hungarian thesis' could be summed up in the following way. In the absence of a real bourgeoisie, it is the state in Eastern Europe which becomes the actual driving force of economic modernization; the intelligentsia naturally identifies with the state and, more than elsewhere, its nationalist and socialist ideologies acquire a clearly *étatiste* complexion. Seen in this light, the Marxist phase (the triumph of Communism) was no more than the culmination of a lengthy process in which the intelligentsia – as the repositories of teleological and technological knowledge – gradually merged with the modernizing state:

> Whether bureaucrats or revolutionaries, the East European intellectuals had long since taken on board a teleology of either the nationalist or the socialist variety. Thus they forged themselves a redoubtable weapon in the battle to establish their own class power. As victors they married the two brands of teleology to produce the ethics of state-run socialist redistribution.[27]

Marxism, says Haraszti, is the perfect ideology for an intelligentsia which, by identifying with the state, becomes the sole repository of the keys to 'rational distribution' and 'social engineering'.

This is the genealogy of what the Polish sociologist Paulina Preiss called 'total bureaucracy'. A basic trait of this phenomenon is the elimination of the autonomy of subsystems. Bihari analyses this 'descent' of politics into the economic sphere and its consequent 'incorporation into the political system':

> The result of the total politicization of the economic system and the economization of the political system was the fusion of these two subsystems and the total disappearance of their relative autonomy.[28]

According to another Hungarian author (Polok), Communism (particularly in its Stalinist phase), by homogenizing the agents of the different spheres of social action, has represented a regression: the suppression of the achievements of several centuries of modernization.

At this point discussion of the totalitarian phenomenon merges with a critique of the *étatisme* which made the Central-Eastern European societies vulnerable to Communist takeover. While aware of the specific nature of these systems and the break they represented with the cultural and political tradition of those countries, the discussion does not omit an analysis of the endogenous factors which could have played a role in the establishment of Communist systems. This leads to an idea which has its roots in the thinking of Hayek and von Mises. The latter based their critique of modern *étatisme* on its Austrian incarnation, of which several countries now incorporated in the Soviet bloc were the legatees.

The other aspect of this approach, which one finds in the writings of historians, philosophers and writers alike, is the idea that the twin phenomena of war and revolution brought about the totalitarian systems of the twentieth century. These phenomena not only provoked enormous political changes but also rocked the values which were the very basis of civilization. Hence Solzhenitsyn's fixation, in *The Red Wheel,* upon the way in which the interaction of war and civil war paved the way for the first Communist state. One finds a similar preoccupation among several Central-Eastern European historians, for whom the establishment of the Communist system after the Second World War was not the unfortunate outcome of the 'Cold War' but the continuation of the work of destroying or reshaping social, political and cultural structures which started with the war and the Nazi occupation.[29]

In his celebrated essay 'The Wars of the Twentieth Century

and the Twentieth Century as War', Jan Patočka places the problem fully in a philosophical perspective. He views the problem of totalitarianism as symptomatic of the crisis of the European cultural identity and the triumph of a metaphysics of History, which identifies existence with the force which in turn paves the way for the totalitarian Night, in which an external 'state of war' goes hand in hand with an internal 'state of war':

> In the twentieth century war has become a revolution against existing everyday values. ... War is a universal declaration that 'everything is permitted'; as savage freedom, war invades states and becomes 'total'. Everyday life and the orgy are organized by one and the same hand. The author of five-year plans is also the director of show trials which form part of the witch-hunt of modern times. War represents at one and the same time the greatest project of industrial civilization: the product and the instrument of total mobilization (as Ernst Junger saw so well) and the release of an orgiastic potential which nowhere else could cause destruction to such an extreme limit of intoxication.[30]

Beyond Totalitarianism

When a social order survives for more than sixty years, says Agnes Heller, it is relevant to raise the question of its legitimacy. Clearly the Hungarian philosopher regards it as a negative legitimacy derived from the absence from society's consciousness of a recognized alternative to the existing social order; here too is a fundamental difference between the Soviet Union and Central Europe in the experience and perception of totalitarianism. Indeed, Poland, Czechoslovakia and Hungary differ from the Soviet Union, in Heller's view, in being in a 'state of permanent crisis of legitimacy', which in a period of open crisis (1956, 1968, 1980) not only affects society but also provokes the decomposition of the Communist Party itself. It is a crisis of legitimacy fuelled both by the 'demise of ideology' and the economic crisis.

According to Vajda the chief contradiction of the system is

> the fact that it can maintain its totalitarian power structure only by channelling all human activity into the private sphere; to this end, however, it is forced to introduce a mechanism which threatens the system as much as the socially oriented initiatives.[31]

In the face of the 'disintegration of Leninist totalitarianism' (of which Djilas speaks), the consequent risks of militarization and 'power projection' that holds out on the Soviet side, the gulf is widening between the centre of the empire and its peripheries. A reflection of this can even be detected in oppositional analyses of totalitarianism and civil society.

Tolstoy's novel *Anna Karenina* begins with the famous sentence: 'All happy families are alike; each unhappy family is unhappy in its own way.' One is tempted to say that (in the view of the dissident writers) all regimes of the 'radiant future' are alike in terms of their political system, while each of the societies concerned has its own particular experience of the 'unhappy' realities of totalitarianism. While most of the writings refer to the concept of totalitarianism, each defines it differently and the approaches of the various authors often reflect the situation of their own country and the characteristics of their political culture.

The notion of civil society is clearly at the centre of the divide between images of totalitarianism (and alternatives to it) in the Soviet Union and East-Central Europe. In Polish oppositional thinking of the 1970s and 1980s Communist power – invariably defined as totalitarian – is to be 'rolled back' by the revival or reconstitution of civil society. Adam Michnik's famous 'new evolutionism' was the key turning point when the opposition ceased addressing the Party-state and turned rather to society itself. The Party was to be driven back into the state by the steady emancipation of civil society through an ongoing process of self-organization. The corollary of this idea is that one can try to 'undo' totalitarianism at the peripheries of the empire so long as one keeps the Party-state as a necessary umbrella and intermediary with the 'centre',

General Jaruzelski's military coup, of course, cut short the Solidarity debate about the limits of 'new evolutionism', but without being able to restore the *ancien régime*. To the extent that Solidarity represented a 'self-limiting' revolution, what followed was a 'self-limiting counter-revolution'. Thus the situation of the opposition has changed, but not its basic strategy. To be sure, there is no longer a powerful social movement such as Solidarity, but there are a variety of old and new ways in which the society of Poland (as well as those of Hungary and Czechoslovakia) try (with mixed results) to sustain their aspirations for autonomy. The economic decay of the system opened new spaces for market and privatization; and the collapse of the Marxist ideology enhanced the search for autonomy in the sphere of culture. This leads Kuron to reformulate the idea of the autonomy of civil society:

Today Polish society is outside the totalitarian system. Now we have to bring ourselves to inject our independence into dependent state structures. Now is the time for what I call the 'interdependent economy'. It is the time to form self-management workers' councils in factories, to make state enterprises autonomous, to replace administrative control with the market.[32]

This is very much in line with Hungarian political thinking of the last decade, in which references to totalitarian features of the system are a by-product of discussions concerning the political obstacles to a genuine evolution in the direction of a market economy. Hungarian economic thinking (by no means confined to the democratic opposition) identifies the economy with society and calls for its independence from the Party-state. Whether belonging to the liberal variant (Tibor Liska as a 'Friedmanite' proponent of the integral market) or to the more socially aware libertarian self-managing one (T. Bauer, Forintos), the Hungarians tend to agree that a Polish-style solution is to be avoided and that in Hungary the economy (the local equivalent of society) should become an autonomous sphere while keeping the Party-state involved in a self-limiting process of retreat.

In Czechoslovakia, too, thinking about totalitarianism and civil society reflects a specific situation. In the face of the apparently unending 'normalization', considerations tend to focus on the 'metaphysics' of totalitarianism: on spiritual and cultural resistance to the totalitarian language and mode of thinking relentlessly imposed by the system on the society. Hence the importance of the emergence of a 'parallel' or 'underground' culture as a backbone to the remarkable attempt of the last decade or so to rebuild, around Charter 77, a community of citizens, a 'parallel *polis*' as Václav Benda called it. As in the 'Age of Darkness', the period of the counter-reformation in the seventeenth century, culture tends to become the substitute for politics. From this angle totalitarianism's victory over society can never be lasting so long as the national culture has not been quelled, so long as the 'resistance of the typewriter' continues.

There are, however, two mutually reinforcing theses concerning totalitarianism in East-Central Europe which tend to challenge the notion of civil society. The first, put forward by several Hungarian historians and sociologists, stresses that the weakness of civil society in the region actually predates Communism (and sometimes even contributed to its introduction). The second is a reminder that totalitarian systems have systematically attempted to destroy whatever civil society there was left at the end of World War II.

The first thesis tends to lump together Russia and Central Europe: the idea is to seek in social history the rationale for post-1945 Eastern Europe under Soviet rule (the boundaries of the so-called 'second serfdom' roughly coinciding with those of the Warsaw Pact!). Stimulating answers to this view can be found in Jeňo Szücz's essay in this volume. He shows that there were (if one wishes to go back to historical arguments about civil society) not two but at least three historical regions in Europe.

The history of the Hungarians, the Poles or the Czechs might not fit the Western model but it certainly had even less to do with the Eastern or Russian model. Kundera's theses on the 'tragedy of Central Europe', which is viewed as torn between its cultural allegiance to the West and its political 'kidnapping' by the East, takes the argument one step further: the 'Caesaro-papist' tradition of subservience to the state and its ideology, the very absence in Russia of the notion of civil society, are seen as central historical/cultural features in the divide between Russia and Europe.[33]

The second, less 'loaded' argument is that, as Raymond Aron once said, 'fortunately or unfortunately, political systems rarely entirely fulfil their essence.' This was all the more so in Central Europe, where a political culture radically different from that of Soviet Russia helped to sustain the idea of society as something distinct from the state and thus created the conditions for the emergence of new society-centred dissent after 1968.

Georges Nivat, a leading French expert on Russian culture, has argued that the key word for understanding Russia was '*narod*', the people. In contrast, one could say that the key word for understanding contemporary Poland is society. It could also be argued that most lands of East-Central Europe represent an intermediate situation between the atomized people, Soviet-style, and the civil society of the Polish type. Václav Benda's parallel *polis* or Elemer Hankiss's 'second society' are the nearest Czech and Hungarian approximations to the Polish model of the emancipation of civil society in the post-totalitarian era.

There is no better illustration of the gulf that separates Central European and Russian ideas about totalitarianism than the thinking of Solzhenitsyn or his *alter ego*, Alexander Zinoviev. The latter sees a totalitarianism from below, a *Homo sovieticus* belonging to a 'community' but certainly not a 'society'. The former believes that Communism came from without, that it has 'stifled Russia'. The origin of the catastrophe is that people have 'forgotten God'. Communism is the fruit of unbelief, which results from a secularization of the state which can be traced back to the Renaissance. Whereas Communism has stifled the spirituality of the Russian people, it is the West, source of the 'disease' of atheism and secularization, which is now in a state of internal decay ...

In contrast, the Central Europeans stress their Western cultural ties even in the field of political or economic thought. The Poles significantly centre their thinking on the notion of 'civil society'; the Hungarians on the market economy and the liberal tradition; and the Czechs on their attachment to Western culture. In other words, here are three complementary aspects of their European and Western heritage, which are all obstacles to the ambitions of totalitarian power. As far as the Russian participants in the debate are concerned these are mostly writers of genius who, when it comes to thinking about politics, turn into prophets of doom who blame their 'misfortune' either on the hated West or on a Sovietized people who, when all is said and done, have got just what they deserve.

However, above and beyond their different analyses of the 'essence' of totalitarianism, its mechanisms or its strengths, the authors we have mentioned, who represent the emergence of independent political thinking in Russia and East-Central Europe, are united in contradicting Orwell's vision of *Nineteen Eighty-Four* on one point. In contrast with the case of Winston Smith, who ends up 'loving' Big Brother, Solzhenitsyn's entire *oeuvre* consists in proving that resistance to totalitarianism (even in the Gulag) is both possible and necessary. This stance is echoed in the rejection of 'enslavement to banality' and the 'solidarity of the shaken' of which Patočka speaks, not to mention Michnik's 'living in dignity' or Havel's 'living in the truth'. But at this point we have already gone beyond political analysis of the totalitarian phenomenon to enter the field of ethics and 'spiritual resistance'. It is symptomatic that this should happen, because it suggests that it is precisely this ethical unity of resistance which in the end is the common denominator (among dissident thinkers) of reflections on totalitarianism. If that is so, we can justifiably conclude that we are not dealing with a 'scientific' concept – fitting the criteria of Weberian sociological objectivity – but with a 'subjective' notion which, like 'democracy' or 'liberty', rests on a value judgement and inevitably commits those who employ it.

Notes

1. Czeslaw Milosz, *La pensée captive*, Paris 1953.

2. Peter Meyer, under his his real name Josef Guttman, was one of the first 'dissidents' in the Czechoslovak Communist Party to denounce the 1936 Moscow trials. After emigrating to the USA during the war, Guttman published a study of Nazi anti-Semitism in the light of the Nuremberg Trials before eventually becoming the leading Western expert on Communist anti-Semitism. See especially his interpretation of the 1952 Prague Trials in P. Meyer, ed, *The Jews in the Soviet Satellites*, Syracuse, NY 1953. This theme is also central to the vision of Communism in V. Grossman's monumental work *Life and Fate*, Paris 1983. In Grossman's view, it was during the war that Communist internationalism degenerated into state nationalism and converged with Nazi ideology. Anti-Semitism was the catalyst that brought about a fusion of the two apparently antagonistic forms of totalitarianism.

3. Hannah Arendt, *Le Système totalitaire*, Paris 1972 (1951); J.L. Talmon, *The Origins of Totalitarian Democracy*, London 1952.

4. Milosz, p. 72.

5. For example the Polish KDS in 1983, Václav Racek, 'Lettre à E.P. Thompson', *L'Alternative*, 24, 1983, pp. 11-12, and 'In Search of Central Europe', *The Salisbury Review*, Spring 1983, pp. 30-32.

6. The concept of totalitarianism is considered here chiefly in the light of the plentiful *samizdat* publications. But even in official documentation it is possible to come across the concept of totalitarianism within articles refuting Western sociological or Sovietological arguments. For instance, the Polish political scientist Jerzy Wiatr has criticized Friedrich and Brzezinski's analysis of totalitarianism; see 'Socjologizcne teorie antykomunistycznaj sowietologii', in *Studia socjologiczne*, no. 3/4, 1968, pp. 5-20; compare, by the same author, 'Etapy sowietologii', in *Wspolczesnosc*, no. 11, 1968, pp. 1-17. And in the margin of S. Ehrlich's study of the various models of pluralism one can find an interesting analysis of Western literature on totalitarianism; see his 'Symptoms of the Abandonment of the Totalitarian Model of Socialist Societies in Western Political Science', in Ehrlich, *Oblicza pluralismu*, Warsaw 1980. Similarly, F. Ryszka's study of the state (*Panstwo jako zmienna niezalezna*, Warsaw 1983) deals with totalitarianism as 'an ideal example of the subordination of citizens to the state'. But it is revealing that nowadays it is in Hungary and Yugoslavia that we are seeing, in academic publications, the most serious and direct analyses of the totalitarian phenomenon. See, for instance, Hungarian articles on the regime's crisis of legitimacy and the negative effects of the suppression of the autonomy of subsystems by the Communist regime (for example B. Polok, 'Stabilité et legitimité, *Valosag*, no. 1, 1983; M. Bihari, 'Politikai mechanizmus es demokracia', in H. Wass, ed., *Valsag es magujales*, Budapest 1982) or the recently published Yugoslav study by V. Koštunica and K. Čakovski, on the means employed to destroy political pluralism after the war, *Party Pluralism or Monism*, Belgrade 1983.

7. L. Kolakowski, *Main Currents of Marxism*, Oxford 1978, vol. 3, p. 465.

8. A. Solzhenitsyn, *Des voix sous les décombres*, Paris 1975, p. 20.

9. Milosz, p. 72.

10. L. Kolakowski, 'Totalitarianism and the Virtue of the Lie', in I. Howe, ed., *1984 Revisited*, New York 1983, p. 127.

11. Solzhenitsyn, p. 275.

12. L. Kolakowski, 'Totalitarianism and the Virtue of the Lie. The theme of the eclipse of memory is central to the novel by the Khirgiz writer Cingiz

Aitmatov, *A Day Longer than an Age*, published in *Novy Mir* (November 1980), which tells of a people reduced to slavery by the destruction of its memory. A slave of this kind – a *mankurt* – was ten times more valuable than an ordinary slave. The novel has been awarded the Lenin Prize, as a work asserting the 'dignity of labour' ...

13. M. Simecka, 'Muj soudruh Winston Smith', *Svedectvi*, no. 70-71, 1984, pp. 247-69.

14. M. Heller, 'Le socialisme mur', *Esprit*, no. 2, 1983, p. 41.

15. Simecka, 'Muj soudruch Winston Smith'.

16. Václav Havel, ed., *O svobodě a moci*, Cologne 1980.

17. P. Fidelius, *Jazyk a moc*, Munich 1983.

18. Karl Deutsch, *The Nerves of Government*, New York 1966, p. 111.

19. Deutsch, p. 129.

20. Simecka, *Le rétablissement de l'ordre*, Paris 1979, p. 80.

21. Simecka, ibid., p. 145.

22. György Konrád, 'L'écrivain étatisée', *Lettre Internationale*, 2, 1984, pp. 40-44.

23. J. Wiatr, 'To Achieve a Genuine Accord the Party Must Give up its Monopoly of Power', in *Gazeta Krakowska*, 10-12 December 1981. Soviet criticism of Wiatr's ideas can be found in *New Times*, May 1983, and *Voprosy Filosofii*, December 1983.

24. Michael Walzer, 'On "Failed Totalitarianism"', in I. Howe, ed., *1984 Revisited*, pp. 103-21.

25. J. Kuron, 'Pour une plate-forme unique de l'opposition', in Z. Erard, ed., *La Pologne: une société en dissidence*, Paris 1978, p. 116.

26. Václav Bělohradský, *Krize eschatologie neosobnosti*, London 1982.

27. G. Konrád and I. Szelényi, *La marche an pouvoir des intellectuels*, Paris 1979, p. 88.

28. Bihari, 'Politikai mechanizmus es demokracia', p. 13.

29. The historian J. Mlynarik discusses the profound implications of the transfers of populations (chiefly the Germans) from Czechoslovakia after the Second World War (though the problem could be extended to Poland). In the twentieth century, the transfers of national minorities have been the work of great totalitarian powers – Nazi Germany and Stalinist Russia. In depriving the German minority of their civil rights on the grounds of their 'collective guilt', was not the restored Czechoslovak democracy actually succumbing to the terrifying logic set in motion by its two totalitarian neighbours and successive invaders? See Danubius, 'Tézy o vysídlení sudetských němcov', *Svdectvi*, no. 1, 1978.

30. J. Patočka, *Essais hérétiques sur la philosophie de l'histoire*, Paris 1981.

31. Mihály Vajda, *The State and Socialism*, London 1981.

32. Interview with Helena Luczywo, 1987.

33. Milan Kundera, 'Un occident kidnappé', in *Le Débat*, November 1983, pp. 3-22.

Three Historical Regions of Europe
An Outline[1]

Jenö Szücs

The Birth of European Regions

Where do the internal boundaries of Europe lie? One very pronounced line runs southwards across Europe from the lower course of the Elbe-Saale, along the Leitha and the western border of ancient Pannonia: the eastern border of the Carolingian Empire around 800 AD. The region to the west of that line had witnessed, in the previous three centuries, an organic symbiosis between elements of late Antiquity and Christianity, on the one hand, and Barbarian Germanic elements on the other. The first (premature and transitional) synthesis of that symbiosis was the 'renovated' *Imperium* itself. The name often applied to that block even in those days was the West. Of course, the term *Occidens* did not refer originally to something removed from other parts of Europe, for example from 'Eastern Europe' – a term with little meaning or content before the turn of the millennium, even in retrospect. *Occidens* referred to the ancient 'world' that formed a belt around the Mediterranean in opposition to Byzantium and Islam, which had expropriated the southern half of that ancient world. Many consider that one can speak of European history as such from about 800, when the centre of historical development was shifted northwards to Europe by the Arab conquests, which robbed Graeco-Roman civilization of a southern swathe stretching from Syria through North Africa to Hispania. Europe, to the Ancients, had been a purely 'geographical' entity. At precisely this time a new type of structure was beginning to crystallize in its western parts. It was neither Ancient nor German, but a 'Christian and feudal society'. To express that new structure, the region began as early as the death of Charlemagne (814) to appropriate the term *Europe* exclusively to itself, although this was unjustified in that it represented only one pole of the Europe that was being born.

The other pole was Byzantium, although initially Byzantium entertained no European aspirations; and since its geographical centre was in Asia Minor it was not a European entity in the geographic sense either. Until the turn of the millennium, Byzantium's firm intention was to defend the eastern heritage of the 'Romans' (as they continued to call themselves) from the 'Barbarians', even at the expense of territorial losses, and to do so by carrying out thorough, ancient-style reforms and maintaining a defensive rigidity. Thus the history of Europe after the turn of the millennium started to develop out of those two poles by absorbing the intermediate region and the heterogeneous world that lay still further to the north: the *Occidens* had been transformed from a western pole of a putative Europe into 'Western Europe', and Byzantium had abandoned its defensive rigidity. From that time onwards one can talk of European regions.

Particularly after the Great Schism of 1054, there was added to that dual radiation another, no less pronounced border running roughly parallel to it, but to its east. It stretched from the region of the Lower Danube to the eastern Carpathians and further north along the forests that separated the West Slavs from the East Slavs, reaching the Baltic regions in the thirteenth century. The comprehensive term used as early as the twelfth century for the region west of this line was *Europa Occidens (Occidentalis)*, the Elbe-Leitha lines obviously having been forgotten. Hardly had *Europa* advanced from being a mere geographical entity to being a synonym for Christendom than it was split into two by the influence of Rome and Byzantium. During the Middle Ages there were fewer and fewer scruples about speaking of Western Europe as the region that stretched from the Elbe to the curve of the Carpathians, and from the Baltic to the Adriatic: that is, the new region which had been annexed to the area of the former 'Carolingian Europe', including Scandinavia. Did that region really become Western Europe?

The workings of medieval Europe remained at their crudest and least complete in the east. The overwhelming majority of what was to become Russia (which would eventually occupy exactly half the entire territory of Europe), the area to the south and east of the Russian land, was not called either the 'Russian land' or 'Europe' until modern times. It formed a wedge-shaped western extension of the Euroasian steppe region and the world of nomads that extended like a wedge into geographical Europe, and which the predecessors of today's Hungarians and others had crossed to the Carpathians. But after the turn of the millennium the thin end of that wedge broke off and joined the area we are discussing. From the thirteenth century that huge wedge was acknowledged to be identical with the Mongol Empire. There was a succession of developments, starting with a loosening of dependence on the Golden Horde (1480), continuing with the Russian conquest of the khanates of Kazan and Astrakhan (in 1552 and 1556) and the annexation of the territories in the southern Ukraine under Polish rule (1667-86), and concluding with the annihilation of the Crimean Tatar khanate (in 1783). These have no less meaning in terms of European history than they have for the history of the Russian state, since they created (and simultaneously assimilated into the notion of Russia) the homogeneous formula of Eastern Europe *par excellence* out of the heterogeneous swathe between the Poles and the Ural mountains. These developments continued, in early modern times, the internal expansion of Europe and the conquest by the plough and towns, which in the Middle Ages had reached only to the Russian lands around Kiev and the Moscow. This accomplishment in the eighteenth and nineteenth centuries in the region of the Dnepr, Don and Volga was similar to what 'Europeanized' Europe had accomplished (albeit in a more extensive way) 500 years earlier between the Rhine and the Vistula, Memel, Tisza and Maros. When comparing the structural models of European regions, one cannot disregard that final inclusion of the eastern half of Europe.

Nor can one disregard the penetration into Europe during the waning of the Middle Ages of another, Asian wedge. This particular invasion was stronger than ever before and entered from the south-east into South-Eastern Europe, where the process of 'Europeanization' was almost complete (if in a rougher form than elsewhere). This provided a whole area with the name of Rumelia, used for several centuries to refer to Byzantium, the Asia Minor portion of which had long before been swallowed up by the Seljuk advance, thereafter receiving the new name of Anatolia. Since the point of the wedge of the Ottoman Empire was blocked in its advance in Hungary, the latter's new role as a 'border area' became an important factor in the development of regions, at the same time releasing Eastern Europe from that role.

So, roughly speaking, the co-ordinates were as follows: the first expansion of the Barbarian peoples, having engulfed the western heritage of Rome, led to the birth of the notion of the 'West' (500-800); the first great eastward and northward expansion of the West (1000-1300) then enlarged the bounds of *Europa Occidens* (to include Northern and East-Central Europe), while in the meantime a 'truncated' Eastern Europe and South-Eastern Europe took shape under the sphere of influence of Byzantium, which had inherited Rome's mantle in the east. Since this latter area was to secede from the European structure (during the gradual decline of Byzantium) by the end of the Middle Ages, I shall disregard it.

Modern times arrived from two directions: one was the second great expansion of the West (1500-1640) which, by stretching over the Atlantic, connected America to itself (and later absorbed Scandinavia too); the other was the great expansion of 'truncated' Eastern Europe, which created a 'complete' Eastern Europe by annexing Siberia, which stretched to the Pacific. East-Central Europe became squeezed between these two regions. At the dawn of modern times, it was obliged to notice with some defensive amazement that while history had redrawn a border that had been thought to have faded, from the south the last (and strongest) wave of one thousand years of invasions from Asia Minor was lapping against its borders, and that it no longer knew whether it still belonged within the framework of *Europa Occidens*.

The original position of the regions, their movements and their responses to the challenges of history produced the structural models that have defined modern Europe ever since.

Western Europe

How did the original Western model look – at least from the viewpoint of István Bibó? His viewpoint (one of several possible) amounts to a search for the deepest roots of a 'democratic way of organizing society'. All that Bibó emphasized about these beginnings (the customary, personal and mutual obligations and rights; the balancing structure of 'narrow circles of freedom' that prevents a concentration of power and provides a counterweight to the 'brutally expedient' methods of unilateral subordination; and so on) were real and important elements, although they were shared with the successive structures of the Middle Ages. Yet something more comprehensive is at work. This can be shown by glancing backwards from the centuries of modern times to the Middle Ages in the West.

When considering concepts like natural law, social contract and popular sovereignty, the transfer of power or the separation of powers, most people will recall names such as Hobbes, Locke, Montesquieu and Rousseau, and, of course, the French Revolution and its aftermath. There are certainly few who know that these key problems were first pondered a good 500 years earlier in Bologna, Paris and Oxford, even if in a context fairly remote from and alien to the modern era. At the height of the Middle Ages, in the 'great' thirteenth century, such ideas were as much at the centre of political theory as they were in the great preparatory period of modern times, the eighteenth century. If one searches for the roots of 'social development in the Western sense' (as Bibó put it) or seeks to identify the 'original characteristics' of the West (as Marc Bloch would have put it), this consideration is important, since one such characteristic of the West is the structural – and theoretical – separation of 'society' from the 'state'.

This kind of separation is not an endogenous feature of human history. Of course, all states are built upon some society, but it is in the gravitational field of 5,000 years of high cultures that the emerging state finds a justification for itself 'beyond the bounds' of society, thus creating an operational mechanism in which society appears to be the derivative of the state, and not vice versa. For any sector of society to exist autonomously, independent of the state (even when functionally connected with it) is a rare exception. And exceptions are the luxury products of history. A well-known example is the Greek *polis*, the primeval model of the autonomous society, in which the *koinōnia* of the free citizens is interpreted as a kind of 'natural' outcome. Another example is the Roman *res publica*, the form of the power of the *populus Romanus* expressed chiefly in the categories of public law. But like the Roman idea of the republic, the practice of Greek democracy was swamped by the Hellenistic empires and, having been transformed into a mere fiction, was confined to an imperial cul-de-sac. These early historical antecedents had no direct influence on the social development of Europe. Nothing, of course, was further removed from the medieval West than democracy; the republic was flirted with by only a handful of Italian city-states, and then in a very aristocratic style. Yet there remained an organic historical continuity that led from there to the development of modern Europe. The reason why Western feudalism was able to posit the category of *populus seu societas civilis* is not that feudalism in the

West held itself to be the heir of Antiquity and had read the works of Aristotle; in these terms, Byzantium was a more faithful successor and, for a while, even Islam seemed a worthier one. The reason is that whereas this category was to some extent familiar to Western feudalism, it had nothing at all in common with the other two civilizations. To establish a correlation with the entirely new formula of the state at the dawn of modern times in Europe, the primeval form of 'civil society' had to be shelled out of its 'feudal context'. However, it is important to point out that that operation was not particularly unusual or entirely new since, much earlier, history itself had both created the category and established its relation to the state. No such thing had happened in Byzantium, in Islam, or in China: that is, in other cultures that for a long time had boasted higher 'indices of civilization'. Nor, indeed, had such a thing happened in Kiev.

The characteristics of Western development are traceable to its genesis, and it can be understood primarily by examining how it contrasts with other civilizations. Byzantium adhered, with a defensive inflexibility, to the half of the old framework of integration formally separated long before (395): to the remains of the Eastern Roman Empire, with its traditionally urban civilization and centralized, bureaucratic state structure. Islam exhibited expansive flexibility in its attachment to Arab traditions, to both the heritage of Mesopotamia and Persia and of the southern half of the *Orbis Latinus*. The world of Islam nevertheless followed the typical ancient development pattern of high cultures, while in the meantime integrating urban civilizations of various origins and amalgamating elements of the Persian and Byzantine centralized state structure into a military and theocratic autocracy of its own. The first 500 years' history of the West exhibit an entirely unusual 'take-off' in the rise of civilizations. This take-off took place amidst disintegration instead of integration, and amidst declining civilization, re-agrarianization and mounting political anarchy.

In fact, what occurred in the West was a peculiar kind of integration, an amalgamation of the ancient and barbarian heritage (which Byzantium had managed to exclude by means of Pyrrhic victories). But it was no simple co-ordination of various elements, as occurred in Islam; indeed, in the Dark Ages it seemed increasingly that these elements had become so intermeshed that they cancelled each other out.

Nowadays it is clear that a crucial precondition of these peculiar dynamics was this very fragmentation of everything. Let me refer to three aspects of a single group of correlations. Squeezed into agrarian relations and local frameworks (where the only source of wealth and prestige was the land), the West was forced to proceed beyond the dead point of Antiquity and every other ancient high culture: the chronic stagnation of agrarian techniques and productivity. It was the 'agrarian revolution' begun during the 'Dark Ages' that prepared the soil for the birth of a new type of urban culture, one which would produce the demographic explosion that almost doubled Europe's population between 1000 and 1300. Secondly, the immanent structural precondition for the specific Western formula of the emerging urban culture and the autonomous town was the breakdown of 'public power' – that is, political sovereignty. Non-existing centralized states could obviously not turn the developing towns into centres of non-existing administrative, military and economic functions, as happened in Byzantium or under Islam. Western towns grew up in the interstices of rival sovereign powers, so blending elements of sovereignty into themselves. They grew up in such a way that, wedged between agrarian economies under different political and legal authorities, they also developed a new economic formula – that of the autonomous urban economy. Thirdly, the combination of the agrarian revolution and the autonomous town produced an urbanized foundation that might not have produced cities with millions of inhabitants until modern times (a few such towns existed in the Islamic world under the Abbasids and in China under the Sung dynasty), but did create a thick network of towns and an intensity of commodity exchange that completely dominated the whole economic and social structure in a way no other previous high culture had seen.

Historians in recent decades have rehabilitated the 'Dark Ages'. Of course, for a long time after the turn of the millennium, the development of the West cannot be measured by any immutable criteria for civilization. The vandalous depredation of Byzantium (1204) still demonstrated the inferiority complex of the Crusaders; meanwhile, the scholars of the 'twelfth-century Renaissance', with their humble admiration of the *orientale lumen*, imbibed the knowledge of Antiquity to be found in Córdoba and Sicily thanks to the Arabs. The secret of Western development lies neither in the 'Faustian soul' of Spengler nor in its 'cumulative' patterns that differ from the cyclical motion of Asian civilizations. It lies, rather, in its possession of a peculiar rhythm of development, whereby cumulative changes always led to changes of structure as well. From another angle one can say that the struc-

tures themselves were of a kind that possessed the innate ability
to surpass their own limits. How right István Bibó was to identify
the Western model with 'motion' and deviation from it with
'immobility'. The precondition for the West's dynamics and integration after the turn of the millennium was its prior disintegration, and in that lies the precondition as well for the separation
of 'society' and 'state'.

In talking of 'society' in remote historical times, one should not
mean 'all the people'; this latter interpretation is *sub specie historiae*
extremely new, being hardly 200 years old. The structure of a
civilization and its rhythm of development are defined by many
different factors in the deeper layers of the economy and society,
but the crystallization of forms always depends directly on the
functional relations within the political sphere, by its internal
conditions and normative values. This political sector of society is
not necessarily identical with the 'ruling class', which itself is
quite hard to define precisely in most cases.

In the high cultures of history the political function is predominantly exercised 'downwards from above'. It makes no difference
whether the legitimacy of power is exclusively theocratic (as in
Islam from the first caliphs), fundamentally secular (as in Confu-
cian China) or a combination of the two (as in Byzantium, where
ancient and oriental legitimacy were combined). It makes no
difference whether the constitutional structure is primarily
military (as in Islam), predominantly civilian and bureaucratic
(as in China), or a balance of the two (as in Byzantium). One
common feature is that the groups directly exercising power are
to a decisive extent both at the centre of the state and locally
present, in what Max Weber called a position of 'prebendal'
dependence, irrespective of whether land is a full state monopoly
(Islam), or only partly so (Byzantium and China). The second
common feature is that the town is at once at the centre of the
civil and military administration, of the state's fundamentally
'tax-levying structure', and of the exchange of goods, which is
usually controlled closely by the state. This results in a settlement
pattern consisting of a conglomeration of landowners exercising
local power, of civil and military functionaries, merchants and
artisans, all without legal homogeneity or autonomy. The third
common feature is that between those exercising state functions
and the peasantry, whose legal status is in most cases heterogeneous, the town contains only a few (if any) 'intermediate' elements
with an independent social standing or legal position; these

elements do not have much weight.

Of course, these political structures are to some extent subject to centrifugal forces, which very typically take the form of a struggle for supremacy between the various groups in the strata that exercise power: for instance, between court cliques (clergy, mandarins or 'Praetorian guards') and regional groups, or between factions in the civil and military groups. These struggles may result in the division of an empire between members of a dynasty (Islam) or contribute to the annihilation of the civilization itself (Byzantium), but under certain circumstances it may also result in successive strengthenings of the imperial centres (China). The essential point is that each part of the empire retains the structure of the original whole: the upheavals generally take the form of court intrigues, palace revolutions and military coups that involve no theoretical changes in the relation of the 'political sector' of society to the state.

In this respect, the West created an entirely new model of political and social power. It began with the virtual dissolution, fragmentation and annihilation within scarcely three centuries (6th-8th) of two state formulae. The experimental executive power of the German *regna*, resting on sacred foundations, was dissolved as surely as the institutional system of the *Imperium* and Roman public law. But the dissolution occurred not just in the 'state' sphere, since there was a radical split in the original 'social' framework as well. The German tribes and peoples disintegrated as fully as the socio-legal community of what remained of the Roman *populus*. The former, despite all the fictions about their origin, were formations dependent on the power framework [*Heerkönigtum*] of the Age of Migrations, while the latter, despite all the fictions about public law, derived from the imperial framework of the Empire period. As public power dissolved, political sovereignty itself became a mere illusion; as society disintegrated, all traditional forces of cohesion disappeared. Initially even the main crystallizing force, the private ownership of land, assisted political and social disintegration.

There remained only one institution that was not torn asunder by development – the Church. That fact is at least as important as the processes of disintegration. In the power chaos and vacuum, the Western Church was released from the dependence which had been assumed since the reign of Constantine the Great in late Antiquity (337) (under this arrangement the *ius sacrum* had formed part of the *ius publicum*) and which later was reproduced more firmly by Justinian in Byzantium (532). The

Roman Church's breakaway from '*cesaropapizmus*' had resulted from the fall of the Roman Empire. It was Saint Augustine who had expressed the idea that the Christian 'society' [*societas fidelium*] had an identity independent of the existing power relations and that by pressure of necessity this society permeated into secular power relations, 'mixing together' [*invicem permixta*]. Pope Gelasius (493) then quickly translated this idea into actual institutions. The West's separation of the sacred and the secular, the ideological and political spheres, was uniquely fruitful, and without it the future 'freedoms', the theoretical emancipation of 'society', the future nation-states, the Renaissance and the Reformation alike could never have ensued.

There was another separation, important from the viewpoint of the original structures. The early Carolingians had attempted to forge a political synthesis out of the symbiosis between Antiquity and the Barbarians. This can also be interpreted as a one-off attempt by the West, prompted by the reflex of most high cultures prior to and contemporary with it, to unite the various heritages: in other words to establish a link between the notion of 'civilization' and an 'imperial' integration. The 'renovation' of the *Imperium* around 800 amounted to an attempt to revive ancient imperial traditions transmitted by the Roman Church, making use of the last reserves of the Frankish institutions. But these reserves had already been exhausted, and the temporary edifice was destroyed once and for all by a new element that arose from below – vassalage. Charlemagne tried to employ this element to balance the fundamentally unstable construction. Thus it was agreed once and for all in the West that 'civilization' and 'political framework' were separated. In this respect, one should not be misled by the survival in the West for another three centuries after 962 of the idea of restoring the *Imperium Romanorum*. In real terms, this amounted to hardly more than an illusory policy towards Italy by the German kings. Its only apparent result was the postponement of the chance to create a unified German state until the nineteenth century, which itself assisted in the crystallization of the new regional notion – Central Europe.

Once reduced to its basic elements, the stability of the West was ensured in the long run precisely by the impossibility of integrating it 'from above'. The integrational lines of force began 'from below', and in the first phase (9th-11th centuries) these displayed a specifically vertical orientation.

The development of vassalage was stimulated not by some glorious motive but by dire need, since the dissolution of public power meant that only some kind of individualized legal dependence could provide defence as well as enhance power. Personal dependence in itself was nothing particularly new; both the Germanic military retinue [*comitatus, Gefolgschaft*] and the late Roman *clientela* had been of such a kind. Indeed, the form had been familiar to all pre-feudal societies, even among the nomads, and had been the binding medium of feudalism from Kievan Russia to Japan. Western vassalage differed from these related structures: first, by fully incorporating all the elements of society that had retained some freedom after the social erosion; secondly, by establishing itself not adjacent to or beneath the state but in its place, so that it supplanted the 'state' formula with that of 'social' relations. But Western feudalism had other specific features. In time, these permeated downwards beneath the actual 'feudal society' and, by means of several transformations, extended through several centuries.

One such specific feature was the 'contractual' nature of vassalage. The ceremony of feudal allegiance always involved the entry into a fundamentally unequal relationship of two persons, one powerful and the other weak. The 'fealty' was always the unilateral obligation of the vassal. But from the outset the liege lord had also been under customary obligations; moreover, the *fidelitas* itself presupposed and was a function of the more powerful partner's fulfilment of his contractual obligations. If he did not fulfil them the charge of *felonia*, of breach of contract, applied with as much force to him as it did to a 'faithless' vassal. An unequal relationship by mutual contract, under which both parties incurred obligations, was an internally developed feature of Western vassalage that might under certain circumstances become a fiction. Yet it was a productive fiction that operated as a norm – in the course of time downwards as well. Of course, the relation of landlord to peasant assumed some kind of contractual nature around 1200 not because contracting appeared in the upper echelons around 900, but because the dynamics of development and a new, horizontal type of integration had also circumscribed, at the level of the peasantry, a limited and conditional type of 'freedom'. This emphatically 'contractual' form is among the characteristic 'conditionings' which, in István Bibó's terminology, were the key term for expressing the reflexes that extend over the ages and are determined not merely psychologically, but also by social structure.

Another specific feature was the presence of human dignity

even under subjection. In general outside Europe – but even in the Russian principalities – a 'man of service' would bow to the ground, kiss the hand of his lord or even throw himself down and kiss the hem of his lord's garment. In the Western ceremony of *homagium* the vassal would go down on one knee with head erect, then place his hands into the clasped hands of his lord. The new relation was finally sealed with a mutual kiss. An age that expressed everything in emphatic symbols and spectacular gestures could not have found a better way to convey the basic model of a relation that strove fully to transplant that symbolism into practice. The effects were far-reaching, for example on the gestures for expressing religious devotion. The Western stance of prayer, with hands clasped, was borrowed by the Church from the vassalage ceremony. (The Christians of Ancient Rome had turned to God with outstretched arms.) In a similar fashion, the Orthodox custom of bowing to the ground and kissing the feet of saints derived from the reflexes of the 'man of service'. Of course human relations were still directly imbued with varying attitudes, yet every peasant revolt in the West was an expression of enraged human dignity at the landlord's breach of contract, and a demand for the right to 'freedom'. The same holds true of moral feelings. The 'honour' of the individual was a central element in the ancient system of values, and the 'fidelity' of the subordinate was of central importance in every society that was based upon systems of dependence. Normally the two were morphologically exclusive: the *honor* of the knight and the *fidelitas* of the vassal fused organically only in Western feudalism. Europe directly inherited human dignity as a constitutive element in its political relations not from Antiquity but from feudalism, and of course preserved it wherever human dignity was present in the process of changes of institutional forms.

The territorial consequence of Western feudalism, a large number of small provinces each with its own customary law, also provided a far more suitable soil for the development of direct legality in general and for the thorough predominance of law as 'custom' [*mos terrae*] than would political and administrative frameworks broken up roughly and superficially from above. Decentralization was the medium through which, at local levels, the 'ascending' principles of law and government could overcome the 'descending' mechanisms of exercising power, as Walter Ullmann indicated in his typology of legal history. The same also applies to the cultural sphere in general. As early as the eleventh and twelfth centuries the multitude of feudal courts, with their colourful milieux, had been forging a Christian, yet autonomous lay culture, scale of values and set of moral principles. Having divested themselves of many affectations, these courts became the source of the reconciliation between 'valour' [*virtus*] and 'temperance' [*temperantia*] in European behaviour.

Once the old formulae had been almost entirely eliminated, the strangely mosaic, ceremonial world of feudalism then began, after its own fashion, to develop a new type of society–state relationship. In the fully developed feudal structure, the state's administrative, military, fiscal and legal functions became entirely divorced from the power of the monarch. They were distributed among the tiers of the feudal society, where they integrated themselves separately at each tier by merging with the similarly tiered system of landownership. The theoretical sovereignty of monarchical power derived from divine grace hung emptily over the whole social fabric, like the Augustinian legitimation of power as the 'safeguarding of peace and justice' on earth. The power of the king was real in so far as the monarch exercised it not as a sovereign but as a suzerain. One might say that sovereignty, having been fragmented, was absorbed into a newly formed 'political' sector of society – if there were much sense in saying so, for the fragmented formula no longer resembled any kind of sovereignty, and the exclusively vertical formula of feudal society had scarcely anything in common with any kind of coherent 'political society'. Territorial status and feudal dependence did not necessarily coincide. In the long run, this paradox had enormous significance: the notion of sovereignty had become entirely relative and its fragments were scattered in an uncertain way into the sphere of 'society'. If they liked, the great liege lords could still consider themselves a kind of 'political society', and it was in this milieu that the embryo of the social contract, destined for so great a future, was conceived.

The social contract, like every child, had two parents: feudalism and the Church. The latter was independent of secular power, yet under Pope Gregory VII it intervened in worldly affairs with more emphatic 'freedom' than ever before. The social contract was first expounded as a theoretical generalization around 1080 in a radical Gregorian treatise. The ruler was said to be tied to the people by some kind of contract [*pactum*]: if the ruler 'broke the contract by which he had been elected', annulment of the contract and resistance were justified. One part of the background to this assertion was the split of Christian universalism into two branches, since that split logically impelled the papacy to argue theoretically for a weakening of the emperor's position, in general for the removal of secular power from the sacred sphere and, thus, for a lay and rational derivation of power. Thus began an unstoppable process: the return of European thinking to ancient sources, the extrication of politics from theology, and the simultaneous shedding of the remnants of 'barbarian' ideas about power. The idea of interpreting the 'people' as the source of power was an argument extracted from Justinian's *Institutiones*, which was initially a merely legal device against a tyrannical emperor. However, the ancient theory of the state had included no precise idea of a 'contract', although Cicero had referred occasionally to a kind of *pactio* between the people and those in power, and the Old Testament had also mentioned a contract between the elders of Israel and King David at Hebron. The other background influence came not from Antiquity but from feudalism, whose contractual basis had begun to permeate the sphere of the 'state' about 200 years earlier. For instance, the Frankish and Aquitainian nobles (who were the highest vassals of Charles the Bald) said that if the king 'acted against the contract in any matter' [*contra tale pactum*] he should be removed (856). This idea grew directly out of the feudal *felonia*. The relation between the king (as suzerain) and his vassals took the form of a pseudo-contract as early as the ninth and tenth centuries, just as the oath of allegiance sworn to the king echoed the feudal formula ('I shall be faithful as a man who owes fealty to his liege lord ...'). Subsequently, the idea of social contract managed to free itself of its feudal trappings, since the previous two centuries had seen the formation of a society able to relate itself to the state by partly assuming the role of the ancient *populus*.

That process could never have started had the West not achieved the dethronement of political sovereignty in the first three centuries of its history, and had it not begun to distribute the remnants of sovereignty into a social formula that developed vertically 'from below' during the three centuries that followed. During these three centuries the process gathered strength because the particularly strong dynamism of Western development in the 'second age of feudalism' (1050-1300) evolved horizontal lines of force that broke through the vertical ties of dependence – initially through the new integrating forces of society and then through those of the state – so that the division of sovereignty between the emerging 'political society' and the rulers of the strengthening monarchies could again become possible.

* * *

The structure which had evolved by the turn of the millennium had the basic and unique historical feature of being at once amply universal from the viewpoint of civilization and narrowly local from the viewpoint of its political relations. The productive tension between the universal and particular produced such explosions of energy as the Crusades, the reconquest of the Mediterranean Basin and the expansion of Europe, and these led necessarily to the idea that chivalry, which had been 'vertically' incorporated into the relations of feudalism, was at the same time the 'horizontal' force supporting Christianity. In the ninth and tenth centuries, the view crystallized that alongside the secular powers the members of the Church formed a unified order [*oratores*] in the world, an autonomous and corporate institutional unit, a 'mystic body' [*corpus mysticum*]. This view led to the idea that the warriors [*bellatores*] of the very same world, irrespective of their political allegiances, were also parts of an autonomous and corporative unit, an 'order' of a related kind purely by virtue of their 'functional' existence in society. Propagation of the notion of orders was begun by the Church around 1000, and included the tacit acknowledgement that those who laboured [*laboratores*] also formed a kind of 'functional order'. The structural precondition of orders was the absence of centralized state powers that would have deduced that 'functionality' from the organism of the state. The material precondition was provided by the sudden increase in the living standards and prestige of the knights as a result of the agrarian revolution and urbanization, which made them realize that as 'Christ's warriors' they should be entitled to freedom of the same type as that enjoyed by 'Christ's mystic body'. Once the 'freedom of the Church' [*libertas ecclesiae*] had become a central slogan during the investiture struggle, the idea of the freedom of the nobility [*libertas nobilium*] sprang forth from the same soil.

But the logic of these matters did not end there. It has already been mentioned how the sharing out of sovereignty led to the unique feature of urbanization in the West – urban autonomy and a combination of rights and spheres of influence. In the Dark Ages the urban model of ancient times had not been submerged entirely in Northern Italy, and from there it radiated north-westwards towards Flanders and then eastwards with the expansion of the urban areas; this ensured that in the West a new idea of freedom [*libertas civium*] would be selected out of the *laboratores'* 'functional' scheme of ideals. The new stratum of burghers could not been seen as a kind of heterogeneous urban 'populace'.

Although around the year 1120 the French abbot Guibert de Nogent remarked indignantly that the whole of Western Christendom echoed the 'new and infernal names of the communes ... which have been established by servants in the face of all legal and divine ordinances', this really proved that the structure had evolved fully. Two or three generations later, the successors of the irate abbot considered the existence of communes in the shape of a plurality of 'freedoms' in the world as one of the most natural things – something that followed even theoretically from natural (that is, divine) law.

There was no other period between the Roman *res publica* and the French Revolution that so loudly and frequently proclaimed the slogan of freedom as the twelfth and thirteenth centuries in the West. Also audible in the chorus was the voice of the peasantry – at first the voice of the settlers of lands newly placed under cultivation, and then, with increasing volume, the voice of others, since they possessed a weapon in the shape of a threat to move into the towns, which served as models of positive rights. But the peasants were also supported by various arguments concerning the economic dynamism of the 'second age of feudalism', and these influenced the landlords of the time. The combined weight of all these factors logically extended 'freedoms' to the lowest levels; these 'freedoms' constituted the organizing principle of the structure, even though at the lower levels of the social hierarchy it became increasingly clear that the coin of 'freedom' bore the word *libertas* only on one side, and that its value was qualified and relativised on the other side as 'privileged legal status'. Of course, feudal systems in other regions were also familiar with some notion of freedom, even at the level of the peasantry. But the elimination of servitude so as to provide the whole of the peasantry with homogeneous and positive, if limited rights, not only consecrated by 'custom' but guaranteed in a written contractual form, was a clearly Western characteristic. 'No tax can be levied unless it is in writing' was the principle (of 1142) which spread from northern France to the very borders where *Europa Occidens* ended.

The 'plurality of small spheres of freedom' which István Bibó identified with the foundation of Western development was grouped around a few basic models. Unity in plurality meant that 'freedoms' became the internal organizing principles of the structure and led to something which drew the line so sharply between the medieval West and many other civilizations: the birth of 'society' as an autonomous entity. The boundaries between the hierarchically divided groups were always drawn by some higher authority, but since authority was not identical with sovereignty there were everywhere ascending legal maxims and 'customs' imposed upwards from below. The more succinct the 'freedoms' became, the stronger they grew. Even in the smallest village it was the local community that applied many lesser laws, starting with the regulation of land use. Those rights grew in parallel with the higher levels of the hierarchy, to such an extent that the ruler could do nothing substantial without the *consilium et auxilium* of his vassals. It was precisely the sum of those collective rights, legitimated by custom, that were called 'freedoms'.

The twelfth and thirteenth centuries added three types of theoretical liberation to the existing basis of 'freedoms'.

First, the *various groups* subordinated to various authorities had to be liberated theoretically from their unilateral quality of being subjects [*populus subditus*]. Consequently, a model was devised by which all possible 'people' who existed legitimately formed at the same time a community [*universitas* or *communitas*] of a corporate nature [*corpus*]. These communities were built into the comprehensive organisms of the Christian society as autonomous 'societies', each fulfilling a separate public function [*societas publica*]. The most radical thinkers, such as Baldus de Ubaldis, went as far as canonizing the existence of any social group of public utility as legitimate without the permission or privilege of a superior authority [*sine auctoritate principis, absque licentia superioris*]. Each such autonomous society was to possess, according to the principle of 'representation' and in opposition to the superior authority, the quality of a legal or political personage [*persona ficta* or *politica, representata*] endowed with communal rights. Certainly the thinkers of that period took the view that Christendom was an organism of variously sized societies operating under internally identical principles.

Secondly, the *individuals* subordinated to various powers had to be liberated theoretically from their unilateral quality of being subjects [*fidelis subditus*]. This requirement followed logically from the previous idea of liberation. By squeezing the formative relations of real life into normative categories, it was pointed out theoretically that every individual was part of the world by virtue of a dual quality: besides being a subject, he [sic] was also an equal 'member' of some social community [*membrum communitatis, societatis*] and thus was to be accorded specific communal rights; the individual formed part of a horizontal legal formula independent of his [sic] ties of dependency.

Thirdly, man, the natural being, subject and Christian believer, also had to be liberated theoretically as an Aristotelian 'political being' [*animal politicum*]. For this purpose it was necessary to extricate the notion of politics from ethics, where it had long been consigned by theology. That was done not by the jurists but by the philosophers, who first interpreted politics as *ethica publica* and then clearly pointed out (Thomas Aquinas) that man was a political being 'by nature' and that 'political virtues' were – apart from the Christian and 'theological virtues' of faith, hope and love – themselves factors in the formation of the community. The word *politizare* appeared in the common language of the West around 1250. At the same time there was a break in thinking from the naturalism of Aristotle. By adopting the Neo-stoic model of the Romans, man's political quality was interpreted as more than a 'natural' quality, since it was expressed by the contrasting pair, *naturalis–civilis*. Thus the notion of a *societas civilis* appeared in the West in the mid thirteenth century as a synonym for the autonomous society outlined above; it appeared in the shape of a reproduction of the ancient *populus*, viewed as a 'unity of law and public utility' [*unitas iuris et publicae utilitatis*], as the basic model of a 'political society' and *civilis* relations.

In the medieval West the notion of 'society' naturally took the shape made possible by the existing structure. Nevertheless, the basic model contained an inherent capability of narrowing or widening. When in the West it became a normal principle for the ruler to be responsible to the 'people', that naturally did not mean he was responsible to his 'subjects' in general, nor that he was responsible to the physically present representatives of the Estates. The ruler was under the control of the *populus*, which every lawyer knew to be a corporate identity and a legal entity that amounted to more than the sum of its members, an entity that 'never dies' [*nunquam moritur*]. Although the distinction was subtle it opened up certain prospects, since the model specified that the ruler was responsible to 'society' in the abstract.

Absolutism and the 'First Crisis' of Feudalism (1300-1450)

The luckier regions of Europe can mark the beginning of modern times with success dates like 1492 – the discovery of America. Less fortunate regions fix on the dates of catastrophes like 1526 – the Battle of Mohács and the advent of the Habsburgs. Russian historians could also open a new era with success dates such as

the 'gathering of the Russian lands' or any of the starting dates
for the annexation of the whole of Eastern Europe (1478, 1480,
1502, 1552 or 1556) if they did not insist on treating modern times
as a category of inner 'formational' change, as synonymous with
the rise of capitalism.

Of course, such dates are symptomatic. Nevertheless, if there
has been a thoroughgoing change in the perception of eras it
certainly lies in the realization that in order to comprehend
modern times one must start with the 'first crisis' of feudalism
(1300-1450). Ever since European historians began reconstructing
it in more detail and within a perspective which points to the
establishment of an early modern 'world economy (lasting from
1450 to 1640), there has emerged some justification for supposing
an identity between the regions of Europe and the types of
response to the challenges posed by the crisis. Since Immanuel
Wallerstein's theoretical attempt at a synthesis has appeared only
in recent years, no one can fault Bibó for blaming the distortion
of the historical structure of Hungary on certain catastrophic
occurrences. But it would be inappropriate to start, as he did,
with the great peasant revolt (1514), since that catastrophe was an
effect and not a cause. Nor would it be wise to start with the
acceptance of the Habsburgs, since by doing so one would set
oneself a kind of trap by posing a question from which it would
then be difficult to escape. A third group of phenomena has come
recently to be seen in a new light in the Marxist account of Perry
Anderson, which indicates a fresh approach. This emphasizes the
morphology of the early modern state system, the 'Age of
Absolutism'. The societies of the historical regions largely trans-
posed the task of responding to the challenges posed by the crises
to their states, while the states themselves largely reflected the
different regional opportunities, so that the act of 'transposition'
made them the most active factors in the crystallization of the
regions – whose validity extends to the present day.

The medieval model in which the social and state co-ordinates
of the Western type were drawn up bears a resemblance to the
unfinished cathedrals, the torsos of 'Gothic Titanism' (Le Goff)
that stood for centuries without tower, nave or façade in the
squares of Beauvais, Narbonne, Cologne, Milan, Siena and
elsewhere, until in the nineteenth century a start was made on
completing them. The reason is also shared: the *civilis societas* and
corpus politicum of the state rose upwards for centuries as torsos,
indicating only the conceivable outlines of the gigantic apse, since
the crisis in the whole structure had brought the building itself to

the brink of ruin after 1300.

Europe was extricated from its 'first crisis' because the state – either temporarily or permanently – outstripped the society. How it did so varied from region to region. The region determined whether the new workshop that could complete the gigantic torso of the Middle Ages came together in the nineteenth century, and whether matters went as far as Marx so expressively put it in 1875:

> Freedom consists in the conversion of the State as an organ superimposed on society into one completely subordinated to it, and today, too, the forms of the State are more or less free to the extent that they restrict the 'freedom' of the State.

The crisis occurred at the time (the eve of the fourteenth century in the West) when growth became constrained in almost every direction by the limitations of the structure. As a consequence, the 'growth crisis' turned into a group of phenomena that reflected a slump (agrarian and monetary crisis, desertion of villages, drastic fall in population, political anarchy, and so on) but did not gather sufficient force to dismantle the structure radically. The precondition for overcoming the crisis was economic expansion, while the nature (or impossibility) of that expansion determined whether feudalism, having been prolonged in one way or another, turned into capitalism or reproduced itself. The crisis first affected the most developed and thickly populated regions. Around 1300, three-quarters of Europe's population lived in the west: that is, in one-fifth of Europe's territory. Afterwards, the first waves of famine (1315-18), exacerbated by relative overpopulation, revealed with elemental force the various crisis phenomena. The eastern regions continued for a good while to show an ambivalent growth trend and the wave of crisis finally arrived about a century and a half later, when the West was already recovering from its own crisis.

Ultimately, the salient point in the West's recovery was the fact that even before 1300 the whole structure's centre of gravity shifted once and for all to the urban economy. The urban economy was the first of the affected forces (and the crisis affected all strata) to recover. This it managed to do chiefly by discovering East-Central Europe as the place where its market crisis could be solved and its demand for precious metals satisfied. The regions beyond the Elbe paid, in the long run, for the West's recovery. At the same time, the regeneration of the Western towns forestalled the attempt or inclination of the nobility to push the crisis down beneath the '*corpus politicum*' and on to its own peasantry. The armed vengeance with which the nobility reacted to the great peasant revolts of the fourteenth century was in vain, since the deeper reflex of the economy proved stronger; one of the main achievements during the overcoming of the crisis was the elimination of serfdom in the West by the end of the Middle Ages. The regulating principles of peasant–landlord relations became money rent and tenancy. Another reflex of the nobility failed as well – its attempt to fight its way out of the crisis and compensate itself for its decreased income by 'chivalrous banditry' and the devastating anarchy of the type of warfare shown in the Hundred Years War and the Wars of the Roses: in other words, by disrupting the states.

Eventually the *corpus politicum* emerged from the crisis through a specific rearrangement of forces. At the end of the Middle Ages the monarchies, relying on the towns (and more or less subordinating the Church) found themselves facing a nobility whose income and social standing had been exhausted by civil wars, a nobility that expected the state both to provide it with offices and military positions and to safeguard its privileges. In that framework and in due proportion, the West found the energy it needed for an expansion on a far greater scale than that after the turn of the millennium. This expansion led, via geographical discoveries and colonization, to the laying of the foundations of the 'world economy' in early modern times. Of course, another long century passed between the strengthening of new monarchies like the France of Louis XI (1461-83) or the England of Henry VII (1483-1509) and the emergence of 'absolutism' and its threefold solution: preserving whatever was preservable from feudalism, preparing for capitalism, and forming the framework of the nation-state system.

The reaction in East-Central Europe to the crisis was organically correlated to the reaction of the West. Yet the type of reaction was similar to that specifically produced by Eastern Europe – due to the latter's emergence, if nothing else. This was the other expansive model after the programme of 'gathering the Russian lands' under the leadership of the Grand Duchy of Moscow (fourteenth century) had been adopted and carried out effectively by Ivan III (1462-1505). It was nothing less than a parallel answer of 'incomplete' Eastern European feudalism to the crisis of the late Middle Ages. The crisis had analogous symptoms to those in the West: devastated villages, decrease of population and political anarchy; while the situation was further worsened by subjection to the Tatars. The overall result was not only three centuries of Russian expansion (resulting in the internal colonization of Eastern Europe). The fact is that a gigantic eastern 'appendage' was also attached to the formula, forming in a sense a partner of the western (North American) appendage to the *Occidens*. While the *conquistadores* were expanding the western world economy to the 'Indies', the Cossacks, after the first expeditions to Siberia (1581-84), advanced as far as Kamchatka, thus outlining the possibilities of another 'world economy'. One can talk about a 'Russian world economy' in early modern times in the sense that there existed some other world economies besides the European one (for example the Chinese), each with its own centre, peripheries and outer zones. The parallel lies not in their relative weight but in their internal structure, and in the fact that the Russian economy experienced growth albeit extremely slow, in the decisive sixteenth and seventeenth centuries, during the time when decline was deforming the regions between Russia and the West.

Apart from all the obvious contrasts, there were two basic differences that turned Russia against the West. One was the West's insistence on certain separations. Just as it became obvious after the death of Charlemagne that the imperial frameworks of 'civilization' could not be maintained, so it became obvious soon after the death of Charles V that the attempt to fuse the 'world economy' with the '*Imperium*' was incompatible with the model that by then had extended over the Atlantic to America. By contrast, the Eastern European model that extended through Asia to the Pacific was based on a fusion of categories. Its 'economy' was identical with the 'imperial' framework which had been based on the concept of 'civilization' of the Third Rome (Moscow) – until the eighteenth and nineteenth centuries, when it became a periphery of the European world economy. The other basic difference was that the Western model was based on eliminating serfdom, while the Eastern was based on prolonging it. The decisive element in Russian expansion was the agrarian colonization of large areas that offered practically unlimited space for the peasantry's mobility. The Russian nobility was forced under the authority of the state, with even more elemental force than the Western nobility was by its existential crisis, by participating in the expansion and drastically effective prevention of the peasantry's mobility. The codification dates of the first radical restriction and then the full abolition of the peasantry's migration and other minimal rights to freedom (1497 and 1649) were just as clearly milestones in the development of Russian absolutism as were the dates of territorial expansion (1480 and 1679) already mentioned.

East-Central Europe lay between these two zones of expansion. Its defensive position was due not merely to its lack of space in which to break out, nor even to the pressure of the Ottoman military offensive. It was too much a part of the Western 'world economy'; ever since the Middle Ages it had served as its periphery, and therefore had a weak infrastructure and economic basis. After the temporary stimulating effect of the Western urban economy's solution of the crisis (export industry, capital exports), the weakness and permanent stagnation of the Eastern urban economy was among the factors that decided the peasantry's fate. Coupled with that was the growing demand of the urbanizing West for agricultural produce, causing the great estates cultivated by forced labour to become the typical Eastern partner in the East–West division of labour that developed. Consequently, the nobility of the Eastern European region succeeded after 1500 in doing what the paralysed nobility of the West had failed to do after 1300: shifting the burdens of the crisis on to the peasantry. The legislative omens of the 'second serfdom' appeared with awesome synchrony in Brandenburg (1494), Poland (1496), Bohemia (1497), Hungary (1492 and 1498), and also in Russia (1497), although the background and causes there were different. The great mass of the Russian peasantry had never in the Western sense been liberated from the 'first serfdom', and the Russian economy was not dependent on the West either.

There were two common denominators after 1500 that began to erase the Eastern border of *Europa Occidens* (which had become more pronounced after 1200) while progressively strengthening the Elbe-Leitha line (which after 1200 had begun to fade). One was that the nobility there had weighty reasons for accepting the authority of a strong state, since it was the power of the state that could most effectively enforce the laws binding the peasantry to the soil, without which the latter escaped or rebelled by lawfully referring to its 'ancient freedoms'. The other was the presence in both regions of Eurasian wedges. At the height of its power, the Ottoman Empire pressed forward as far as the region of the Száva and the Danube and was a far stronger opponent than the weakening Golden Horde in the Dnepr–Don–Volga region. Turkish conquest was a serious problem for Poland as well as Hungary and Croatia, for it threatened Poland's eastern wing, in the Ukraine. Despite these common denominators, there was one important difference. The nobility of this region – by contrast to the Russian nobility – had a clear and precise (though one-sided) idea, rooted in the system of institutions, that in the state's *corpus politicum* it 'represented the country' and the 'freedom of the country'. The more the crisis increased the nobility's power over the peasantry and afflicted the towns, the more one-sided the nobility's ideas became. That makes its easy to understand why the nobility in this defensive region hesitated – far more than in the two expansive regions in the twilight of the Middle Ages – over whether to act in accordance with its own fundamental interests or whether to insist on its 'freedom'. Initially it inclined towards the latter, as can be seen from its rejection of the attempts by monarchs in Bohemia, Hungary and Poland (in 1471, 1490 and 1492 respectively) to strike root in ways parallel to those in the West. Later, the region's main characteristic was its experience of all the possible variations.

Fundamentally, this was the situation in Europe around 1500. Concerning the outcome, 'the Age of Absolutism', another important circumstance must be noted. It was not just that the superstructure of the early modern state system created a certain 'convergence' in Europe out of a divergent basis. The newly born state system also strove to balance itself out by mustering its immanent power resources. Since the state had become ascendant over 'society' and the regulator of the economy, and had as its means the seventeenth century's 'military revolution' (only seven years in that century passed without any major international conflict), the result was that the strength of the economic basis decreased in an easterly direction in parallel with an increase in the size of the state apparatus. Eventually, the balance of arms evened out the unbalanced relations of the economic base. Around 1680, the armies of the Romanovs and Frederick II each numbered about 200,000; this was the same number as, say, the French army of the *grand siècle*, although the former placed a much greater burden on the treasury and, more importantly, on the national income. Armies of this size could be reached and maintained only when the state's influence 'from above' over the economy and society was exercised more directly and drastically the further east the country lay. Similarly, the basic 'competitive' attitude with which Europe was imbued was progressively more spasmodic as one moved towards the east. It became still more spasmodic as the Western societies swelled with energy (despite state attempts to control them), right up until the French Revolution. The reduction of this energy was the specific aim of 'enlightened absolutism' and the idea of 'revolution from above'; the latter had been in the air long before Stein, Gneisenau, Hardenberg and others expressed it explicitly after 1806 in Prussia. This formulation was an older historical phenomenon whose borders coincided with those of the old Carolingian Empire.

The absolute state in the West was 'a compensation for the disappearance of serfdom', while in the East it was 'a device for the consolidation of serfdom' (Perry Anderson). Despite the vain mood of consolidation and 'convergence' with which the ruling circles of eighteenth-century Europe supplemented their competitive relations, the divergent regional constructions meant that three different types of relation between the state and society resulted. The bases of the two outward and equally pronounced models were the two expansive regions, while the variant models in the middle reflected the desperate efforts of East-Central Europe in the zone between these two outer regions.

Today hardly anyone would think that the difference between the Western and Eastern absolutisms in Europe was that the former kept a kind of balance between the nobility and bourgeoisie, while the latter was an out-and-out 'feudal' formation. Both were feudal. The fundamental difference between them was that Western absolutism defended the retrievable elements of feudalism against the corrosive effects of capitalism, and in such a way as to contribute in turn to their very erosion in the interests of its own aims and functions, while Eastern absolutism contained no such 'contradiction', since there were scarely any (or no) corrosive forces at work. Aside from this difference, other aims and functions besides the defence of the retrievable elements of feudalism were shared in common by these states. All absolute states had close functional correlations with the 'world economy', since they were simultaneously its principal beneficiaries and the prominent factors in its development. On that basis the absolutist states implemented their immediate air of subordinating society and 'reorganizing' (or 'modernizing') it in preparation for modern times – which amounted, in the end, to laying the foundations of modern times. The means invoked were also similar. The development of the bureaucracy and the army, the centralization of the state administration (the homogenization of the 'subjects'), economic protectionism, and a new kind of legitimation of power – all these were common denominators of Western and Eastern absolutisms.

Yet despite all these similarities every structural element of the two outer models displays sharp contrasts, due to the great differences in their medieval infrastructure of state–society relations and in the new basis of their economy.

The sharp differences appeared in the rhythm of development and in the overall temporal dimension. In the West the feudal components of the medieval '*corpus politicum*' gave up their struggle gradually and unwillingly, and at a price of recurrent rebellion against the rulers with their increasing (but not yet absolute) power. The state was therefore able to come out on top only in the seventeenth century. In France, the clearest *terminus post quem* of absolutism was the last assembly of Estates (1614-15). Only afterwards did the real builders of absolutism such as Sully, Richelieu or Colbert gain ground on the basis of Bodin's plans, which had until then remained merely a scrap of paper. Moreover, the most developed areas either abandoned the system early (as in the Netherlands) or survived with only an incomplete absolutism lasting less than half a century (as in England). In the West the structure outlived the eighteenth century only in areas (Spain, Portugal and southern Italy) where the shifting of the centre of the world economy to the Atlantic region and the consequent internal regional rearrangement of the West in early modern times had created a 'semi-periphery' of economic and social structures. Moreover, even if this was exceptional the medieval *corpus politicum*, which had been undergoing internal change, developed through a specific dialectical unity of revolutionary conflict and organic continuity into the basis of modern parliamentarianism via the Long Parliament of the English Revolution. In England the Stuarts constituted something of an obstacle to the organic transformation of the medieval *civilis societas* into a modern civil society, while in other places the part absolutism played was to help that process. At least in the West, absolutism was a decisive yet episodic historical event, forming one of the productive 'cumulative' changes that prepared further structural changes.

By contrast, Russian absolutism in the East was itself the structure that served as a framework for subsequent cumulative changes down through the centuries. It created – albeit somewhat roughly – all the basic elements between the reigns of Ivan III and Ivan IV (1462-1584); it was preceded by formations like the *oprichnina* of Ivan the Terrible, 'a state within the state', a terror organization that kept an eye on all opposition, exterminated the refractory boyars and confiscated their lands. Before

1905 the only considerable shock to the foundations of Russian absolutism in four centuries was the 'Time of Troubles' in 1605-13. After 1613, the Romanovs managed to consolidate the structure to such an extent that Count Stroganov could write in his memorandum to Alexander I: 'It has been the peasantry that was the source of all disturbances in our whole history, while the nobility never stirred. If the government has any force to fear and any group to watch, it is the serfs and not any other class.' The weak and short-lived Estates Assembly [*zemskiy sobor*] was created by Ivan IV by decree 'from above' for manipulative, tactical reasons – to win over the nobility of the Western and Ukrainian territories under Polish and Lithuanian influence. After the assembly had codified the binding of the serf to the soil for eternity (1649), thus fulfilling its role, it faded into oblivion. A similar pact was produced by the Prussians only some years later (in 1653). In both cases, the nobility resigned in theory from its role in the state structure in exchange for a state guarantee of the *corvée* and the deprivation of the serfs' civil rights. Consequently, modern Russian history was marked in part (as Stroganov said) by the Bolotnikov, Razin, and Pugachov type of peasant uprisings that swept periodically, with elemental force, across the vast territories of Russia. One of the models of absolutism consisted of an integrative episode that transformed the West; the other assumed a lasting form of existence that integrated the whole of Eastern Europe.

It has been mentioned already that one tool of absolutism in both West and East was the organization of a bureaucracy that ensured its smooth operation, and of the army, which caused a multiplication of the bureaucracy. But East and West followed two different models, even though the common basis was the nobility. In the West the state divided the nobility: it gave offices and a military role to one part while neutralizing the other and leaving it to vegetate in exchange for guaranteeing its privileges. But in the West the typical form of the 'bureaucratization' of the nobility was the sale of offices (the French *paulette*), by which the state killed three birds with one stone: it raised income, blocked the clientèle system of the magnates, and – by buying off one part of the old nobility and turning it into professional holders of office – opened the way for infiltration of the state apparatus by the bourgeoisie [*noblesse de robe*]. Through the purchase of offices the bureaucracy became a type of capital investment and a vehicle for social mobility, while the practice of farming out taxes and other fiscal machinations incorporated the developing bourgeoisie into the state's 'staff of cadres'. Behind its aristocratic courtly milieu, the 'feudal' state was shaped on capitalist operating principles; as was the army, whose reorganization likewise became a business 'enterprise'. Apart from that, the nobility remained a corporation outside the 'state' sphere. In the East, on the other hand, absolutism made its first move after 1478 when Ivan III created a 'service nobility' [*pomeshchiki*] which depended exclusively on the power of the tsar and had primary interests in both territorial expansion and the processes of confiscation. The next stage occurred when this new nobility came to predominate over the old nobility with free estates [*votchina*]. Absolutism was fully consolidated when Peter the Great merged the two types by extending the principle of service to all, thus creating a unified service nobility incorporated into the bureaucracy and the army in fourteen ranks. Thus it was the 'archaic' relationship of service that sustained (with subsequent slight modernizations) the 'modernized' absolutist structure even under Nicholas I (1831), and until the great revolution. A nobleman was *eo ipso* either a civil servant or an army officer; social rank and bureaucratic hierarchy were fused. The West, turning the whole nobility into interested parties, selectively built it (and elements of the bourgeoisie) into the state, while the East implemented a kind of 'nationalization' of the entire nobility.

The West subordinated society to the state; the East 'nationalized' it. Absolutism everywhere strove to homogenize its 'subjects', and there was no difference in principle between, for instance, the views of Louis XIV [*mes peuples*] and that of the tsars concerning indivisible unity. But in practice the various local autonomies and 'freedoms' were not eliminated anywhere in the West. At most they were curtailed and subjected to state control. Corporate particularism and provincial variety were far more motley under every *ancien régime* than under the loose structure of a modern state. Periodically there would be a joint revolt of the nobility, the bourgeoisie and the peasantry in favour of restoring the various 'freedoms' of each, as in France from the period of the 'religious wars' to the *Fronde* (1648-53). Between these 'freedom movements' of the medieval type and the French Revolution some 150 years elapsed (punctuated in the main by local peasant movements against the burden of taxation). This gap was caused not by any strengthening of absolutism but by the fact that the earlier campaigns had become anachronistic. The new bourgeoisie, strengthened by mercantilism, had no need of any peculiar 'autonomies'. Centralization was not strong enough to homogenize the subjects thoroughly, but it was effective enough to encourage the relativized traditional 'freedoms' to begin to converge underneath the state; their content became more homogeneous with the strengthening of the new bourgeoisie. István Bibó aptly observed that the early modern state 'administered together rather than annihilated' the colourful world of the existing traditional organizations. The first deed of Russian absolutism was in the spirit of unifying the Russian lands: Ivan III occupied Novgorod (1478), which had enjoyed an exceptional degree of autonomous government. He deported the entire leading strata, the boyars and the merchants, confiscated their property, and placed the city state under the tsarist governor. The pattern was taken from Moscow, the centre of administration and military power, which contained an agglomeration of boyars, civil servants, soldiers, merchants, artisans and agrarian people, each group (as was general in all towns in the Russian lands) depending separately on the principal power. Even the privileged rich merchants [*goshti*] were chiefly business agents of the tsar. In the ensuing centuries, all towns in the newly colonized territories, from Tsaritsyn to Archangelsk, and from there to Ufa and further to the East, adopted this model. The declining remnants of the local boyar self-government [*guba*] were eliminated by the first Romanovs, who annexed all territories to the central apparatus of state by organizing them into provinces. One of Western absolutism's contradictions was that its 'subjects' sooner or later began to turn their *libertates* into a unified *liberté* within the leeway remaining under the state. The direction taken by tsarist absolutism precluded that contradiction, such that the concept of 'society' meaning an amorphous mass of subjects, was consistently realized.

Everywhere the absolute state became the largest economic 'entrepreneur' of the period. Whereas the typical form of Western mercantilism was the capitalist company, organized under state protection, the logic of Russian mercantilism was the expansion of the traditional commercial and manufacturing monopolies of the tsar. Under Peter the Great and his descendants this assured state dominance in all key industries, especially those of war (iron in the Urals and shipbuilding) and foreign trade. Whereas in France, for instance, the growth of industrial capital was around 60 per cent (allowing the bourgeoisie to act as the catalyst of the above-mentioned process by which freedoms were unified) even in the century when the *ancien régime* had already turned its back on mercantilism, economic growth in Russia always primarily assisted the state itself. In 'competitive' terms this was the really effective means by which, in its final hours, tsarist Russia had outpaced France to become the world's fourth largest steel producer and fifth in overall industrial production.

'Absolutism' itself is an imprecise concept in two directions. It says both too much and too little. Neither in practice nor in principle was the power of any of the Western monarchies limitless or free of every kind of law [*legibus solutus*]: that is, 'absolute' in the true sense. Theoreticians of absolutism like Grotius, Bodin or Hobbes were far from sweeping 'society' off the theoretical table. In fact, they interpreted and developed the ideas assembled at the height of the Middle Ages (from natural law through the social contract to Roman law), making out of them a modern version of the medieval principle of divine grace and the late ancient 'irrevocable' transfer of power. But the 'absolute' power of the sovereign over legislation, levying taxes and other decisions was not 'unrestricted' in principle but 'uncontrolled' in practice – a big difference. On the one hand, the 'people' did not control the sovereign *pars pro toto*, since in the 'contract' the people transferred the natural rights that were its due in principle to him. On the other hand (as Bodin put it) the sovereign 'had no right to infringe upon natural law' or do anything 'without just or reasonable cause'. No attribute that could be made good use of by society was dropped; each was merely 'subordinated' in principle to the structure (just as the remains of the 'body politic' were condemned in practice to passivity), while the limitations on the power of the sovereign were transferred to the moral sphere (whose practical guarantee was the existence of those remains). As soon as conditions were ripe, all these theoretical elements could be pulled out from under the feet of the sovereign by one single movement and arranged around the principle of the sovereignty of the people. It was almost symbolic that Montesquieu (who was for a while president of the Bordeaux *parlement*) should have been at once a pioneer of 'modern' state theory and a representative of the aristocratic opposition to absolutism.

The legitimization of Russian absolutism followed an entirely different formula. On behalf of Ivan III, monks went to work around 1480. They dug out from manuscripts the elements of the Byzantine, autocratic mysticism of the state, centring it around the mission of the 'Tsar of all Russians' to be God's vicar on earth and linking this with the idea of Moscow as the 'Third Rome', the function of whose subjects was to 'service' it. Since the great boyars had no institutional or theoretical traditions of social autonomy to supplement their *de facto* (though less articulated) participation in power, the only remaining ideological opposition consisted of the constant renewals in the Orthodox Church, which inclined towards a profound mysticism. But from the outset the Church tended to be subordinated to the state after the Byzantine pattern. The Gordian knot was cut by Peter the Great, who created the Holy Synod that ultimately subordinated the Eastern Church to the state (1721). Not even in theory was any leeway left to any stratum under the state ideology that crystallized out of the indissoluble trio of autocracy, orthodoxy and the Russian people. This trio converged upon one single focus, the personal power of the tsar, and from there radiated outwards as 'truth' through the sphere of influence of 'true' power to the 'true' unity of the people. The legitimization of Western absolutism consisted in declaring the 'legitimacy' of power. That of Eastern absolutism amounted to declaring the mystic 'truth' of power and forcing its opponents into the same conceptual framework. In the West, the opponents of absolutism referred constantly to the rights to freedom and progressively simplified the slogan (so much so that in the decade before the French Revolution the terms 'freedom' and 'representation' converged in the parlance of both conservatives and radicals); in the East, the opposition similarly revolved around the one true total 'truth', never managing to break loose from it even by modern times.

The divergence between the Western and Eastern models increased within the framework of 'convergence' that had set in by the eighteenth century. The turning point was marked by the outcome of the War of the Spanish Succession (1701-15) and by the reforms of Peter the Great (1689-1725). The war (the 'first world war in modern times') gave a new dimension to the 'competitive' relation that had imbued the early modern state within the West itself, since England and Holland, whose revolutions had eliminated them from the system of absolutism, emerged as the real winners, while the strongest model of absolutism, France, emerged as the real loser. The result was an ossification of French absolutism which shifted the competitiveness within the model state itself into a battle between the state's retrograde structure and the emancipating forces in society. Enlightenment in the West was the concern of 'society', not of the 'state'. The Western parabola of absolutism was then completed by the French Revolution, after which the state, which had gained ascendancy over the premature and crisis-ridden medieval *societas civilis* on the basis of the expansive 'world economy', helped liberate society from the crisis as a 'subject'; as a result, a higher *société civile* gained ascendancy over the state in crisis.

The Eastern parabola of absolutism looked quite different. To hold its ground in competition with the West, the Russian Empire was forced to 'open a window' to Europe, give up its own separate 'world economy' and become part of the European economy, and at the same time to make enlightenment a state concern by 'civilizing' its subjects in such a way that, in terms of their social character, they still remained subjects (and not '*civiles*'). That process of modernization was initiated very deftly by Peter the Great. His reforms (and their continuance, particularly during the reign of Catherine the Great) can be assessed not so much from the customary point of view as Russia's Europeanization but as the accomplishment of a consistent 'Eastern-Europeanization', in that that formula was extended in every possible direction. It was Peter the Great who said: 'Now we need Europe for a few decades, so that we can turn our back on it later.' Beyond various indicators of how restricted opportunities for movement of a structure (and a 'nationalized' European region) directed exclusively from 'above' had been opened up amidst circumstances of fundamental social and political inertia, the result was that a Russian nation was forged from within the Russian 'imperial' framework, just as in the West nations were forged from absolutism. But this convergence concealed a difference as well. Under the Western model national society freed itself from absolutism as the theoretical depositee of sovereignty, so that it could then control the state in practice. Under the Eastern model, the Russian nation remained both in theory and practice a social framework subordinated to the 'freedom of the state' (Marx).

Eastern-Central Europe

The region that lies between those two models, as we have seen, crossed the threshold of modern times amidst newly developing 'Eastern European' conditions, but with defective 'Western-like' structures. Precisely because of that duality, early modern times produced in this middle region a number of variant models instead of one unified one, as if all the permutations and possible combinations were being experimented with.

In the northern half of the region, two extreme variants were attempted. This was the area destined by its location to be the first to connect, via the Baltic trade, with the industrial and agrarian division of labour in the expanding global economy of Europe, and to do so to the greatest extent in terms of volume. Thus it was the first area to adopt the 'second serfdom', and the one to do so most consistently. During the great boom (1550-1620) grain was chiefly (and to an increasing degree) shipped to Brugge and Amsterdam from the ports of Stettin, Gdańsk and Königsberg by the German *Gutswirtschaft* from over the Elbe and by the Polish great estates cultivated by forced labour. The beneficiaries were the nobility of one very large and one very small state. The Polish–Lithuanian kingdom was the largest state formation in sixteenth-century Europe, extending from the Baltic to the Black Sea and from Silesia to the regions of Kiev and Smolensk. The Electorate of Brandenburg was, at the beginning of modern times, one of the smallest part-states in the region – one of the least urbanized territories of the Holy Roman Empire with a feudal structure predominantly determined by the *Herrenstand* and *Ritterstand*. Some political significance was gained only after the Hohenzollern dynasty had obtained the other pole of their future power, the heritage of the Teutonic knights: East Prussia (1618).

It was precisely because of the prosperity of the Baltic and the extra weight of Eastern Europe that the selective 'political society' of the Polish nobility set out on an extreme road: by reducing *ad absurdum* its unilaterally 'Western' situation inherited from the Middle Ages, it established a kind of noble *res publica* entirely unprecedented in Europe. Relying on the initial strength of the *Rzeczpospolita Polska* that organized the Polish–Lithuanian union into one of political law (1569), and radically rejecting the dynastic principle and subordinating the elected ruler to the Estate Assembly (the *Sejm*) from which the towns were excluded (1573), the Polish nobility tried to behave as if it were living in an expansive region. In fact that was so, since by incorporating large areas of White Russia and the Ukraine territories beyond Volhynia and Podolia, this state was in part responsible for initiating Eastern Europe's 'internal colonization' as far as the Dnepr area. Subsequently, it remained the dominant political factor in the region until the last third of the seventeenth century. In the field of culture, this situation provided the background for Copernicus and the Polish renaissance, known as the 'Polish Golden Age', with Cracow as its centre. As if it were meant to illustrate the contradiction between the models of the West and East, this noble *res publica* developed a strange 'anti-mercantilist' policy that in principle excluded Polish merchants from marketing the grain of Polish landlords, and gave the business to foreign (mainly Dutch) merchants (1565). The attempt to have a 'Western-type' noble society running the state on a kind of 'anti-absolutist' basis ran into hopeless impasses in every direction. By the end of the seventeenth century the general economic depression had ruined the manorial economy, the urban basis having already been destroyed. The extreme noble 'freedom' of feudal parliamentarianism [*liberum veto*], which bound the ruler hand and foot and paralysed the state, also excluded the noble state from the 'military revolution' of the period. Lacking a well-trained infantry and artillery – and a standing army of any kind – the noble cavalry, hopelessly outdated, suffered easy defeat at the hands of the Swedish, Prussian and Russian armies in quick succession. After this, the revenge of the Orthodox peasantry led by the Cossacks led to the annexation of the Ukraine to Russia under the banner of Chmelnicky (1648 and 1654). What all is led to is widely known: after a series of partitions (in 1772, 1793 and 1795), Poland disappeared from the European map. Its place was taken by three neighbouring absolutisms: Prussia and Russia, which in the meantime had become factors of European significance, and the Habsburg state. It was symbolic that over the grave of Poland stood the three greatest figures of 'enlightened absolutism': Fredrick II, Catherine the Great and Joseph II. The absurd and overextended attempt by the nobility in East-Central Europe to preserve a medieval 'Western' structure when 'Eastern European' conditions were more and more predominant resulted in complete failure.

The smallest state formation in the region, the Electorate and Principality of Brandenburg, followed a completely different road. The Hohenzollerns and the Junkers interpreted (although not without initial frictions) the 'Eastern European' turn of history in a quite different way. Abandoning the distorted 'Western' situation they had inherited, they adopted a model of absolutism whose military and bureaucratic structure approximated to the Eastern model more closely than that of any other European absolutist state, although they implemented this model with the precision characteristic of the West. Brandenburg–Prussia – due to its methodical expansion northward and eastward (into Pomerania) and westward (into Magdeburg, Altmark, and so on), its systematic redevelopment of the feudal mechanism, its consistent cementing of the nobility into the bureaucratic machine and the army (making the Junkers an exemplary Western variant of the 'service noblemen' in the East), and its effective adaptation of mercantilism – became a factor of European significance as early as the reign of Frederick I, the Great Elector (1640-80). His successor and namesake turned the country into a kingdom and military power (1713-30), after which Fredrick the Great (1740-86) acquired Silesia and raised the Prussian kingdom to the level of a model absolutist state and a major political force that also proved flexible enough to transpose (under Napoleon's influence in 1806) the ideas of 'revolution from above' into practice. This proved to be a precondition for this variant of the East-Central European model – whose diametrical opposite, Poland, disappeared from the map, its western part becoming Prussia – to seize the sole realistic opportunity for successfully unifying Germany, which had existed thus far only on the map as a conglomeration of several hundred territories straddling three great historical regions of Europe. Of course the success of the Prussian kingdom was ambivalent by comparison with the successes of the two regions on either side of it. Bibó appropriately remarked that somewhere, at some time and by some means, the region's countries always had many a cruel trick played on them by the distortions of their history. Eventually Fascism and its consequences were the currency in which Germany was obliged to pay for having won its unity from 'above', under the stamp of an 'Eastern' initiative and by way of internal aberrations and obstacles to democracy; that conclusion forms the theme running through Bibó's work *Német hisztéria* [*German Hysteria*] (1942).

The hybrid variant produced by the region between the two extremes was the *domus Austriae*. The Austrians' irony about themselves helps to explain the fact that the Habsburg house managed to squeeze the whole southern part of East-Central Europe into a single imperial conglomerate for almost four centuries under the motto *Tu felix Austria nube*, and by means of the pursuit of a successful policy of dynastic marriages. In the long run the Czechs' irony about themselves could cope with the consequences, after the style of Švejk. But the Hungarians are perhaps less able to laugh at themselves because, in order to do so, they would have had to resolve the contradiction whereby the real sufferings of Hungarian society at the hands of this historical framework resulted from the unfailing, effective contribution of the Hungarian ruling strata to its maintenance. As far as the origin of this framework is concerned, it is not explainable purely in terms of clever marriages (1515), constitutional considerations, catastrophic turns of history (1526), or of the fatal historical errors or 'treachery' of the feudal system in one country or another. What finally helped the Eastern branch of the House of Habsburg to obtain the Bohemian and the Hungarian kingdoms was the fact that the 'political society' of the region was compelled to acknowledge – since it lacked the temporary scope for expansions and the illusions of the Poles – that it lived in a 'defensive' region. Menacing the Czech nobility was Hussitism, the region's main 'Western' type of reaction to the first crisis of feudalism. The traditions of the Hussites threatened the entire nobility with dire setbacks after the 'Eastern European' change in the relationship of landlord and peasant. The Hungarian nobility, on the other hand, had to bear in mind both the nightmarish memory of 1514 and the very real knife in its back, placed there by an Eastern despotism. But the majority of the Hungarian nobility was 'Western' in so far as it was unable to imagine either compromising with Ottoman power or conceding its feudal freedoms and collective political rights and cultural traditions in the widest sense – its 'Christian freedom' [*Christiana libertas*], as the whole complex had been called since the mid fifteenth century. Of course, there were all sorts of manoeuvrings going on. Little Transylvania, for instance, managed to adapt to a permanent process of manoeuvring at the mercy (and by the consent) of the Sultan, who needed such a small, remote buffer state. No such mercy was extended to the rest of Hungary. There, meanwhile, the House of Habsburg won its case with the powerful argument that experience from the times before 1526 showed the annual income of the Crown in the whole of the independent Hungarian kingdom to be merely sufficient to cover the annual costs of the border-castle system in the south 'in time of peace', and certainly not enough to repel the Sultan's 100,000 strong army – unique in Europe – on its doorstep. In 1526 and thereafter, the Habsburgs were the only power who coud have altered that imbalance.

The Habsburg dynasty was marked for almost four centuries by a specific and even ambiguous position between the Western and Eastern prototypes of the developing system of European states. Although the geographic boundary of the 'second serfdom' passed through its territory, the agrarian structure of the Austrian hereditary provinces remained basically Western, leading in two isolated areas (Tirol and Vorarlberg) to a political consequence that was exceptional even in the West: the incorporation of the representatives of the peasantry within the provincial *corpus politicum.* The state formula was of 'an Eastern type', in that its 'imperial' character linked it to the Russian formula. However, it was also markedly different in that the degree of centralization of the empire as a whole remained no more than a mere plan. The traditional autonomy of the individual 'countries' (and even provinces) never ceased to penetrate the dynastic unity and the centralization of the military and financial administration, in most places with a force exceptional even in the West. Moreover, the temporal rhythm of the development of Habsburg absolutism showed a definite similarity to that of the West. The conflicts between the strengthening state and the defensive forces of the Estates took the form of 'religious wars' and occasional 'national' slogans that were overcome only by the real 'absolutist' turn of the state in the seventeenth century. The first fairly decisive turn took place – at least in Bohemia (1620) – with a truly 'Eastern' brutality and was continued in Hungary with a similar attempt (1670) that met stiffer resistance than expected and led, within half a century, to a compromise that would have been impossible in the East, and had no parallel in the West. There was no precedent for the way the Austrian hereditary provinces retained the massive remains of their autonomies and disagreements with medieval freedoms for the nobility, burgesses and peasantry, while simultaneously developing the basis of absolutism in the spirit of unconditional faith in the dynasty. At the same time, this 'semi-Western' formula took the matter of enlightenment into its own hands in the eighteenth century in the Eastern European way (although by then the state had become the bastion of papal clericalism); having completed the programme of enlightenment half successfully, the state became, after the great historical turning point of 1789 in Europe, a 'prison of nations' [*népek börtöne*], just as Russia was. This fundamental fact persisted even when, a century later, the Habsburg Empire became a framework for rapid capitalization and modernization – again in a 'semi-Western' way. Its inevitable dissolution was caused precisely by the fact that in the age of nationalism it was too late to turn a 'prison of nations' into a framework for the free association of peoples. It also followed that the dissolution of this four-centuries-old hybrid structure was followed by mounting chaos, and not by relaxation. This absolutism was by nature unsuited to making its 'peoples' into modern nations – either clearly defined nation-states or linguistic nations – although in both the West and the East that was one of the fundamental (if unevenly completed) historic tasks of absolutism.

The whole history of the Habsburg state was an attempt to balance the unbalanceable while being squeezed between the two extremes of East-Central Europe: the Polish and the Prussian variants. The only consequent structural element in that formula that might be called heterogeneous in every respect – apart from the total domination of the dynastic element – was the setting up by the Habsburgs of a diminished 'East-Central European', 'imperial scale' version of the division of labour generated by the nascent 'world economy' on a large scale. The decisive warning had been provided by the Peace of Westphalia (1648), after which the Habsburgs were driven politically out of Western Europe. Their failure in the following half-century to set up monopolistic commercial companies modelled on the West showed clearly that the Habsburgs had no chances in the Western sector of the world economy. So the House of Habsburg settled for a division of labour between West (industrial) and East (agricultural) within its own, East-Central European, political framework. In its hybrid Western sector, the political precondition for this was provided partly by the fact that the Habsburg *Hausmacht* managed to gain the upper hand over its dismembered 'hereditary provinces' fairly easily; and partly by the fact that this Western dynasty never hesitated to eliminate the 'political society' of a country by means more absolute than in the East. After the Battle of the White Mountain (1620), it did exactly this in Bohemia – cleverly selecting one of its 'countries' which in the sixteenth century had already doubled the economic potential and incomes of the original *Erbländer*. By annihilating the cream of the Bohemian nobility, confiscating more than half of their lands and 'replacing' the old Bohemian ruling class with a new, cosmopolitan aristocracy loyal to the dynasty, the Habsburgs made three gains.

First, they ensured an uncontrolled, absolutist government in Bohemia connected to the hereditary provinces. Secondly, the imperial bureaucracy and high command obtained a high-ranking set of cadres which resembled neither the Western (office-buying) nor the Eastern (service nobility) type; it was a third variant that lacked the nation-forming ethnic unity that was a common feature of the other two. Thirdly, the Habsburgs obtained a territory which they could develop into a complex model area of the Eastern-type 'second serfdom', subordinated to a new aristocracy and to the state's Western type of industrial mercantilism. Consequently, it was mainly in Bohemia, under a foreign dynasty, with an aristocracy that remained foreign and an autochthonous nobility of diminishing significance, that East-Central Europe's most bourgeois modern nation would be formed, almost accidentally – as the result of Habsburg absolutism's only unintended and indirect 'nation-building' activity. (It did not even cement the mass of the *Österreichische Erbländer* into a real 'Austrian nation'.) Then, far more conspicuously and with more clamour, there was another nation of a quite unbourgeois character: the Hungarian nation, existing not so much by the favours of the Habsburgs as in spite of them. In the 'Habsburg division of labour' Hungary was cast in the East's role, partly because of her geographical situation and partly because of her system of Estates, which was stronger than Bohemia's. Eventually the ambivalent reward granted her 'political society' proved to be a punishment for Hungary, whereas for Bohemia the punishment that followed the collapse of her system of Estates turned out to be a reward.

After 1526 Hungarian history did not simply experience 'impasses', as Bibó pointed out. It became stuck in a deadlock whose contours in modern times were precisely surveyed by Bibó himself with his merciless candour. In essence, the deadlock was the Hungarian history, with its 'Western' type structure (albeit defective, ineffective and warped), became trapped during its 'Eastern European' turn in an 'East-Central European' model that in principle excluded the state from effectively overcoming the attendant crisis by following clearly either the Western or the Eastern models. The severely defensive situation in the region excluded the possibility of a Western type of 'national monarchy' while the existence of the Western type of *corpus politicum* essentially prevented a Russian type of unilateral subordination to any kind of imperial absolutism. The warped political society of the nobility, which stubbornly preserved the feudal pole of the state, was occasionally able by fits of effort to rally the masses from 'beneath' the *corpus politicum* and behind the banner of the 'freedom of the country'. But it was necessarily unable to modernize itself from within. It cannot be blamed or this failure, since nowhere else in Europe, apart from the Netherlands and England, was the medieval *civilis societas* able to perform unaided such a self-modernization. So there remained the anachronism: while the West set out towards national absolutism and the East towards imperial autocracy, Hungary's noble society did not (and could not) imagine any other option than that of sticking to the medieval dualism of royal power and Estates – even in the face of the imperial framework and changing conditions.

Apart from the widely recognized historical distortions in the structure of its economy and society, Hungary also paid for its warped development with a typical 'malaise' in its mental structure. Some of these maladies – diagnosed accurately by Bibó – did not (as he thought) stem from infections after the healing processes of the Age of Reform had been halted in 1848-9. Rather, they stemmed from old constitutional diseases. Was not a symptom of these diseases that all the leading strata of a society living within a political structure based fundamentally on compromise (within which every uprising was ultimately aimed at political compromise) should for centuries delude themselves into believing they were constantly rebelling and 'resisting'? The delusion was so strong that it still exerts an influence on us. Was not another symptom of those diseases the intensified hereditary 'ruling spirit', as distinct from the 'humility of the serf'? Another symptom of the disease was that passivity of *nil admirari* emphasized by the poet Mihály Babits: the resigned submission that assumes that all major decisions are made somewhere 'up above'. The source of such symptoms was not merely the Eastern European model. More directly, they derived from the warped structure based on compromise, in which local frameworks of power controlled from the centre could serve as a compensation for the full exercise of state functions, whereas in other regions the absolute state itself began to produce some competent balance between central and local powers.

Of course, Western-type structures – albeit in a distorted form – did appear in Hungary. They help us to understand how the strong Estates system of Hungary could exempt the country from the reforms initiated 'from above' by the state around the turn of the eighteenth and nineteenth centuries to a far greater extent than was the case in Austria, Bohemia or Prussia. Yet within scarcely a quarter of a century, the best of the nobility became ready for a renewal that made them take the matter of reform and then revolution 'from below' in hand, so opening probably the most European period in Hungarian history – 'the greatest attempt to return to the main course of Western development' (Bibó). Since that was the point from which Bibó followed in detail and in a very evocative way the hopes and the newer impasses of historical development – Hungary's further warping in the 'East-Central European' model – it seems the appropriate point at which to end this sketch.

Notes

1. This essay appeared originally in Hungarian as 'Vázlat Európa három régiójáról', *Történelmi Szemle*, no. 24, 1981, pp. 313-69. This study is dedicated to István Bibó (1911-79). He was a political scientist and thinker, not a historian, although history forms an organic part of his work. He set an example for historians by realizing that behind 'events' lie certain structures that are essential in the long term and, in the present day, also define limits and possibilities. Within the sphere of these real limits and possibilities can be found the essence of István Bibó's life's work: What could or should be done to maximize the possibility of a society whose historical and structural limits have generated a demand for revolution and democratic transformation, even if history has provided the possibilities for revolutionary change and democracy in a situation which is not revolutionary?

In terms of these long-term limits and possibilities, István Bibó envisaged Hungarian history as a progression in three phases. Expressed simply: in the first 500 years after the turn of the millennium, Hungarian society belonged in its structure to the West, or at least approximately so – 'in a fairly simplified context with some provincial characteristics' and 'with differences of degree'. But it was then dislodged from that position by historical catastrophes, and for more than 400 years was forced into an Eastern European type of development marked by 'inertness in the power relations of society', 'deadlocks' and hopeless attempts to return to the West until the latter half of the nineteenth century, when these processes came to a weird 'impasse'. It became possible to reopen the road '(to rejoin Western social development')' in 1945, Bibó considered. The backbone of his work consists of gauging the limits and possibilities of escaping from this 'history of impasses'.

Starting this study with reference to István Bibó, who died in 1979, moving within the sphere of his ideas at several points and returning to his thoughts at the end, is not merely a matter of timeliness of form, or intended as an *in memoriam*. Many have held views on Hungary's historical and regional position, but scarcely anyone else's whole system of thinking has been so determined by the view taken of it as Bibó's. His view itself is evocative enough to stimulate the historian to consider it further, in precisely the dimensions where the late Bibó, a legal theorist and political thinker, principally sought the regional position of Hungarian history: in the relation between state and society. In that sense, of course, this study is timely, since another organizing principle might have been chosen. And as far as the form is concerned, this study is really no more (and could not within the given limits have been more) than what is indicated in the title – an outline.

At the same time, these circumstances have also decided the method of documentation. It would hardly be in style, or to the point, to burden the text with a vast bibliographical appendix or to attempt to document every detail referred to. The breadth of the subject would necessarily make such an attempt subjectively selective and serve no purpose, since the emphasis is not on the details but on the place of the details in a certain co-ordinate. Thus I shall not dwell on all the details of European or Hungarian history referred to in the text, since they are available in every textbook. Here I shall mention only a purposefully selected group of works which have had a decisive influence in forming my notions on the salient points of the subject.

István Bibó's ideas on the subject, born of profound and extensive outlook on modern history, can be read in two large studies: *A kelet-európai kisállamok nyomorúsága* [*The Poverty of the Small States of Eastern Europe*] (particularly in the chapter 'A politikai kultúra deformálódása' ['The Warping of Political Culture'], Budapest

1946; and 'Eltorzult magyar alkat, zsákutcás magyar történelem' ['A Distorted Hungarian Frame, a Hungarian History Full of Impasse'], *Válasz*, no. 8, 1948, pp. 289-319. The most condensed exposition of the concept can be found in 'A magyar tarsadalom fejlödése és az 1945 évi változás értelme ['The Development of Hungarian Society and the Meaning of the Change in 1945'], *Válasz*, no. 7, 1947, pp. 493-504. Of course there are shorter or longer excursions into this subject in other works of his (including those still in manuscript).

On the conceptual background see H. Gollwitzer, 'Zur Wortgeschichte und Sinndeutung von "Europa"', *Saeculum*, no. 2, 1956, pp. 161-172; G. Barraclough, 'Die Einheit Europas im Mittelalter', *Die Welt als Geschichte*, no. 11, 1951, pp. 97-122.

On the 'first agrarian revolution' and its demographical and social correlations, essential readings are G. Duby, *L'Économie rurale et la vie des campagnes dans l'Occident Médiéval*, 2 vols, Paris 1962; and B.H. Slicher van Bath *The Agrarian History of Western Europe, 500-1850*, New York 1963.

The 'external' and 'internal' expansion of the West has been expressively described in J. Le Goff, *La Civilisation de l'Occident Médiéval*, Paris, pp. 87 ff., and in *Das Hochmittelalter*, Frankfurt am Main 1965.

East-Central European Perspectives*

Mihály Vajda

The 'De-Europeanization' of East Central Europe

Europe has ceased to be a purely geographical concept. We take the term 'Europe' to mean a specific value system, a way of thinking, and during recent decades, it has gradually taken on the character of a political concept.

Quite a few people and nations, having failed to establish a 'democratic' political system in their countries, find themselves – willy-nilly – excluded from Europe. Western Europe seems to have accepted this state of affairs. Barbed wire divides Europe from 'not-yet-Europe' or 'not-any-more Europe': a barrier erected in the aftermath of the Second World War, consolidating a new status quo. Whether these countries did this voluntarily or were forced to do so is another matter. But it is a fact that these states are now automatically excluded from the EEC, from the Council of Europe, and so on. The fence (in the East German case, an actual wall) is supposed to 'protect' them from European influences.

Eastern Europe proper seems to have willed this exclusion in a quite deliberate manner. It appears that Russia has finally settled the dispute that has raged among its intellectuals for over a century. Russia is *not* Europe: it is not the socially, culturally and economically backward part of Europe. It is a world system going

---

*Translated by Julian Schopflin.

its own sweet way, which in many of its facets is quite different from the ways of Europe.

In this sense, political division is only the (ideological) confirmation of an existing cultural and social divide. Communism – which ideally wanted to eliminate the negative consequences of European individualism carried to excess (whilst at the same time trying to maintain its more positive features) – is no longer a 'spectre haunting Europe'.

The short-lived upswing – followed by the virtually final flop – of Eurocommunism seems to prove one thing: after Stalin's death the so-called Communist world hesitated for a brief moment, but then decided *not* to choose the road leading to the 'Europeanization' of Soviet Russia – the road towards increasing adherence to Europe in cultural and societal terms. It opted instead for the paradoxical-sounding route of 'expansive isolation'. Its dream of 'renewing Europe' had already been given up much earlier.

'Expansive isolation'? Yes, indeed, On the one hand this involves a rejection of all the ideas essential to what we call European civilization: its value system, its ways of thought, its concepts of freedom and of the individual (excepting, of course, the crucially important areas of natural science and modern technology). On the other hand, 'expansion' means infiltration of all those parts of the world that have not been 'corrupted' by European individualism. It looks as if Russia is finding the opportunity to realize its values almost exclusively in the Third World.

Between the two great Russian traditions – one a craving for 'Europe' emanating from a deeply felt inferiority complex; the other a sense of mission, offering the world salvation based on the purity and superiority of the 'Russian soul' – the one preaching Russian aloofness has gained the upper hand.

It would be beyond the scope of my subject to analyse the reasons for this. Here, I only offer the commonplace opinion that the Russian Empire could not and cannot become a suitable framework for the unfolding of autonomous social institutions. The non-existence of autonomy – indeed, the lack of even a *desire* for autonomy – is the main distinguishing characteristic of Eastern Europe, in contrast to Europe proper. The development of social autonomy, in its infinitely varied forms, has led to the disintegration of empires throughout Europe. By contrast, the current Russian Empire – the Soviet Union – which has in its hands all possible means of industrial civilization, is capable of shackling and fully controlling its society: there is no chance for the evolution of any kind of social autonomy.

This momentous choice became, to all intents and purposes, irreversible at the time when Brezhnev came to power and has resulted in the current state of affairs in the world. Europe's traditions acquired their multicoloured hues through the blossoming of varied social autonomies; now this continent has become wedged between two world powers of less variegated tints.

One of these powers – America – can more or less rightly claim to be the inheritor of European traditions; indeed, sometimes it seems inclined to believe that it alone can carry on with and defend the values, ways of thinking and ethos of European civilization. However, it has been successful in transplanting only one main trend in European traditions: that of rationalism and pragmatism. It is true that without this particular trend Europe would not have become what it is, but the American standpoint seems to lack one fundamental feature of European traditions: the constantly critical scrutiny of social attitudes, allied to a conscious effort to reach back to historical origins.

The infiltration of American values – the gradual Americanization of Europe – has created a kind of uncertainty and hesitation, a defensive posture, a confused European consciousness. Europe somehow fails to assert those parts of her traditions missing from the American view of the world. The result of all this is that Europe's value system is seen as endangered by the *other* world power, Russia. Any kind of thoroughgoing critique of Europe's existential values is suspected nowadays of being little more than a disguised manifestation of Soviet expansionism.

Europe is thus forced to accept the status quo. Either it accepts American attitudes uncritically, or it becomes subjected to Soviet imperialism. The Western half of Europe has fallen into the first kind of bondage, the East-Central half has to suffer the second. 'If we want to sustain whatever has been left of Europe, we have to stick to this status quo' seems to be the unspoken slogan.

This, however, means that Europe is throwing to the wolves those integral parts of its geography which have been stubbornly struggling against their 'de-Europeanization' and whose basic historical and social traditions must be destroyed before people can resign themselves to the idea: 'We do not belong to Europe any longer.'

Sad evidence of this Western European attitude is offered by the West's reaction to the events of 1980-81 in Poland, or in its behaviour towards the Hungary of Kádár. Alas, one cannot really be surprised at the very lukewarm enthusiasm shown by Western public opinion – ranging from right-wing conservatives to left-wing socialists – towards the struggles of KOR and Solidarity, or at the relief (and the formal protests symbolizing Europe's shame) visible at the introduction of martial law in Poland.

There is no need to beat about the bush. Western Europe is convinced that the main condition of its freedoms is the subjection of East-Central Europe. After all, if the status quo worked out at the end of the Second World War was once upset, anything might happen. And the picture of Hungary today greatly eases the guilty conscience. Just look at it: there is really no need for the wholesale 'de-Europeanizing' of a country in order to allay any Russian feeling of threat from that source. Who can deny that Hungary today is, in many respects, *more* European than it was in the interwar years? And if this is indeed the case, the other peoples of the East-Central European area can blame only themselves if they cannot work out a sort of 'European' existence, within the constraints of political vassalage. After all, meddling with the status quo would be a crime against humankind! Why could the Poles not accept the limitations of action, forced upon them by the status quo? Why has the 'European' element in Bohemia been unwilling to make its peace with the regime…as the Hungarians have done?

There may not be many people who are honest enough to raise these questions so bluntly, but few can deny that questions of this nature lurk behind every reaction by Western public opinion to developments in East-Central Europe.

Those of us who live in East-Central Europe must also raise these questions, though not in a spirit of recrimination. After all, even though we struggle against its acceptance we must reckon with the existence of this status quo. And if we do not want to resign our adherance to Europe, we must do our utmost to sustain this belonging, within the possibilities (however limited they may be) of this status quo. Let me add that – however paradoxical this may sound – precisely because we in East-Central Europe are nonconformists, we may also strike a blow for the renascence and creativeness of European culture. In my view, Western Europe seems to be in danger of throwing these very values overboard in order better to protect its pragmatic and rationalistic individuality. We who live in that region have much less to lose.

Western Europe ought to pay more attention to what goes on in East-Central Europe. It should realize that the repeated rebellions do not actually challenge the political status quo. Our peoples are desperately fighting for the European idea, and are forced to deny the status quo only when there seems to be no other chance to show that they also belong to Europe.

Both the events of Prague in 1968 and the Polish crisis in the 1980s prove this. The Czechoslovak reform movement did not even dream of changing the dual defensive system of NATO and the Warsaw Pact. Up to August 1968 the Czechoslovaks looked upon the Russians as their only natural ally, the only power that stood up for Czechoslavakia in 1938. The change in the situation whereby they do not 'love' the Russians any more was brought about purely and simply by the brutal manner in which the Soviets strangled the cautious reform movement.

In Poland, of course, the situation is rather different. There had been very little love lost between Poles and Russians throughout their history. The horror of Katyn, the tragedy of Warsaw in 1944 and the years following that have not improved this relationship. In spite of this, questions of national independence did not play a decisive part during the rise of Solidarity; indeed, up to the last moment the movement did not want to replace the political power of the Communist Party by a pluralistic democratic system, although there was no doubt whatsoever that the Communists represented the interests of the Soviet Union. Solidarity thus imposed a severe limitation upon itself. Perhaps this was one of the reasons for its failure.

When we look at the anti-totalitarian movements of East-Central Europe that have arisen since the end of the war, we have to point out that the Hungarian revolution of 1956 was to some extent an exception. No one can deny that the demand for national independece played a very strong part in it, in contrast to the later Czechoslovak and Polish reform movements.

There is one thing that cannot and must not be forgotten: the armed intervention of the Soviet Union, and the reaction to it, made it crystal clear that the Western powers had accepted the status quo established in the late 1940s. In fact they cling to it still with great tenacity.

The issue, therefore, has nothing to do with upsetting the status quo. If it were possible to remain 'Europeans' whilst belonging to the Soviet sphere of influence, the peoples of East-Central Europe would accept this without any further ado. So far, however, this has not proved possible. The Finns may be the only exception; but for reasons that go beyond our discussion they have never been *forced* to accept the East European pattern, and their social liberties have remained intact.

Sometimes one has the impression – from the Russian point of view – that the most important issue is a complete denial of the emergence of any kind of European-style social autonomy within their sphere of influence. For instance, the Russians seem to accept Romania's excursions in foreign affairs without any ruction. They feel certain that the Romanian regime will crush any manifestation of this European spirit (mostly attempted by the national minorities) with an iron hand.

Although we are wont to challenge the historical justification of the status quo we reluctantly accept it, having learnt our lesson from the three great upheavals and their failure. Does the lesson not imply that we should pay more attention to Hungary? What is the use, as far as we are concerned, of parading our old grievances about the lack of those freedoms that have gained ground in Europe ever since 1789? Knowing that we cannot change this status quo, it is utterly futile just to complain, occasionally to protest, sometimes to appeal to an indifferent democratic West…

What we should do is to pinpoint the remaining possibilities in our European consciousness. It would be self-defeating if the only lessons we could draw from the failure of the three noble attempts at liberty would be the hopeless conclusion that only a miraculous transformation of the Soviet Empire could promise relief from our spiritual serfdom. It is very praiseworthy that there are still some among us, however small in number, who refuse to sell the proud conviction 'We are Europeans' for the proverbial mess of pottage… but it is not enough. My fear is that these defiant gestures (often at the risk of one's personal liberty) may turn into gestures of despair, a poor substitute for possible action that actually may enlarge our freedom of movement.

Explanations of 'Existing Socialism'

Most attempts at defining 'existing socialism' have a basic weakness: they try to describe it by a sort of structural method.[1] These investigations usually concentrate on the organizational framework within which 'social reproduction' takes place – in the formal mechanisms of the economy, cultural life and in the political structure, upon which all mechanisms of these systems depend. In most cases these descriptions are quite satisfactory, as far as they go. It is not too difficult to assess the organizational structure of these societies. However, having described these 'socialist' structures – which are more or less the same in all these countries – the observers usually go on to analyse the specific differences between countries under the same dispensation. These analyses nevertheless cannot really penetrate the essence of these differences. Drawing upon the structural approach, they usually disregard those differences which are embedded in history and which affect attitudes and behaviour, first and foremost in the relationship of people to the structure.

Behaviour, with its underlying formative attitudes, is hardly ever capable of modifying the formal structures imposed on these countries by force. After all, these structures represent the essence of 'socialism' in the eyes of the Soviet rulers and the Communist elites in power. (Of course, if socialism means the rule of these elites and nothing else, then they are right.) No one is allowed to touch these structures, let alone change them. In consequence, the structural approach cannot illuminate the real differences and gets into a quandary – after all, these countries *are* all fundamentally different.

If we have to admit that the structuralist method is incapable of explaining the differences between societies in East-Central Europe, then we have to turn to another method: the historical one. Only by constantly keeping in view the very different historical developments of these countries can we perceive that there is a profound difference between East-Central Europe and Eastern Europe – first and foremost in social and personal attitudes. And this means that largely identical (forcibly imposed) political structures however correctly described by structural analysis, simply cannot have the same effect everywhere.

In my view, political structure and society are more or less congruent in Eastern Europe. Throughout the history of this region there have never been important independent social movements affecting the deepest layers of society, within the framework of the political state. In contrast to this, in the East-Central European region a totalitarian state must continually coerce society, in order that it should outwardly conform to the Eastern model.

The Communist Party–state assumes responsibility for every thing that is happening in society; therefore it feels obliged to direct and control the whole of social life ('ideally' including the life and fate of each individual). This inevitably leads to a chronic conflict with the traditional conditioning of people, expressed in their attitudes and behaviour.

In these societies the traditional communities that tended to define, in a rigid manner, their members' behaviour and way of life are well on the way to dissolution – indeed, many have already vanished completely. The individual has cut the umbilical cord tying him or her to a community. Men and women want to make the essential decisions about their lives themselves, in as sovereign a manner as possible. Understandably, they are rebelling against the all-embracing power of the totalitarian state. What forms this rebellion takes is another matter.

In East-Central Europe there is an ongoing conflict between the state – claiming total power – and civil society. Society may have been shackled and no autonomous organization may be permitted, but its instinctive behaviour stubbornly survives. Sometimes this conflict breaks out in a confrontation shaking the system to its foundations (as in Poland); elsewhere, political power is strong and resolute enough to crush the rebellion (as in Czechoslovakia); whilst in a third case (Hungary or Yugoslavia) the state is successful in maintaining the formal framework of total power, but in order to avoid damaging confrontation reduces its claims to total control and allows some scope for quasi-independent stirrings.

It seems to me that this third kind of resolution – the attempt to smooth out the conflict between state and society – is, by and large, in accord with common East-Central European traditions. Of course, whatever promise this 'dynamic' solution may hold, it is still only a tendency and not yet a well-established method of conflict resolution. No one can be certain that the attempt will succeed. Historically, these traditions simply mean that these societies have in many ways wrested a measure of independence from political power: that is, have ceased to be purely 'statal societies' on the Eastern model. It is true that their attempts at demanding a share of political decision-making, their efforts at making the state representative, have mostly been unsuccessful. Politics has always been a preserve of the elite, of 'our masters'.

Three European Regions

If we look at the map of Europe, passing from west to east, we can discern two historically decisive (although geographically somewhat blurred) boundaries. The westernmost part of Europe extends to the eastern frontiers of the Carolingian Empire; the eastern boundary marks the division of Latin and Byzantine Christianity. I do not propose to discuss the origins and repeated re-establishments of these boundaries. However, if we want to understand the current situation in Europe – especially the perspectives of the East-Central region – we must concentrate on the central issue: the particular historical evolution which characterizes the societies in this central area. The features outlined above, including the social attitudes and behaviour of peoples, were already clearly discernible towards the end of the Second World War. This societal stance is an integral part of the *Gestalt* of these peoples; it is fashioned by their history and is therefore ineradicable – one may even say hereditary.[2]

The really important feature of West European development from the Middle Age onwards is the gradual separation of state and society. The origins of this cleavage lie in the slow disintegration of traditional, self-supporting peasant communities in which individuals could hardly ever break their bonds and the whole of their lives, so to speak, was determined from birth to death.

Whilst this disintegration was going on there arose new urban communities within which the attitudes and behaviour of individuals were shaped less and less by tradition. Human relations came to be regulated in a more or less deliberate manner. And – most importantly – relations among various groups in society were settled increasingly by contract.

There was a kind of contract between a feudal lord and his vassals; between barons and the central power of kings; between kings and independent cities. In the beginning, tradition and unchallengeable decisions from above had regulated all relationships within society. Later, the pattern tended to move towards settlement by negotiation, between groups representing different interests. Agreements and compromises were embodied in legal forms; thereby the abstraction of the Law became the criterion of social and political relationships.

This sea-change was the result of social movements as well as the framework for further developments. Ever more intricate social relationships and conflict or co-operation among social groups and territorial units made this new kind of societal regulation imperative (albeit at the price of serious struggles and upheavals). On one side stood the great variety of social autonomies; on the other a central power to some extent distinct from society: the state.

For a long time, central power was not yet genuinely representative of society. However, gradually it became responsible to society: its decisions eventually emerged as a result of a social consensus (and, of course, not without a struggle).

It would take us too far afield to analyse this process in detail, to examine whether the increasing divergence of ideology and politics was cause or effect. Perhaps it will be enough to point to the very early divorce of state power and church power. In itself, this development made it possible to challenge the decisions of secular authority and offered some scope for independence, both for social groups and for individuals.

The decay of traditional communities, the divided power of church and state, a system of rights and duties – the result of hard-fought social conflicts – all contributed to the development of individualism. Western man ceased to believe that his social conditions were God-given and unchangeable. Whenever he was forced into relationships not freely chosen, or found himself constrained in behaviour or action, he resented it as a restriction of his individuality. Gradually, he took it for granted that he himself should make the important decisions about his own life. At the same time, being a member of a complex network of social relationships, he increasingly claimed a voice in matters affecting society as a whole.

The end result of this process is well known. On the one hand we have the 'self-evident' freedom of individuals and social groups, limited only by the freedom of other groups; on the other, we see a central power not attached to any group or class, to some extent separate from society proper, responsible to the whole of society. This is the modern state.

In the Eastern region of Europe, no trace of any such development can be found. In the lower layers of society there remained the stagnant, traditional communities, lorded over by a strong central power which brooked no limitation of its grasp. Society was structured from the top downwards. No social group could claim any kind of autonomy. Even the nobility had no rights, only privileges; in exchange for these, it had to serve the central power – as a 'servile nobility'. There was no scope for the emergence of dynamic, free towns, the usual seedbed for progress. The ideological power, the Church, was part and parcel of the state. There was no single element in the whole of society capable of acquiring a shred of independence. The state was Society, all-embracing and omnipotent.

It is not my task to examine the reasons for this immobility. It is obvious that the different ethos of Byzantine Christianity – the fossilization of the Eastern church over the centuries – played an important part in this throughout. Another reason – probably the main one – was the onslaught of Barbarians from the east throughout the formative centuries of Eastern Europe. In a constant 'state of siege', no social grouping can afford the luxury of fighting for its autonomy: a strong central power is essential for survival. This contention seems to be strengthened by the observation that in Western Europe an external threat usually led to the reinforcement of the central power, to the detriment of autonomous groups. As far as the intermediate area, East Central Europe, is concerned it was the advance of Turkish power that as good as stopped the kind of Western-style development that had been discernible in this region up to the end of the fifteenth century.

The outstanding characteristic of this East-Central European area is the fact that it did set out along the same route as the Western model. True, this development was slower and more uncertain than that of the West, even before the wave of Turkish conquest blocked this process. Following the withdrawal of the Turk, a new – and much less favourable – constellation arose. On one side we had the by now strong and confident Western nation-states with their internal network of autonomous social groups; on the other side the Russian Empire, still with its original rigid structures (though overlaid by some elements of modernization). These factors – among others – put a brake on the resumption of Western-style development in our region. Nevertheless, those autonomies that had struck root in the first half of the millenium did not wither away. The societies in that region never relapsed into Russian-style 'statal societies'.

In East-Central Europe the estates remained vigorously alive; some urbanization did take place, even though this was less widespread than in the West; last but not least, the consciousness and attitudes of individualism were alive and well, the desire and demand for autonomy ever present. In spite of these promising signs, however, the countervailing forces were too strong and civil society was unable to gain more than a limited measure of social autonomy.

Society as such was never strong enough to challenge that group which retained its grip upon political power. Certain liberties were obtained, but there was no possibility of reaching the stage where political power is delegated by society and made responsible to it. Western-style individualism did exist, but without the democratic self-confidence of the citizen. The *bourgeois* failed to grow into a *citoyen*. It is no coincidence that the only philosophy that accords the state the role of a 'natural force' – the philosophy of Hegel – was born in this region.

Another key to the understanding of the ethos of East-Central Europe is nationalism. For a Western observer it is well-nigh impossible to understand the baleful role that nationalism has played in this region, tragically distorting every chance for clarity, even in the simplest social problem areas. In Western Europe, the social development indicated above was already well on its irresistible way before the problem of nationalism arose. There the state, more or less secure within estabished boundaries, succeeded in kneading a given variety of language groups into a nation.

In Central Europe, however, this model of the modern state that embraces a network of autonomies and, to some extent, is responsible to it did not manage to come into being *before* the national consciousness of multifarious language groups awoke. These peoples were unwilling to reach a compromise with a 'foreign' central power, especially those (for example the Czechs) who had enjoyed independence as a state in their past history. Or – in a different constellation – the ruling social group, the power elite, had a strong national consciousness and simply could not grasp that other (mainly peasant) groups, speaking a different language, should be taken into account at all (for example the Hungarians versus Slovaks and Romanians, or the Poles versus the Ukrainians).

This tangled skein of national problems led to the really tragic result – exposed brilliantly by István Bibó – that the matter of the community (the nation) and the matter of liberty (the emergence of autonomy) became opposing forces, instead of reinforcing one another.

The peace treaties following the First World War only made matters worse. In their well-intentioned but ill-judged attempt to create viable nation-states in place of the dissolved Habsburg Empire, they violated the principle of self-determination by disregarding ethnic boundaries in the process of setting up national frontiers. Instead of striving to achieve a maximum of peaceful coexistence among the squabbling nations of the region, they punished – or rewarded – real or contrived historical grievances or merits.

In consequence the problems of nationality became open sores, with two fateful results. One has been the curious relationship of nations with their states. The dominant nationality in each country indiscriminately looks upon the state as its very own, however undemocratic it may be. This can be observed even in those situations where society seems to be mature enough to allow individuals to develop, and where the paternalistic rule of an elite could well be transformed into a democratic political structure. 'My state, right or wrong,' is their slogan. A striking example of this state of affairs was the more or less blind trust most Poles had in the 'national army' of General Jaruzelski in 1981. But in a similar manner Czechs, Slovaks and Romanians also co-operate willingly with their governments in oppressing their national minorities. Hungarians, in their turn, tend to believe that a 'strong' state would be better fitted to protect 'our kith and kin' living beyond the national frontiers.

The other discouraging result of this tangled web is the frightening indifference of the peoples towards their neighbours' aspirations. Popular apathy was the reaction to the struggles for freedom – and their defeat – in Hungary in 1956, in Czechoslovakia in 1968 or in Poland in 1980-81. Sometimes there was even a whiff of hostility in the air. Alas, this is nothing new, it has been the traditional response ever since 1848. This behaviour of peoples in our region is not just selfish (Western Europe is just as selfish towards East-Central Europe): it is totally irrational.

Traditions and Social Dynamism

This very sketchy historical review was meant only to support my main thesis: whilst in Eastern Europe proper there is a relative harmony between society and political structure, in the East-Central region all that exists is a fundamental conflict between state and society. This conflict will persist and can be resolved in only one of two ways: either the totalitarian state succeeds in extirpating all traditions of individual and social autonomy, or – yielding to social pressure – the political structure will be transformed...not into democratic rule, but at least into a paternalistic system that would be consonant with the traditions of the region.

I trust I am justified in casting a backward glance at history to support my thesis. Whether the system is good enough for the Russians or the Romanians is not at issue here; nor is the problem of whether the Poles, Czechoslovaks and Hungarians deserve something better, even though it is not as good as what the French or the Dutch enjoy. Nor is the ideal society or ideal political system anywhere in question. The issue is: To what extent are our possibilities determined by our historical traditions?

They are certainly *not* determined by the wishes of the individual. But, it may well be asked, how do these traditions actually evolve and change? Is there any chance of a radical change in structures and attitudes? Although there is no easy answer, one must tackle these questions. What follows, of course, is my own personal view of the matter.

History offers ample proof of one basic fact: the fanatical faith in progress so characteristic of nineteenth-century Europe was more the exception than the rule. The European value system, rooted in the Jewish-Greek-Christian tradition, achieved an almost unbelievably fast breakthrough in the wake of the Great French Revolution, with all its practical consequences, giving rise to a spurious belief in its universality.

The fundamental trait of human societies is, in fact, *stagnation*, not dynamism. As long as a society can reproduce itself along the lines of its traditions, change will be minimal. Traditions – meaning inherited attitudes, customs, structures – have a tendency towards self-reproduction. Perhaps it is no exaggeration to say that European civilization is the single exception. Its novelty has been the constant scrutiny of its own traditions, the constant challenge to the 'extant' in the name of certain ideals. Ideologically, this attitude has found its best expression in Christianity, whose essence is the denial of earthly life (the 'extant') in the name of an ideal: the Hereafter. Once the Church solidified into an institution and the 'ideal' proved to be beyond reach, heresy raised its head, demanding the 'improvement' of earthly life – a practical challenge. At first, heresy wormed its way into the dogmatic edifice of the Church; later on it found its expression in secular movements. The crucial transformation occurred between the English and French revolutions. European civilization is the only one that constantly aims at transcending itself. Its goal is not just self-preservation but the realization of ideas. It may be painful for this European consciousness to realize that traditions in general 'naturally' resist their own immolation. (The exception is our own. Why the exception? I suspect this is the insoluble riddle of the Greek spirit.)

Of course, non-European societies do not last for ever either. Civilizations collapse and disappear; new ones emerge in their place. This has usually happened as a result of external challenge or impact. Natural catastrophes may sometimes play their part in this, but mostly it is due to the onslaught of external forces. Dynamism may not characterize other cultures, but expansionism certainly does. Natural or man-made cataclysms, however, can hardly be called 'progress'. Cultures simply vanish or coalesce. An external force cannot positively energize existing traditions: it can destroy them, replace them or merge them with its own. The swift disintegration and rebirth of traditions is a specifically European phenomenon. The more 'European' a society is, the more swiftly this happens. Traditions change faster in Western Europe than in the central region; and Central Europe shows a stronger tendency towards change than Eastern Europe.

Nevertheless, in its own way Eastern Europe – Russia above all – has always been a part of Europe as a whole. The fundamental feature of European culture, the tendency to transcend itself, to some extent applies to Russia too. But the identification of the Orthodox Church with the centralized state has blocked the emergence of autonomies. Indeed, even rebellious heresy, and even the secularization of Christianity, have been only sporadic there.

The continuous external threat has made only one ruling idea possible: that of the strong, all-powerful Russian Empire. The sudden secularization of that society was possible only because the Russian Empire of the tsars failed to sustain this ruling idea when it collapsed towards the end of the First World War. The new, strong central power – that of the Bolsheviks – realized that in order to establish its legitimacy it had to adopt the traditional ideal. Never mind the ideology: Russia had to be built up into a world power. The scientific and technological knowhow of the West has been essential to this achievement – in this field, Russia *does* belong to Europe.

Of course, these are not the only 'European ideas' alive in Russia. But (as I pointed out earlier), Brezhnev's coming to power found Russia at a crossroads. A choice had to be made between the Western ethos and the specifically Russian ethos. The former – to overtake and outstrip the West – had to some extent been expressed by Khrushchev. Had this road been chosen, however, Russia would have had to renounce the idea of the all-powerful empire, feared by all its 'enemies'. It would also have led to the bitter acknowledgement of its own backwardness.

It would be difficult to imagine a power elite willingly launching such an experiment. Even an objective bystander would find it difficult to envisage this society without a strong, centralized, indeed totalitarian power structure. After all, its traditional society framework had been largely destroyed from above in the Revolution, and every attempt at shaping new communal forms has been thoroughly choked off. Thus there is no disposition for the self-regulation of society.

Waves of modernization in Russia (attempted so many times...by Ivan the Terrible, Peter the Great and Stalin) have always led to the reinforcement of state power, to the strengthening of bureaucracy and the army. In a curious sense, therefore, Russia has remained faithful to one European tradition: the constant effort towards the increase of state power has latterly not been due to any perceptible external threat; only to the drive to transcend the 'extant'. However, one supreme condition of this drive's success is the necessity for destroying all other European values, first and foremost the central idea of Western development: the flowering of individual and social autonomy. In the Soviet sphere, even the most tentative endeavour towards this ideal must be stamped out ruthlessly.

The Paternalistic Tradition

In East-Central Europe this Russian model simply cannot be enforced fully. Admittedly, the peoples of this area are not completely hostile to a strong central state, as long as it seems to defend national independence. (The Polish myth of Pilsudski is a good example.) A truly democratic polity has not struck strong roots anywhere except in Czechoslovakia. One may say that these peoples are dreaming of the 'good king', not of the mature responsibilities of democracy. This probably explains the curious fact that the strongest, most self-assured movement demanding autonomy, Solidarity in Poland, refused for quite some time to deal with questions affecting the Polish political system. It would be rather naive to believe that this was due only to the sober tactical deliberations of its intellectual and working-class leaders. Genuine mass movements like Solidarity do not usually play at tactics. The ideals of political democracy may not have very deep roots in these societies, but ideals concerning certain autonomies (especially those related to the individual) definitely do.

Social autonomy and political democracy are not one and the same. Of course, a truly autonomous society will not tolerate for long any kind of paternalistic 'guardianship'. Sooner or later it will revolt against a paternalistic political power and establish some kind of democratic political system responsible to society itself. This kind of revolt is usually called a 'bourgeois revolution'. However, there are certain types of social autonomy that will quite easily accommodate themselves within a paternalistic political system. After all – in contrast to a fully totalitarian dictatorship which seeks to control every aspect of social life – a paternalistic system will be satisfied so long as political decisions (albeit those affecting the whole community) remain in the hands of a privileged policy-making group. This kind of system has no need to destroy those autonomies which do not impinge on its privileges.

However, if we consider the immanent forces operating within a system of this nature, we have to note that such a paternalistic political system can be only a transitory phenomenon. As I have said before, a truly autonomous society would revolt against restrictions upon its aspirations. The only situation where state power (based on privileges) remains strong enough to shackle autonomous movements is one where society – even though it has acquired a certain limited autonomy – deliberately accepts and supports a 'strong' state (as, for instance, where there is an apparent conflict between the cause of the nation and the cause of freedom).

If we accept that social autonomy and political democracy are *not* one and the same thing, we must similarly accept that the autonomy of the individual is not tied to the existence of a democratic political system. No political dictatorship can fully extinguish individual freedom of action. In economic life, in culture, in everday contacts and behaviour and so on, citizens may enjoy a measure of freedom. No matter that they have no say in politics – in other words that they cannot change the parameters of their existence or that any kind of apolitical social organizations may also be forbidden.

It is not only in their basic attitudes and behaviour that the peoples of East-Central Europe are 'Europeans'. Not only do they have certain ideas against which they are constantly measuring their reality; these ideals do, in fact, closely resemble those of Western Europe. These peoples also resist all efforts towards the establishment of political systems that would attempt to extinguish their autonomy and deny the individual all movement. The chronic crisis and the occasional revolts of East-Central Europe cannot be explained away by trying to put them into the straitjacket of ideology. Of course, in the heat of revolt ideologies do suddenly spring to life. National independence, democracy, constitutionalism, social justice and the like – they all come alive whenever a people is standing up for its rights. Deep down, however, there is always something much more simple, more palpable, more lifelike than any abstraction: 'Let me be, leave me alone, don't try to tell me how to live.'

In 1956, in 1968 and again in 1980-81, a whole national society – which previously had not existed as a society – rebelled against the totalitarianism of its political system. All societies in our region are artificial creations: in every one of them, the state (that is the Communist Party) insists on setting the rules and exercising control over all social linkages. Apart from the Catholic Church in Poland, there is not a single legally formed social organization that does not conform to the criteria of the totalitarian state. They all accept the 'leading role of the Communist Party'. In spite of this configuration, we have to say that it was 'society' that revolted. Each individual, striving for autonomy, harbours a virtual free society within him or herself.

In a situation where individuals cannot do what they think is right and correct; where they are not allowed to participate in drawing up the rules which regulate their daily life, despite the fact that their actions, lifestyle or thoughts clearly cannot harm anyone else; where those in power can summarily declare that one's actions or words are 'against the public interest' – in such a situation only one avenue is left for effecting or influencing change. This is, simply, to get together with other people who are equally disturbed by this state of affairs, even if their wishes or ambitions differ from one's own. Together, we may win the right to order our affairs in our own way. It should not be the powers that be who decide for us what we should or should not do. Let them leave this to us, the interested parties – we shall agree somehow amongst ourselves.

Our demands are modest. All we want is that if individuals are bored with their jobs, they should be able to acquire new skills. If they feel uncomfortable in their workplace, they should be able to look for another one. If they have some ideas, they should be able to put them down in writing and circulate them to other interested readers. If they are concerned about poverty they should be able to call on others for help, as well as offer help themselves. And if they would like to stay in another country for a while, they should be allowed to try their luck there.

Admittedly, such primitive claims carry in themselves the seeds of autonomous communities, more or less independent of political power. All those who put forward such claims really assert the right to decide what suits them and what does not. In their view, it is not self-evident that the rulers (whomever or whatever they may represent) have a God-given right to decide the lives of their subjects.

These claims for autonomy have no political content in the majority of cases. Most people would not even dream of taking a stand on – for instance – the Iraq-Iran war. They are not really concerned about great matters of policy – for example whether motorways should be built or air traffic extended, or whether heavy industry or the infrastructure should get more money. Such issues may actually affect their lives, but they do not feel competent to make these decisions. After all, it is evident that most people usually cannot be bothered by such questions even in those countries where they have the full right of active intervention.

From Totalitarianism to Paternalism?

Most people draw the line, however, at outside interferences in their private lives, in what affects their families. They believe that one should have the right to lay down the rules for such matters. These views are in sharp contradiction with the very nature of totalitarian systems.

There is a danger that an abyss – encompassing rulers and ruled alike – will open up before a society where mediating mechanisms are suppressed, even though these could eventually help to create a dynamic equilibrium. But political rulers are not strong and self-confident enough to regulate by fiat any and every aspect of communal life. Total suppression of every free move within society requires total dictatorship; and this can operate smoothly only where the members of society exercise no claims for autonomy. Members of most East-Central European societies, however, do have such claims. Therefore, these societies (nurturing their latent claims for autonomy) have revolted time and time again, sometimes breaking out in spectacular revolutions against totalitarian dictatorship...Meanwhile, an imperceptible 'internal' society has been in the making all the time.

The three great revolts of 1956, 1968 and 1980 were bloodily suppressed. There is no reason to think that future revolts would not be equally crushed, in the same way. The Russians are incapable of accepting that their totalitarian system cannot work in the countries of East-Central Europe. After all, it works perfectly well in their bailiwick. And; since it works there, why should they change it fundamentally? Every change carries a threat to the power elite. In all this reasoning, they are probably quite right.

However, the Communist power elites in our region have to start thinking and acting differently if they are to stay in power. They have to recognize that their peoples are different from the Russians, the Romanians or the Albanians. So, either they have to do their best to weed out all the traditions that are the hallmark of these societies, or they must try to refashion the pattern of Communist totalitarianism and adapt it to the fundamentals of their communities. If this latter path were taken, the result would be a paternalistic Communist system.

In considering this possibility, I shall limit myself to three countries only: Poland, Czechoslovakia and Hungary. East Germany and the two westernmost republics of Yugoslavia – Croatia and Slovenia – also belong to our part of the world, and not only geographically. They too share most of our ideas. But when it comes to East Germany, the 'German question' bedevils all problems; whilst in the case of Croatia and Slovenia, their participation in a fairly strong federation creates complications for my analysis. There are also rather different problems affecting the three Baltic republics within the Soviet Union, although these too clearly belong to our area. However, I do not feel competent to extend my sketchy analysis to those communities. The task of writing a comprehensive historical sociology of East-Central Europe still awaits us.

The Polish crisis

The Communist elite in Poland has never been able to come down on the side of either totalitarianism or paternalism. The results of this shilly-shallying – affecting the elite's best interests as well – have been strikingly negative. Since the death of Stalin and the passing of the cohort of Stalinist leaders (who were forced out by the comparatively small-scale Poznan revolt), we have seen the coming – and passing – of four ruling groups, two of which were also swept away by popular uprisings. Perhaps one secret of recent Polish history lies in the fact that the removal of the Stalinist group happened relatively painlessly. Consequently, the successors had no profound lessons to learn. Gomulka did to some extent give way to the pressures from society; as a consequence, in the late 1950s and early 1960s Poland was (relatively speaking) the freest country in the Soviet bloc.

However, the loosening of controls, allowing some autonomy – in cultural matters, foreign travel, a measure of free speech –

did nothing to resolve the fundamental problems of society, whilst at the same time increasing the desire for more freedom. There was absolutely no movement whatsoever in the economy. All efforts towards some sort of autonomy in the various spheres of production were scotched; they dared not introduce co-operative farming, but starved private agriculture. This standstill eventually aroused the justified anger of the working class – the strongest social force in the whole region – and led to the present impasse. Gierek's gang then simply followed the same catastrophic path. One suspects that they knew they were in charge of a bankrupt estate; that they knew their promises would prove to be empty; and that they simply enjoyed the fruits of ten years' misrule and corruption. All decisions were again postponed.

In retrospect, it is fairly clear that Gomulka & Co. had no choice to begin with. Attempts to destroy instinctive autonomy would have carried too great a risk. On the one hand, they never succeeded in subjecting the Catholic Church to state servitude (as happened to all other churches in the region). This has meant the survival of the one really autonomous social organization capable of offering shelter to other autonomous initiatives. On the other hand, the idea of the Great Polish Nation (the Poles are the only truly large nation in East-Central Europe) has been flourishing since time immemorial. Therefore any kind of rule that wanted to subordinate Polish interests to Great Russian interests had to think twice before taking any really drastic measures. This was the main reason why the first Communist military dictatorship has had to appear in the guise of a Ruritanian operetta. Jaruzelski has to fight much more self-assured social forces than his predecessors.

Gomulka, and later Gierek, had no real choice when it came to the other, paternalistic alternative. The reason why Poland has remained a poorly functioning but essentially totalitarian dictatorship probably lies in the relatively peaceful transition in 1956. The successors of the Polish Stalinists did not have the same painful and profound need for trial and error as in Hungary. A little more social freedom, a somewhat more bearable economic policy (less forced accumulation and thus a more tolerable standard of living) – Gomulka may have thought that all this would be enough to head off social discontent.

However, by about 1968 the structural crisis of all the ruling systems in the East-Central European region became apparent. By then it was too late. For a couple of years the appearance of Polish stability was maintained by an attempt to divide the working class from the intellectuals. From 1970 onwards, the crisis broke with irresistible force. It could be solved only by really thorough structural reforms. But two decisive factors would have had to be present if such reforms were to be achieved: a minimal consensus of society and political power, and the quiet self-confidence of the ruling group. Short of a miracle, the Communist leaders of Poland are still incapable of creating the former and unable to acquire the latter.

The destruction of Bohemian tradition

The extirpation of all autonomous traditions and aspirations was the way chosen by the Czechoslovak ruling Communist elite. Two decades after the 'Prague Spring', those who – following a very short period of 're-consideration' – have not relinquished their ideas have not been forgiven. By 1969, everybody had to decide whether or not to accept and co-operate with the new regime. The ruling elite did not need any bloody terror in order to enforce this decision. Superficially, it may almost have looked as if it relied upon a 'free' election, particularly in contrast to what had happened in Hungary in 1957. What may have seemed like a parallel was no parallel at all. At one stroke, all those who supported the ideas of 1968, all those who sustained the traditions of autonomy and democracy, were thrown on to the margins of society. There was no forgiveness, no way back – not even for those who, by now, would be willing to submit. People who go on nurturing the aspirations for autonomy, who actually believe in democracy, are dangerous, and so are their offspring. After all, public behaviour and ways of social thinking are handed down within families – and in Czechoslovakia today, this happens exclusively within families.

This was not really surprising: political 'normalization' had to happen this way in Czechoslovakia. It was the only country in the whole region – at least in the Bohemian heartland – which was truly Western European in its attitudes. Civic autonomies did not exist in aspiration only: they found embodiment in a true democracy.

The reasons for this were somewhat peculiar. In 1620, at the beginning of the Thirty Years War, the Czech nobility revolted against the Empire. They were decisively beaten in the Battle of the White Mountain, and in the aftermath this nobility was virtually exterminated. The new, mostly German, nobles were foreign oppressors in Czech eyes. Whilst in Poland and Hungary the nobility and the rest of society occasionally made common cause, in Bohemia the Czechs saw the removal of this ruling group as one of the main preconditions for national independence. Bohemia was the only country in the region where the cause of liberty and the cause of social progress were not in conflict. This was the main basis for its genuine democracy.

A nation that has experienced a real democratic system, over and above the existence of individual autonomy, simply cannot make a compromise with a totalitarian dictatorship – not even a paternalistic one. The Czechs may not have the instinct for rebellion, but their skills in quiet sabotage could have made the system unworkable. That is why every single person who was suspected of democratic thinking and attitudes had to be thrown on the scrapheap. And in Czechoslovakia this meant much more than a group of cosmopolitan intellectuals.

The sad spectacle of Czech cultural life today bears ample witness to this process. 'Official' culture is nothing but cheap propaganda. If there is anything left of genuine Czech culture, it has been forced underground.

Nobody knows whether deeply rooted democratic traditions can be completely extirpated or not. Let us hope they cannot. But there is no doubt that a stubborn effort is being made in this direction. The fact that the Husák regime has been as successful as it seems to have been is due to something else: the national problem. Historically speaking, Czechoslovakia is not a homogeneous country. Czechs and Slovaks may understand one another verbally, but their ethos has always been radically different. The Slovaks felt themselves to be 'underdogs' both in the interwar democratic republic and in post-war socialist Czechoslovakia. In their own eyes Slovakia was a Czech 'colony', and this view was not without justification. Husák succeeded, therefore, in building his rule on Slovak ascendancy. It was pure luck for his regime that the Slovaks have never had true democratic traditions.

This is, then, another sad farce of Central European history. All these problems in Czechoslovakia, the solutions of which have been on the agenda ever since 1918 – like a properly federated state, or the economic build-up of the underdeveloped Slovak half of the republic – eventually became the means for throttling democracy, instead of for advancement towards autonomy for both nations.

The Hungarian experiment

The third course in East-Central Europe has been the Hungarian experiment. I believe now that it would be a serious historical error to give short shrift to 'Kádárism'. One cannot say that the Hungarian system does not differ substantially from the rest, or that the only difference is that the Hungarian Communists are cleverer – especially in their economic policies – and that this is the sole reason for the improved state of affairs in Hungary, as opposed to what is going on in neighbouring countries.

In order to avoid any misunderstanding, I must make it quite clear that in assessing the case of Hungary I am not thinking of any kind of scientific 'experiment'. No one has ever deliberately *planned* the changes that have occurred in Hungary. One can only say that it appears that the ruling Communist elite there has learnt something from the first, and most spectacular, genuine revolt against totalitarianism, the Hungarian revolution of 1956. It has learnt to listen and to notice certain demands. It has learnt that it is safe to allow some freedom of movement, as long as this does not threaten the monopoly of power. It has learnt how to channel such forces into innocuous outlets, instead of suppressing them.

Western public opinion – and, indeed, the public consciousness in Hungary itself and in East-Central Europe more generally – tends to forget the brutal and bloody terror used by the present rulers following the defeat of the revolution. Thousands were executed, tens of thousands imprisoned, hundreds of thousands thrown into limbo. Then, after a few years, the Communists made a surprisingly radical about-turn (however ambigous it may have been): the rulers offered an olive branch to the defeated nation. And the nation – not for the first time in its history – accepted the peace offering and showed its willingness to co-operate. The first condition of radical reforms, a minimal consensus between an exhausted society and a minimally tolerant ruling group, came into being at a stroke.

Only eight years had elapsed since the revolution when, at the time of the fall of Khrushchev, the nation stood four-square behind the butcher of the revolution in defence of 'socialism with a human face' (although this expression was unknown at the time) and against Soviet demands. Once that conflict was settled, the second condition of reform came gradually into being: the growing self-confidence of the ruling elite. 'It is true that we have thoroughly intimidated them,' its members may have said, 'but now they seem prepared to co-operate, not out of fear but because they realize that what we want is their "well-being".' The ruling group thus developed a kind of paternalistic attitude. 'We genuinely have their well-being at heart and they know it.'

In this way the idea of 'reform' took on material shape. The essence of these reforms has been the unquestioning acceptance of the monopoly of power in the hands of the Communist elite but alongside it, some freedom of movement for autonomous action in society. Of course, these reforms were never allowed to reach the stage of democratic consciousness. All measures have been aimed at giving free rein to people's 'bourgeois selfishness'. A free rein has been given to the fulfilment of personal – material – ambitions. This has led to a modest affluence benefiting the better part of society and, in effect, the whole national economy.

It is not by chance that these reforms are almost exclusively *economic*. The result is the evolution of a new form of property relations. Today, it is often observed that the gradual separation of the state executive from the property system is a necessary condition of a healthy socialist economy. At the same time, a deep silence obscures the fact that, on the one hand, genuine economic reforms would willy-nilly create pressure for the introduction of social and political reforms as well; and, on the other, that radical economic reforms would inevitably have rather negative social consequences too. These, in turn, would necessitate additional social and political changes. Today, even raising questions like these can earn the disapproval of the powers that be.

It is also inevitable that the development of certain economically autonomous trends will create changes in attitudes and behaviour. It would be an exaggeration to say that one can observe the sprouting of some sort of civic consciousness. However, it is noticeable that there are now some people who do not believe that the citizen exists for the state; who – in however limited a way – are beginning to demand their rights, and who are unwilling to accept that others should decide their fate in all aspects of their lives.

These aspirations towards the broadening of individual autonomy are as yet mostly unconscious – they are not yet at the level of a conscious rejection of the system. People are simply trying to improve their lot, to live according to their own ideas – mostly without any kind of political consciousness. All those people who – by making an auspicious start in life or by using their talents later – have gained the chance to extend their autonomous actions are feeling freer than before. This rudimentary 'feeling of freedom' in turn increases the self-confidence of the regime. The rulers have realized that there is no need to apply brute force in every instance.

This development, so far, has accorded mainly economic freedoms. Society may enjoy the paternalistic 'guardianship' of the ruling powers, but some ill effects of these changes are also gradually coming to the surface. Perhaps the most serious of these is a complete lack of the sense of social-communal responsibility. People are becoming less and less afraid of standing up for their own personal interests – for example in making complaints, pointing out their rights, demanding what is their due. On occasion they see that they can even get away with not-quite-legal manoeuvres in order to improve their standards. At the same time, they are fully aware of the fact that any step towards setting up some sort of independent collective association is interpreted as a 'hostile act against the state' (although one has to admit that any attempt at opposition, or at the creation of a 'second public opinion', is being persecuted with relatively civil methods).

One social consequence of these developments is a frightening polarization of society. The more affluent have managed to stay afloat even during the economic difficulties of recent years, whilst the number of those who are incapable of solving their problems by individual effort is growing apace.

Despite the seamy side of things, no one can deny that in the last twenty years the chances for individual autonomy have increased quite considerably in Hungary, more so than in any other country of 'existing socialism'. It is also a fact that various policies in Hungary, however tentatively and reluctantly, do tend to move in the direction of an economy which is more and more 'autonomous' – that is, to some extent independent of state regulations and directives. Even in cultural matters, autonomy and independence are much greater than in any other socialist country, with the exception of Poland. Of course, this does not mean that one can salute a truly autonomous culture.

The Hungarian question may be assessed in the following way: Is it possible to go further along this road? Could these scattered individual autonomies lead to a relatively autonomous global society with genuine trade unions, independent interest groups, a free and open cultural life, an independent judiciary? If so, this hoped-for peaceful process may lead to the emergence of proper social responsibilities in all walks of life.

The stark alternative may be a severe social crisis similar to the Polish one, rendered even more serious by an inevitable economic collapse. The consequences of this second scenario, with the disappearance of all social responsibility, are truly unpredictable. It is also possible, of course, that the current state of affairs may remain stable.

Perspectives within the Status Quo

One snag with all theorizing is the curious discovery that it may not be possible to describe a society properly, even with the most complicated model. It is not my job to make historical prophecies, nor am I trying to assess the social and political conditions that may render the Hungarian alternative possible. I should like only to express my conviction that this alternative can offer the achievable maximum in safeguarding and continuing our 'European essence' – as long as the current status quo remains in force. A concordat of this nature may leave all political power in the hands of the rulers, and at the same time allow a fair measure of independence for society as a whole. It may thus allow various groups in society to arrange their – non-political – affairs amongst themselves, without interference by the ruling powers.

This option, in effect, would largely conform to the traditions of East-Central Europe. After all, the Polish movement aimed at the realization of the same alternative. Its suppression does not mean that this alternative is impossible. First, the previous decades of Polish history, instead of moving towards such a structure, showed a decline into almost total social catastrophe; secondly, the ruling Communist elite in Poland has not been at all prepared for any kind of collaboration with a freer society. Its only reaction has been the determination to sabotage every agreement and be ready to smash them all. Thirdly, whilst Communist regimes may not be as rigid as they seem, it is quite unimaginable that they would give ground to a revolutionary mass movement. There is logic in their reaction: once the masses have come to recognize their own power, who knows when and where they would stop?

Our first alternative would surely fit Hungarian traditions. Apart from a few exceptional instances, there has never been a proper political democracy here on the Western model. Our only question is: Can the Communist elite fulfil the function performed by the historic ruling classes? It is probably a pretty rare event in the history of any country when the majority of the ruling class simply deserts the nation, complete with its army and state administration, as happened in Hungary in 1945. After a few years' gap, the Communists then moved into the same positions, and they have every intention of remaining the unchallengeable practitioners of political power...as their predecessors had been for a thousand years.

The old regime became, in the end, a corrupt, mendacious system without convictions and without vision. Any other ruling group could have taken over and could have functioned better. The Communists, however, are suffering from two grievous disadvantages, and it is difficult to see how they could overcome them. One is the thousand-year-old tradition of the old ruling class, according to which masters will always be masters, regardless of what they are like. The other disadvantage confronting the Communists is their difficulty in proving that they are the best possible guardians and champions of the national interests of the Hungarian people. (Which is not to say that the old regime had a better claim to this role).

For these reasons, the status quo is their only available excuse. And as far as Hungary is concerned, this is all we can have.

Notes

1. Some Hungarian examples include Marc Rakowski, *Towards an East European Marxism*, London 1978; György Konrád and Ivan Szelényi, *The Intellectuals on the Road to Class Power*, Brighton 1979; and Ferenc Fehér, Agnes Heller and György Markus, *Dictatorship over Needs*, Oxford 1983. Despite their very different arguments, these works seek to describe and analyse the *different* existing socialist regimes of East-Central Europe as a unified 'social formation', consisting of identical forms of production and class structure. For further discussion see *Les Temps Modernes*, 468-9, July–August 1985, pp. 88-102.

2. My source for this view of the three historical regions of Europe is the magisterial essay of Jenö Szücs, in this volume. Szücs's work has been influenced by the writings of István Bibó, whose political essays concentrated on understanding and explaining the dead ends and distortions of East-Central European development. My own thinking is also indebted to Bibó's work, in particular to his *Misery of the East European Small States, The Distorted Hungarian Character: the Blind Alleys of Hungarian History and Social Evolution*, and *The Meaning of the Changes in 1945*. My ideas on the indivisibility of social structure and individual attitudes are based largely on Norbert Elias, *Über den Prozess der Zivilisation*, Basel 1939.

Solidarity and 'The Rebirth of Civil Society' in Poland, 1976–81

Z.A. Pelczynski

The term 'civil society' began to be used in the West, and occasionally in Poland, during the late 1970s with reference to a form of political dissent best exemplified by the Committee for the Defence of Workers (KOR), founded in 1976 and renamed in 1978 the Committee For Social defence (KSS-KOR). Writing not long before the emergence of Solidarity, Jacques Rupnik, an émigré Czech intellectual then living in England, characterized the situation in Poland between 1968 and 1978 as 'the end of revisionism and the rebirth of civil society'.[1]

Revisionism, it will be remembered, emerged in a number of East European Communist states about 1956 as a reaction against Stalinism and the limited official measures of de-Staliniz-ation taken in the Soviet bloc. Its aim was to redefine, in theory and practice, the role of the Communist Party *vis-à-vis* culture, society, economy and the state. Instead of its leaders continuing to impose a dogmatic conception of socialism in those spheres, the Party was to reassess Marxian theories in the light of changed conditions. It had to arrive at correct socialist policies through a free, internal-democratic debate, and execute those policies through the *aktiv* rather than the professional party *apparat*.[2] The extinguishing of the remnants of Polish revisionism by the party leadership after the so-called 'March events', and the suppression of the Czechoslovak reform movement by the armed intervention of other Communist states – both of which took place in 1968 – seemed to rule out for good the revisionist scenario for the trans-formation of East European Communism.

While nothing intellectually significant replaced revisionism in the rest of the Soviet bloc (Rupnik argued), the Polish 'democratic opposition' of the late 1970s initiated a completely new strategy for changing the Communist system. In an ever-growing volume of *samizdat* publications, the spokesmen of the democratic opposition argued that society under Communism was not as defenceless and powerless as had been believed, and could act to change the system outside the channels of the Party and the organizations and mass media controlled by it. Generalizing from past examples of intellectual, student and working-class protest, which sometimes produced significant results, from the existence of a free and critical Catholic Church, and from the experience of their own oppositional activity after 1976, KOR and other groups urged the political activation of the intelligentsia and ultimately the whole population. The opposition sharply criticized the official policies which had obviously failed, as well as the general corruption, inefficiency, inegalitarianism, arbitrariness and other patent evils of the system. It urged everybody to do the same, taking immediate advantage of opportunities presented by the so-called 'democratic centralism': that is, official channels of pseudo-popular participation.

In the medium term 'the new evolutionism' (as the strategy was labelled by one of its chief theoreticians, Adam Michnik[3]) postulated the creation of all kinds of independent, self-governing associations and publications alongside the party-controlled institutional framework, through which social pressure could be even more powerfully exercised. In the unspecified long term, the opposition envisaged the official framework itself being modified, under mass pressure, in the direction of genuine autonomy and popular participation. Because the evolution would be gradual and slow and would not totally challenge the position of either nationalist Communist leaders and officials or their Soviet masters, it had a reasonable chance of success.[4]

The 'evolutionist' strategy seemed to rest on two main premises: that Polish society could muster enough courage, determination and faith in itself to keep up pressure long enough to realize those aims, and that the Polish and Soviet party leaders would shrink from the massive resort to terror that would be necessary to stifle large-scale popular pressure. What lent plausibility to the second assumption was perhaps a new sensitivity of the Soviet bloc to western public opinion; indeed, a new relationship between the West and the East that seemed to be emerging in the 1970s. It was expressed in such terms as 'détente' and 'the Helsinki spirit' and was accompanied by substantial borrowing of Western money for the modernization of East European economies.

Although Rupnik and other Western commentators took the emergence of the dissident movement in Poland seriously, as an exciting and significant development within Communism, there was, until August 1980, an air of utopianism and wishful thinking about 'the rebirth of civil society'. The strikes of that month and the signing of the agreements between workers and the government representatives in Gdańsk, Szczecin and elsewhere, which allowed the formation of independent, self-governing trade unions, suddenly turned the dream into reality, or at least the beginning of reality.

The suddenness must be strongly emphasized. The tiny groups of workers and their intelligentsia backers, who in the 1970s had set up committees to spread the idea of free unions, expected years to pass before it became practicable. But for reasons that are still obscure, the discredited Polish party leadership – one must assume with the temporary connivance of the CPSU leaders – gave in to the unprecedented demands of the summer 1980 strikers instead of stifling them by military force, as had happened in the case of the much more moderate demands made by the Baltic Coast strikers in December 1970. Thus, almost miraculously, Solidarity was born and for some fifteen months its existence, development and activities horrified the Communist world and amazed, thrilled and cheered the West.

The changes which the establishment of Solidarity brought about in the Communist power system and in Polish society gave the phrase 'rebirth of civil society' a new and far deeper meaning. A sizeable body of literature interprets the events of 1980–81 in the light of the concept of 'civil society'.[5] The subsumption of the history of Polish dissent, and Solidarity in particular, under the category of civil society is a truly remarkable intellectual development. Few social and political concepts have travelled so far in their life and changed their meaning so much. Originally the term was simply a synonym for the state: Saint Thomas Aquinas spoke of *communitas civilis sive politica*, while John Locke referred to 'civil or political society'. With Hume and the writers of the so-called Scottish Enlightenment, 'civil society', while still synonymous with the state, acquired the connotation of 'civilized society' and was applied to countries at the level of commercial and industrial development which Britain and France had reached in the late eighteenth century.

With Hegel there occurs a theoretical rupture: the terms 'state' and 'civil society' become separated.[6] The 'state' now means the political community in its entirety, pursuing universal or national goals through a central government or supreme public authority. 'Civil society' is an aspect of the modern state, which Hegel further subdivides into the 'system of needs', concerned with the promotion of particular (individual and sectional) goals (the economic sphere of production, exchange and other market relations), the social sphere of classes and autonomous organizations which he calls 'corporations', and the 'civil' sphere of public institutions such as the courts and various regulatory and welfare agencies. Civil society in this sense is an arena in which modern man legitimately gratifies his self-interest and develops his individuality, but also learns the value of group action, social solidarity and the dependence of his welfare on others, which educate him for citizenship and prepare him for participation in the political arena of the state.[7]

Critical though Marx was of the Hegelian conception of the state, he nevertheless appropriated the civil society component of it, reduced it to the economic dimension and made it the foundation of his whole theory of history, society and the state. In the famous passage in 'Preface to *A Contribution to the Critique of Political Economy*', Marx states:

> My investigation led me to the result that the legal relations as well as forms of the state are to be grasped neither from themselves nor from the so-called general development of the human mind, the sum total of which Hegel ... combines under the name 'civil society', that, however, the anatomy of civil society is to be sought in political economy.[8]

In his *Ludwig Feuerbach* Engels put the point concisely as follows: 'the state – the political order – is the subordinate, and civil society – the realm of economic relations – the decisive element.'[9]

With insignificant exceptions, Hegel's followers in mid-nineteenth-century Germany, late-nineteenth- and early-twentieth century Britain and early-twentieth-century Italy – the major centres of Hegelianism – made hardly any use of the civil society concept.[10] Nor did the Marxian version of it play any role in the Marxist movement after the death of Marx and Engels, except of course as an axiom of economic determinism. It was Antonio Gramsci who, in his *Prison Notes*,[11] returned to and revitalized the concept of civil society. Gramsci retained the Marxian idea of the state as a predominantly coercive apparatus, controlled in bourgeois society by the same class which owned the means of production and dominated economic life. But he insisted that in modern, advanced Western countries civil society was not just the economic sphere, nor a mere adjunct to the state. It was a sphere of various autonomous organizations and activities, which by no means merely perpetuated the ideology and class interest of the bourgeoisie. While in the economic and state spheres the modern bourgeoisie exercised more or less full 'domination', in the civil sphere it did not always have a monopoly of political, moral and intellectual influence, or what he called 'hegemony'.

Civil society was therefore, so to speak, the 'soft underbelly' of the capitalist system. It offered other groups and classes – above all the industrial workers ('the fundamental class') and their intellectual spokesmen – a chance to undermine the bourgeoisie's position in the realm of ideas, values, culture, education and voluntary organizations, and thus prepare the way, gradually and over a long period, for a political, revolutionary struggle against the capitalist state and property relations. This political 'war of position' (as Gramsci called it) was a more suitable strategy for a successful seizure of power by the workers of Western Europe than the 'war of movement' or sudden frontal attack on the state apparatus that the Bolsheviks had recently carried out in backward and war-ravaged Russia.

Gramsci's reformulation of the state–civil society relation, which is obviously a synthesis of Marxian and Hegelian elements, did not of course provide a viable action programme in Italy or anywhere else in the West. Although it is widely discussed in the contemporary Western Marxist circles it has proved, from the standpoint of revolutionary praxis, a dead end. Amazingly, however, developments in Eastern Europe, especially Poland, have given the Gramscian approach – albeit in a radically modified form – a new lease of life. It is this so-to-speak revisionist, upside-down, neo-Gramscian version of Gramsci which has been found theoretically fruitful, both by the radical left intellectuals in the West and by the theorists of the 'democratic opposition' or 'new evolutionism' in the East, in order to conceptualize historical developments and to map out a programme of what is sometimes called the 'de-totalization' of socialism. An analytical framework for considering developments in advanced, Western bourgeois society has been transformed into a framework for analysing the situation in the contemporary socialist countries of East Europe.

In the 'classical' Leninist model of post-revolutionary socialism, the state–civil society distinction is obviously meaningless. The state absorbs virtually the whole sphere of the economy; the political superstructure and the economic base merge into one. The realm of social organizations distinct from the state exists on paper, in constitutional theory or party ideology, but in fact is wholly controlled by the Communist Party and integrated into the rest of the base-structure complex. The Party, through its iron grip over the state and the economy, exercises Gramsci's 'domination'; through the implementation of '*partiinost*' in science, literature and the arts, the watertight control over the mass media, and the official universal commitment to Marxism-Leninism, it also exercises Gramsci's 'hegemony' in the realm of culture and ideology.

During Stalinism the unity and cohesion of the whole became cemented even more by the power of the security police and its massive, regular use of terror. This socialist 'bloc' – to adopt another of Gramsci's favourite terms – is so tightly interdependent and monolithic that it is qualitatively different from the bourgeois 'bloc' which Gramsci analysed in the context of inter-war Italy. There is simply no leverage in the Leninist system for any ideological dissent or political opposition, let alone room for a sustained 'war of position' of independent social forces which could lead to an eventual capture of the system. The Western literature of totalitarianism, especially in its heyday in the 1950s, clearly accepted some such view of Soviet-type Communism.

The Leninist-Stalinist model of socialism obviously lost a good deal of its plausibility after Stalin's death, especially in the non-Russian part of the Soviet bloc, and it is worth asking why. The emergence of revisionism was a sign that a number of factors – national hostility to Soviet domination, Western cultural influences, social democratic traditions, the historical role of the intelligentsia, and so on – had survived the relatively short period of Stalinism. It could significantly influence political reality even if, by 1968, revisionism itself was successfully stifled by the Soviet Union.

In Poland there were additional factors, which reinforced the others. Small-scale peasant landownership largely survived Stalinism. The Roman Catholic Church fully recovered its internal autonomy after 1956 – it acted as an independent body in social, cultural and religious matters and, on select issues, even as a political opposition. After 1970 the Polish workers established the practice of strikes over attempted cuts in their standard of living. The Polish Communist Party began losing its hold over the population during the 1960s because of the stagnant living standards, the decline of social mobility (very marked during Stalinism), the growth of inequality and privileges, and the corruption of the power elite. The widespread belief that socialism equalized social positions and opportunities for advance, perhaps the one part of the Party's ideology which the population accepted wholeheartedly, turned in the end against the institutional system of 'real socialism'.

A sort of non-Marxist socialist ideology or popular political culture, composed of both new and traditional elements, became dominant in Poland in the 1970s. There was a strong conviction that more freedom, participation and toleration had to be built into the system as it existed there. It was strikingly revealed by the first two reports of the 'Experience and Future' (DiP) discussion group published in Warsaw at the end of the 1970s.[12] That it was not merely an intelligentsia attitude but was widespread in all sections of Polish society, especially the young generation who grew up in the post-Stalinist period, has been amply shown by attitude surveys conducted by Professor Stefan Nowak and his associates at Warsaw University[13] and by several other sociologists. (Some of the surveys were in fact commissioned by the Communist Party and made public only during the Solidarity period.) The programmes and activities of the 'democratic opposition' of the late 1970s lose some of their apparent utopianism when they are considered against the background of a changing social consciousness and the evident disappointment with Communism.

One might say that in Poland on the threshold of the 1980s the Communist Party's political and economic 'domination' was still intact, but its 'hegemony' was already seriously undermined. There is, as far as I can see, no clear Gramscian explanation for that remarkable Polish phenomenon – the rise of a genuine public opinion, the independent discussion of alternatives to official policies and structures and the crystallization of values perceived to be in sharp conflict with the existing political reality without a fully fledged, institutional civil society to support it.

In fact the Polish phenomenon seems to highlight a weakness in the Gramscian schema, admitted by some of his intellectual admirers on the radical left: the ambiguity of the relation of structural to superstructural factors. Gramsci's civil society contains two indistinctly separated elements: a realm of independent social organizations and non-governmental institutions, corresponding to the Hegelian concept of 'corporation' (civil society in a narrow sense) and a realm of what one might call, following Tocqueville, 'political society',[14] existing outside and in opposition to the state and made possible by the existence of a degree of social autonomy. While 'civil society' in the narrow sense is concerned with egoistic, particular, mainly material interests, 'political society' reflects the critical concern over all kinds of general issues kept off the public agenda of the class-dominated state system. It is here that ideas and values inimical to the system of state and economy domination incubate and develop, and eventually lead to the creation of a new 'historic bloc' [*blocco storico*] which challenges the old 'bloc'.

From the neo-Gramscian perspective, what was puzzling about Poland in the late 1970s was that with the significant exception of the Catholic Church, an independent and powerful body for the past twenty-five years, 'political society' emerged without any corporate, institutional underpinning. The score of intellectual groups organizing petitions, publishing *samizdat* leaflets, periodicals and books, holding academic seminars and occasional discussions with the workers, and producing reports on 'the state of the republic' – critical analyses of the socio-economic crisis of the country – owed their existence to the laxity of party control, the relative toleration of the security police apparatus and a degree of judicial independence, not to an infrastructure of genuinely autonomous social organizations. They were beneficiaries of loopholes in the state structure.[15] Hence the application of the civil society concept to Poland before the rise of Solidarity – any meaningful talk of 'the rebirth of civil society' – is in my view highly misleading; indeed, a piece of mystification and wishful thinking.

The reality implied by the term civil society, in its classical Hegelian but also recognizably Gramscian sense – the realm of independent social organization, activity and pressure on the state – never existed in Poland in the 1970s. The theorists of the 'democratic opposition' in Poland rather implied that it had to be created somehow, sometime, by mobilizing a new consciousness throughout Polish society and by taking advantage of the strange weakness of the apparatus of Communist political and economic domination and the relative 'evaporation' of Marxist-Leninist ideology from intellectual life. Given the lack of independent institutional base, it would be more correct to say that the spread of 'democratic opposition' or dissident movement in Poland at the end of the 1970s represented a rebirth of *political society*, an independent realm of public activity outside the structure of the Communist state. That fledgling political society was groping for ways to institutionalize itself and to become a civil society capable of confronting the Communist Party-state from a position of reasonable strength and pressurizing it in the direction of substantial reforms.[16]

With the sudden and wholly unforeseen rise of the Solidarity trade union in September 1980, and its amazing popularity and rapid growth, the Gramscian framework of analysis began to make better sense. There was now a powerful, organized and entrenched workers' movement which was independent and self-governing; its aims and activities reflected the wishes and interests of its members, not those of the party leaders. But although Solidarity was in name a trade union it was in fact, from the start, a political movement. It perceived itself as a movement for the repair or rescue of the republic from the doldrums of Communist policies and institutions and their malfunctioning for the last thirty years, but especially for the previous decade or so. One of the workers' representatives negotiating in Gdańsk with the government commission expressed the idea very clearly:

> It is essential that there should be control over the authorities' decisions in the social and economic spheres. Reforms of management and planning are imperative. ... We want to create these free, independent trade unions in order to rescue our nation. This is our fundamental duty. We are all Poles.[17]

During the negotiations, speakers on the strikers' side pointed to a host of areas which needed urgent attention and remedy. The protocol of the negotiations, incorporating the twenty-one demands of the Gdańsk Interfactory Strike Committee, reflected not just the sectional concerns of the workers but demands of the Polish society as a whole. The broadcasting of Mass on state radio, the relaxation of control over censorship, the release of political prisoners and the toleration of dissent are examples of the wide-ranging, essentially public interests of the creators of the Solidarity movement. Far from losing these public aims, Solidarity developed them increasingly as time went on. The preamble to its programme, adopted at the National Congress in October 1981, made the public or political character of Solidarity abundantly clear:

> Our union sprang from the people's needs: from their suffering and
> disappointment, their hopes and desires. It is the product of the revolt
> of Polish society against political discrimination, economic exploit-
> ation, and the violation of human and civil rights. It is a protest
> against the existing form of power. ... Our organization combines the
> features of a trade union and a broad social movement: it is this which
> gives us our strength and determines the importance of our role.
> Thanks to the existence of a powerful union organization, Polish
> society is no longer fragmented, disorganized and lost, but has
> recovered strength and hope. There is now the possibility of a real
> national renewal. Our union, representing the majority of workers in
> Poland, seeks to be and will become the driving force of this renewal.[18]

The shock of Solidarity forced the Polish Communist Party to
seek ways of winning back the support of the working class and a
measure of acceptability from society as a whole. Battling against
various internal and external obstacles, it pursued a renewal
policy of its own: 'socialist renewal', as it was called. The government passed several important reform measures, while the Ninth
Party Congress of July 1981 adopted a comprehensive
programme of social, political and economic reform. But the
radicalism of Solidarity's demands made the Party appear a
conservative force, defending the status quo – the entrenched
system of government and economic domination – rather than
meeting genuine popular demands for change.

It is possible to exaggerate the extent of polarization which the
emergence of Solidarity caused within Polish society. There were
important groups, organizations and institutions that tried to
mediate and to help the two antagonists to reach at least temporary agreement. The Catholic Church was essentially such a 'third
force', not an unquestioning supporter of Solidarity. It is nevertheless true that around Solidarity there crystallized a new
'historic bloc' of anti-state and anti-Party elements in Polish
society, elements which now had an organizational base and
therefore constituted civil society in a strong sense. Although
these civil organizations were new and somewhat ramshackle,
they had a broad base in Polish society: most of the industrial
workers, most of the private farmers, most of the humanistic
intelligentsia and most of the students belonged to or supported
Solidarity or one of its allied organizations: support among white-
collar employees and the technical intelligentsia was less widespread, but not insignificant.

It is not surprising that Solidarity perceived itself as a *national*
movement and dismissed the Party-state 'bloc' (not quite

correctly) as merely a representative of the privileged bureaucracy. Although the use of the army to smash Solidarity in December 1981 had an obvious practical utility, it had the additional advantage of weakening Solidarity's claim to exclusive national legitimacy. The army had been traditionally perceived in Poland (and highly respected) as a national institution, not just as a coercive arm of the ruling bureaucratic elite, which the police clearly seemed to be. It would not be stretching Gramsci's terms too much to say that during 1981 Solidarity's ideas achieved 'hegemony' over Polish society, but the state's 'domination' over the economy – and, even more, the police and the army – remained intact.

The opposition between the Communist Party 'bloc' and the Solidarity 'bloc', captured in Arato's phrase 'the state versus civil society', evolved into a struggle for power of the kind Gramsci postulated. But it will be remembered that he ruled out the possibility of a quick assault on the state-economy domination system by the radical-social forces developing within civil society. Instead he visualized a slow 'war of position' in which struggle would shift from one sector of the front to another, involved capturing and temporarily losing key positions, but in the long run tilt the balance of power from the state to civil society. We may pursue the neo-Gramscian analysis of the Polish situation along this new line with interesting, if rather unexpected results.

The original Gramscian interpretative schema has two major aspects, and they should be distinguished. First, it is a way of conceptually analysing existing and emerging empirical relations between social and political forces and their organizational (structural) and ideological (superstructural) manifestations. Secondly it is a 'pragmatic' analysis, seeking to formulate a political strategy or action programme for the 'progressive' forces in civil society, the 'new historical bloc'. Norberto Bobbio calls the two aspects respectively the 'historiographical and practico-political use of the concept of civil society'.[19] Rather than examine the impact of the Solidarity movement on the Communist Party-state 'historiographically', let us consider some aspects of the 'practico-political' or pragmatic aspect. In the context of global state–society conflict, what kind of strategy guided Solidarity's actions? How far did it have a clear strategy at all? In what ways, if any, did the strategy change and for what reasons?

But a preliminary objection may be raised. Solidarity was not just a pragmatic, sociopolitical movement, organized to achieve specific goals or even the large goal of transforming the institutional environment in which it lived and worked. It had also the aspect of a moral crusade. Its members and leaders sometimes thought primarily in moral or religious categories of the struggle of good against evil. Philosophical theories of 'immanent evil' in Communism had long been widespread among Polish intellectuals, while the masses inclined to consider Communism evil in so far as it violated the national, pluralistic and Catholic traditions of the country. Calculated political action, with its weighing of advantages and disadvantages, the rational choice of means appropriate to a chosen end and the necessity to compromise with reality, do not square well with such a view of Solidarity. The insistence on fundamental principles, an 'all or nothing' attitude, are inherent in 'moralism'; moral victories are compatible with political defeats – indeed, sometimes presuppose such defeats. It is undeniable that such ideas circulated within the heyday of Solidarity and are still widespread in Poland today, serving perhaps as a kind of psychological compensation for the disaster of martial law and the official dissolution of Solidarity.

The other objection to the pragmatic way of looking at Solidarity's activities comes from what one might call a 'fatalistic' outlook, also widespread in Poland today among the former activists and supporters of Solidarity. According to this view it was impossible for Solidarity to pursue a rational strategy during 1980–81 because it was an incoherent, elemental mass movement, a kind of social avalanche or political landslide which could not be meaningfully controlled and guided. Perhaps over time it would have become a unified and disciplined movement prepared to submit to the authority of its leaders, willing to wait and make sacrifices for the sake of eventual victory, pursuing an evolutionist, gradualist course. But during the fifteen months of its existence Solidarity had not managed to acquire that character; indeed, towards the end of 1981 it was becoming more rather than less elemental. It was propelled more than ever before by the bitter popular mood of exasperation with the disastrous economic conditions and the frustration of the activists at the inflexibility of the entrenched party–state institutions. During the final stages of the struggle with the government, Walesa was clearly being carried on a wave of radicalism towards a confrontation with the Party-state which he feared but was powerless to prevent. Like 'moralism', 'fatalism' existed and played an important role in Polish events. But neither of them decisively determined the overall situation; questions about strategy are thus perfectly legitimate.

We may recall that the dominant theoretical conception current within the 'democratic opposition' before Gdańsk was called 'new evolutionism'. It applied a long-term strategy of (1) transforming the existing and creating new, independent social organizations capable of defending vital interests and resisting the domination of the Party-state; and (2) extending the arena in which public opinion could criticize existing policies, formulate alternatives and consider various systemic issues which the Party-state had for too long excluded from the official political agenda. The strikers' victory in Gdańsk achieved substantially both goals, but few leaders and advisers of Solidarity (largely prominent members of the 'democratic opposition') believed that the movement's most important task was to entrench itself within the existing system and to enjoy the enormous gains of the August 1980 agreements. It was principally the Church hierarchy, dominated by the personality of the aged and ailing Cardinal Wyszyński (who was to die of cancer in May 1981), which believed in consolidation.

Wyszyński wanted Solidarity to pause and take stock of the situation, to streamline its organization, to train a large cadre of activists and officials, to focus its attention on various social and economic grievances of the population, and to help other social groups – especially the peasant farmers, with whom the Catholic Church had always had a particularly close relationship – to set up independent unions to protect their interests. In other words, Wyszyński favoured concentration on civil society issues and treading gently in the realm of political society. His favourite motto was 'not everything at once'. He publicly chided Solidarity for having the typical characteristics of a juvenile – rashness, impatience, overoptimism, excessive zeal, and so on.[20] In several private meetings with Wałesa and his Catholic advisers, through his own permanent representative at the Solidarity headquarters in Gdańsk and during various public audiences for Solidarity delegations he preached the same message: be or behave as if you were just an independent trade-union movement and, having mastered that difficult task, extend your activities gradually to broader, more political issues. When the triumphant National Delegation of Solidarity, after scoring a great political victory over registration, called on him in November 1980 to receive his blessing, Wyszyński typically gave them this advice:

First of all you must organise yourselves well. ... In order to be well organized you must put yourselves through a training course. ... It

> seems to me that the basic, preliminary task of every Solidarity collective must be the education of union members in the knowledge of the Labour Code and Labour legislation. ... One of the most important areas to which attention must be paid are conditions of labour. They leave much to be desired. ... Although you might have various temptations of a political nature, remember that your first aim is the realization of professional and social tasks: the defence of the working environment, conditions of hygiene and work safety, the observance of the Labour Code, social legislation – these are your most important tasks.[21]

Some of Solidarity's advisers did follow Cardinal Wyszyński's ideas and also advocated the depoliticization of the union's activity, but on the whole the leaders and militants of the new union were not prepared to listen to such advice, or were unable to put it into practice in the tense political atmosphere of 1981. And the regularity with which the Communist Party backed down during confrontations with Solidarity in the first year of its existence suggested that the movement would be able to carve out a more substantial sphere of activity than the one the Church was recommending.

The Catholic Church, which had traditionally acted as a guardian of the country's fate during the chequered and unhappy history of the Polish nation, thus sought to introduce an element of stability to the situation in the early 1980s; this was in line with Gramsci's conception of 'positional war', although the role of the Church is hard to fit into the neo-Gramscian framework of analysis. It is bizarre to suggest, as it sometimes has been suggested, that the Church's own conservative past and authoritarian hierarchy somehow inclined it to collaborate with the equally conservative and authoritarian Party-state 'bloc'. The Church had shown that it could defend its institutional interests quite well against Communism. As an institution it had nothing to fear from the weakening of the Communist state; it would have flourished even more in a Solidarity-dominated Poland than it had done under Communism. But the victory of Solidarity, or even the appearance of victory, spelt for Wyszyński a Soviet armed intervention and a national tragedy, as well as a setback for the Church.

After the legalization of the union in November 1980 the activities of its leaders and militants focused increasingly on the political tasks which Wyszyński had advised them to ignore: branding the privileges of party bosses, curbing police arbitrariness, relaxing censorship, getting access to mass media, bringing the union's views on every subject to the attention of the country. In other words, their dominating concern was the extension of political society, rather than the consolidation of civil society. Until the Party Congress in July 1982, Solidarity's attitude was still relatively restrained. The union was not sure how far the Party was willing to go in reforming itself and the established political system, and although Solidarity rejected any idea of an alliance with the reformists in the Party it was prepared to wait and see how much they could achieve. However, as formulated and enshrined in the Party's new programme, the conceptions of 'socialist renewal' and 'socialist democracy' fell far short of the minimum which Solidarity was prepared to regard as a basis for negotiation. It seemed that the old hegemonic apparatus of power was not prepared to yield to the nation's wishes expressed through the alternative political society established by Solidarity and its allies.

Having found itself stymied by the Party-state 'block', the Solidarity movement eventually adopted the idea of a 'self-governing republic', enshrined in the programme of the Solidarity Congress in October 1981. The idea was an extension of the objectives of the self-management movement, which emerged within Solidarity in June 1981. It advocated transferring the control of factories from the state and the Party (which dominated them through the *nomenklatura* system) to democratically elected workers' councils, which would have been dominated by the members or sympathizers of Solidarity. According to Solidarity's programme, 'social' ownership and control was to be applied to other parts of the state mechanism. Self-management was to be introduced into education, culture and mass media. The residual legal and financial powers of the state in those fields were to be controlled by democratically elected 'national' or 'social' councils. There was also going to be such a national council in the sphere of economy, to debate and approve government proposals and to scrutinize the evidence on which they were based.

The theory of the 'self-governing republic' was a highly original contribution to the Gramscian strategy of 'positional war' in the realm of theory, however hopelessly utopian it was in practice. Gramsci did not visualize a gradual, piecemeal takeover of the state by the social and political forces entrenched in civil society. He was enough of a Marxist to believe that a ruling class never surrendered power voluntarily. A revolution was inevitable to overthrow the system of domination and give power to the working class and its allies. But a revolution would be quick and painless because the structure of the bourgeois state and property relations had been undermined by the advances of the working class within civil society. What Solidarity was proposing was a negotiated takeover of several parts of the old hegemonic state structure by civil society, leaving the Communist state in those areas largely a façade beyond which the newly emancipated, democratically organized social forces would in fact exercise predominant influence. The rest of the old state structure – the army, the police and the courts – were for the time being not to be included in the schema, nor were ministries dealing with foreign policy, and so on. This was certainly an exciting theoretical possibility, but what chance did it have of being realized?

Solidarity's theoreticians and the congress delegates seemed to have imagined that their scheme of social self-management, although drastically restricting the power of the Party-state, would preserve enough of the 'leading role of the Party' to appease the Kremlin and enable the Polish ruling elite to relinquish most of its traditional power without losing face. They saw it as a kind of 'historical compromise' which recognized Poland's geopolitical realities and the security interests of the Soviet Union, but also accepted the fact which was evident to them: that Poland could no longer be governed in the old way. Confident that the country was behind it, Solidarity left the Party the choice of either surrendering much of its power peacefully or provoking a civil war and risking a Soviet intervention. If negotiations did not achieve peaceful surrender Solidarity proposed to organize a referendum on its constitutional proposals, followed by organizing free parliamentary elections with new parties opposing the Communist Party. Should one or both initiatives be obstructed by the government, Solidarity threatened to use the weapon of the general strike.

The commitment to a negotiated solution within the framework of the existing state constitution, and only in the last resort appealing to the population directly, showed how non-revolutionary the Solidarity movement basically was. This is confirmed by the fact that no measures whatever were taken to prepare for a violent seizure of power. The idea of a general strike had an air of Sorelian myth about it; it was a moral threat to paralyse the ruling elite, rather than a practical political tactic. Neither did Solidarity have a practical contingency plan in case of a state of emergency or any kind of violence against itself. This commitment to non-volence was probably a 'liberal bourgeois' fetish with which Gramsci would have had little sympathy. As for the idea of a self-governing republic, it was – needless to say – flatly rejected by the Polish Politburo as wholly incompatible with the Party's own programme of 'socialist renewal'. The threats of a referendum or a general strike, still no more than theoretical possibilities in early December 1981, were met with the pre-emptive military strike and General Jaruzelski's introduction of martial law.

The creation of the Solidarity trade-union movement gave a boost to the historically unique process of developing a genuine civil society within the framework of an economy dominated by the state, which was in turn dominated by the Communist Party. Had economic conditions been different, more akin to the prosperous early 1970s than the hungry early 1980s, civil society and the state might have found a reasonable *modus vivendi*. The institutions of self-management and autonomous social organiz-ations would not necessarily have become bases for radical politi-cal demands. Individual and group energies could have been channelled into further essentially private and material interests, and political society need not have developed into a challenge to the rule of the Communist Party.

The bad and worsening conditions of the economic crisis caused by the failures of a growth policy based on massive foreign loans, with the added social evils of corruption and inequality, politicized the situation in 1980–81 to such a degree that concen-tration on what one may call civil society issues became extremely difficult. Nevertheless, one may speculate what would have happened if Cardinal Wyszyński's gradualist strategy had prevailed within Solidarity, and the movement had managed – by a feat of heroic self-limitation – to restrict itself to a largely trade-union role and to press for social and economic reforms. With the Catholic Church as a partner – and allied to a host of other autonomous and semi-autonomous corporate bodies which emerged after September 1980 – Solidarity could have defended the gains of civil society for many years beyond 1981. No doubt there would have been a 'retreat from August' (1980) in due course, but the course would have been a very long one, far longer than 'the retreat from October' (1956).

The tremendous weakness of the Communist Party, one-third of whose members joined Solidarity with perhaps another third remaining completely passive, precluded any quick political offen-sive. The need to compensate society with political reforms for the inevitable drastic economic austerity – and the necessity to placate the West, if new credits were to be obtained and the repayment of old debts postponed – would have acted as powerful brakes on a return to full-scale Leninism. Meanwhile, the Communist leaders and state and party officials could have learned how to play the new political game and might well have found rules to regulate the relations between the state and civil society. Inevitably the existing boundaries of the official, party-controlled political society would have been greatly extended, reflecting the much freer public opinion and the need to consult with the new independent bodies. The Polish Parliament, already remarkably energetic and assertive in 1981, could have developed still further along those lines, especially under a liberalized electoral system. It could have become an increasingly genuine intermediary between the Communist-controlled state and the partly autonomous society.

Arguably, the political instincts of the Catholic hierarchy, grounded in the Church's long and valuable experience of dealing with the Communist state between 1956 and 1980, would have been a better guide to practice than the short experience of dissident activity and industrial strikes, and the miracle of Gdańsk. As for theory, there was nothing wrong with the conception of the 'new evolutionism' of Adam Michnik and his fellow KOR members, except that both those who had propounded it and those whom they sought to influence after Ausgust 1980 became 'dizzy with success' and *de facto* abandoned the gradualist path they had advocated so persuasively in the late 1970s.

Notes

1. Jacques Rupnik, 'Dissent in Poland, 1968-78: the End of Revisionism and the Rebirth of Civil Society in Poland', in Rudolf Tőkés, ed., *Opposition in Eastern Europe*, London 1979.

2. See, for example, Leszek Kolakowski's article 'Intellectuals and the Communist Movement', in his collected essays *Marxism and Beyond*, London 1968, a statement of the revisionist case by one of its former leading champions.

3. Adam Michnik, 'The New Evolutionism', first published in Paris in October 1976. English translation in A. Michnik, *Letters from Prison and other Essays*, Berkeley, CA 1985.

4. See the programme of the KSS-KOR published in Warsaw in October 1977 and in an English translation as 'Declaration of the "Democratic Movement"', in Peter Raina, *Political Opposition in Poland 1954-1977*, London 1978.

5. Perhaps the best examples are two articles by Andrew Arato, 'Civil Society against the state: Poland 1980-81', and 'Empire versus Civil Society: Poland 1981-82', published respectively in *Telos*, nos 47, 1981 and 50, 1982. See also the article

on civil society by Maria Markus in Robert Miller, ed., *Poland in the Eighties*, Canberra 1985.

6. See Manfred Riedel, '"State" and "Civil Society": Linguistic Context and Historical Origin', originally published in Germany in 1962. English translation in M. Riedel, *Between Tradition and Revolution: The Hegelian Transformation of Political Philosophy*, Cambridge 1984.

7. See my editorial introduction to the collection of essays published under the title of *The State and Civil Society: Studies in Hegel's Political Philosophy*, Cambridge 1984.

8. Karl Marx, 'Preface to *A Contribution to the Critique of Political Economy*', in K. Marx and F. Engels, *Selected Works*, Moscow 1969, vol. 1, p. 503.

9. Frederick Engels, 'Ludwig Feuerbach and the End of Classical German Philosophy', in *Selected Works*, Moscow 1970, vol. 3, p. 396.

10. One significant exception was Lorenz von Stein, whose work *The History of the Social Movements in France 1779-1850* (published in German in 1850; abridged English text trans. and ed. K. Mengelberg, Tototwa, NJ 1964) makes frequent use of the concept.

11. Gramsci's ideas on civil society can be found conveniently in *Selections from the Prison Notes*, ed. and trans. Q. Hoare and G. Nowell Smith, London 1971. They are illuminatingly discussed by Norberto Bobbio in 'Gramsci and the Concept of Civil Soviety', in this volume.

12. Published in the West as *Poland: The State of the Republic*, London 1981.

13. See Stefan Nowak's analysis of the main results in 'Values and Attitudes of the Polish People', *Scientific American*, July 1977.

14. Outside the Hegelian and Marxian tradition the only thinker who made a significant (though not explicitly systematic) contribution to the relevant conceptual analysis was Alexis de Tocqueville. Throughout *Democracy in America* Tocqueville uses a *triad* of concepts: the state, political society and civil society. 'State' in his terminology is the centralized, bureaucratic apparatus which nineteenth-century France inherited from absolute monarchy (Marx makes the same point in, for example, *The Eighteenth Brumaire of Louis Napoleon*). 'Political society' is the realm of citizens' involvement in politics or public affairs – the realm of local self-government, parties, newspapers, public opinion, etc., undeveloped in continental Europe but flourishing in the United States; neither Hegel nor Marx clearly recognizes it as a distinct aspect of social life. 'Civil society' (for Tocqueville as for the other two) is the realm of the citizens' private, mostly economic activities based on self-interest. While he believed that contemporary Americans had achieved a unique balance between civil and political society, in France there was a danger of the state and civil society growing closely together and stifling the public-spirited activities ('the republican virtues') required by the nascent political democracy in Europe. I am grateful to Jeffrey Weintraub, who helped me to see the Tocquevillean 'tripartite model' clearly when we discussed these matters at Harvard in 1982-83.

15. Interestingly, the first 'DiP' report was produced by an officially sanctioned group involving party and non-party intellectuals. Only when the party authorities refused to publish it was it circulated privately and eventually led to other, wholly unofficial inquiries and publications. On the evolution of the 'democratic opposition' out of small intellectual groups and campaigns until it culminated in KOR, see J.J. Lipski, *KOR: A History of the Workers' Defense Committee in Poland, 1976-1981*, Berkeley, CA 1984. Lipski records how astonished he and other organizers of the so-called 'constitutional petition' were when the party authorities not only did not repress it but actually made significant concessions to the

demands of public opinion in the text of the new constitution of 1976.

16. The evolution of the strategy of using the opportunities of existing institutions of 'democratic centralism' and supplementing them with new, wholly independent organizations such as 'initiative committees of free trade unions' can be traced through the publications of KOR and its successor, the Social Self-Defence Committee (KSS), especially the *samizdat*, *Robotnik* [*The Worker*]. See the documents printed in Peter Raina, *Independent Social Movements in Poland*, London 1981.

17. For a full account of the Gdańsk negotiations and the issues raised, see A. Kemp-Welch, trans. and ed., *The Birth of Solidarity: The Gdańsk Negotiations, 1980*, London 1983.

18. This text is included in Peter Raina, *Poland 1981: Towards Social Renewal*, London 1985, pp. 326ff.

19. 'Gramsci and the Concept of Civil Society'.

20. Stefan Kardynał Wyszyński, *Kościół w służbie Narodu* [*The Church in the Service of the Nation* – addresses, August 1980-May 1981], Rome 1981, pp. 252ff.

21. Ibid., pp. 107, 109.

Anti-Political Politics*

Václav Havel

As a boy, I lived for some time in the country and I clearly
remember an experience from those days: I used to walk to
school in a nearby village along a cart track through the fields
and, on the way, see on the horizon a huge smokestack of some
hurriedly built factory, in all likelihood in the service of war. It
spewed dense smoke and scattered it across the sky. Each time I
saw it, I had an intense sense of something profoundly wrong, of
humans soiling the heavens. I have no idea whether there was
something like a science of ecology in those days; if there was, I
certainly knew nothing of it. That 'soiling of the heavens' nevertheless offended me spontaneously. It seemed to me that in so
doing, humans are guilty of something, that they destroy something important, arbitrarily disrupting the natural order of
things, and that such doings cannot go unpunished. Certainly,
my revulsion was largely aesthetic; I knew nothing then of the
noxious emissions which would one day devastate our forests,
exterminate game and endanger the health of people.

Were a medieval man suddenly to see something like a huge
smokestack on the horizon – say, while out hunting – he would
probably think it the work of the Devil and fall on his knees, to
pray that he and his kin be saved. What is it, actually, that the

---

*Text of an address forwarded to the University of Toulouse in 1984, on the occasion
of an honorary doctorate which, since he lacks a passport, he was unable to receive in
person. Translated by E. Kohák and R. Scruton, amended by A.G. Brain.

world of a medieval peasant and that of a small boy have in common? Something substantive, I think. Both the boy and the peasant are rooted far more intensely in what some philosophers call 'the natural world', or 'life-world' [*Lebenswelt*] than most modern adults.* They have not yet grown alienated from the world of their actual personal experience, the world which has its morning and its evening, its *down* (the earth) and its *up* (the heavens), where the sun rises daily in the east, traverses the sky and sets in the west, and where concepts like 'at home' and 'in foreign parts', good and evil, beauty and ugliness, near and far, duty and work, still mean something living and definite. They are still rooted in a world which knows the dividing line between all that is intimately familiar and appropriately a subject of our concern and that which lies beyond this horizon, that before which we should bow down humbly because it partakes of a mystery.

Our 'I' attests primordially to that world and personally certifies it. This is the world of our lived experience, a world to which we are not yet indifferent, since we are bound to it personally in our love, hatred, respect, contempt, tradition, in our interests and in that pre-reflective meaningfulness from which culture is born. It is the realm of our induplicable, inalienable and non-transferable joy and pain, a world in which, through which and for which we are somehow answerable, a world of personal responsibility. In this world, categories like justice, honour, treason, friendship, infidelity, courage or empathy have a wholly tangible content, relating to actual persons and actual life. At the basis of this world are values which are simply there, perennially, before we ever speak of them, before we reflect upon them and inquire about them. It owes its internal coherence to something like a 'pre-speculative' assumption that the world functions and is generally possible at all only because there is something beyond its horizon, something beyond or above it that might escape our understanding and our grasp but, for just that reason, grounds this world firmly, bestows order and measure upon it, and is the hidden source of all its rules, customs, commandments, prohibi-

---

Editor's note: The concept of *Lebenswelt* was first developed by Edmund Husserl, a Moravian-born philosopher, in *Die Krisis der europäischen Wissenschaften und die transzendentale Phänomenologie* (most of which was published in Belgrade in 1936). It refers to the horizon which is shared by all experiencing beings, but which recedes from their efforts to grasp or define it absolutely, even though through this life-world they make judgements, reach decisions and engage in various other actions.

tions and norms. The natural world, in virtue of its very being, bears within it the presupposition of the Absolute which grounds, delimits, animates and directs it, and without which it would be unthinkable. This Absolute is something which we can only quietly respect; any attempt to spurn it, master it or replace it with something else appears, within the framework of the natural world, as an expression of *hybris* for which humans must pay a heavy price, as did Don Juan and Faust.

To me, personally, the smokestack soiling the heavens is not just a regrettable lapse of a technology that failed to include 'the ecological factor' in its calculation, one which can be corrected easily with the appropriate filter. To me it is more the symbol of an age which seeks to transcend the boundaries of the natural world and its norms and to make it into a merely private concern, a matter of subjective preference and private feeling, of the illusions, prejudices and whims of a 'mere' individual. It is a symbol of an epoch which denies the binding importance of personal experience – including the experience of mystery and of the Absolute – and displaces the personally experienced Absolute as the measure of the world with a new, man-made absolute, devoid of mystery, free of the 'whims' of subjectivity and, as such, impersonal and inhuman. It is the absolute of so-called objectivity: the objective, rational cognition of the scientific model of the world.

Modern science, constructing its universally valid image of the world, thus crashes through the bounds of the natural world, which it can understand only as a prison of prejudices, from which we must break out into the light of objective truth. The natural world appears to it as no more than an unfortunate leftover from our backward ancestors, a fantasy of their childish immaturity. With that, of course, it abolishes as mere fiction even the innermost foundation of our natural world: it kills God and takes His place on the vacant throne, so that henceforth it might be science which, as sole legitimate guardian, holds the order of being in its hand. For, after all, it is only science that rises above all individual subjective truths and replaces them with a superior, trans-subjective, transpersonal truth, which is truly objective and universal.

Modern humans, whose natural world has been conquered properly by science and technology, objects to the smoke from the smokestack only if the stench penetrates their apartment. In no case, though, do they take offence at it *metaphysically*, since they know that the factory to which the smokestack belongs manufactures things they need. As people of the technological era, they can conceive of a remedy only within the limits of technology – for instance, a catalytic scrubber fitted to the chimney.

Lest you misunderstand, I am not proposing that humans abolish smokestacks or prohibit science or generally return to the Middle Ages. Besides, it is not accidental that some of the most profound discoveries of modern science render the myth of objectivity surprisingly problematic and, via a remarkable detour, return us to the human subject and his or her world. I wish no more than to consider, in a most general and admittedly schematic outline, the spiritual framework of modern civilization and the source of its present crisis. And although the primary focus of these reflections will be the political rather than the ecological aspect of this crisis, I might perhaps clarify my starting point with one more ecological example.

For centuries, the basic component of European agriculture had been the family farm. In Czech, the older term for it was *grunt* – which itself is not without its etymological interest. The word, taken from the German *Grund*, actually means ground or foundation and, in Czech, acquired a peculiar semantic colouring. As the colloquial synonym for foundation it points out the 'groundedness' of the ground, its indubitable, traditional and pre-speculatively given authenticity. Certainly, the family farm was a source of endless and intensifying social conflict of all kinds. Still, we cannot deny it one thing: it was rooted in the nature of its place, appropriate, harmonious, tested personally by generations of farmers and certified by the results of their husbandry. It also displayed a kind of optimal mutual proportionality in extent and kind of all that belonged to it: fields, meadows, bounds, woods, cattle, domestic animals, water, roads and so on. For centuries no farmer made it the topic of a scientific study. Nevertheless, it constituted a generally satisfactory economic and ecological system within which everything was bound together by a thousand threads of mutual and meaningful connection, guaranteeing its stability as well as the stability of the agricultural product.

Unlike present-day 'agribusiness', the traditional family farm was energetically self-sufficient. Although it was subject to common calamities, it was not guilty of them – unfavourable weather, cattle disease, wars and other catastrophes lay outside the farmer's province. Certainly, modern agricultural and social science could also improve agriculture in a thousand ways, increasing its productivity, reducing the amount of sheer drudgery, and eliminating the worst social inequalities. But this is possible only on the assumption that modernization, too, will be guided by a certain humility and respect for the mysterious order of nature and for the appropriateness which derives from it and which is intrinsic to the natural word of personal experience and responsibility. Modernization must not be simply a megalomaniac and brutal invasion by an impersonally objective Science, represented by a newly graduated agronomist or a bureaucrat in the service of the 'scientific world-view'.

That, however, is exactly what happened to our country: our word for it was 'collectivization'. Like a tornado it raged through the Czechoslovak countryside thirty years ago, leaving no stone unturned. Among its consequences were, on the one hand, tens of thousands of lives devastated by prison, sacrificed on the altar of a scientific utopia; on the other hand, a certain diminution in the level of social conflict and the amount of drudgery in the countryside and a certain quantitative increase in agricultural productivity. That, though, is not why I mention it. My reason is different: thirty years after the tornado swept the traditional family farm off the face of the earth, scientists are amazed to discover what even a semi-literate farmer previously knew – that human beings must pay a heavy price for every attempt to abolish, radically, once and for all and without trace, that humbly respected boundary of the natural world, with its tradition of scrupulous personal acknowledgement. They must pay for the attempt to seize nature, to leave not a remnant of it in human hands, to ridicule its mysteries; they must pay for the attempt to abolish God and to play at being God. The price, in fact, fell due. With hedges ploughed under and woods cut down, wild birds have died out and, with them, a natural, unpaid protector of the crops against harmful insects. Huge unified fields have led inevitably to the annual loss of millions of cubic yards of topsoil that had taken centuries to accumulate; chemical fertilizers and pesticides have catastrophically poisoned all vegetable products, the earth and its waters. Heavy machinery systematically presses down the soil, making it impenetrable to air and so infertile; cows in gigantic dairy farms suffer neuroses and lose their milk, while agriculture siphons off ever more energy from industry – manufacture of machines, artificial fertilizers, rising transportation costs in an age of growing local specialization; and so on and on. In short, the prognoses are terrifying and no one knows what surprises coming years and decades might bring.

It is paradoxical: people in the age of science and technology live in the conviction that they can improve their lives, because they are able to grasp and exploit the complexity of nature and the general laws of its functioning. Yet it is precisely these laws which, in the end, tragically catch up with them and get the better of them. Humans thought they could explain and conquer nature, yet the outcome is that they destroyed it and disinherited themselves from it. But what are the prospects for humans 'outside nature'? It is, after all, precisely the most recent leading sciences that are discovering that the human body is actually only a particularly busy intersection of billions of organic microbodies, of their complex mutual contacts and influences, together forming that incredible megaorganism we call 'the biosphere', in which our planet is blanketed.

The fault is not one of science as such but of the arrogance of humankind in the age of science. Humans simply are not God, and playing God has cruel consequences. Humans have abolished the absolute horizon of their relations, denied their personal 'pre-objective' experience of the lived world, while relegating personal conscience and consciousness to the bathroom, as something so private that it is no one's business. We have rejected our responsibility as a 'subjective illusion' and in its place installed what is now proving to be the most dangerous illusion of all: the fiction of objectivity stripped of all that is concretely human, of a rational understanding of the cosmos, and of an abstract schema of a putative 'historical necessity'. As the apex of it all, we have constructed a vision of a purely scientifically calculable and technologically achievable 'universal welfare', demanding no more than that experimental institutes invent it while industrial and bureaucratic factories turn it into reality. The fact that millions of people will be sacrificed to this illusion in scientifically directed concentration camps is not something that concerns our 'modern person' unless by chance he or she lands behind barbed wire and is thrown back drastically upon his or her natural world. The phenomenon of empathy, after all, belongs with that abolished realm of personal prejudice which had to yield to Science, Objectivity, Historical Necessity, Technology, System and the '*Apparat*' – and since they are impersonal, they cannot worry. They are abstract and anonymous, always utilitarian and, thus, also always innocent a priori.

And what for the future? Who, personally, would care about it or even personally worry about it when matters concerning eternity are locked away in the bathroom, if not actually exiled into the realm of fairy tales? If a contemporary scientist thinks at all of what will be in two hundred years, he or she does so solely as a personally disinterested observer who, basically, could not care less whether he or she is doing research on the metabolism of the flea, on the radio signals of pulsars or on the global reserves of natural gas. And a modern politician? He or she has absolutely no reason to care, especially if it might interfere with his or her chances in an election, as long as he or she lives in a country where there are elections ...

The Czech philosopher Václav Bělohradský has persuasively developed the thought that the rationalist spirit of modern science, founded on abstract reason and on the presumption of impersonal objectivity, has, in addition to its father in the natural sciences, Galileo, a father in politics – Machiavelli, who first formulated, albeit with an undertone of malicious irony, a theory of politics as a rational technology of power.[1] We could say that, for all the complex historical detours, the origin of the modern state and of modern political power may be sought precisely here, that is, in a moment when human reason is beginning once again to break free of humanity, of personal experience, personal conscience and personal responsibility and so also from the framework of the natural world, to which all responsibility had been uniquely related as its absolute horizon. Just as the modern natural scientists set aside the actual human being as the subject of the lived experience of the world, so, ever more evidently, do both the modern state and modern politics.

To be sure, this process of anonymization and depersonalization of power, and its reduction to a mere technology of rule and manipulation, has a thousand masks, variants and expressions. In one case, it is covert and inconspicuous while in another it is just the contrary, entirely overt; sometimes it sneaks up on us along subtle and devious paths, at other times it is brutally direct. Essentially, though, it is the same universal trend. It is the essential trait of all modern civilization, growing directly from its spiritual structure, rooted in it by a thousand tangled roots and inseparable even in thought from its technological nature, its mass characteristics and its consumer orientation.

Rulers and leaders were once personalities in their own right, with a concrete human face, still in some sense personally responsible for their good and evil deeds – whether they had been installed by dynastic tradition, the will of the people, a victorious battle or by intrigue. But they have been replaced in modern times by the manager, the bureaucrat, the *apparatchik* – a professional ruler, manipulator and expert in the techniques of obfuscation, filling a depersonalized intersection of functional relations, a cog in the machinery of state caught up in a predetermined role. This professional ruler is an 'innocent' tool of an 'innocent' anonymous power, legitimated by science, cybernetics, ideology, law, abstraction and objectivity – by everything, that is, except personal responsibility to human beings as persons and neighbours. A modern politician is transparent: behind his or her judicious mask and affected diction there is not a trace of a human being rooted in the natural order by loves, passions, interests, personal opinions, hatred, courage or cruelty. All that he or she, too, locks away in his or her private bathroom. If we glimpse anything at all behind the mask, it will be only a more or less competent power technician. System, ideology and *apparat* have deprived us – rulers as well as ruled – of our conscience, our natural understanding and natural speech and, with these, of our actual humanity. States grow ever more machine-like; people are transformed into casts of extras, as voters, producers, consumers, patients, tourists or soldiers. In politics, good and evil, categories of the natural world – and therefore obsolete remnants of the past – lose all absolute meaning; the sole method of politics is quantifiable success. Power is a priori innocent because it does not grow from a world in which words like guilt and innocence retain their meaning.

This impersonal power has achieved its most complete expression so far in the totalitarian systems. As Bělohradský points out, the depersonalization of power and its conquest of human conscience and human speech have been linked successfully to an extra-European tradition of a 'cosmological' conception of the empire which identifies the empire as the sole true centre of the world, with the world as such, and considers the human as its exclusive property. But, as the totalitarian systems illustrate clearly, this does not mean that the modern impersonal power is itself an extra-European affair. The truth is the very opposite: it was precisely Europe, and the European West, that provided and frequently forced on the world all that today has become the basis of such power: natural science, rationalism, scientism, the Industrial Revolution, and revolution as such, as a kind of fanatical abstraction from the natural world. And it is Europe – democratic Western Europe – which today stands bewildered in the face of this ambiguous export. The contemporary dilemma – whether to yield to or resist this reverse expansionism of its erstwhile export – attests to this. Should rockets, now aimed at Europe thanks to its export of spiritual and technological potential, be countered by similar and better rockets, thereby demonstrating a determination to defend such values as Europe has left, at the cost of entering into an utterly immoral game? Or should Europe retreat, hoping that the responsibility for the fate of the planet demonstrated thereby will infect, by its miraculous power, the rest of the world?

In the relation of Western Europe to the totalitarian systems, I think that no error could be greater than the one looming largest – that of a failure to understand the totalitarian systems for what they ultimately are: a convex mirror of all modern civilization and a harsh, perhaps final call for a global recasting of that civilization's self-understanding. If we ignore that, then it does not make any essential difference which form Europe's efforts will assume. It might be the form of taking the totalitarian systems, in the spirit of Europe's own rationalistic tradition, for some localised idiosyncratic attempt at achieving 'general welfare', to which only people of ill-will attribute expansionist tendencies. Or – in the spirit of the same rationalist tradition, though this time in the form of a Machiavellian conception of politics as the technology of power – it might perceive the totalitarian regimes as a purely external threat by expansionist neighbours, who can be driven back within acceptable bounds by an appropriate demonstration of power, without having to be considered more deeply. The first alternative is that of the person who reconciles him- or herself to the chimney belching smoke, even though that smoke is ugly and smelly, because in the end it serves a good end: the production of commonly needed goods. The second is that of the person who thinks that it is simply a matter of a technological flaw which can be eliminated by technological means, such as a filter or a scrubber.

The reality, I believe is unfortunately more serious. The chimney 'soiling the heavens' is not just a technologically corrigible design error, or a tax paid for a better tomorrow, but a symbol of a civilization which has renounced the Absolute, which ignores the natural world and disdains its imperatives. So, too, the totalitarian systems warn of something far more serious than Western rationalism is willing to admit. They are, most of all, a convex mirror of the inevitable consequences of rationalism, a grotesquely magnified image of its own deep tendencies, an extreme outcropping of its own development and an ominous product of its own expansion. They are a deeply informative reflection of its own crisis. Totalitarian regimes are not merely dangerous neighbours and, even less, some kind of an avant-

garde of world progress. Alas, just the opposite; they are the
avant-garde of a global crisis of this civilization, one which is
European, then Euroamerican, and ultimately global. They are
one of the possible futurological studies of the Western world, not
in the sense that one day they will attack and conquer it but in a
far deeper sense – that they illustrate graphically the possible
consequences of the 'eschatology of the impersonal', as Bělohradský calls it.

It is the total rule of a bloated, anonymously bureaucratic
power, not yet irresponsible but already operating outside all
conscience, a power grounded in an omnipresent ideological
fiction which can rationalize anything without ever having to
confront the truth. It is power as the omnipresent monopoly of
control, repression and fear, a power which makes thought,
morality and privacy a state monopoly and so dehumanizes
them. It is a power which long ago has ceased to be the matter of
a group of arbitrary rulers but which, rather, occupies and
swallows everyone, so that all should become integrated within it,
at least through their silence. No one actually possesses such
power since it is the power itself which possesses everyone; it is a
monstrosity which is not guided by humans but which, on the
contrary, drags all persons along with its 'objective' momentum –
objective in the sense of being cut off from all human standards,
including human reason – to a terrifying, unknown future.

Let me repeat: this totalitarian power is a great reminder to
contemporary civilization. Perhaps somewhere there may be
some generals who think that it would be best to dispatch such
systems from the face of the earth and then all would be well. But
that is no different from a plain girl trying to get rid of her plain-
ness by smashing the mirror which reminds her of it. Such a
'final solution' is one of the typical dreams of impersonal reason –
capable, as the term 'final solution' reminds us graphically, of
transforming its dreams into reality and thereby reality into a
nightmare. Not only would it fail to resolve the crisis of the
present world but, assuming anyone survived at all, it would only
aggravate that crisis. By burdening the already heavy account of
this civilization with further millions of dead, it would not block
its essential tendency to totalize but, rather, would accelerate it. It
would be a Pyrrhic victory, because the victors would emerge
from such a conflict inevitably resembling their defeated
opponents far more than anyone today is willing to admit or able
to imagine. Just a minor example of this: imagine what a huge
Gulag Archipelago would have to be built in the West, in the

name of country, democracy, progress and military discipline, to contain all who refused to take part in such an enterprise, whether out of naiveté, principle, fear or ill-will!

No evil has ever been eliminated by suppressing its symptoms. We need to address the cause itself.

From time to time I have a chance to speak with various Western intellectuals who visit our country and decide to include a visit to a dissident on their itinerary. Some visit out of genuine interest, or a willingness to understand and to express solidarity; others simply out of curiosity: beside the Gothic and Baroque monuments, dissidents are apparently the only thing of interest to a tourist in this uniformly dreary context. These conversations are usually instructive: I learn much and realize much. The questions most frequently asked are these: Do you think you can really change anything, when you are so few and have no influence at all? Are you opposed to socialism, or do you merely wish to improve it? Do you condemn or condone the deployment of the Pershing II and cruise missiles in Western Europe? What can we do for you? What drives you to do what you are doing when all it brings you is persecution, prison – and no visible results? Would you want to see capitalism restored in your country?

Those questions are well intended, growing out of a desire to understand and showing that those who ask do care about the world, about what it is and what it will be.

Still, precisely these and similar questions reveal to me ever anew how deeply many Western intellectuals do not understand – and in some respects, cannot understand – just what is taking place here, what it is that we, the so-called 'dissidents', are striving for and, most of all, what is the overall meaning of our situation. Take, for instance, the question 'What can we do for you?' A great deal, to be sure. The more support, interest and solidarity of free-thinking people in the world we enjoy, the less the danger of being arrested, and the greater the hope that ours will not be a voice crying in the wilderness. And yet somewhere deep within the question, there is a built-in misunderstanding. After all, in the last instance the point is not to help us, a handful of 'dissidents', to keep out of jail a bit more of the time. It is not even a question of helping these nations, Czechs and Slovaks, to live a bit better, a bit more freely. We need first and foremost to help ourselves. We have waited for the help of others far too often, depended on it far too much, and far too many times come to grief: either the promised help was withdrawn at the last moment or it turned into the very opposite of our expectations. In the deepest sense, something else is at stake: the salvation of us all, of myself and my interlocutors equally. Or is it not something that concerns us all equally? Are not my dim prospects or, conversely, my hopes, their dim prospects and hopes as well? Was not my imprisonment an affront on them and the deception to which they are subjected an attack on me as well? Is not the destruction of humans in Prague a destruction of human beings everywhere? Is not indifference to what is happening here, or even illusions about it, a preparation for the same kind of misery elsewhere? Is not their misery the precondition of ours? The point is not that some Czech dissident, as a person in distress, needs help. I could best help myself out of distress simply by ceasing to be a 'dissident'. The point is what those dissidents' flawed efforts and their fate tell us and mean; what they attest about the condition, destiny, opportunities and problems of the world; the respects in which they are or could be food for thought for others as well; for the way they see their and so our shared destiny; and in what ways they are a warning, a challenge, a danger or a lesson for those who visit us.

Or the question about socialism and capitalism! I admit that it gives me a sense of emerging from the depths of the last century. It seems to me that these thoroughly ideological and many-times-mystified categories have long since been beside the point. The question is wholly other, deeper and equally relevant to all. Shall we, by whatever means, succeed in reconstituting the natural world as the true terrain of politics, rehabilitating the personal experience of human beings as the initial measure of things, placing morality above politics and responsibility above our desires, making human community meaningful, returning content to human speaking, reconstituting, as the focus of all social activity, the autonomous, integral and dignified human 'I', responsible for him- or herself because he or she is bound to something higher? It really is not all that important whether, by accident of domicile, we confront a Western manager or an Eastern bureaucrat in this very modest and yet globally crucial struggle against the momentum of impersonal power. If we can defend our humanity, then perhaps there is a hope of sorts that we shall also find some more meaningful ways of balancing our natural rights to participate in economic decision-making, and to a dignified social status, with the tried driving force of all work: human enterprise realized in authentic market transactions. However, as long as our humanity remains defenceless we shall not be saved by any technical or organizational trick designed to produce better economic functioning, just as no filter on a factory smokestack will prevent the general dehumanization. To what purpose a system functions is, after all, more important than how it does so. Might it not function quite smoothly, after all, in the service of total destruction?

I speak in this way because, looking at the world from the perspective which fate allotted me, I cannot avoid the impression that many people in the West still understand little of what is actually at stake in our time.

If, for instance, we take a second look at the two basic political alternatives between which Western intellectuals oscillate today, it becomes apparent that they are no more than two different ways of playing the same game, proferred by the anonymity of power. As such, they are no more than two diverse ways of moving toward the same global totalitarianism. One way of playing the game of anonymous reason is to keep on toying with the mystery of matter – 'playing God' – constantly inventing and deploying weapons of mass destruction, all, of course, intended 'for the defence of democracy', but in effect degrading democracy to the 'uninhabitable fiction' which socialism has long since become on our side of Europe.

The other form of the game of anonymous reason is the tempting vortex that draws into itself so many good and sincere people, the so-called 'struggle for peace'.[2] Often I have the impression that this vortex has been designed and deployed by that same treacherous, all-pervasive impersonal power as a more poetic means of colonizing human consciousness. Please note that I have in mind impersonal power as a principle, globally, in all its instances, and not only in Moscow – which, if the truth be told, lacks the capability to organize something as widespread as the contemporary peace movement. Still, could there be a better way of rendering ineffectual in the world of rationalism and ideology an honest, free-thinking person, the chief threat to all anonymous power, than by offering him or her the simplest thesis possible, with all the apparent characteristics of a noble goal? Could you imagine something that would more effectively fire a just mind – preoccupying it, then occupying it and ultimately rendering it intellectually harmless – than the possibility of 'a struggle against war'? Is there a cleverer means than deceiving people with the illusion that they can prevent war if they interfere with the deployment of weapons (which will be deployed in any case)? It is hard to imagine an easier way to a totalitarianism of the human consciousness. The more obvious it becomes that the weapons will indeed be deployed, the more rapidly does the mind of a person who has totally identified with the goal of preventing such deployment becomes radicalized, fanaticized and in the end alienated from itself. So a person sent off on his or her way by the noblest of intentions finds him- or herself, at the journey's end, precisely where anonymous powers needs to see him or her: in the rut of totalitarian thought, where he or she is not his or her own and where he or she surrenders individual reason and conscience for the sake of another 'uninhabitable fiction'!

As long as that totalitarian goal is served, it is not important whether we call that fiction 'human well-being', 'socialism' or 'peace'. Certainly, from the standpoint of the defence and the interests of the Western world, it is not very good when someone says 'better red than dead'. Still, from the viewpoint of the global impersonal power, and as a boost to its devilish omnipresence, there could be nothing better. That slogan is an infallible sign that the speaker has given up his or her humanity. For he or she has given up the ability personally to guarantee something that transcends him or her and so even to sacrifice, in the extreme, life itself to that which makes life meaningful. Patočka once wrote that a life not willing to sacrifice itself for what makes it meaningful is not worth living.[3]

It is exactly in the world of abandoned lives and just such a 'peace' – that is, under the humdrum conditions of 'everydayness' – that wars happen most easily. In such a world there is no moral barrier against them, no barrier guaranteed by the courage of supreme sacrifice. The door stands wide open for the irrational 'securing of our interests'. The absence of heroes who know what they are dying for is the first step on the way to the mounds of corpses of those who are then slaughtered like cattle. The slogan 'better red than dead' does not irritate me as an expression of surrender to the Soviet Union, but it terrifies me as an expression of the renunciation by Western people of any claim to a meaningful life and of their acceptance of impersonal power as such. For what the slogan really says is that nothing is worth giving one's life for. However, without the horizon of the highest sacrifice, all sacrifice becomes senseless. Then nothing is worth anything. Nothing means anything. The result is a philosophy of sheer negation of our humanity. In the case of Soviet totalitarianism, such a philosophy does no more than offer a little political assistance. In the West, it directly creates totalitarianism.

In short, I cannot overcome the impression that Western culture is threatened far more by itself than by SS–20 rockets.

When a French leftist student told me, with a sincere glow in his eyes, that the Gulag was a tax paid for the ideals of socialism and that Solzhenitsyn is just a personally embittered man, he cast me into a deep gloom. Is Europe really incapable of learning from its own history? Can't that pleasant young man ever understand that even the most tempting project of 'general well-being' convicts itself of inhumanity the moment it demands a single involuntary death – that is, one which is not a conscious sacrifice of a life to its meaning? Is he really incapable of comprehending that until he finds himself incarcerated in some Soviet-style jail near Toulouse? Has latter-day newspeak so penetrated natural human speech that two people can no longer communicate even such a basic experience?

I presume that after all these stringent criticisms, I am expected to explain just what I consider to be a meaningful alternative for Western humanity today, in the face of the political dilemmas of the contemporary world.

As all I have said suggests, it seems to me that all of us, East and West, face one fundamental task from which all else should follow. That task is one of resisting – vigilantly, thoughtfully and attentively, but at the same time with total dedication, at every step and everywhere – the irrational momentum of anonymous, impersonal and inhuman power: the power of Ideologies, Systems, *Apparats*, Bureaucracy, Artificial languages and Political Slogans. We must resist its complex and wholly alienating pressure, whether it takes the form of consumption, advertising, repression, technology, or cliché – all of which are the blood brothers of fanaticism and the wellspring of totalitarian thought. We must draw our standards from our natural world, heedless of ridicule, and reaffirm its denied validity. We must honour with the humility of the wise the bounds of that natural world and the mystery which lies beyond them, admitting that there is something in the order of Being which evidently exceeds all our competence. We must relate constantly to the absolute horizon of our existence which, if we but will, we shall constantly rediscover and experience. Values and imperatives must become the starting point of all our actions, of all our personally attested, openly contemplated and ideologically uncensored lived experience. We must trust the voice of our conscience more than that of all the abstract speculations, while contriving no other responsibility than the one to which that voice calls us. We must not be ashamed that we are capable of love, friendship, solidarity, sympathy and tolerance. On the contrary: we must set these fundamental dimensions of our humanity free from their 'private' exile and accept them as the only genuine starting point of meaningful human community.

I know all that sounds very general, very indefinite and very unrealistic, but I assure you that these apparently naive words stem from a very concrete and not always easy experience with the world and that, if I may say so, I know what I am talking about.

The vanguard of impersonal power, which drags the world along its irrational path, lined with devastated nature and launching pads, is composed of the totalitarian regimes of our time. It is not possible to ignore them, to make excuses for them, to yield to them or to accept their way of playing the game, thereby becoming like them. I am convinced that we can face them best by studying them without prejudice, learning from them and resisting them by being radically different, with a difference born of a continuous struggle against the evil which they may embody most clearly, but which dwells everywhere and so even within each of us. That evil is endangered less by rockets aimed at this or that state than by our own determination to negate it, by the return of humans to themselves and to their responsibility for the world. The best defence against totalitarianism is simply to drive it out of our own souls, our own circumstances, our own land: to banish it from contemporary humankind. The best help to all who suffer under totalitarian regimes is to confront the evil which a totalitarian system constitutes, from which it draws its strength, and on which its 'vanguard' is nourished.

If there is nothing whose vanguard or extreme outcrop a totalitarian regime could be, it will also have no basis. A reaffirmed human responsibility is the most natural barrier to all irresponsibility. If, for instance, the spiritual and technological potential of the advanced world is spread truly responsibly, not solely under the pressure of a selfish interest in profits, we can prevent its irresponsible transformation into weapons of destruction. It surely makes much more sense to operate in the sphere of causes than simply to respond to their effects: otherwise, as a rule, the only possible response is to use equally immoral means. To follow that path means to continue spreading the evil of irresponsibility in the world, and so to produce precisely the poison on which totalitarianism feeds.

I favour 'anti-political politics': that is, politics not as the technology of power and manipulation, of cybernetic rule over humans or as the art of the useful, but politics as one of the ways of seeking and achieving meaningful lives, of protecting them and serving them. I favour politics as practical morality, as service to the truth, as essentially human and humanly measured care for our fellow-humans. It is, I presume, an approach which, in this world, is extremely impractical and difficult to apply in daily life. Still, I know no better alternative.

When I was tried and then serving my sentence, I experienced directly the impotance and beneficial force of international solidarity. I shall never cease to be grateful for all its expressions. Still, I do not think that we who seek to proclaim the truth under our conditions find ourselves in an asymmetrical position, or that it should be we alone who ask for help and expect it, without being able to offer help in the direction from which it also comes.

I am convinced that what is called 'dissent' in the Soviet bloc is a specifically modern experience, the experience of life at the very ramparts of dehumanized power. As such, 'dissent' has the opportunity and even the duty to reflect on this experience, to testify to it and to pass it on to those fortunate enough not to have to undergo it. Thus we, too, have a certain opportunity to help in some ways those who help us, to help them in our deeply shared interest, in the interest of humankind.

One such fundamental experience is that anti-political politics is possible and can be effective, even though by its very nature it cannot calculate its effect beforehand. That effect, to be sure, is of a wholly different nature from what the West considers political success. It is hidden, indirect, long-term and hard to measure. Often it exists only in the invisible realm of social consciousness, and therein it can be almost impossible to determine what value it assumes and to what extent, if any, it contributes to shaping social development.

It is, however, becoming evident – and I think this is an experience of an essential and universal importance – that a single seemingly powerless person who dares to cry out the word of truth and to stand behind it with all his or her person and life, has, surprisingly, greater power, though formally disenfranchised, than do thousands of anonymous voters. It is becoming evident that even in today's world, and especially on this exposed rampart where the wind blows most sharply, it is possible to oppose personal experience and the natural world to 'innocent' power and to unmask its guilt, as the author of *The Gulag Archipelago* has done. It is becoming evident that truth and morality can provide a new starting point for politics and can, even today, have an undeniable political power. The warning voice of a single brave scientist, besieged somewhere in the provinces and terrorized by a goaded community, can be heard over continents and can address the conscience of the mighty of this world more clearly than can entire brigades of hired propagandists speaking to themselves. It is becoming evident that wholly personal categories like good and evil still have their unambiguous content and, under certain circumstances, are capable of shaking the seemingly unshakable power and its army of soldiers, policemen and bureaucrats. It is becoming evident that politics by no means need remain the affair of professionals and that one simple electrician, with his heart in the right place, honouring something that transcends him and free of fear, can influence the history of his nation.

Yes, anti-political politics is possible. Politics 'from below'. Politics of people, not of the apparatus. Politics growing from the heart, not from a thesis. It is no accident that this hopeful experience has to be lived just here, on this grim battlement. In conditions of humdrum 'everydayness', we have to descend to the very bottom of a well before we can see the stars.

When Jan Patočka wrote about Charter 77, he used the term 'solidarity of the shaken'. He was thinking of those who dared resist impersonal power and confront it with the only thing at their disposal: their own humanity. Does not the perspective of a better future depend on something like an international community of the shaken which, ignoring state boundaries, political systems and power blocs, standing outside the high game of traditional politics, aspiring to no titles and appointments, will seek to make a real political force out of a phenomenon so ridiculed by the technicians of power – the phenomenon of human conscience?

Notes

1. Václav Bělohradský, *Krize Eschatologie Neosobnosti* [*The Crisis in the Eschatology of the Impersonal*], London 1982.

2. *Editor's note*: The background of Havel's important contributions to the trans-European dialogue within the peace movement are discussed in Jan Kavan and Zdena Tomin, eds, *Voices From Prague. Documents on Czechoslovakia and the Peace Movement*, London 1983. His most important essay on the subject is *Anatomy of a Reticence. East European Dissidents and the Peace Movement in the West*, Stockholm 1985 and London 1987.

3. Jan Patočka, *Kacířské Eseje*, Munich 1980, translated as *Essais hérétiques*, Paris 1981.

Select Bibliography

The following bibliography contains a selection of recent essays, books and research publications on the subject of civil society and the state. Most items have appeared during the past two decades, and have been printed mainly in English, German and French. Additional references are listed throughout the footnotes to both this volume and its companion, *Democracy and Civil Society*, London and New York 1988.

Richard Adamiak, 'State and Society in Early Socialist Thought', *Survey*, vol. 26, no. 1, 1982, pp. 1-28.

Maurice Agulhon, ed., *Sociabilité et société bourgeoise*, Paris 1986.

Robert R. Alford, 'Paradigms of Relations Between State and Society', in Leon N. Lindberg et al., eds., *Stress and Contradiction in Modern Capitalism*, Lexington, Mass. 1975.

Erich Angermann, 'Das "Auseinandertreten von Staat und Gesellschaft" im Denken des 18. Jahrhunderts', *Zeitschrift für Politik* vol. 10, 1963, pp. 89-101.

Andrew Arato, 'Civil Society Against the State: Poland 1980-81', *Telos*, vol. 47, 1981, pp. 23-47.

Andrew Arato, 'Empire vs. Civil Society: Poland, 1981-82', *Telos*, vol. 50, 1981-2, pp. 19-48.

Andrew Arato and Jean Cohen, 'Social Movements, Civil Society, and the Problem of Sovereignty', *Praxis International* vol. 4, no. 3, 1984, pp. 266-83.

Milan Balažic, 'Civilna družba skozi "samoupravno" mikrofiziko oblasti', *Problemi*, vol. 25, no. 1, 1987.

Laura Balbo and Helga Nowotny, eds, *Time to Care in Tomorrow's Welfare Systems*, Wien 1986.

Zwi Batscha and Hans Medick, 'Einleitung', in Adam Ferguson, ed., *Versuch über die Geschichte der bürgerlichen Gesellschaft*, Frankfurt am Main 1986.

Zygmunt Bauman, 'On the Maturation of Socialism', *Telos*, vol. 47, 1981, pp. 48-54.

Zygmunt Bauman, 'On the Origins of Civilisation: A Historical Note', *Theory and Society*, vol. 2, no. 3, 1985, pp. 7-14.

Zygmunt Bauman, 'Intellectuals in East-Central Europe: Continuity and Change', unpublished paper, Leeds University 1986.

C.B.A. Behrens, *Society, Government and the Enlightenment: the Experiences of Eighteenth-Century France and Prussia*, London 1985.

Robert Bellah, 'Civil Religion in America', *Daedalus*, vol. 96, 1967, pp. 1-21.

R. Bendix, ed., *State and Society. A Reader in Comparative Political Sociology*, Berkeley 1973.

Seyla Benhabib, 'The "Logic" of Civil Society: A Reconsideration of Hegel and Marx', *Philosophy and Social Criticism*, vol. 8, no. 2, 1981, pp. 152-66.

Jean-Marie Benoist, *Les outils de la liberté*, Paris 1985.

J.A. Bergougnoux and B. Manin, *La social democratie ou le compromis*, Paris 1979.

R.N. Berki, 'State and Society: An Antithesis of Modern Political Thought', in Jack Hayward and R.N. Berki, eds, *State and Society in Contemporary Europe*, Oxford 1979.

Richard J. Bernstein, 'Rethinking the Social and the Political', in *Philosophical Profiles. Essays in a Pragmatic Mode*, Cambridge 1986.

Homi K. Bhabha, 'Sly Civility', *October*, no. 34, pp. 71-80.

Adolf Bibič, *Zasebništvo in skupnost. Civilna družba in politična država pri Heglu in Marxu*, second enlarged edn, Ljubljana 1984.

Adolf Bibič, 'Civilna družba v socializmu?', *Teorija in praksa*, vol. 23, no. 11, 1986.

Adolf Bibič, 'Civilna družba je samoupravljanje', *Delo*, Ljubljana, 28 November 1986.

Pierre Birnbaum, 'La fin de l'état?', paper presented to the Congrès de L'IPSA, Paris 1985.

Norberto Bobbio, 'Italy's Permanent Crisis', *Telos*, vol. 54, 1982-3, pp. 123-33.

Norberto Bobbio, *The Future of Democracy*, Cambridge 1987.

Norberto Bobbio, 'Grandeur et decadence de l'idéologie Européenne', *Lettre internationale*, vol. 12, 1987, pp. 8-11.

Norberto Bobbio, 'Sulla nozione di società civile', in *Studie Hegeliani*, Torino 1981, pp. 147-58.

Norberto Bobbio, 'Società civile', in *Enciclopedia Einaudi*, vol. 13, pp. 53-68.

Ernst-Wolfgang Böckenförde, *Staat und Gesellschaft*, Darmstadt 1976.

Martin Boddy and Colin Fudge, eds, *Local Socialism? Labour Councils and New Left Alternatives*, Basingstoke and London 1985.

Angelo Bolaffi and Massimo Ilardi, eds, *Fine della Politica?* Roma 1986.

Dieter Borchmeyer, *Höische Gesellschaft und französische Revolution bei Goethe. Adliges und bürgerliches Wertsystem im Urteil der Weimarer Klassik*, Kronberg 1977.

Eberhard Braun, 'Was ist bürgerliche Gesellschaft?', *Das Argument*, vol. 143, 1984, pp. 26-39.

Marilyn Butler, ed., *Burke, Paine, Godwin, and the Revolution Controversy*, Cambridge 1984.

Carlo Carboni, ed., *Classi e Morimenti in Italia, 1970-1985*, Bari 1986.

Fernando Henrique Cardoso, 'Democracy in Latin America', *Politics and Society*, vol. 15, no.1, 1986-7, pp. 23-41.

Manuel Castells, *The City and the Grassroots. A Cross-Cultural Theory of Urban Social Movements*, Berkeley and Los Angeles 1983.

H. Caygill, 'Aesthetics and Civil Society: Theories of Art and Society 1640-1790', doctoral dissertation, University of Sussex 1982.

B. Cazès, 'L'Etat protecteur contraint a une double manoeuvre', *Futuribles*, vol. 40, 1981.

Pierre Clastres, *La société contre l'état*, Paris 1974.

Jean Cohen, *Class and Civil Society. The Limits of Marxian Critical Theory*, Oxford 1983.

Lucio Colletti, 'Rousseau as Critic of "Civil Society"', in *From Rousseau to Lenin. Studies in Ideology and Society*, London 1972.

Werner Conze, ed., *Staat und Gesellschaft in deutschen Vormärz 1815-1848*, Stuttgart 1978.

Lewis A. Coser, 'The Notion of Civility in Contemporary Society', *Archives européennes de sociologie*, vol. 21, no. 1, 1980, pp. 3-13.

Critica y Utopia, vol. 6: *Sociedad Civil y Autoritarismo*, March 1982.

Otto Dann, ed., *Lesegesellschaften und bürgerliche Emanzipation. Ein europäischer Vergleich*, Munich 1981.

Gábor Demszky, 'Parliamentarism in Eastern Europe - The Chances of the Independent Candidate', *East European Reporter*, vol. 1, 3, Autumn 1985, pp. 23-5.

Mehmet Ali Dikerdem, 'A Turkish Tug-of-War. The State of Human Rights in Turkey Today', *Index on Censorship*, vol. 16, 6 June 1987, pp. 15-19.

Horst Dippel, 'Die Theorie der bürgerlichen Gesellschaft bei Benjamin Franklin', *Historische Zeitschrift*, vol. 220, 1975, pp. 568-618.

Ronald Dore, 'Goodwill and the Spirit of Market Capitalism', *The British Journal of Sociology*, vol. 34, no. 4, 1983, pp. 459-82.

Helmut Dubiel, *Was ist Neokonservatismus?* Frankfurt am Main 1985.

Hans Peter Duerr, *Traumzeit. Über die Grenze zwischen Wildnis und Zivilisation*, Frankfurt am Main 1978.

Kenneth H. F. Dyson, 'Die Ideen des Staates und der Demokratie. Ein Vergleich "staatlich verfasster" und "nicht staatlich verfasster" Gesellschaften', *Der Staat*, vol. 19, 1980, pp. 485-515.

Norbert Elias, *Die höfische Gesellschaft*, Neuwied and Berlin 1969.

Gösta Esping-Andersen, *Social Class, Social Democracy and State Policy*, Copenhagen 1980.

402

Lucien Febvre, 'Civilisation: Evolution of a Word and a Group of Ideas', in Peter Burke, ed., A New Kind of History, London 1973, pp. 219-57.

Ferenc Féher et. al., Dictatorship over Needs, Oxford 1983.

Peter Flora, State, Economy and Society in Western Europe 1815-1975. A Data Handbook, vol. 1: The Growth of Mass Democracies and Welfare States, Frankfurt am Main 1983.

Boris Frankel, Beyond the State? Dominant Theories and Socialist Strategies, London 1983.

Ute Frevert, Frauen-geschichte. Zwischen bürgerlicher Verbesserung und neuer Weiblichkeit, Frankfurt am Main 1986.

Ute Frevert, 'Deutungen und Bedeutungen - Das "bürgerliche" Geschlechterverhältnis als Forschungsproblem', unpublished paper, Zentrum für interdisziplinäre Forschung, Bielefeld 1987.

Milton Friedman, The Tyranny of the Status Quo, London 1985.

Lothar Gall, 'Liberalismus und "bürgerliche Gesellschaft". Zu Charakter und Entwicklung der liberalen Bewegung in Deutschland', Historische Zeitschrift, vol. 220, 1975, pp. 324-56.

Peter Gay, The Bourgeois Experience. Victoria to Freud, New York 1984.

Ernest Gellner, State and Society in Soviet Thought, Oxford 1987.

Ute Gerhard, 'Den Sozialstaat neu denken? Voraussetzungen und Preis des Sozialstaatskompromisses', Vorgänge, May 1987, pp. 14-32.

Jeffrey Goldfarb, 'Social Bases of Independent Public Expression in Communist Societies', American Journal of Sociology, vol. 4, 1978, pp. 920-39.

Alenka Goljevšček, 'Arhaičnost: civilnost', Nova revija, vol. 6, no. 57, 1987.

Zagorka Golubović and Svetozar Stojanović, The Crisis of the Yugoslav System, Cologne 1986.

Phil H. Goodstein, The Theory of the General Strike from the French Revolution to Poland, New York 1985.

André Gorz, Farewell to the Working Class. An Essay on Post-Industrial Socialism, London 1982.

Dieter Grimm, Die verfassungsrechtlichen Grundlagen der Privatrechtsgesetzgebung, Munich 1982.

Anne-Marie Guillemard, 'State, Society and Old-Age Policy in France: From 1945 to the Current Crisis', unpublished paper, Paris 1986.

Anne-Marie Guillemard, Le declin du social, Paris 1986.

Anne-Marie Guillemard, La vieillesse et l'état, Paris 1986.

John Gyford, The Politics of Local Socialism, London 1985.

Jürgen Habermas, Strukturwandel der Öffentlichkeit. Untersuchungen zu einer Kategorie der bürgerlichen Gesellschaft, Neuwied 1962.

Jürgen Habermas, 'New Social Movements', Telos, vol. 49, 1981, pp. 33-7.

Stuart Hall and Martin Jacques, eds., The Politics of Thatcherism, London 1983.

Utz Haltern, Bürgerliche Gesellschaft. Sozialtheoretische und sozialhistorische Aspekte, Darmstadt 1985.

Hevré Hamon and Patrick Rotman, La deuxieme gauche: histoire intellectuelle *et politique de la CFDT*, Paris 1982.

Elemér Hankiss, *The 'Second Society'*, Budapest 1986.

Roger Harris, 'Socialism and Democracy: Beyond State *and* Civil Society', *Radical Philosophy*, vol. 45, 1987, pp. 13-22.

Václav Havel et al., 'The Power of the Powerless', in *Citizens against the State in Central-Eastern Europe*, edited by John Keane, London 1985.

Jack Hayward and R.N. Berki eds., *State and Society in Contemporary Europe*, Oxford 1979.

David Held et al., eds., *States and Societies*, Oxford 1983.

David Held, *Models of Democracy*, Cambridge 1987.

David Held and John Keane, 'Socialism and the Limits of State Action', in James Curran, ed., *The Future of the Left*, Cambridge 1984.

Agnes Heller, 'The Great Republic', *Praxis International*, vol. 5, no. 1, 1985, pp. 23-34.

Agnes Heller, *The Power of Shame*, London 1985.

Wilhelm Hennis, ed., *Regierbarkeit: Studien zu ihrer Problematisierung*, Stuttgart 1977.

Helga Maria Hernes, 'Care Work and the Organization of Daily Life', unpublished paper, Oslo 1986.

Ulrich Herrman, ed., *'Die Bildung des Bürgers'. Die Formierung der bürgerlichen Gesellschaft und die Gebildeten im 18. Jahrhundert*, Weinheim 1982.

Barry Hindess, *Parliamentary Democracy and Socialist Politics*, London 1983.

Ulrich Im Hof, *Das gesellige Jahrhundert. Gesellschaft und Gesellschaften im Zeitalter der Aufklärung*, Munich 1982.

Stanley Hoffmann and George Ross, eds., *The Mitterand Experiment. Continuity and Change in Modern France*, Cambridge 1987.

Istvan Hont and Michael Ignatieff, eds., *Wealth and Virtue. The Shaping of Political Economy in the Scottish Enlightenment*, Cambridge 1983.

Joseph Huber, *Wer soll das ändern. Die Alternativen der Alternativbewegung*, Berlin 1981.

Geoffrey Hunt, 'Gramsci, Civil Society and Bureaucracy', *Praxis International*, vol. 6, no. 2, 1986, pp. 206-19.

J.K. Hyde, *Society and Politics in Medieval Italy. The Evolution of the Civil Life, 1000-1350*, London 1973.

Jean Hyppolite, 'Marx's Critique of the Hegelian Concept of the State', in *Studies on Marx and Hegel*, New York 1969, pp. 106-25.

Claude Lefort, *The Political Forms of Modern Society. Bureaucracy, Democracy, Totalitarianism*, Cambridge 1986.

Günther Lottes, *Politische Aufklärung und plebejisches Publikum: zur Theorie und Praxis des englischen Radikalismus im späten 18. Jahrhundert*, Munich 1979.

John Keane, *A Letter on Why Civil Society is Important to Socialists ... And Others*, New York 1983.

John Keane, *Public Life and Late Capitalism. Toward a Socialist Theory of Democracy*, Cambridge and New York, 1984.

John Keane, 'Civil Society and the Peace Movement in Britain', *Thesis Eleven*, vol. 8, 1984, pp. 5-12.

John Keane, 'Hegel Against Marx; The State and Civil Society', *New Society*, 16 August, 1985, pp. 237-38.

John Keane, 'More Theses on the Philosophy of History', in James Tully, ed., *Meaning and Context. Essays in Honour of Quentin Skinner*, Cambridge 1988.

John Keane, 'The Modern Democratic Revolution', *The Chicago Review*, vol. 35, no. 4, 1987, pp. 4-19.

John Keane and John Owens, *After Full Employment*, London 1986.

John Keane, Tomaž Mastnak et al., 'Yugoslavia's Permanent Crisis', *East European Reporter*, vol. 2, no. 2, 1986, pp. 46-50.

János Kenédi, *Do It Yourself: Hungary's Hidden Economy*, London 1981.

Rainer Koch, *Grundlagen bürgerlicher Herrschaft. Verfassungs- und sozialgeschichtliche Studien zur bürgerlichen Gesellschaft in Frankfurt am Main (1612-1866)*, Frankfurt am Main 1983.

Leo Kofler, *Zur Geschichte der bürgerlichen Gesellschaft. Versuch einer verstehenden Deutung der Neuzeit*, Neuwied and Berlin 1966.

Leszek Kolakowski, 'The Myth of Human Self-Identity: Unity of Civil and Political Society in Socialist Thought', in Stuart Hampshire and Leszek Kolakowski, eds., *The Socialist Idea. A Reappraisal*, London 1977, pp. 18-35.

Leszek Kolakowski, 'Marxism and Human Rights', *Daedalus*, vol. 112, no. 4, 1983, pp. 81-92.

György Konrád, *Anti-Politics*, London 1984.

Walter Korpi, *The Working Class in Welfare Capitalism*, London and Boston, Melbourne and Henley 1978.

Walter Korpi, *The Democratic Class Struggle*, London, Boston, Melbourne and Henley 1983.

Reinhart Koselleck, *Preussen zwischen Reform und Revolution*, Stuttgart 1967.

Reinhart Koselleck, 'Staat und Gesellschaft in Preussen 1815-48, in Werner Conze, ed., *Staat und Gesellschaft in deutschen Vormärz 1815-1848*, Stuttgart 1978, pp. 79-112.

Vojislav Koštunica and Kosta Čavoški, *Party Pluralism or Monism. Social Movements and the Political System in Yugoslavia 1944-1949*, Boulder 1985.

Lawrence Krader, *Dialectic of Civil Society*, Assen 1976.

Jan Krouzil, 'The Social Relation of Power. Are there Symptoms of an Incipient Civil Society in the Soviet Union?', unpublished paper, Toronto 1983.

Jan Krouzil, 'On the State, Economy and Civil Society and the Current Stage of Capitalist Development in Canada', unpublished paper, Toronto 1985.

Helmut Kuzmics, 'Verlegenheit und Zivilisation. Zu einigen Gemeinsamkeiten und Unterschieden im Werk von E. Goffman und N. Elias', *Soziale Welt*, vol. 37, no. 4, 1986, pp. 465-86.

Jan Józef Lipski, *KOR. A History of the Workers' Defense Committee in Poland, 1976-1981*, Berkeley 1985.

Heinz Lubasz, 'Too Clever by Half: Review of Jean Cohen's *Class and*

Civil Society', *Times Higher Education Supplement*, 20 January 20, 1984.
Aladar Madárász, 'Politics and the Civilising Process. The Rise, Fall and Revival of the Concept of Civil Society in the Languages of European Political Thought', mimeograph, Vienna 1987.
Louis Maheu, 'Les mouvements de base et la lutte contre l'appropriation étatique du tissu social', *Sociologie et société*, vol. 15, 1 April, 1983.
Michael Mann, 'The Autonomous Power of the State', *Archives Européennes de Sociologie*, vol. 25, no. 2, 1984, pp. 185-213.
Michael Mann, *The Sources of Power*, London 1985.
Michael Mann, 'State and Society, 1130-1815: An Analysis of English State Finances', *Political Power and Social Theory*, vol. 1, 1986, pp. 165-208.
Maria Márkus, 'Formation and Re-structuration of Civil Society. Is there a General Meaning in the Polish Paradigm?', unpublished paper, Haverford College 1985.
Maria Márkus, 'Constitution and Functioning of Civil Society in Poland 1980-1981', paper delivered at the conference *Poland After Martial Law. The Search for 'Normalisation'*, Canberra November 1983.
Maria Márkus, 'Women, Success and Civil Society: Submission to or Subversion of the Achievement Principle', *Praxis International*, vol. 5, no. 4, 1986, pp. 430-42.
Antonio Marongiu, *Medieval Parliaments. A Comparative Study*, trans. S.J. Woolf, London 1968.
Andrew Martin, 'Trade Unions in Sweden: Strategic Responses to Change and Crisis', in Peter A. Gourevitch et al., eds., *Unions, Change and Crisis: Britain, West Germany and Sweden*, London 1984.
Andrew Martin, 'Wages, Profits, and Investment in Sweden', in Leon Lindberg and Charles S. Maier, eds., *The Politics of Inflation and Economic Stagnation*, Washington DC 1985.
Tomaž Mastnak, 'Za anarholiberalizem', *Problemi*, vol. 22, nos 1-3, 1984.
Tomaž Mastnak, 'H kritiki "Židovskega vprašanja"', *Problemi*, vol. 23, no. 1, 1985.
Tomaž Mastnak, ed., *Socialistična civilna družba?*, Ljubljana 1985.
Tomaž Mastnak, 'De la démocratie en Yougoslavie', *Problemi*, vol. 23, no. 7, 1985.
Tomaž Mastnak, 'Perspektive demokracije v Jugoslaviji', *Problemi*, vol. 24, no. 2, 1986.
Tomaž Mastnak, 'Socialistična civilna družba', *Valj*, vol. 18, 1986.
Tomaž Mastnak, 'Socialistična civilna družba, demokratična opozicija', *Tribuna*, vol. 35, no. 12, 1986.
Tomaž Mastnak, 'Machen wir uns diese Stadt wieder rein', *Mladina*, vol. 30, no. 26, 1986.
Tomaž Mastnak, 'H kritiki Marxovega pojma "bürgerliche Gesellschaft" v Očrtihh kritike politične ekonomije', *Vestnik*, vol. 7, nos 1-2, 1986.
Tomaž Mastnak, 'Dalje od istočnoevropskog marksizma', *Medjunarodni radnički pokret*, vol. 29, nos 3-4, 1986.
Tomaž Mastnak, 'Socialistična civilna družba? Skica aktualnega stanja

diskusije', *Katedra*, vol. 28, nos 6-7, 1987.

Tomaž Mastnak, 'Pred koncem revizionizma in ponovnim rojstvom civilne družbe', introduction to Marc Rakovski, *Vzhodnoevropskemu marksizmu naproti*, Ljubljana 1987.

Alberto Melucci, *Altri Codici*, Bologna 1984.

Alberto Melucci, 'Challenging Codes', in *Social Movements in Complex Societies*, edited by John Keane and Paul Mier, London 1989.

Alberto Melucci, ed., *Movimenti sociali e sistema politica*, Milan 1986.

Adam Michnik, *L'Eglise et la gauche. Le dialogue Polonais*, Paris 1979.

Adam Michnik, 'What We Want to Do and What We Can Do', *Telos*, vol. 47, 1981, pp. 66-77.

Adam Michnik, *Letters From Prison and Other Essays*, London 1986.

Adam Michnik, 'Gorbachev – as Seen from Warsaw', *East European Reporter*, vol. 2, no. 4, 1987, pp. 32-4.

Keith Middlemas, *Politics in Industrial Society*, London 1983.

Ferenc Miszlivetz, *An Essay on Nationalism*, Budapest 1985.

Bronislaw Misztal, ed., *Poland After Solidarity*, London 1985.

Pierre-François Moreau, 'Société civile et civilisation', in François Chatelet, ed., *Histoire des idéologies*, vol. 3: *Savoir et pouvoir du XVIIIe au XXe siècle*, Paris 1978.

Robin Murray, 'New Directions in Municipal Socialism', in Ben Pimlott, ed., *Fabian Essays in Socialist Thought*, London 1984, pp. 206-29.

A.R. Myers, *Parliaments and Estates in Europe to 1789*, London 1975.

Wolf-Dieter Narr et al., *SPD – Staatspartei oder Reformpartei?*, Munich 1976.

Thomas Nipperdey, 'Verein als soziale Struktur in Deutschland im späten 18. und frühen 19. Jahrhundert. Eine Fallstudie zur Modernisierung I', in *Gesellschaft, Kultur, Theorie. Gesammelte Aufsätze zur neuren Geschichte*, Göttingen 1976, pp. 174-205.

Thomas Nipperdey, 'Der Umbruch zur bürgerlichen Gesellschaft seit der amerikanischen und französischen Revolution', in Klaus W. Hempfer and Alexander Schwan, eds., *Grundlagen der politischen Kultur des Westens*, Berlin and New York 1987, pp. 169-89.

Ernst Nolte, *Was ist bürgerlich?*, Stuttgart 1979.

Eric A. Nordlinger, *On the Autonomy of the Democratic State*, Cambridge 1981.

Klaus Novy, *Die Diskussion der Wirtschaftsreform in der Weimarer Republik*, Frankfurt am Main 1978.

Robert Nozick, *Anarchy, State and Utopia*, Oxford 1974.

Guillermo O'Donnell, 'Tensions in the Bureaucratic-Authoritarian State and the Question of Democracy', in David Collier, ed., *The New Authoritarianism in Latin America*, Princeton 1979, pp. 285-318.

Guillermo O'Donnell, 'A mi que me importa. Notas sobre sociabilidad y politica en Argentina y Brasil', *Kellogg Institute Working Paper 9*, January 1984.

Claus Offe, 'Konkurrenzpartei und kollektive politische Identität', in R. Roth, ed., *Parlamentarisches Ritual und politische Alternativen*, Frankfurt am Main 1980, pp. 26-42.

Claus Offe, *Contradictions of the Welfare State*, edited by John Keane, London 1984.

Claus Offe, 'Korporatismus als System Nichtstaatlicher Makrosteurung?', *Geschichte und Gesellschaft*, vol. 10, no. 2, 1984, pp. 234-56.

Claus Offe, *Disorganized Capitalism*, edited by John Keane, Cambridge 1985.

Claus Offe, 'New Social Movements: Challenging the Boundaries of Institutional Politics', *Social Research*, vol. 52, no. 4, 1985, pp. 817-68.

Claus Offe, 'Zwischen Bewegung und Partei. Die Grünen in der politischen "Adoleszenzkrise"?', in Otto Kallscheuer, ed., *Die Grünen – Letzte Wahl?*, Berlin 1986, pp. 40-60.

Claus Offe and Rolf G. Heinze, 'Am Arbeitsmarkt vorbei. Überlegungen zur Neubestimmung "haushaltlicher" Wohlfahrtsproduktion in ihrem Verhältnis zu Markt und Staat', *Leviathan*, vol. 14, no. 4, 1986, pp. 471-95.

Johan P. Olsen, *Organized Democracy*, Bergen 1983.

Michael Opielka and Georg Vobruba, eds., *Das garantierte Grundeinkommen. Entwicklung und Perspektiven einer Forderung*, Frankfurt am Main 1986.

Józef Orzet, 'Civil Society as a Desire', unpublished paper, Warsaw 1987.

Gianfranco Pasquino, 'Partiti, società civile, istituzioni: il caso italiano', *Stato e Mercato*, vol. 8, 1983.

Gianfranco Pasquino, 'Party Government in Italy: Achievements and Prospects', in Richard S. Katz, ed., *Party Governments: European and American Experiences*, Berlin and New York 1987, pp. 202-42.

Z.A. Pelczynski, ed., *The State and Civil Society in Hegel*, Cambridge and New York 1984.

Victor Perez-Diaz, *State, Bureaucracy and Civil Society. A Critical Discussion of the Political Theory of Karl Marx*, London 1978.

Christopher Pierson, 'New Theories of State and Civil Society', *Sociology*, vol. 18, no. 4, 1984, pp. 563-71.

Hanna F. Pitkin, 'Justice: On Relating Private and Public', *Political Theory*, vol. 9, 1981, pp. 327-52.

J.G.A. Pocock, 'Cambridge Paradigms and Scotch Philosophers: a Study of the Relations between the Civic Humanist and the Civil Jurisprudential Interpretation of Eighteenth-century Social Thought', in Istvan Hont and Michael Ignatieff, eds., *Wealth and Virtue. The Shaping of Political Economy in the Scottish Enlightenment*, Cambridge 1983, pp. 235-52.

Darka Podmenik, 'Za civilno družbo', *Tribuna*, vol. 35, no. 15, 1986.

Darka Podmenik, 'Civilna družba ni samoupravljanje', *Delo*, 28 November 1986.

Darka Podmenik, 'Ali je mogoče razvijati koncept civilne družbe', *Problemi*, vol. 25, no. 1, 1987.

Nicos Poulantzas, *Repères. Hier et aujourd'hui*, Paris 1980.

Nicos Poulantzas, 'Research Note on the State and Society', *International*

Social Science Journal, vol. 32, no. 4, 1980, pp. 600-8.

Ivan Prpić, *Država i društvo. Odnos 'gradjanskog društva' i 'političke države' u ranim radovima Karla Marksa,* Beograd 1976.

Jože Pučnik, 'Politični sistem civilne družbe', *Nova revija,* vol. 6, no. 57, 1987.

Marc Raeff, *Understanding Imperial Russia: State and Society in the Old Regime,* New York 1984.

Joachim Raschke, ed., *Bürger und Parteien. Ansichten und Analysen einer schwierigen Beziehung,* Opladen 1982.

Zbigniew Rav 'Some Thoughts on Civil Society in Eastern Europe and the Lockean Contractarian Approach', *Political Studies,* vol. 35, 1987, pp. 573-92.

Jean-François Revel, *Le rejet de l'état,* Paris 1984.

Revue de l'Institut de Sociologie, special issue: 'Etat et société en Amérique Latine', Brussels 1981.

Manfred Riedel, *Bürgerliche Gesellschaft und Staat. Grundproblem und Struktur der Hegelschen Rechtsphilosphie,* Neuwied and Berlin, 1970.

Manfred Riedel, 'Hegels Begriff der bürgerlichen Gesellschaft und das Problem seines geschichtlichen Ursprungs', in *Materialien zu Hegels Rechtsphilosophie,* vol. 2, Frankfurt am Main 1974, pp. 247-75.

Manfred Riedel, 'Gesellschaft, Bürgerliche', in O. Brunner et al., eds., *Geschichtliche Grundbegriffe. Historisches Lexikon zur politisch-sozialen Sprache in Deutschland,* vol. 2, Stuttgart 1975, pp. 719-800.

Manfred Riedel, 'Bürgerlichkeit und Humanität', in Rudolf Vierhaus, ed., *Bürger und Bürgerlichkeit im Zeitalter der Aufklärung,* Heidelberg 1981, pp. 13-34.

Manfred Riedel, 'Transcendental Politics? Political Legitimacy and the Concept of Civil Society in Kant', *Social Research,* Autumn 1981, pp. 588-613.

John Robertson, 'The Scottish Enlightenment at the Limits of the Civic Tradition', in Istvan Hont and Michael Ignatieff, eds., *Wealth and Virtue. The Shaping of Political Economy in the Scottish Enlightenment,* Cambridge 1983, pp. 137–78.

Pierre Rosanvallon, *Le capitalisme utopique,* Paris 1979.

Pierre Rosanvallon, *La crise de l'état-providence,* Paris 1981.

Pierre Rosanvallon, 'Politique en liberté. La dérégulation sociale', *Intervention,* vol. 2, January-February, 1983, pp. 87-94.

Mort Rosenblum, *Mission to Civilize. The French Way,* New York 1986.

Jacques Rupnik, 'Dissent in Poland, 1968-78', in Rudolf Tökes, ed., *Opposition in Eastern Europe,* London 1979.

Richard Sakwa, 'The State and Civil Society in the USSR', mimeograph, London 1986.

Richard Sakwa, *The Party and Opposition in Moscow, 1920-Early 1921,* University of Essex Discussion Paper 7, 1986.

Richard Sakwa, 'The Commune State in Moscow in 1918', *Slavic Review,* vol. 46, nos 3-4, 1987.

Richard Sakwa, *Soviet Communists in Power: A Study of Moscow during the*

Civil War, 1918-21, London 1988.

Arnaud Sales, 'Champs sociaux et structures de pouvoir', paper presented to the conference, *L'Etat contemporain: au coeur de la société*, Lennoxville June 1986.

Slobodan Samardžić, 'Društvo i država u socijalizmu', *Književne novine*, vol. 32, no. 719, 1986.

Steven Sampson, 'The Informal Sector in Eastern Europe', *Telos*, vol. 66,
· Winter 1985-86, pp. 44-66.

G. Savran, *Rousseau, Hegel and the Critique of Civil Society*, doctoral dissertation, University of Sussex 1983.

Theodor Schieder, *The State and Society in Our Times: Studies in the History of the Nineteenth and Twentieth Centuries*, London 1962.

M. Schmolz, 'Societas civilis sive Respublica sive Ropulus', *Österreichisches Zeitschrift für Öffentliches Recht*, vol. 14, 1964, pp. 28-50.

Gerhard Schulz, 'Die Entstehung der bürgerlichen Gesellschaft. Zur Genesis politischer Ideen und Begriffe', in G.A. Ritter, ed., *Entstehung und Wandel der modernen Gesellschaft. Festschrift für H. Rosenberg zum 65. Geburtstag*, Berlin 1970.

Laslo Sekelj, 'Politički sistim i model socijalističkog gradjanskog društva', *Problemi*, vol. 23, no. 1, 1985.

James J. Sheehan, 'Wie Bürgerlich war der deutsche Liberalismus?', mimeograph, Stanford University 1987.

Hannes Siegrist, ed., *'Bürgerliche Berufe'. Beiträge zur Geschichte der akademischen und freien Berufe im internationalen Vergleich*, Göttingen 1988.

Allan Silver, 'The Demand for Order in Civil Society', in David Bordua, ed., *The Police*, New York 1967, pp. 1-24.

Milan Šimečka, *The Restoration of Order. The Normalization of Czechoslovakia 1969-1976*, London 1984.

Brian Singer, *Society, Theory and the French Revolution: Studies in the Revolutionary Imaginary*, London 1986.

Carmen Sirianni, 'Councils and Parliaments: The Problems of Dual Power and Democracy in Comparative Perspective', *Politics and Society*, vol. 12, no. 1, 1983, pp. 83-123.

H. Gordon Skilling, *Charter 77 and Human Rights in Czechoslovakia*, London 1981.

H. Gordon Skilling, *Samizdat and an International Society in Eastern Europe*, London and Basingstoke 1988.

Theda Skocpol, *States and Social Revolutions. A Comparative Analysis of France, Russia and China*, Cambridge and New York 1979.

Theda Skocpol, 'Bringing the State Back In: Strategies of Analysis in Current Research', in Peter B. Evans et al., eds, *Bringing the State Back In*, Cambridge 1986.

Bernardo Sorj and Maria Herminia, eds., *Sociedade e Politica no Brasil Pós-64*, São Paulo 1983.

Jonathan Sperber, 'State and Civil Society in Prussia', *Journal of Modern History*, vol. 57, no. 2, 1985, pp. 278-96.

Jadwiga Staniszkis, 'Poland: The Self-Limiting Revolution', *The Bulletin of Scottish Politics*, vol. 1, no. 2, 1981, pp. 87-110.

Jadwiga Staniszkis, *Poland's Self-Limiting Revolution*, Princeton 1984.

Peter Steinfels, *The Neoconservatives. The Men Who Are Changing America's Politics*, New York 1979.

Alfred Stepan, *State and Society: Peru in Comparative Perspective*, Princeton 1978.

Wolfgang Streeck and Philippe C. Schmitter, eds., *Private Interest Government. Beyond Market and State*, London, Beverly Hills and New Delhi 1985.

Jerzy Szacki, 'The Utopia of Civil Society in Poland Today', mimeograph, Warsaw 1987.

Jenö Szücs, *Vázlat Európa három történeti régiojáról*, Budapest 1983.

Jan Tesař, 'Totalitarian Dictatorships as a Phenomenon of the Twentieth Century and the Possibilities of Overcoming Them', in H. Gordon Skilling and Vilém Prečan, eds., *Parallel Politics: Essays from Czech and Slovak Samizdat, International Journal of Politics*, vol. 60, no. 1, 1981, pp. 85-100.

E.P. Thompson, 'Comment', *Praxis International*, vol. 5, no. 1, 1985, pp. 75-85.

Gregor Tomc, 'Civilna družba pod slovenskim socializmom', *Nova revija*, vol. 6, no. 57, 1987.

Alain Touraine, *Production de la société*, Paris 1973.

Alain Touraine, *Lutte étudiante*, Paris 1978.

Alain Touraine, *L'Après-socialisme*, Paris 1980.

Alain Touraine, *The Voice and the Eye. An Analysis of Social Movements*, Cambridge 1981.

Alain Touraine et al., *Solidarity. Poland 1980-81*, Cambridge and New York 1983.

Alain Touraine, *Le retour de l'acteur*, Paris 1984.

Keith Tribe, 'Cameralism and the Science of Government', *Journal of Modern History*, vol. 56, 1984, pp. 263-84.

John Urry, *The Anatomy of Capitalist Societies. The Economy, Civil Society and the State*, London 1981.

Robert J. van der Veen and Philippe Van Parijs, 'A Capitalist Road to Communism', *Theory and Society*, vol. 15, no. 5, 1986, pp. 635-56.

Robert J. van der Veen and Philippe Van Parijs, 'Universal Grants versus Socialism: Reply to Six Critics', *Theory and Society*, vol. 15, no. 5, 1986, pp. 723-58.

Rudolf Vierhaus, ed., *Bürger und Bürgerlichkeit im Zeitalter der Aufklärung*, Heidelberg 1981.

Gerhard Vowinckel, *Von politischen Köpfen und schönen Seelen. Ein soziologischer Versuch über die Zivilisation der Affekte und ihres Ausdrucks*, Munich 1983.

Michael Walzer, 'Civility and Civic Virtue in Contemporary America', in *Radical Principles. Reflections of an Unreconstructed Democrat*, New York 1980, pp. 54-72.

Michael Walzer, *Spheres of Justice. A Defense of Pluralism and Equality*, New York 1983.

Mihály Vajda, *The State and Socialism*, London 1981.

Thomas E. Wartenberg, 'Poverty and Class Structure in Hegel's Theory of Civil Society', *Philosophy and Social Criticism*, vol. 8, no. 2, 1981, pp. 169-82.

Richard D. Winfield, 'Capital, Civil Society and the Deformation of Politics', *History of Political Thought*, vol. 4, no. 1, 1983, pp. 111-55.

Kasimierz Wojcicki, 'The Reconstruction of Society', *Telos*, vol. 47, 1981, pp. 98-104.

Sheldon Wolin, 'The People's Two Bodies', *democracy*, vol. 1, no. 1, 1981, pp. 9-24.

Sheldon S. Wolin, 'America's Civil Religion', *democracy*, vol. 2, no. 2, 1982, pp. 7-17.

Isser Woloch, 'Napoleonic Conscription: State Power and Civil Society', *Past and Present*, vol. 111, 1986, pp. 101-29.

Ellen Meiksins Wood, 'The Separation of the Economic and the Political in Capitalism', *New Left Review*, vol. 127, 1981, pp. 66-95.

Alexander Yanov, *The Origins of Autocracy*, Los Angeles 1980.

Perez Zagorin, *Rebels and Rulers, 1500-1660*, vol. 1: *Society, States, and Early Modern Revolution. Agrarian and Urban Rebellions*; vol. 2: *Provincial Rebellion. Revolutionary Civil Wars. 1560-1660*, London and New York 1982.

Notes on Contributors

NORBERTO BOBBIO is Italy's foremost political theorist. He was born in Torino in 1909. He taught jurisprudence and political philosophy at the Universities of Camerino (1935-38), Siena (1938-40), Padova (1940-48) and Torino (1948-79). Since 1984 he has been a member of the Italian Senate. His works in English include *The Philosophy of Decadentism* (1948), *On Mosca and Pareto* (1972), *The Future of Democracy* (1987) and *What is Socialism?* (1987).

NORBERT ELIAS, born in 1897, studied medicine, philosophy (with Edmund Husserl) and psychology in Breslau, Freiburg and Heidelberg. He did his postgraduate studies with Alfred Weber and taught at Frankfurt with Karl Mannheim. He went on to posts in Paris and at the London School of Economics, becoming Reader in Sociology at the University of Leicester, Professor of Sociology at the University of Ghana and Professor Emeritus at the University of Frankfurt. He presently lives in Amsterdam. His English publications include *The Civilizing Process* (1978, 1982), *The Court Society* (1983) and *The Loneliness of the Dying* (1985).

AGNES HELLER was born and educated in Budapest. She was a student, close associate and friend of György Lukács. In 1977, after years of political dissent and political unemployment, she emigrated to Australia, where she lectured for nearly a decade at La Trobe University in Melbourne. She is currently Professor of philosophy and political science at the New School for Social

Research in New York, and is the author of many essays and books, including *The Power of Shame* (1985), *Beyond Justice* (1987) and (with Ferenc Feher) *Eastern Left-Western Left* (1987).

KARL HINRICHS was born in 1951. He was first employed as a bank clerk, went on to study economics and sociology at the University of Bielefeld, and was for several years a secondary school teacher in Bremen. Since 1984 he has lectured and researched in the Department of Sociology at the University of Bielefeld. He is the author of numerous essays on the welfare state, trade unions and working time policy, and is the co-editor of *Arbeitszeitpolitik. Formen und Folgen einer Neuverteilung der Arbeitszeit* (1982).

JOHN KEANE, born in 1949, is the author of *Public Life and Late Capitalism* (1984), *Democracy and Civil Society* (1988) and (with John Owens) *After Full Employment* (1986). He is the editor of a volume of essays by Czechoslovak writers, *The Power of the Powerless* (1985), as well as the editor and translator of Claus Offe's *Contradictions of the Welfare State*. He is a regular contributor to the *Times Literary Supplement* and the *New Statesman*. He has taught and researched at Monash University, the University of Toronto, the Freie Universität Berlin and Cambridge University; in 1987 he was a Fellow at the Centre for Interdisciplinary Research, Bielefeld. He lives in London, where he is a Fellow at the Centre for Communication and Information Studies and teaches political theory and sociology at The Polytechnic of Central London.

HELMUT KUZMICS was born in 1949. He studied economics and sociology at the University of Graz and the Institute for Advanced Studies in Vienna. Since 1974, he has lectured in sociology at the Institute of Sociology at the University of Graz. His main research interests include comparative perspectives on modernity and theories of the civilizing process. He has published numerous studies of the modern civilizing process and co-edited *Korruption. Zur Soziologie nicht immer abweichenden Verhaltens* (1985).

ALBERTO MELUCCI is Professor of Sociology at the University of Milano as well as a practising psychotherapist. He is among the foremost European writers on social movements. He is the author of many essays and nine books, including *Altri codici* (1984), *Corpi estranei* (1984) and *Challenging Codes. Social Movements in Complex Societies* (1988).

CLAUS OFFE was born in 1940 in Berlin. He studied sociology, economics and philosophy in Köln and at the Freie Universität Berlin; he held a Harkness Fellowship at the University of California, Berkeley and at Harvard University during 1969-1971. He has lectured widely throughout Europe and North America, and has held teaching posts in Frankfurt, Konstanz, Vienna, Bielefeld, Boston and Berkeley. He was a Fellow at the Centre for Advanced Study in the Behavioral Sciences, Stanford during 1987-88. He has authored numerous books and essays, including (in English) *Industry and Inequality* (1976), *Contradictions of the Welfare State* (1984) and *Disorganized Capitalism* (1985).

CAROLE PATEMAN was an adult student at Ruskin College, Oxford, then read Philosophy, Politics and Economics at Lady Margaret Hall, Oxford. She emigrated from Britain to Australia in 1973. She is presently Reader in Government at Sydney University and a Fellow of the Academy of Social Sciences in Australia. Her main field of teaching and research is modern political theory, especially democratic theory, feminist theory and political economy. She is the author of *Participation and Democratic Theory* (1970), *The Problem of Political Obligation* (1979) and *The Sexual Contract* (1988). In 1985 she presented the Jefferson Memorial Lectures at the University of California, Berkeley, on the subject of Women and Democratic Citizenship.

ZBIGNIEW PELCZYNSKI was born in Grodzisk Mazowiecki, Poland in 1925. After participating in the Polish resistance movement and serving in the Polish armed forces under British command, he emigrated to England in 1946. He was educated at the Universities of St. Andrews and Oxford. He is presently a Fellow and Tutor in Politics at Pembroke College, Oxford and Oxford University Lecturer in Politics. He has written essays on modern political thought, totalitarianism and contemporary Polish history, and is the editor of *Hegel's Political Philosophy* (1971) and *The State and Civil Society: Studies in Hegel's Political Philosophy* (1984), and joint editor of *Conceptions of Liberty in Political Philosophy* (1984) and *Hegel's Political Writings* (1964).

VÁCLAV HAVEL was born in Prague in 1936. After military service, he embarked on a career at the renowned Theatre of the Balustrade, where he became resident playwright. He published essays on theatre in the 1950s, before the success of his first play, *The Garden Party* (1963). Among his most well-known plays are

The Memorandum (1965), *The Increased Difficulty of Concentration* (1968), an adaptation of *The Beggar's Opera* (1976), *Largo desolato* (1984) and *Temptation* (1987). He is also a contributor to *The Power of the Powerless* (1985) and author of *Letters to Olga* (1988). He has received numerous literary awards, including the prestigious American Obie Prize (1968 and 1970), and he holds honorary doctorates from York University (Toronto) and the University of Toulouse, France. Since 1969 the Czechoslovak authorities have prohibited the publication or performance of his work. In 1977 he was arrested and jailed for four months for his Charter 77 activities. In 1979, together with nine fellow members of VONS, a citizens' group working for the protection of democratic rights, he was again convicted and sentenced to four-and-a-half years in prison. After an international protest campaign, and owing to serious illness, his sentence was suspended in early 1983. He is presently under surveillance by the state authorities and, if the authorities so wished, he could be returned to prison at any time to serve the remaining ten months of his sentence.

PIERRE ROSANVALLON was born in 1948. He is a graduate of the Ecole des Hautes Etudes Commerciales. From 1969 to 1977 he was an economic adviser to the French trade union, CFDT, as well as founder and editor of its journal, *CFDT — Aujourd'hui*. He has researched and taught at the University of Paris-Dauphine and is presently a member of the Ecole des Hautes Etudes en Sciences Sociales in Paris. Since 1981 he has been general secretary of the Fondation Saint-Simon. His main publications include *L'Age de l'autogestion* (1976), *Le Capitalisme utopique* (1979), *Misère de l'économie* (1983) and *Le Moment Guizot* (1985).

JACQUES RUPNIK was born in Prague in 1950. He studied at the University of Paris and Harvard University. He is a Senior Fellow at the Fondation Nationale des Sciences Politiques in Paris. He is the author of *A History of the Czechoslovak Communist Party* (1981) and of many essays on the political systems of eastern-central Europe. He is presently writing a book on the theme of central Europe.

JENÖ SZÜCS is a member of the Institute of History at the Hungarian Academy of Sciences, Budapest. His main fields of interest are the mediaeval history of Hungary, social history and the history of ideas. His recent publications include studies of households in thirteenth-century Hungary, mediaeval political thought, the formation of the Hungarian gentry, and two books, *Nation und Geschichte. Studien* (1981) and a full length version of his contribution to this volume, *Les trois Europes* (1985).

MIHÁLY VAJDA was born in 1935 in Budapest, where he studied philosophy and German literature. He was a pupil and close associate (with Agnes Heller and other members of the Budapest School) of György Lukács. From 1961-1973 he was a research fellow in the Institute of Philosophy at the Hungarian Academy of Sciences. He was dismissed from this post for political reasons, and since then has engaged in various forms of 'freelance' employment in Budapest. He has been a visiting professor at the University of Bremen, Columbia University and the New School for Social Research. His present main fields of research include phenomenology, Heideggerian philosophy and eastern-central Europe. His books in English include *Fascism as a Mass Movement* (1976) and *The State and Socialism. Political Essays* (1981).

HELMUT WIESENTHAL, a former engineering firm executive, studied philosophy and sociology in Bochum and Bielefeld. He is presently a research fellow at the University of Bielefeld. He is also a well-known activist in die Grünen. His main research interests include the welfare state, working time policy, industrial relations and new social movements. He is the author of *Die Konzentierte Aktion im Gesundheitswesen (1981)* and *Strategie und Illusion* (1987).

Index